CHEVROLET POWER

Foreword

It is an honor to write the foreword to the seventh edition of the *Chevrolet Power* manual. No family of engines has had a greater impact on the racing, high-performance, and custom parts industry than Chevrolet. The star of the family, the small-block V8, is the most universally accepted and most successful racing powerplant in the world.

The roots of Chevrolet's success can be traced to the inherent design genius of the basic engines—designs that not only met the requirements of mass production, but more importantly could be modified to meet more demanding performance parameters. These timeless engine designs have endured changes in displacement and output, the introduction of electronic controls, and the advent of federally mandated fuel economy and emission standards. The availability of factory-engineered heavy-duty parts and good information about how to use them has made the dreams of enthusiasts and racers a reality!

No single individual is responsible for the incredible success of Chevy Power. Within Chevrolet, Zora Arkus-Duntov saw the potential impact of performance that extended far beyond the production automobile business. Vince Piggins continued Chevrolet's success story in a working environment that was not always sympathetic to his efforts. On the outside, engine builders like Smokey Yunick always had ideas about making better parts. Talented writers like John Thawley and Jim McFarland told millions of enthusiasts how to modify their Chevrolets for improved performance.

In reality, Chevy Power is a continuing saga—a story that will never be finished. With leading engine builders and the dedicated engineers of the GM Motorsports Technology Group writing new chapters daily, the script changes with every dynamometer run.

Chevy Power is an amazing story. It's been healthy for the industry. It's a story that everyone who loves cars has had the opportunity to be a part of in one way or another. I'm honored that I've had the privilege several times throughout my career with General Motors.

Herbert A. Fishel
Executive Director
GM Motorsports Technology Group

Contents

Introduction to Engine Building

Crankshaft stroke gauge

Blueprinting is a term that means different things to different people who are involved in performance engine building. As used in this manual, "blueprinting" refers to assembling an engine to very precise specifications. These specifications may be determined by the manufacturer, by experience, and by the intended use for the engine. If an engine is to be used in competition, the rules and regulations of the sanctioning body must also be considered when selecting, modifying, and installing engine components.

Chevrolet shop manuals are highly recommended as reference sources for specifications and assembly procedures for production engines. These manuals provide valuable information that can be applied to even highly modified competition engines. Shop manuals are available by mail from:

Helm, Inc.
Chevrolet Manual Distribution Dept.
P.O. Box 07130
Detroit, MI 48207

Many of the recommendations contained in this publication are based on the experiences of GM Motorsports Technology Group engineers and successful Chevrolet competitors. They have been culled from years of involvement in motorsports and high-performance activities. These recommendations are intended only as general guidelines, however, and they may or may not be appropriate for a particular engine or application. The skill, craftsmanship, and mechanical aptitude

Sonic testing a block will reveal its cylinder wall thickness. Select a block that has maximum thickness on the major thrust axes.

Preassemble the engine and measure the piston deck height. Mill the block to produce the desired deck clearance.

Check the diameter and roundness of the main bearing bores with an accurate dial bore gauge. Caps should fit their registers tightly.

A deck plate recreates the stresses produced by torquing the head bolts. Hone the cylinders with 400 grit stones to produce a smooth finish.

of the engine builder also determines whether or not a particular procedure will produce the desired result.

An engine's intended usage is an important consideration when selecting specifications and components for any

Metal Removal

Machine the intake manifold as shown in the charts to restore the gasket spaces and port alignment after decking the engine block or cylinder heads.

Small-Block V8, V6/90

Cylinder Head/Block	Intake Manifold	
	Side	Bottom
.005"	.006"	.009"
.010"	.012"	.017"
.015"	.018"	.025"
.020"	.025"	.034"
.025"	.031"	.043"
.030"	.037"	.052"

Big-Block V8

Cylinder Head/Block	Intake Manifold	
	Side	Bottom
.005"	.004"	.010"
.010"	.007"	.019"
.015"	.011"	.029"
.020"	.014"	.038"
.025"	.018"	.048"
.030"	.021"	.058"

Chevrolet competition engine. The required power level, durability, cost, and sanctioning body rules must all be considered when preparing an engine. The builder should be thoroughly familiar with the regulations governing the particular type of motorsport in which the engine will be used.

"Blueprinting" also implies scrupulous attention to cleanliness, careful inspection of components (especially used parts), and the proper use of tools during assembly. This section outlines general procedures that apply to many engines and components. Refer to the appropriate chapter of this manual for information and recommendations that apply to specific Chevrolet engines.

Block Preparation

A wide variety of production and heavy-duty Chevrolet engine cases are suitable for high-performance and competition applications. Whether you are starting with a new or a used cylinder block, it should be carefully inspected. Examine the block closely for hidden defects before you invest your time and money in expensive machine work.

A used block will have to be cleaned before inspection. A visual examination will reveal stripped bolt holes, spun bearings, and other obvious flaws. A Magnaflux inspection will highlight any cracks in the water jackets, cylinder walls, and main bearing bulkheads.

After a block passes this preliminary inspection, check the main bearing bores for roundness and size. Make sure the main caps fit tightly in their notches.

Check the cylinder wall thickness if you plan to bore a production block more than .030-inch oversize. If any core shift has occurred during the casting of the block, the block may be susceptible to cracks in the thin areas after it is overbored. Sonic testing is an accurate

method of determining cylinder wall thickness, and many machine shops have the equipment to perform such tests. Select a block that has minimal core shift. A block with greater wall thickness on the major thrust side of the bores (outboard side on the right bank, inboard side on the left bank) is preferred.

If a straight crankshaft will spin freely in new main bearings with .002 to .0025-inch clearance, the block does not need to be align bored. The main bearing saddles can also be checked for alignment using a machinist's straight edge and a .0015-inch feeler gauge. With the straight edge in place you should not be able to insert or remove a .0015-inch feeler gauge at any main bearing bore.

After you are satisfied that the block is basically sound, you are ready to begin the machining phase. Chevrolet engine blocks should be bored and honed with the main bearing caps torqued in place. A deck plate ("torque plate") should be installed on the head surface to simulate the stresses normally created by the head bolts. Hone for final piston clearance with a medium grit stone, establishing a good cross-hatch pattern in the cylinder bores. Finish hone with 400 to 500 grit stones to produce a very smooth bore finish.

To determine how much material must be removed from the cylinder block deck surfaces to produce the desired deck clearance, you must install the pistons, rods, and crankshaft that you intend to use. Assemble these parts in the block and measure how far the piston is above or below the deck. You can also measure all the component dimensions (piston compression height, rod center-to-center length, block height, and crankshaft stroke) with instruments and then calculate the final deck clearance figure.

The minimum acceptable clearance between the piston top (not the dome) and the cylinder head is .035/.040-inch with steel connecting rods. The compressed thickness of the cylinder head gasket of the type being used must be included in this calculation. This minimum deck clearance dimension may have to be adjusted in engines operated at high speeds, engines with large piston-to-wall clearances, and engines equipped with aluminum connecting rods.

Keep in mind that if an appreciable amount of material is removed from the engine block or cylinder heads, the intake manifold may have to be machined to restore gasket spaces and port alignment.

Epoxy screens over the oil drainback holes and install magnets in the lifter valley and cylinder heads to catch metal particles.

Check for taper and out-of-round journals when measuring the crankshaft's main bearing and connecting rod journals.

Measure the inside diameter of the bearing insert and subtract the crankshaft journal diameter to calculate the bearing clearance.

The block should be thoroughly deburred using a small hand grinder and rotary file or abrasive rolls. The objective is to remove casting flash that can impede the flow of oil and to eliminate sharp edges that may break off and cause engine damage. Enlarge and smooth the oil drainback holes. Chamfer the head bolt holes with a countersink or similar tool.

After all machining operations are completed, the block should be thoroughly cleaned. Clean all oil passages using a rifle cleaning brush or other long, stiff bristle brush. Scrub the cylinder bores with hot, soapy water, then coat them immediately with oil to prevent rust.

After cleaning, the block's unmachined surfaces can be painted with high-quality paint. Replace the oil gallery plugs and cam bearings. You may also want to positively retain all welch plugs (freeze plugs) with small self-tapping screws or drive pins. Soft plugs can also be epoxied in place to prevent coolant leaks.

The final step in preparing a Chevrolet block is to install protective screens over the oil drainback holes. Any fine wire screen can be cut and shaped to conform to the oil drainback holes; stainless steel screen is preferred. Glue the screens in place with good quality epoxy after carefully cleaning the block surface to insure a good bond. Epoxy small magnets near the cylinder head oil drain back holes to catch small metal particles that have worn off the valve springs and shims.

Crankshaft Preparation

A production Chevrolet crankshaft should be Magnaflux inspected for cracks before installation. Cast and forged cranks should be carefully deburred to eliminate stress risers. Check the crankshaft straightness by supporting the crank in Vee blocks (or in the cylinder case with only the front and rear bearings installed). Set up a dial indicator on the center or intermediate main journal and slowly rotate the crankshaft. The center main journal should have less than .003-inch runout after all operations are completed.

To check the thrust clearance, install the crankshaft in the block with the main bearings. Tighten the main cap bolts for the thrust bearing. Set up a dial indicator with its plunger parallel to the crank axis. Pry the crankshaft forward and backward to measure the clearance.

To check the bearing clearances, first measure the diameter of the crankshaft's rod and main journals. Install the bearing inserts in the main bearing bores and the connecting rods, torque the fasteners, and measure their inside diameters. (Measure the inside diameter 90 degrees from the bearing's parting line.) To calculate the bearing clearance, subtract the diameter of the crankshaft journal from the inside diameter of its respective bearing.

Specialty crankshaft shops can index the throws and equalize the strokes when regrinding a crankshaft. Minor changes in crankshaft stroke can be achieved by offset grinding the rod journals. Lead-in grooves can also be machined in the main bearing journals to channel oil to the rod bearing oil feed holes. If you regrind a production nodular iron crankshaft, it *must* be thoroughly polished in a lathe, *turning the crankshaft in the direction of engine rotation.* The final step in preparing a crankshaft is to hand polish all the journals with #400 grit sandpaper.

If you are using non-stock components, the crankshaft assembly should be balanced before final installation. Your machinist will need the pistons and connecting rods you intend to use, plus samples of the wrist pins, bearings, and piston rings. If your engine is externally balanced, you must also furnish the torsional damper and flywheel (or flexplate).

Connecting Rod Preparation

Production Chevrolet connecting rods are suitable for many high-performance and limited competition applications. The following modifications are recommended to improve the durability of production rods used in high-output engines:

1. Round all sharp edges from the beam section of the rod and grind off excess flash at the forging parting lines on the sides of rod.

BOW TIE TIPS — Balancing Act

The GM Motorsports Technology Group recommends the following bobweight formulas when balancing Chevrolet crankshafts.

Small-block V8, big-block V8, V6/60, and V6/90 with *odd-fire* crankshaft:

$$W_{BOB} = W_{ROT} + 0.5\ W_{REC}$$

V6/90 with *even-fire* crankshaft:

$$W_{BOB} = W_{ROT} + .366\ W_{REC}$$

W_{BOB} = Bobweight attached to crankpin for balancing

W_{ROT} = Rotating weight (includes big end of connecting rod and rod bearings)

W_{REC} = Reciprocating weight (includes small end of connecting rod, piston, wrist pin, and piston rings)

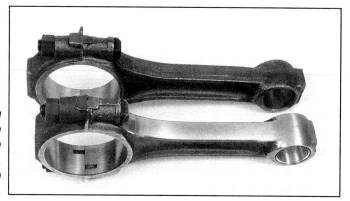

Grind the connecting rod beams to remove excess flash at the forging lines. Shotpeen the rods to prevent cracks.

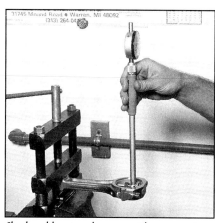

Check rod bearing clearance with an accurate dial bore gauge after tightening the rod fasteners to their recommended torque.

Drill a ⅛-inch hole in the top of the connecting rod to lubricate a floating wrist pin. Hone the bore for .0008/.001-inch clearance.

Measure the connecting rod side clearance by inserting a feeler gauge between the rods on a common crank pin.

2. Round all sharp edges around the rod bolt head and nut seats, and smooth any nicks in the radius of the bolt and nut seats with a small hand grinder.

3. Qualify the big end of the connecting rod in a precision rod reconditioning machine. Specifications for rod bearing bore diameters are as follows:

Engine	Journal Diameter	Rod Bearing Bore
Small-block V8, V6/60	2.00"	2.1247/ 2.1252"
Small-block V8, V6/90 (odd-fire)	2.10"	2.2247/ 2.2252"
Big-block V8	2.20"	2.3247/ 2.3252"
V6/90 (even-fire)	2.25"	2.3747/ 2.3757"

4. Shotpeen the entire rod and cap, including bolt and nut seats. A satisfactory shotpeening specification for connecting rods is .012-.015-inch Allmen "A" arc height using #230 cast steel shot. Shotpeening compresses the metal's surface and reduces its susceptibility to cracking.

5. For full-floating pins, drill a single ⅛-inch diameter hole in the top of the connecting rod to supply additional oil to the piston wrist pin. Hone the pin bore as necessary to produce .0008/.0010-inch wrist pin clearance. (Wrist pin clearance should be reduced to .0005/.0008-inch if the small end is bushed.)

6. Production connecting rod bolts and nuts should be Magnaflux inspected and tested with a Rockwell hardness tester (36-40 on the "C" scale). A hardness test is generally a reliable indication of whether the bolts will pull up to the proper torque.

7. Before final assembly, check the connecting rod side clearance. This can be done by inserting a feeler gauge between each pair of rods which share a crankshaft journal (common pin crankshafts only). Rod side clearance can also be calculated by subtracting the combined width of each rod pair from the distance between the crankshaft cheeks on their respective journal.

8. Check the rod bearing inserts for clearance when using crankshafts with oversize fillet radiuses. The outer edges of the bearing inserts may require chamfering for proper clearance and oil flow.

If you are using heavy-duty Chevrolet or aftermarket connecting rods with a long-stroke crankshaft, preassemble the crank assembly to check block and camshaft clearance. Relieve the block and/or rods to eliminate interference.

Piston Preparation

When assembling pistons and connecting rods with pressed wrist pins, heat the small end of the rod and quickly install the pin. It is necessary to have at least .001-inch (preferably .0012-inch) press fit between wrist pins and rods to insure that the pins will not loosen.

Round wire pin retainers are preferred for all pistons using floating pins. This pin retaining system is more resistant to pound-out than other types of pin locks. Many heavy-duty Chevrolet pistons are equipped with round wire pin retainers. Regardless of the type of pin retainer used, *wrist pin retainers should never be reused after the engine has been run and disassembled.*

High compression pistons should be checked for adequate valve-to-piston clearance by assembling one piston and rod with the other engine components (camshaft, crankshaft, rocker arms, etc.) you intend to use. Piston-to-valve clearance can be measured by laying strips of clay across the valve notches in the piston dome and then turning the crankshaft at least two complete revolutions.

The absolute minimum piston-to-valve clearance required to prevent engine damage is .045-inch, measured with the recommended valve lash. This minimum piston-to-valve clearance assumes that the engine will never operate in valve float. It is good practice to allow more than the minimum piston-to-valve clearance in a racing engine to allow for occasional valve float. A minimum of .080-inch intake valve clearance and .100-inch exhaust valve clearance should be maintained to prevent contact during overspeed conditions.

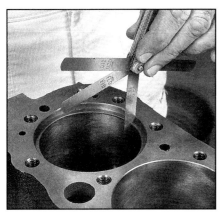
Piston rings must be square in their cylinder bores when measuring the end gaps with a feeler gauge.

Pistons should be thoroughly deburred before installation, paying particular attention to the edges of the skirts. Lightly radius any sharp corners on the dome and valve reliefs with sandpaper.

Piston Ring Preparation

Always measure the piston ring end gaps before installation with each ring square in its assigned cylinder bore. If the end gaps are less than the minimum recommended dimension shown in the engine specification charts, the end gaps must be filed to prevent ring scuffing.

File from the outside of the ring toward the inside to prevent chipping the moly or chrome face on compression rings. After filing the end gaps, break the sharp edges on the ends of the ring with a whetstone.

Check the piston rings for adequate side and back clearance in their grooves. Shim material is available from aftermarket ring manufacturers to reduce excessive back clearance. The rings must not protrude above the piston's ring lands.

A smooth cylinder wall finish is recommended for competition engines, using 400/500 grit stones for the final hone. Modern ring manufacturing techniques virtually eliminate the need for a lengthy break-in time to seat the rings. A smooth cylinder bore finish produces a significant power increase due to decreased internal engine friction.

Camshaft Installation

Several aftermarket manufacturers offer kits to alter the camshaft phasing from the production timing locators. As a general rule, advancing the camshaft improves low-speed torque, while retarding it increases high rpm horsepower.

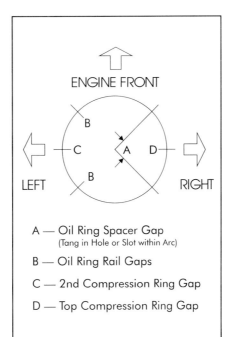

ENGINE FRONT

LEFT   RIGHT

A — Oil Ring Spacer Gap
   (Tang in Hole or Slot within Arc)

B — Oil Ring Rail Gaps

C — 2nd Compression Ring Gap

D — Top Compression Ring Gap

Install the piston rings with their end gaps in the positions shown when assembling Chevrolet high-performance engines.

The camshaft timing can be changed with offset crankshaft keys or offset cam sprocket bushings. The camshaft phasing must be rechecked and verified after installing either an offset crank key or an eccentric timing gear bushing. This procedure requires an accurate degree wheel and a precision dial indicator.

Advancing or retarding the camshaft from its stock timing specifications also affects piston-to-valve clearance. As the camshaft is advanced, intake valve-to-piston clearance is reduced; retarding the cam reduces exhaust valve-to-piston clearance. To prevent the possibility of valvetrain and piston damage after changing camshaft timing, the piston-to-valve clearance should be verified before final engine assembly. If the clearance is insufficient, the valve reliefs in the piston should be deepened, or the camshaft timing readjusted to provide an adequate safety margin.

The first step in degreeing a camshaft is to accurately locate Top Dead Center (TDC) for the piston in cylinder No. 1. This can be done using a piston stop or dial indicator. TDC is located exactly halfway between the points where the piston contacts the stop when the crank is rotated clockwise and counterclockwise.

Adjust the degree wheel or its pointer so that the piston stops at the same number of degrees before and after the wheel's Top Dead Center mark. (If you

Check the camshaft timing with a degree wheel and a dial indicator. Adjust the timing with offset crank keys or cam sprocket bushings.

are using a dial indicator to determine Top Dead Center, note the readings on the degree wheel when the piston is at an arbitrary distance—.100-inch, for example—below the deck surface. TDC is exactly halfway between these two points. Adjust the degree wheel accordingly.)

The camshaft specification charts in the engine chapters contain information on the valve timing for various profiles. To determine whether the camshaft in your engine is advanced or retarded, compare the cam's actual intake centerline to the figure given in the specification chart.

The intake centerline is the point of maximum valve lift. To measure the intake centerline, set up a dial indicator on the intake lifter for cylinder No. 1. Because there is very little lifter movement as the tappet approaches its maximum lift, you should note the points when the tappet is .050-inch below its maximum lift as the crankshaft is turned in its normal direction of rotation. For example, record the reading on the degree wheel when the rising tappet is .050-inch from its maximum lift. Then continue turning the crank until the lifter begins to fall; note the reading again when the tappet is .050-inch below its maximum lift. The intake centerline is exactly halfway between these two readings.

In installations where high-lift camshafts and heavy-duty springs, retainers, and valve stem seals are used, all parts should be checked closely for adequate clearance. Make a temporary assembly of the complete valvetrain on the engine and check for possible interference between the spring retainer and seal at maximum valve lift, bottoming of the inner, outer, and damper coils at maximum lift, and possible interference between the rocker arm and valve spring retainer. Any of these conditions will result in very short engine life if not corrected.

Measure the installed height of the valve springs with a telescoping gauge or a machinist's rule. Also measure the valve spring tension at the installed height using an accurate spring tester. Hardened shims can be installed under the valve springs to increase seat pressure. If the installed height is reduced by inserting shims under the valve springs, make sure that the spring coils and dampers do not stack solid at maximum valve lift.

A molydisulfide-based grease should be applied to the lobes of Chevrolet hydraulic and mechanical flat lifter camshafts during final engine assembly. This high-pressure lubricant reduces the risk of premature wear on the camshaft lobes and tappets during the first minutes of engine operation. Initial run-in is very critical with high-performance flat tappet camshafts. The engine should not be allowed to idle below 2000 rpm for the first ½ hour of running time. Replace the oil filter on an engine assembled with this grease after initial break-in to prevent possible engine damage caused by molydisulfide grease plugging the filter.

If you have trouble with early cam lobe failure on a flat tappet cam, then it may be necessary to break in the replacement camshaft by running it with reduced valve spring loads. The cam should be run-in for approximately one hour with low-tension springs; after this break-in period, racing springs can be installed.

Record Keeping and Teardowns

Maintaining accurate records on dimensions and components is an essential part of engine building. These records can be an invaluable aid when rebuilding and overhauling competition engines. Many professional engine builders use standardized "build sheets" to record clearances, camshaft phasing, valve spring tension and other pertinent information. Sample sheets are included in the appendix of this manual. Photocopy these sheets and record the information for each engine you build.

The teardown phase is often overlooked by inexperienced engine builders. Barring an outright failure, the only way to accurately evaluate the durability and longevity of many engine components is to carefully examine them during disassembly. Measurement and inspection of the following items will give you valuable information about the engine's operating conditions and help pinpoint potential problems:

Valve lash. Significant changes in valve lash are an indication that the rocker arms or other valvetrain components are distressed.

Head bolt breakaway torque. You must use a beam-type torque wrench to measure head bolt breakaway torque; click-type torque wrenches cannot be used. Low breakaway torque readings are a sign of possible head gasket problems, since good gasket sealing requires adequate bolt torque. Low breakaway readings can also indicate that the engine was severely overheated.

Rod bolt torque. Low rod bolt torque readings are an indication that the engine has been over-revved sufficiently to stretch the fasteners. Stretched rod bolts should be replaced during reassembly.

Valve spring tension. Loss of valve spring tension indicates potential durability problems caused by the camshaft profile or the valve spring manufacturer. Over-revving the engine can also cause a loss of valve spring tension.

Bearing condition. Careful examination of the rod and main bearing inserts will reveal whether the oil filter and lubrication system are adequate. Distressed bearings may also indicate a warped or bent crankshaft, misaligned main bearing saddles, or improperly sized housings.

Piston condition. Excessive carbon below the top ring indicates poor ring seal or detonation. Erosion of the piston top and/or the ring land on the side of the piston opposite the spark plug is a sign of detonation. Small cracks in the lower corners of the piston skirt are frequently the result of excessive piston-to-bore clearance; cracks under the piston head are produced by excessively high piston temperature. Uneven coloring on the underside of the pistons indicates poor fuel mixture distribution to the cylinders. If the pistons appear to have run hotter from the front to the rear of the block, the cooling system circulation may be inadequate. Pin bore scuffing indicates insufficient clearance, inadequate lubrication, or out-of-round bores. Scuffing or excessive wear at the center or corners of the piston skirts indicates improper piston cam design. An absence of carbon on the piston squish areas may be caused by too little piston-to-head clearance.

Component inspection. In addition to the visual inspections described above, you may wish to Magnaflux or Zyglo inspect critical components during teardown. You should perform the same inspection on crankshafts, connecting rods, and similar parts when new to prevent confusing forging flaws with newly developed cracks. ⌐☰⌐

Chevrolet Small-Block V8

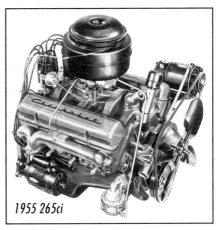

1955 265ci

The small-block Chevrolet V8 is America's most popular and most successful production-based racing engine. Since its debut in 1955, more than 60 million small-blocks have been manufactured, a feat unmatched by any other automotive engine. The amazing small-block Chevrolet V8 has powered more winning race cars and won more championships than any other motor.

During its lifetime, the small-block Chevrolet V8 has been produced in ten different displacements to suit a wide variety of tasks and applications. Despite the numerous improvements and design updates that have been made in the small-block's history, the engine's basic dimensions have remained fundamentally unchanged since its introduction. This continuity in design has contributed greatly to the small-block V8's tremendous popularity among performance enthusiasts. As a result, there is a huge selection of factory-produced and aftermarket high-performance hardware available for the small-block V8. Chevrolet's line of Bow Tie performance parts is designed to meet the needs of racers, engine builders, and enthusiasts for high-quality components.

The specifications and procedures in this chapter are intended primarily to aid Chevrolet enthusiasts in preparing the small-block V8 engine for "off-highway" and emission-exempt operation. This information applies to road racing, oval track competition, drag racing, heavy-duty marine use, off-road racing, and tractor pulls. Due to the diversity of sanctioning bodies' rules and the special demands of various types of motorsports, an

- America's Favorite Performance Engine
- Four Decades of Development
- Valvetrain and Cylinder Head Innovations

Many heavy-duty factory components for the Chevrolet small-block V8 were originally developed for high-performance Corvettes.

The small-block V8 is a mainstay of stock car racing. Chevrolet won ten NASCAR manufacturer's championships in 11 years (1983-93), and Dale Earnhardt won his sixth Winston Cup title in 1993.

Small-block V8s swept the SCCA Trans-Am manufacturer's and driver's championships three consecutive seasons (1991-93). Chevy has won 13 Trans-Am manufacturer's titles in the series' 28-year history.

TECH SPECS: SMALL-BLOCK V8 DESIGN FEATURES

Engine Displacement (ci)	Model Year	Bore (in.)	Stroke (in.)	Main Journal Dia. (in.)	Rod Journal Dia. (in.)	Main Bearing Cap
262	1975-76	3.671	3.10	2.45	2.10	2 Bolt
265	1955-56	3.750	3.00	2.30	2.00	2 Bolt
265	1994	3.740	3.00	2.45	2.10	2 Bolt
267	1979-81	3.500	3.48	2.45	2.10	2 Bolt
283	1957-67	3.875	3.00	2.30	2.00	2 Bolt
302	1967	4.000	3.00	2.30	2.00	2 Bolt
302	1968-69	4.000	3.00	2.45	2.10	4 Bolt
305	1976-94	3.736	3.48	2.45	2.10	2 Bolt
307	1968-73	3.875	3.25	2.45	2.10	2 Bolt
327	1962-67	4.000	3.25	2.30	2.00	2 Bolt
327	1968-69	4.000	3.25	2.45	2.10	2 Bolt
350	1967-94	4.000	3.48	2.45	2.10	2 & 4 Bolt
400	1970-72	4.125	3.75	2.65	2.10	4 Bolt
400	1973-80	4.125	3.75	2.65	2.10	2 Bolt

engine may require specific preparation procedures and accessories not covered in this manual. These specifications and recommendations are intended as general guidelines that have been tested and proven by leading competitors.

Many of the points discussed in this chapter apply specifically to the small-block V8. For additional information on engine building and blueprinting procedures, ignition systems, and lubrication requirements, refer to the chapters on these topics.

Small-Block V8 Interchangeability

The basic architecture of the small-block Chevrolet V8 has been unchanged since the engine's introduction in 1955. Many major and minor components are readily interchangeable among the millions of small-block Chevy V8s that have been produced. There are, however, several significant differences between various production engines.

The internal dimensions and design features of various Chevrolet small-block V8 engines are summarized in the accompanying chart. Chevrolet also offers several heavy-duty engine blocks and components that have never been installed in production vehicles. Technical details on these heavy-duty parts are included throughout this chapter.

LT1 Small-Block

A second-generation small-block V8 was introduced in the 1992 Corvette as the 5.7-liter (350ci) LT1. (The "LT-1" designation was also used in the early Seventies for an optional 350ci high-performance small-block, but the two engines are unrelated.) Production of this second-generation design was subsequently expanded in the 1994 model year to include a 4.3-liter (265ci) version. Although many internal components are

The L98 Corvette small-block was equipped with tuned-port fuel injection, aluminum cylinder heads, and tubular exhaust manifolds.

The second-generation small-block V8 is installed in late-model Corvettes, Camaros, and Caprices. A 4.3-liter version debuted in 1994.

Chevrolet small-blocks are hard to beat in the badlands. Larry Ragland drove Nelson & Nelson Racing's full-size Chevy pickup to back-to-back Class 8 off-road championships.

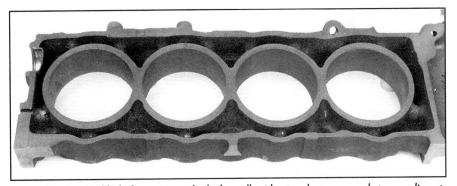

Heavy-duty Bow Tie blocks have siamesed cylinder walls without coolant passages between adjacent cylinders. This feature allows larger cylinder bores.

interchangeable between the first- and second-generation engines (including crankshafts, pistons, connecting rods, etc.), there are several significant differences between the two designs.

Features of the second-generation small-block include:

- Reverse flow cooling
- Gear-driven water pump
- Front-mounted optical distributor
- Short-runner electronic fuel injection intake manifold (with sequential fuel injection and mass airflow sensor in 1994 model year)

Due to these revisions, some components are not interchangeable between first- and second-generation small-block V8s. These parts include blocks, cylinder heads, intake manifolds, distributors, and water pumps.

It should be noted that second-generation small-blocks are installed only in specific production vehicles (Corvette, Camaro, Caprice). The original small-block V8 design continues to be used in other applications, including Chevrolet over-the-counter high-performance engine assemblies.

Block Selection

For high-performance and competition applications, the essential points to consider when selecting a block are material, cylinder bore diameter, cylinder wall thickness, main bearing diameter, main cap design, rear seal type, and lifter boss machining. The following is a summary of the chief differences between Chevrolet blocks.

Material

All production Chevrolet small-blocks are cast iron. Heavy-duty Bow Tie blocks are available in cast iron (GM 232-M specification) and aluminum (A-356 alloy, T6 heat treat). Although an aluminum blocks offers a substantial weight savings (approximately 100 pounds over a heavy-duty cast iron block), the cost of an aluminum block is significantly higher.

Cylinder Bores

For optimum performance and durability, the cylinder walls should be as thick as possible to minimize bore distortion and to reduce the risk of failure under severe loads.

In general, production blocks have thinner cylinder walls than heavy-duty Bow Tie castings. Production blocks are therefore lighter, but they are not as durable as heavy-duty castings under the stress of competition.

The largest cylinder bore diameter currently available in a production Chevrolet block is 4.00 inches. A production block's comparatively thin cylinder walls limit how far the cylinders can be overbored—an especially important consideration when preparing a used block. In most instances, production blocks can be

Weight Watchers

The following comparison highlights the weight differences between Chevrolet small-blocks. All weights are for bare blocks with main caps and cylinder liners (where applicable):

Description	Weight
Bow Tie aluminum small-block	90 lbs.
Production cast iron small-block V8	152 lbs.
Bow Tie cast iron small-block V8	183 lbs.

safely overbored .060-inch for street and moderate competition uses if the block does not have significant core shift. Boring a production block more than .060-inch oversize is not recommended.

Cast iron Bow Tie blocks are available with two types of cylinder barrels: "siamesed" and "non-siamesed." A block with non-siamesed cylinder walls has coolant passages between adjacent cylinders; a siamesed block has no water between its cylinders.

Siamesed cylinder walls allow larger bore diameters than cylinder barrels with coolant passages between them. For example, the cylinders in a cast iron Bow Tie block with siamesed cylinders can be safely bored to 4.150-inch diameter, while a non-siamesed version is limited to a maximum recommended bore diameter of 4.060-inch. Siamesed cylinder walls allow an engine builder to build an engine with more displacement than would be possible within the limitations of a production cylinder block.

Main Bearing Diameter

As the chart on page 2 points out, all small-blocks produced from 1955 through 1967 had 2.30-inch diameter crankshaft main bearing journals. These are commonly referred to as "small journal" blocks.

In 1967-68, blocks with larger 2.45-inch diameter mains were introduced. These blocks replaced the early-model small journal engines, and are known today as "medium journal" blocks. All current production engines (and most heavy-duty Bow Tie blocks) have 2.45-inch diameter mains.

In 1970 a 400-cubic-inch version of the small-block V8 was released. The 400 block's main journal size was increased

---

Second Generation Small-Block

The original 1970 LT-1 had a mechanical lifter camshaft, 11:1 compression, and a high-rise aluminum intake manifold with a four-barrel carburetor.

Major changes in the second-generation LT1 introduced in 1992 included reverse-flow cooling, a gear-driven coolant pump, a front-mounted optical distributor, and a one-piece manifold.

The legendary LT-1 small-block V8 enjoys a special place in the history of Chevrolet performance engines. For more than two decades, the 1970 LT-1 reigned as the most powerful production small-block ever offered. In 1992, a new and improved small-block replaced the LT-1 at the top of the horsepower chart. When Chevrolet's second-generation LT1 V8 debuted in the 1992 Corvette, it earned the distinction of being Chevrolet's most powerful production small-block.

The second-generation LT1 has a factory rating of 300 net horsepower—more than the original LT-1 and the fuel-injected 327s of the Sixties delivered under the same "real world" test conditions. But power is only a part of the story. The reborn V8 bristles with features that will propel America's favorite engine into the 21st century.

The second-generation small-block benefits from engineering advances in its cooling, ignition, induction, and exhaust systems. The new LT1's list of improvements includes reverse-flow cooling, a gear-driven water pump, a front-mounted optical distributor, a short-runner EFI intake manifold, and a high-lift hydraulic roller camshaft. The second-generation small-block is a more compact package than its predecessors, thanks to its relocated distributor, low-profile intake manifold, and redesigned accessory drive.

The most striking visual difference in the new engine design is the switch to a front-mounted distributor. The secto 2.65-inch diameter to enhance the durability of its long-stroke cast iron crankshaft. Among production engines, these "large journal" cranks are specific to the 400ci small-block, which was last produced in 1980. Aluminum Bow Tie blocks are also available with 2.65-inch diameter main bearings.

When selecting components for a high-performance small-block, it is important to match the block, crankshaft, and connecting rod dimensions to the engine's intended usage. Small journal crankshafts and connecting rods are suitable for some street high-performance and drag racing engines, but serious oval track, marine, and endurance racing applications require the additional durability provided by the larger rod and main bearing journals found in 1968 and later blocks.

400-type main bearings are recommended for large displacement (400+ cubic inch) small-block engines equipped with long stroke crankshafts. The larger main bearing diameter provides additional overlap between the crankshaft's main and rod bearing journals, thereby improving crankshaft durability.

Special main bearing inserts and spacers are available from aftermarket suppliers to accommodate non-standard block and crankshaft combinations. For example, a 3.48-inch stroke medium journal crankshaft can be installed in a large journal 400ci block using extra-thick main bearing inserts. Chevrolet also offers heavy-duty unfinished crankshaft forgings that can be machined for non-standard block/crank combinations. These forgings are described in the crankshaft section.

Main Bearing Caps

Three types of main bearing caps are available on Chevrolet small-block V8s:

Cast iron Bow Tie blocks are available with two-bolt main bearing caps for engine builders who prefer to install their own four-bolt caps.

two-bolt, parallel four-bolt, and splayed four-bolt.

Two-bolt cast iron main bearing caps are installed on standard production engines and some cast iron Bow Tie blocks. Two-bolt caps are suitable for street usage. Two-bolt caps are offered on Bow Tie blocks to allow engine builders to install four-bolt main bearing caps with-

The LT1's block and cylinder head castings were extensively revised from previous designs to accommodate reverse-flow cooling—coolant circulates through the cylinder heads before returning to the block.

ond-generation small-block's distributor is mounted on a precision-machined aluminum front cover and driven by a shaft from the camshaft sprocket. The sealed distributor housing contains a slotted shutter wheel and an optical sensor. A light source shines through the rotating shutter wheel to provide precise information on the crankshaft's position to a pre-processor in the computer-controlled ignition. The Powertrain Control Module (PCM) then determines the optimum spark timing.

The LT1's aluminum cylinder heads have free-flowing intake and exhaust runners, and feature high-efficiency heart-shaped combustion chambers. A one-piece aluminum fuel injection intake manifold enhances engine airflow and contributes to the engine's wide, flat power curve. Maximum camshaft lift is .450-inch, and the compression ratio is 10.2:1. Compared to the L98 small-block installed in 1991 Corvettes, the second-generation LT1 offers more torque below 2000 rpm, and increased power above 4000 rpm. The LT1's redline is 5700 rpm, up from the L98's 5000 rpm redline.

The LT1's reverse-flow cooling system is a dramatic departure from the traditional small-block design. Coolant enters the front of the block and is immediately channeled to the cylinder heads, where it cools the combustion chambers, spark plugs, and exhaust ports. The pre-heated coolant then returns to the block, where it circulates around the cylinder barrels before re-entering the water pump. Vapors formed in the cooling system are scavenged through vents at the rear of the cylinder heads, ensuring that only liquid coolant circulates through the system.

This reverse-flow cooling system offers several advantages. The potential for leaks is reduced by eliminating several gaskets and the intake manifold coolant cross-over. The vapor elimination system provides a solid coolant stream that improves heat transfer and reduces cavitation. Routing the coolant to the cylinder heads first also promotes higher cylinder bore temperatures and reduced friction.

The centerpiece of the LT1's reverse-flow cooling system is a gear-driven water pump. The pump shaft is turned by a spur gear on the camshaft sprocket. This drive system eliminates the side-loads on the pump's seals and bearings produced by a conventional belt drive. The water pump casting routes coolant into and out of the block. Its two-way thermostat mixes hot coolant from the block with cool liquid from the radiator to reduce thermal shock to the engine.

The LT1's block and cylinder head castings were extensively redesigned to accommodate the changes in the cooling and ignition system. As a result, these components are not interchangeable with previous small-blocks. The 5.7-liter small-block's familiar 4.00-inch diameter cylinders and 3.48-inch stroke crankshaft were retained, however. The Corvette LT1's bottom end is bolstered with four-bolt caps on the three center main bearings.

After 37 years of continuous production, the Chevrolet small-block V8 was given an invigorating infusion of advanced technology. GM Powertrain engineers have updated a classic design while respecting the small-block's legendary virtues of simplicity, reliability, and performance.

Production gray iron four-bolt main bearing caps have parallel bolt holes. Four-bolt caps are installed on the three middle main bearings.

Small-block Chevrolets manufactured from 1955-85 used a two-piece rear crankshaft seal and a four-piece oil pan gasket.

The lifter bosses in pre-1987 small-blocks are not machined for production hydraulic roller lifters.

Steel four-bolt main bearing caps are available on "race-prepared" Bow Tie blocks. The four-bolt front cap will clear a standard oil pan.

1986 and newer blocks are machined for one-piece rear seals. This seal design required a revised crankshaft flywheel flange and oil pan.

Late-model blocks have tall lifter bosses for hydraulic roller lifters. The tops of the bosses are machined flat.

out having to plug holes in the main bearing bulkheads.

Four-bolt gray cast iron main bearing caps are installed on the three middle main bearings on some production blocks. These caps have four parallel

BOW TIE TIPS
Main Cap Guidelines

Four different types of main bearing caps are available for Chevrolet small-block V8 engines. The following are recommended usages for these main cap designs:

Type	Application
Two-bolt grey iron	Street
Four-bolt grey iron (Parallel bolts)	High-performance
Four-bolt nodular iron (Parallel bolts)	Moderate competition
Four-bolt steel (Splayed bolts)	Maximum effort competition

These are general guidelines for main cap usage; various types of main caps may provide satisfactory performance in a wide range of operating conditions, depending on engine speed, power output, and other factors.

("straight") bolt holes. The four-bolt caps' increased clamping force and their larger interface with the block's main bearing bulkheads reduce bearing cap movement under high loads.

Four-bolt nodular iron main bearing caps are similar in appearance to gray cast iron caps. These intermediate bearing caps also have four parallel bolt holes, but the nodular iron material provides superior strength. Nodular caps are installed on some Bow Tie blocks intended for limited competition applications.

Four-bolt steel main bearing caps are recommended for maximum competition. Chevrolet steel main bearing caps for the three middle main bearings (No. 2, 3, and 4) have splayed outer bolt holes. These angled outer bolts anchor the cap to the strongest part of the block structure to reduce cap movement and minimize bearing bore distortion under the stress of racing. Steel front main bearing caps with four parallel bolts and two-bolt steel rear main caps are installed on some cast iron and all aluminum Bow Tie blocks.

Rear Seals

Production Chevrolet small-block V8 engines produced from 1955 through 1985 used a two-piece rear crankshaft seal. (Engines produced before 1959 used a rope-type seal; later engines used a more effective two-piece wiper seal.) In

1986, a leak-resistant one-piece rear was introduced. This new seal design required revisions in the crankshaft flywheel flange, rear main bearing cap, block, oil pan, and flywheel. Consequently these components are not interchangeable with engines manufactured before 1986.

Crankshafts that use a one-piece rear oil seal have a smaller flywheel flange bolt pattern than pre-1986 cranks designed for two-piece seals (3.00-inch vs. 3.58-inch bolt circle). The old-style large diameter flywheel flange bolt pattern is preferred for high-performance and competition applications. Production crankshafts used with one-piece seals also require counterweighted flywheels or flex-plates for proper engine balance.

Various Chevrolet Bow Tie blocks are machined for one-piece and two-piece rear seals as described later in this chapter. Seal adapters are available to allow the use of early-style crankshafts and flywheels with blocks machined for one-piece seals.

Lifter Boss Machining

Hydraulic roller lifters were introduced on Chevrolet production small-block V8 production engines in 1987. Blocks designed for hydraulic roller lifters have taller lifter bosses than conventional blocks. The tops of the lifter bosses are machined flat to accommodate roller lifter guides. Three mounting bosses in the lifter valley attach a lifter guide retainer. The front cam bearing boss also has mounts for a camshaft thrust plate.

Conventional flat tappets can be installed in a block machined for hydraulic roller lifters. However, production roller lifters cannot be installed in a block that does not have provisions for them.

Design Revisions

Minor design revisions have been made to the small-block Chevrolet V8 during its long production run. While these changes do not significantly impact a particular block's performance potential, they may require changes in related components. These revisions include:

Oil Dipsticks

Production blocks have been manufactured with right-hand (passenger's side) and left-hand (driver's side) oil dipsticks. If you are using an oil pan with a dipstick relief, it must match the block's oil pan rail to seal properly. Cast iron Bow Tie blocks have dipstick bosses on both pan rails; neither boss is drilled.

Clutch Pivot Balls

On some production blocks, the mounting hole above the oil filter pad is not drilled and tapped for a clutch linkage pivot ball.

Starter Mounting Holes

Chevrolet starter motors have two different bolt patterns to accommodate two flywheel diameters. Some production blocks are not machined for both starter bolt patterns.

Engine Assemblies

Chevrolet offers two complete engine assemblies that can be the basis for a high-performance street or limited competition small-block V8. The chief advantage of purchasing an engine assembly is that all components are in new condition, eliminating the uncertainty and cost of reconditioning used components.

Special Performance 350ci/300hp Engine Assembly—PN 12355345

The 300hp special performance 350ci engine assembly is designed for street use in emission-exempt 1968 and older cars and trucks. It can also replace any 265ci to 400ci small-block for off-highway use.

This block has dipstick holes on both oil pan rails; most blocks have only a single hole on the left-hand or right-hand oil pan rail. This block also has two starter motor bolt patterns.

This engine's nominal compression ratio is 9.1:1. The block has four-bolt main bearing caps and a one-piece rear seal. The cast iron cylinder heads have 64cc combustion chambers and non-swirl intake ports for enhanced performance.

This assembly also includes a chrome-plated timing cover and chromed rocker covers with the Chevrolet Bow Tie emblem. An intake manifold, distributor, flywheel, balancer, water pump, and exhaust manifolds are not included in this engine assembly.

The 350ci/300hp engine uses a one-piece rear main seal, and requires a counterweighted flywheel; see the flywheel section for recommended part numbers. Two balancers are recommended for this engine assembly: PN 6272221 (6.75-inch diameter) and PN 6272224 (8-inch diameter). The oil dipstick is located on the right-hand (passenger) side of the block; check for clearance in early-model chassis. Two four-barrel intake manifolds with dual pattern carburetor flanges are recommended: PN 14096011 (cast iron) and PN 10185063 (aluminum). A 600cfm to 650cfm four-barrel carburetor will provide satisfactory performance.

5.7L (350ci) High Output Engine Assembly—PN 10185072

The 350ci High Output (H.O.) Chevrolet small-block V8 offers outstanding performance at an affordable price. It is intended primarily for emis-

The 350ci/300hp special performance engine assembly is an affordable alternative to a rebuilt motor for emission-exempt vehicles.

sion-exempt and off-highway applications. However, when installed with a complete H.O. 350 performance package (PN 10185077), the H.O. 350 meets emission requirements under EPA Memorandum 1A for operation in 49 states (excluding California). The conversion is legal in California under California Air Resources Board Exemption Order #D-278. (The H.O. 350 performance package is described in detail at the end of this chapter.)

The H.O. 350 small-block V8 was introduced in 1989 as PN 10134338. This original H.O. engine was known as the "ZZZ" version, a reference to the manufacturing code stamped on the block's serial number pad just above the water pump. The H.O. engine package was subsequently updated and released as the "ZZ2" (PN 10185025).

BOW TIE SPECS
H.O. 350 Engine

Part Number:	10185072 ("ZZ3")
Displacement:	5.7-liter (350 cubic inches)
Horsepower:	345 @ 5250 rpm
Bore/Stroke:	4.00" x 3.48"
Compression Ratio:	9.8:1
Engine Block:	Cast iron with parallel four-bolt main bearing caps (#10105123)
Crankshaft:	Forged 1053 steel with one-piece rear seal (#14096036)
Connecting Rods:	1053 forged steel, heat-treated, shotpeened, "pink" color code (#14096846)
Pistons:	Cast hypereutectic (high silicon) aluminum with offset pins (#10181389)
Camshaft:	Hydraulic roller tappet (#10185071)
Valve Lift (Intake/Exhaust):	.474"/.510"
Duration (Intake/Exhaust):	208/221 degrees @ .050" tappet lift
Cylinder Heads:	Cast aluminum, 58cc chambers, angled spark plugs, screw-in rocker studs (#10185056)
Valve Diameter (Intake/Exhaust):	1.94"/1.50"
Valve Springs:	Chrome silicon wire with damper, orange color code (#10134358)

The 345hp H.O. 350 engine is assembled and tested at the factory. The H.O. 350's components include aluminum cylinder heads, a dual-plane intake manifold, and a high-performance hydraulic roller cam.

An H.O. 350 engine assembly is a good choice for bracket racing, autocross, and other emission-exempt performance applications.

The latest version was introduced in 1992 with numerous improvements as the "ZZ3" (PN 10185072). For a detailed list of changes, see the sidebar on page 20.

The H.O. 350 engine assembly is a bolt-in replacement for all 265-400ci small-block Chevrolet V8s. This assembly combines proven small-block components with the latest advances in engine technology, including lightweight aluminum cylinder heads, low-friction hydraulic roller tappets, and hypereutectic (high-silicon) pistons.

High Output 5.7-liter engines are assembled using brand new, premium quality components. All H.O. small-blocks are fire-tested and final balanced at the factory to ensure their quality and performance. A prototype H.O. 350 engine equipped with a Quadrajet carburetor, 1¾-inch headers, and low-restriction mufflers produced 345 horsepower (at 5250 rpm) and 387 lb.-ft. of torque (at 3250 rpm).

The following are some of the features of the H.O. 350 engine assembly:

Intake Manifold

A low-profile dual-plane aluminum intake manifold (PN 10185063) produces the same horsepower as previous high-rise designs, but provides increased hood clearance and more versatility. The new manifold has a dual-pattern flange that accommodates both standard-flange Holley and spread-bore Quadrajet four-barrel carburetors. It also has provisions for all late-model accessory brackets, EGR (exhaust gas recirculation), and an integral hot air choke. (Block-off plates are installed on the EGR and choke stove on H.O. 350 engines.)

Camshaft

A hydraulic roller camshaft (PN 10185071) bolsters mid-range torque and improves driveability without sacrificing peak horsepower. This dual-pattern profile has .474-inch intake lift and .510-inch exhaust lift. Intake duration is 208 degrees (at .050-inch tappet lift), and exhaust duration is 221 degrees.

Valvetrain

The H.O. 350 valvetrain uses lightweight valve spring retainers that have half the mass of the previous design. Valve stem seals are installed on the exhaust valves to enhance oil control, and the aluminum cylinder heads are outfitted with radiused valve seat inserts.

Rocker Covers

The H.O. engine's stamped steel rocker covers orient the PCV valve properly for most applications.

Accessories

The 5.7-liter High Output engine assembly also includes a torsional damper, a cast iron water pump (standard rotation, long-style), a 12¾-inch diameter automatic transmission flexplate (153 tooth ring gear), and a dipstick. It does not include spark plug wires, pulleys, exhaust manifolds, a starter motor, an oil filter, an oil filter adapter, a fuel pump, or external accessories.

An H.O. 350 partial engine assembly is available as PN 10185065. This "short block" assembly includes the block, crankshaft, pistons, rings, and connecting rods only.

H.O. engines are equipped with hypereutectic (high silicon) pistons with 9.8:1 compression and forged steel connecting rods.

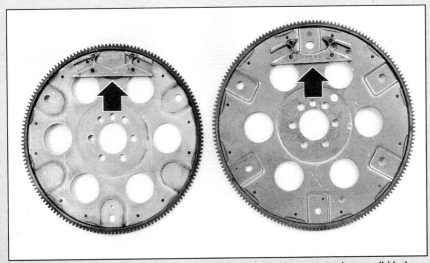

Flexplate alternatives: Automatic transmission flywheels for High Output 5.7-liter small-blocks have a 3.00-inch diameter bolt circle and a counterweight for proper engine balance.

A 750cfm carburetor with mechanical or vacuum-operated secondaries will perform well on an H.O. 350 small-block.

H.O. 350 Installation Notes

Wheel Deal

Like all Chevrolet small-block V8 and V6/90 engines produced since 1986, the High Output 5.7-liter Chevy has a 3.00-inch diameter flywheel flange bolt pattern. Small-block V8 and V6/90 engines produced from 1955 through 1985 have a 3.58-inch diameter flywheel flange bolt pattern. This change in the bolt circle diameter was made to accommodate a leak-resistant one-piece rear main seal. 1986 and newer cranks also require a counterbalanced flywheel (or flexplate) for proper engine balance.

The High Output engine assembly includes a 12¾-inch diameter automatic transmission flexplate (PN 14088765). The flexplates and manual transmission flywheels listed below have the correct bolt pattern and counterweight for High Output engine installations. (For additional information on parts interchangeability, see the crankshaft and flywheel sections in this chapter.)

P/N	Description
14088761	Automatic transmission flexplate, 14-inch diameter
14088767	Automatic transmission flexplate, 14-inch diameter, heavy-duty
14088650	Manual transmission flywheel, 12¾-inch diameter
14088646	Manual transmission flywheel, 12¾-inch diameter, lightweight
14088648	Manual transmission flywheel, 14-inch diameter

Carburetor Calibrations

Holley engineers conducted a series of carburetor tests on a 1989 Camaro equipped with a 350 H.O. engine to determine recommended calibrations. Various 750cfm and 600cfm four-barrel carburetors were evaluated. The following calibrations produced the best quarter-mile performance:

Model 4010 750cfm double-pumper: List 84013 carburetor equipped with air cleaner spacer #17-14 (included with carburetor) and a 14-inch diameter air cleaner with a 2-inch tall element. Primary and secondary accelerator pump shooters were hand drilled from .026-inch to .040-inch to improve throttle tip-in and quicken response at cruising speed. Carburetor was equipped with No. 70 primary jets, No. 80 secondary jets, and a stock power valve. Connecting the HEI distributor's vacuum advance mechanism to a spark-ported vacuum source enhanced throttle response. Related components: Electric choke kit #45-223 (grind secondary pump cam lever for clearance); center-hung nitrophyl float #116-3 (prevents fuel slosh from bowl vents on hard acceleration).

Model 4010 750cfm vacuum secondary: List 84011 carburetor equipped with air cleaner spacer #17-14 and 14-inch air cleaner with a 3-inch tall element. Primary main jets increased from #75 to #78 (Holley PN 122-78) to improve part-throttle driveability. Accelerator pump shooter hand drilled from .026-inch to .035-inch. Related components: Secondary spring kit #20-13 (best performance with white spring—not recommended for street use); quick-change diaphragm cover kit #20-59; center-hung nitrophyl float #116-3.

BOW TIE TIPS

Charting the Changes

The H.O. 350 small-block V8 was introduced in 1989. Three different versions have been produced to date. The following summary highlights the significant revisions made to H.O. engines:

PN 10134338 ("ZZZ")

Cast hypereutectic (high-silicon) pistons with 9.8:1 compression and no wrist pin offset. Single-pattern camshaft with 235 degrees duration (at .050-inch tappet lift) and .480-inch maximum lift.

PN 10185025 ("ZZ2")

Revised piston design with offset pins for quieter cold-start operation. Minor intake manifold casting revisions to accommodate late-model accessory mounting brackets.

PN 10185072 ("ZZ3")

New low-profile intake manifold with dual-pattern carburetor flange and provisions for exhaust gas recirculation (EGR) and hot air choke. New dual-pattern camshaft profile with 208/221-degree intake/exhaust duration and

The original ZZZ H.O. 350 engine debuted in 1989 with a high-rise intake manifold and a single-pattern hydraulic roller camshaft.

.474"/.510" valve lift. Revised cylinder head assembly with reduced mass spring retainers, exhaust valve stem seals, and radiused valve seat inserts. Stamped rocker covers with revised PCV valve location.

Peak output for all three versions is 345 horsepower. However, the dual-pattern camshaft installed in the ZZ3 engine improves low-speed and mid-range torque compared to the single-pattern profile used in earlier engines.

Engine Blocks

Chevrolet offers a variety of production and heavy-duty engine blocks that are suitable for high-performance and competition applications. The following is an overview of small-block choices:

Production 350 Block
PN 10105123

This block is used in 1986 and newer high-performance applications, including the H.O. 350 engine assembly. It has 4.00-inch diameter cylinder bores and four-bolt cast iron intermediate main bearing caps with parallel bolt holes. This block is machined for hydraulic roller lifters; conventional flat tappets can also be installed in this block. It uses a one-piece crankshaft rear seal. The oil dipstick hole is on the right (passenger) side of the casting.

Production 305 Block
PN 10066098

This block is identical to the production 350 block except for its 3.74-inch diameter cylinder bores and two-bolt gray iron main bearing caps.

TECH SPECS: ENGINE BLOCKS

Part Number	10066098	10105123	10066034	10051181	10051183	10185047
Description	Production 305	Production 350	Goodwrench	Bow Tie	Bow Tie	Bow Tie
Block Material	Cast iron	Cast iron	Cast iron	Cast iron	Cast iron	Cast iron
Cylinder Wall Type	Non-siamesed	Non-siamesed	Non-siamesed	Non-siamesed	Siamesed	Siamesed
Cylinder Deck Height	9.025"	9.025"	9.025"	9.025"	9.025"	9.025"
Cylinder Bore Range	3.740–3.770"	4.000–4.030"	4.000–4.030"	3.725–4.020"	3.980–4.090"	3.980–4.090"
Bearing Cap Bolts	2	4	4	2	2	4
Cap Bolt Orientation	Straight	Straight	Straight	Straight	Straight	Straight
Bearing Cap Type	Gray cast iron	Gray cast iron	Gray cast iron	Gray cast iron	Gray cast iron	Nodular cast iron
Crankshaft Journal Diameter	2.45"	2.45"	2.45"	2.45"	2.45"	2.45"
Oil Sump Type	Wet	Wet	Wet	Wet	Wet	Wet
Crankshaft Seal Type	1 piece	1 piece	2 piece	1 piece	1 piece	1 piece
Design Max. Stroke	3.75"	3.75"	3.75"	3.75"	3.75"	3.75"
Weight (lbs., bare)	N/A	N/A	N/A	181	181	182
Intended Max. HP @ RPM	300 @5500	350 @ 5700	350 @ 5700	375 @ 5750	400 @ 5750	450 @ 6500
Intended Usage	Street	Street	Street	Street	Street	Amateur Competition

A Goodwrench replacement block with four-bolt main bearing caps and 4.00-inch cylinder bores is recommended for engine builders on a budget.

The Goodwrench block has gray iron four-bolt bearing caps with parallel bolt holes on the three middle main bearings.

The front bulkhead of a Goodwrench block can be drilled for an inlet line to supply oil directly to the center oil gallery.

Goodwrench Block
PN 10066034

The "Goodwrench" cast iron bare block is designed for limited racing applications that do not require the strength of a heavy-duty Bow Tie casting. This block has 4.00-inch diameter cylinder bores with the same cylinder wall thickness as a production case. It is approximately 40 pounds lighter than a heavy-duty Bow Tie casting—a weight savings that can significantly improve handling in some racing vehicles. Its features include:

Main Bearing Caps

This block has production-type four-bolt gray iron main bearing caps with parallel outer bolt holes on the three intermediate main bearings. The two-bolt front and rear main bearing caps are cast iron. The rear cap is machined for a pre-1986 two-piece crankshaft seal and a pre-1986 oil pan.

Oiling System

Material is added to the front bulkhead to accommodate a front oil inlet line. This boss can be drilled and tapped to route oil directly to the central oil gallery from an external oil pump. The oil pan rail has provisions for a dipstick on both sides of the block. The oil filter pad is machined for an early-style large diameter filter.

Accessories

The Goodwrench block has provisions for front and side motor mounts and a mechanical fuel pump.

Cast Iron Bow Tie Blocks

Heavy-duty Bow Tie cast iron blocks are recommended for maximum-effort small-block competition engines. These blocks offer outstanding durability under the stress of racing. The cylinder walls in Bow Tie blocks are significantly thicker (and therefore stronger) than production engine cases. This feature promotes a more effective ring seal and reduces cylinder wall failures under sustained high loads. The deck surfaces in Bow Tie blocks are also thicker than the decks in production blocks to improve head gasket sealing. The head bolt holes are blind tapped, and do not penetrate the water jacket to prevent coolant leaks.

All cast iron Bow Tie blocks are machined for crankshafts with 2.45-inch diameter main journals. The main bearing bulkheads in Bow Tie blocks are reinforced to resist cracking with long-stroke crankshafts.

TECH SPECS: ENGINE BLOCKS

Part Number	24502501	24502503	24502525	10134399	10134400	10185075
Description	Race-Prepared Bow Tie	Race-Prepared Bow Tie	Race-Prepared Bow Tie	Aluminum Bow Tie	Aluminum Bow Tie	Aluminum Bow Tie
Block Material	Cast iron	Cast iron	Cast iron	A356-T6	A356-T6	A356-T6
Cylinder Wall Type	Non-siamesed	Siamesed	Siamesed	Siamesed	Siamesed	Siamesed
Cylinder Deck Height	9.025"	9.025"	9.150"	9.025"	9.025"	9.025"
Cylinder Bore Range	3.750–4.020"	3.995–4.160"	3.995–4.160"	4.000"–4.125"	4.125"	4.000"–4.125"
Bearing Cap Bolts	4	4	4	4	4	4
Cap Bolt Orientation	Splayed 20°	Splayed 20°	Splayed 20°	Splayed 20°	Splayed 20°	Splayed 20°
Bearing Cap Type	8620 steel	8620 steel	8620 steel	8620 steel	8620 steel	8620 steel
Crankshaft Journal Diameter	2.45"	2.45"	2.45"	2.45"	2.65"	2.45"
Oil Sump Type	Wet	Wet	Wet	Dry	Dry	Wet
Crankshaft Seal Type	2 piece	2 piece	2 piece	2 piece	2 piece	2 piece
Design Max. Stroke	3.75"	3.75"	3.75"	3.75"	4.00"	3.75"
Weight (lbs., bare)	183	183	186	90	89	90
Intended Max. HP @ RPM	700 @ 8500	800 @ 8500	800 @ 8500	700 @ 8500	800 @ 8600	500 @ 6800
Intended Usage	Professional Competition	Professional Competition	Professional Competition	Professional Competition	Professional Competition	Amateur Competition

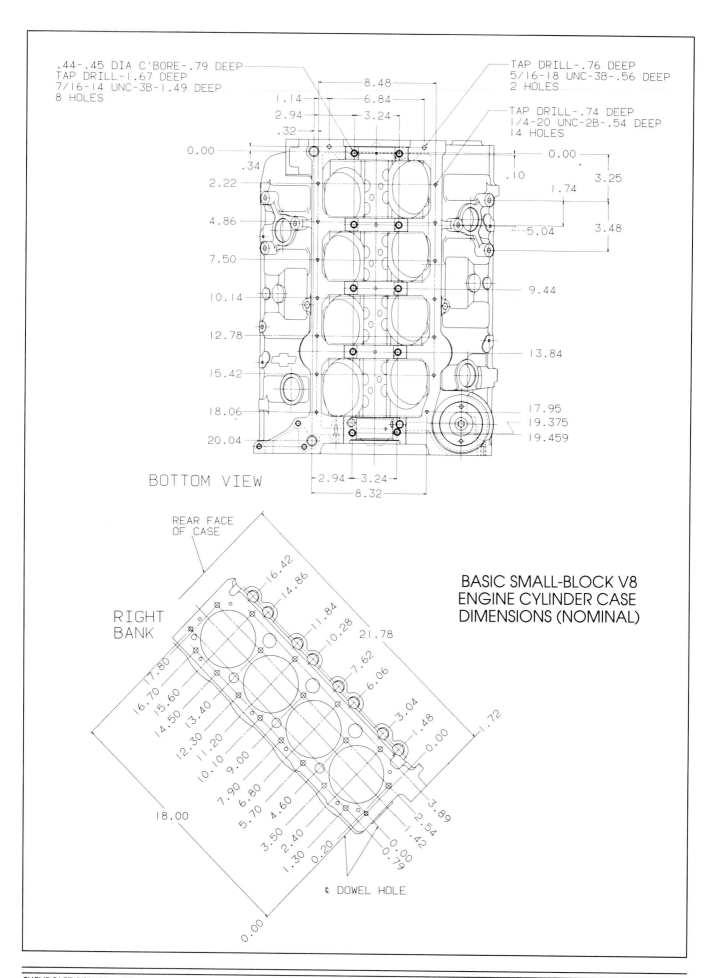

.44-.45 DIA C'BORE-.79 DEEP
TAP DRILL-1.67 DEEP
7/16-14 UNC-3B-1.49 DEEP
8 HOLES

TAP DRILL-.76 DEEP
5/16-18 UNC-3B-.56 DEEP
2 HOLES

TAP DRILL-.74 DEEP
1/4-20 UNC-2B-.54 DEEP
14 HOLES

BOTTOM VIEW

REAR FACE
OF CASE

RIGHT
BANK

BASIC SMALL-BLOCK V8
ENGINE CYLINDER CASE
DIMENSIONS (NOMINAL)

¢ DOWEL HOLE

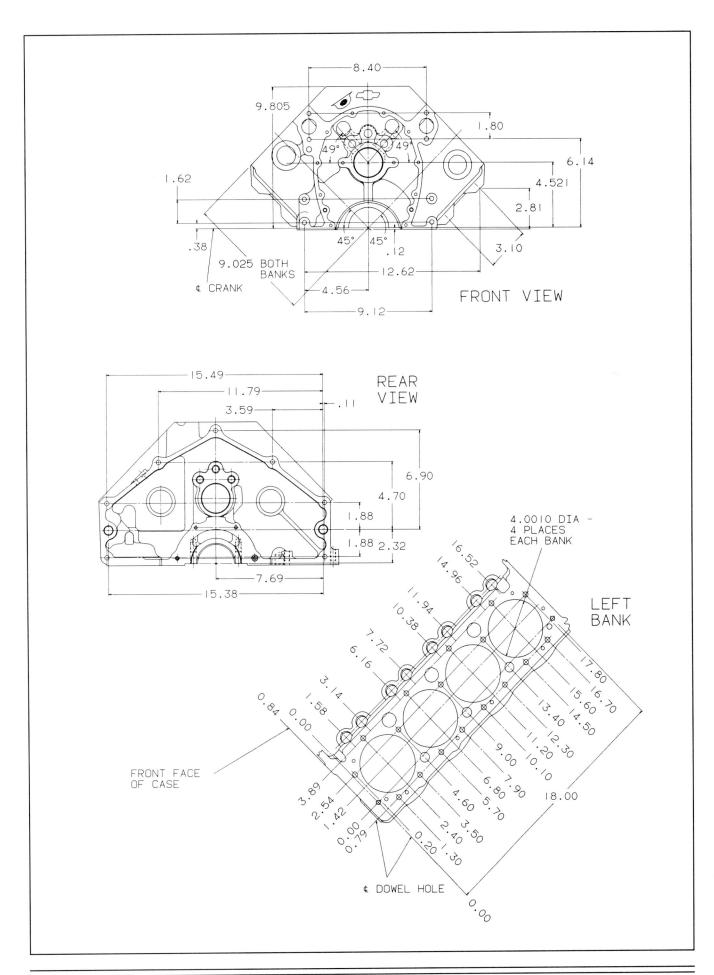

8.40

9.805

1.80

6.14

4.521

2.81

3.10

1.62

.38

.12

45° 45°

49° 49°

9.025 BOTH
BANKS

¢ CRANK

12.62

4.56

9.12

FRONT VIEW

15.49

11.79

3.59

.11

REAR
VIEW

6.90

4.70

1.88

1.88 2.32

7.69

15.38

4.0010 DIA –
4 PLACES
EACH BANK

16.52

14.96

11.94

10.38

7.72

6.16

3.14

1.58

0.84 0.00

LEFT
BANK

17.80

16.70

15.60

14.50

13.40

12.30

11.20

10.10

9.00

7.90

6.80

5.70

4.60

3.50

2.40

1.30

0.20

18.00

FRONT FACE
OF CASE

3.89

2.54

1.42

0.00

0.79

¢ DOWEL HOLE

0.00

Cast iron Bow Tie blocks are available in several configurations. Three part numbers are machined on production tooling, and offer a choice of two-bolt and four-bolt cast iron main bearing caps. In addition, three "race-prepared" versions are offered for engine builders who require a ready-to-assemble block.

The following are technical highlights of Chevrolet cast iron Bow Tie blocks:

10051181	3.73" Bore Bow Tie Block, 2-Bolt Main Bearing Caps
10051183	3.98" Bore Bow Tie Block, 2-Bolt Main Bearing Caps
10185047	3.98" Bore Bow Tie Block, 4-Bolt Iron Main Bearing Caps

Cylinder Bores

Cast iron Bow Tie small-block engine blocks are available with two different cylinder bore diameters. The castings are externally similar, but there are important differences in the two blocks' internal water jackets. The 3.73-inch "small-bore" block (casting number 10051182) has fully jacketed cylinders with .110-inch water passages between its cylinder barrels. The small-bore Bow Tie block's cylinder walls will "clean up" when bored to 3.875-inch diameter; the maximum recommended bore diameter for this casting is 4.030-inch. The 3.98-inch "big bore" version (casting number 10051184) has siamesed cylinder walls with no water passages between adjacent bores. The big-bore version can be finished with 4.00-inch diameter cylinders, and the maximum recommended cylinder bore diameter for these blocks is 4.160-inch.

Both siamesed and non-siamesed Bow Tie blocks have a nominal cylinder wall thickness of .340-inch at the casting parting line (measured two inches below the deck surface). These extra-thick cylinder walls resist distortion under high loads, improving ring seal and reducing cylinder wall failures.

These Bow Tie blocks give competition engine builders a wide choice of displacements. The small-bore Bow Tie block is an excellent starting point for small displacement engines used in many drag racing and road racing classes. The small-bore Bow Tie block will also appeal to engine builders who prefer full water jackets for endurance racing.

A big-bore Bow Tie engine block with siamesed cylinder walls is the ideal foundation for a large displacement small-block. Even at its maximum recom-

"Small-bore" Bow Tie blocks have non-siamesed cylinder walls; "big-bore" versions have siamesed cylinders that can be bored to 4.150-inch.

The machined main bearing bulkheads in cast iron Bow Tie blocks are .900-inch thick. The front and rear bulkheads are ribbed for strength.

Bow Tie blocks with two-bolt main bearing caps can be upgraded with factory or aftermarket four-bolt caps. The rear of the block is machined for a one-piece seal, and the casting has dipstick bosses on both sides of the oil pan rail. The oil filter pad uses an early-model large filter.

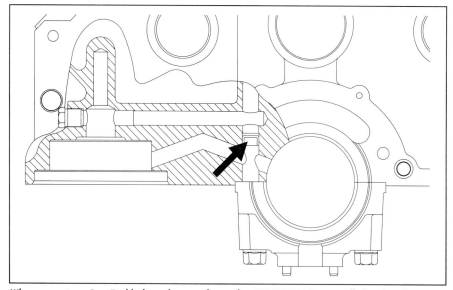

When preparing a Bow Tie block, make sure that a plug (PN 3701638) is installed in the oil passage above the rear main cap as shown. If this plug is missing, oil will not be routed to the filter and the engine will not have satisfactory oil pressure.

mended bore diameter of 4.160-inch, the Bow Tie block's nominal wall thickness on the cylinder thrust surfaces is at least .250-inch.

Main Caps

Production gray iron two-bolt main bearing caps are installed on Bow Tie blocks available as PN 10051181 and 10051183. This simplifies the installation of main bearing caps with angled outer bolt holes by eliminating the need to plug unused bolt holes in the main bearing bulkheads. The GM Motorsports Technology Group (GM MTG) recommends the installation of steel four-bolt main bearing caps on all Bow Tie blocks used in competition.

For engine builders on a budget, a Bow Tie block with nodular iron four-bolt main bearing caps (PN 10185047) is an affordable alternative that eliminates the expense of installing replacement caps. The three intermediate four-bolt iron caps have straight bolt holes.

The Bow Tie block's oil galleries extend to the rear face of the engine case. The latest castings have provisions for a camshaft block-off plate.

A production camshaft thrust plate can be installed on the front cam bearing to limit forward cam movement in a Bow Tie block.

The fully machined main bearing bulkheads are .900-inch thick. Additional ribs strengthen the front and rear bulkheads. Bow Tie blocks have dipstick bosses on both sides of the crankcase; neither boss is drilled for a dipstick tube.

Reinforced Decks

The Bow Tie blocks' deck surfaces are thicker than production castings. Blind tapped head bolt holes enhance head gasket sealing and prevent coolant leaks around the fasteners.

Valley Scavenge System

A Bow Tie block has a boss below the bellhousing flange behind the No. 8 cylinder that can be drilled and tapped for a lifter valley oil scavenge line. This is a popular modification on competition engines equipped with dry sump oiling systems.

Oil drainback holes in the lifter valley are drilled instead of cast. This reduces casting flash, and simplifies sealing the valley with pipe plugs when installing a scavenge system.

Cooling System

Bow Tie blocks have bosses on the outer water jacket walls to accommodate cooling system modifications. Large bosses in the center of the block can be drilled and tapped for auxiliary water inlet lines from the water pump. Smaller bosses just below the deck surfaces provide starting points for drilling coolant holes between the siamesed cylinders in 3.98-inch bore blocks.

Rear Seal

Cast iron Bow Tie blocks are machined for one-piece rear main seals described previously in the "Block Selection" section. A crankshaft designed for a two-piece rear seal can be installed in a Bow Tie block using an aluminum seal adapter (PN 10051118). Refer to the "Crankshaft Seal Adapter" section in this chapter for installation instructions.

Oil Galleries

The Bow Tie block's oil galleries extend to the front and rear faces of the cylinder case. The ends of the galleries are machined flat, providing a smooth starting surface for the drill bits that bore the oil holes from the front and rear of the block. These extended front galleries can interfere with some camshaft drive systems, however; clearance should be checked before engine assembly.

Approximately .070-inch of material has been added around the oil galleries to allow engine builders to enlarge the passages for increased flow. The larger oil gallery bosses may not clear some timing sets and aftermarket camshaft drives; check for interference before final assembly.

Camshaft Anti-Walk Plate

The flange around the front camshaft bearing has provisions for a production camshaft thrust retainer. Two bosses on the sides of the cam bearing are drilled and tapped to mount the "anti-walk" plate. This feature provides a reliable method of controlling camshaft movement, and eliminates the need for a stopbolt on the bottom of the water pump to limit camshaft thrust.

Cam Bearings

Additional material has been added around the front and rear camshaft bearing bores. This extra iron allows engine builders to enlarge the cam bearing bores to accommodate roller cam bearings or big-block Chevrolet V8 cam bearing inserts for endurance racing applications.

Camshaft Block-Off Plate

Bosses have been added to the sides of the rear camshaft bearing to allow the installation of a block-off plate. This is a more reliable method of sealing the camshaft tunnel in a competition engine than a production soft plug. The holes for the block-off plate are drilled and tapped.

Lifter Bosses

The Bow Tie block's lifter bores are finish machined to production specifications; bushed lifter bores are not required in most applications. The lifter bosses are .150-inch wider per side than a production block. These bosses can be machined for offset or large diameter lifters.

Race-Prepared Bow Tie Blocks

24502501	3.750" Bore Race-Prepared Bow Tie Small-Block
24502503	3.995" Bore Race-Prepared Bow Tie Small-Block
24502525	3.995" Bore Race-Prepared Tall-Deck Small-Block

These three "blueprinted" engine blocks simplify the task of preparing a Chevrolet small-block V8 for competition. The external surfaces are machined in a series of operations performed by automated CNC equipment. The decks, oil pan rails, bellhousing flange, and the front face are precision machined to ensure that they are square and true. The cylinder head dowel holes are accurately located in relation to the crankshaft thrust surface. This feature is a boon to engine builders who rely on the position of the cylinder head dowels as reference points for subsequent machining operations.

The cylinder walls in race-prepared Bow Tie blocks are sonic tested to ensure consistent high quality. The cylinders are bored to within .007-inch of the specified diameters, leaving sufficient material for an engine builder to hone the cylinders to a standard bore size using his preferred honing procedure.

These race-prepared blocks incorporate all of the casting revisions of the Bow Tie blocks described above. They also have the following features:

Priority Main Oiling

Oil is routed directly from the center oil gallery to the main bearing saddles through two intersecting $5/16$-inch diameter passages. This system eliminates the restrictive annular grooves in the cam bearing bores, and minimizes internal oil leakage. The diameter of the main oil

Race-prepared Bow Tie blocks simplify engine building. All external surfaces are precision-machined to close tolerances. The cylinders are sonic tested and bored to within .007-inch of the specified diameter.

The intermediate steel main bearing caps on race-prepared blocks have splayed outer bolt holes. The front cap will clear a standard oil pan.

Dowel pins accurately register the three middle caps on the main bearing bulkheads. Ball end studs are used in the outer bolt holes.

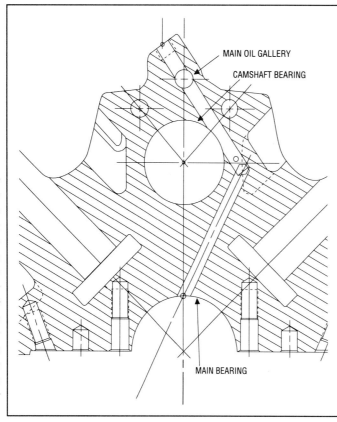

MAIN OIL GALLERY

CAMSHAFT BEARING

MAIN BEARING

Race-prepared Bow Tie blocks have a priority main oiling system that routes oil directly from the center oil gallery to the main bearing saddles. The upper passages intersect the cam bearing bores tangentially; the oil holes in the cam bearing inserts must be aligned with these openings for proper lubrication.

The rear main bearing cap and seal adapter allow a pre-1986 two-piece rear seal and oil pan to be installed on a race-prepared Bow Tie block.

gallery is increased to $^{37}/_{64}$-inch. Pipe plugs seal the three oil galleries above the camshaft tunnel.

The water jacket cores in race-prepared cast-iron Bow Tie blocks have been revised to accommodate the priority main lubrication system. The upper oil passages intersect the cam bearing bores tangentially to provide single-point lubrication for the cam bearings. Eliminating

the annular grooves behind the bearings also significantly increases support for the cam bearing inserts.

Steel Main Bearing Caps

Race-prepared Bow Tie blocks are equipped with 8620 steel main bearing caps. The caps are secured with premium quality centerless ground studs and 12-point nuts. The three center caps have splayed outer bolt holes that are angled

20 degrees from vertical. Ball-end $^{3}/_{8}$-inch studs anchor these middle caps to the strongest part of the block structure. Dowel pins register the caps on the main bearing bulkheads, and machined pry slots make cap removal easy.

The four-bolt front cap has $^{7}/_{16}$-inch inner studs and $^{3}/_{8}$-inch outer bolts, and will clear a standard oil pan. The two-bolt steel rear cap is machined to accept a two-piece crankshaft seal with adapter kit PN 10051118. This cap has provisions for an internal wet sump oil pump.

All Bow Tie small-block V8s are machined for crankshafts with 2.45-inch diameter (350-type) main bearing journals. The bolt holes in the steel main caps installed on race-prepared versions are spread far enough apart to allow engine builders to bore the main bearing saddles for 2.65-inch (400-type) bearing inserts.

Radiused Main Bearing Bulkheads

The machined radii between the main bearing bulkheads and the bottoms of the cylinder barrels are enlarged to forestall cracking in this highly stressed area.

Aluminum Bow Tie Blocks

10134399	Bow Tie Aluminum Block (350-type Main Bearings)
10134400	Bow Tie Aluminum Block (400-type Main Bearings)
10185075	Bow Tie Aluminum Block (350-type Main Bearings, Wet Sump)

These aluminum Bow Tie engine blocks combine light weight with the strength to withstand the power levels of today's racing engines. All three members of this family of aluminum blocks are identical except for main bearing diameters and oiling systems. The following are some of the technical features of these state-of-the-art engine blocks:

Premium Materials

Aluminum Bow Tie blocks are cast from premium A-356 alloy, heat-treated to T6 specifications. This high-quality material has an ultimate strength of 37,000 psi. It resists cracking under severe loads and provides extended fatigue life.

Light Weight

A bare aluminum Bow Tie small-block V8 weighs 90 pounds, including cylinder liners and main bearing caps. This is approximately 92 pounds lighter than a comparable cast iron Bow Tie block.

Main Bearing Diameters

Aluminum blocks are available with standard 2.450-inch diameter main bearings (350-type) and extra-large 2.650-inch (400-type) main bearings. The larger 400-type bearings enhance reliability when using a long-stroke crankshaft.

Main Bearing Caps

Four-bolt steel caps are used on all five main bearings. The front and rear caps have straight outer bolt holes, and will clear conventional oil pans. The interme-

Chevrolet aluminum Bow Tie blocks are available with a choice of main bearing diameter and oiling system type (wet or dry sump). The ductile iron cylinder liners are pressed in place.

Aluminum blocks have four-bolt steel bearing caps with splayed outer bolts. Threaded AN plugs with "O"-rings seal the water jackets.

The rear main bearing cap uses a two-piece seal and a pre-1986 oil pan. The bearing saddles are grooved to increase oil flow.

diate caps have widely spaced outer bolts that are angled at 20 degrees; this design anchors the caps to the strongest part of the block structure.

All bearing caps are precisely registered with dowel pins. The main bearing saddles are grooved to accommodate additional oil supply holes drilled in the upper main bearing inserts. The rear main bearing accepts a two-piece (pre-1986) crankshaft seal and early-style oil pan.

Cylinder Liners

The centrifugally cast ductile iron cylinder liners are pressed in place with 5,000 pounds of force to prevent movement. These heat-treated liners are rough-honed to 4.118-inch diameter, and will "clean up" at a 4.125-inch finished bore diameter. The liners are .077-inch thick, and are supported by .250-inch thick aluminum on the major and minor thrust axes. Stepped top flanges register the lin-

ers in the block and provide a rigid sealing surface for the head gaskets.

Reinforced Decks

The deck surfaces are .620-inch thick. The head bolt holes are blind-tapped to prevent coolant leaks. The head bolt bosses between adjacent cylinders extend to the bottom of the cylinder barrels, and can be drilled to full depth for highly stressed applications.

Oiling System

Oil is routed directly from the central oil gallery above the camshaft tunnel to the intermediate main bearing saddles through intersecting passages, eliminating the restrictive annular oil grooves behind the camshaft bearing inserts. Oil can be fed directly into the central oil gallery from an external oil pump through a threaded boss at the front of the block. The oil filter pad accepts a late-model small diameter filter.

Oil can be pumped directly into the central oil gallery from an external pump through a threaded hole above the timing chain cover.

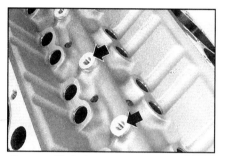

Aluminum blocks have a priority main oiling system. Plugs in the lifter valley seal the oil passages that feed the main bearings.

The oil pan rails are machined for connecting rod clearance with long-stroke crankshafts. Minor modifications may be required.

Oil Pan Rail

The oil pan rail will clear a 4.00-inch stroke crankshaft (minor modifications may be required for rod clearance). Solid aluminum above the pan rails eliminates the need for supplemental girdles and main bearing supports.

Lifter Bosses

The oversize lifter bosses can be offset-bored and bushed to optimize the valvetrain geometry when using highly modified cylinder heads. The lifter bores are roller burnished to produce an extremely smooth surface finish.

Cooling System

The fuel pump boss is eliminated to improve coolant flow around the No. 2 cylinder. Threaded AN plugs with "O"-rings seal the water jackets.

BOW TIE TECH All-Aluminum Small-Block

The all-aluminum 6.5-liter splayed-valve Chevrolet V8s that powered MTI Racing's Intrepid GTPs to four poles in 1991 were among the most sophisticated small-blocks in motorsports.

After a decade of domination by exotic engines from Europe and Japan, Chevrolet's all-American small-block V8 emerged as a potent force in the 1991 IMSA Camel GT road racing series. Chevy's venerable V8 propelled MTI Racing's Intrepid GTPs into the forefront of IMSA's GT Prototype category.

The engines that powered the Intrepid GTPs redefined the state-of-the-art in small-block technology with aluminum Bow Tie blocks, splayed-valve Bow Tie cylinder heads, and electronic engine management.

These leading-edge engines were assembled at Katech, Inc. in Mt. Clemens, Michigan, using heavy-duty components developed by the GM Motorsports Technology Group. The MTI Racing team used 6.0-liter (366ci) and 6.5-liter

(396ci) engines that produced more than 740 horsepower. The splayed-valve small-blocks won four poles in 1991, and driver Wayne Taylor put the revolutionary Chevy in the winner's circle at the inaugural New Orleans Grand Prix.

Chevrolet's Bow Tie aluminum blocks were the centerpiece of the GTP engine program. GM engineers specified aluminum blocks with 2.650-inch diameter main bearings (PN 10134400). These blocks' large 400-type main bearings enhanced the durability of the long-stroke crankshafts used in the Intrepid GTPs by increasing the overlap between the cranks' main journals and rod throws.

The expansion characteristics of the aluminum blocks required several adjustments in Katech's standard engine

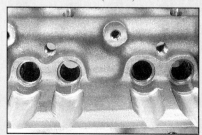

Katech machinists offset the aluminum block's lifter bores with bronze bushings to minimize pushrod angularity.

Shaft-mounted 1.7:1 ratio aluminum rocker arms were mounted on the splayed-valve Chevrolet Bow Tie aluminum heads.

The splayed-valve heads' 45cc combustion chambers were outfitted with 2.20/1.625-inch diameter titanium valves.

building procedures. "An aluminum block 'grows' approximately two-thousandths of an inch as it is heated from room temperature to operating temperature," explained Katech technician Ted Spehar. "This means that a main bearing clearance that measures .002-inch in the shop will expand to .004-inch when the engine is hot and running on the track."

Spehar set the clearances at .001-inch for the No. 1 through 4 main bearings; the rear main bearing clearance was slightly larger at .0015-inch. The rod bearing clearance was .002 to .0025-inch, the same as a cast iron block. "The recommended rod bearing clearance doesn't change because we use the same steel connecting rods in both aluminum and cast iron racing engines," Spehar said.

The relatively tight initial main bearing clearances required a careful warm-up procedure. The MTI team preheated the oil in the dry sump tank and circulated hot water through the block before starting the engine.

The GTP small-blocks used 3.70-inch stroke crankshafts. These crankshafts began life as a 4340 steel Chevrolet raw forging (PN 10051168). The long stroke required careful checking to prevent interference between the crankshaft counterweights, pistons, block, and camshaft. The aluminum block's oil pan rails and cylinder liners were notched at the factory for rod clearance, and required only minor modifications to clear the rod bolts.

Katech tapered the crankshaft's No. 2 and No. 4 counterweights to clear the block's main bearing bulkheads, and

chamfered the piston skirts to clear the bottoms of the cylinder barrels and the crankshaft counterweights. The steel connecting rods' shoulders and bolts were also relieved for camshaft clearance.

The GTP engines were equipped with splayed-valve Bow Tie cylinder heads (PN 10185040). The titanium intake valves were 2.20-inch in diameter, and the titanium exhausts 1.625-inch. A roller tappet camshaft lifted the valves .700-inch off their seats. Aftermarket 1.7:1 ratio aluminum rocker arms were installed on Chevrolet rocker mounting bars (PN 10185041). Heavy-duty Chevrolet composition head gaskets (PN 10185054) sealed the cylinders.

Katech's machinists offset the lifter bores in the GTP aluminum blocks with bronze bushings to minimize pushrod angularity. Katech also installed aftermarket roller tappets with .060-inch offset pushrod cups to align the pushrods and rocker arms. The 5/16-inch diameter pushrods were custom-made from .080-inch wall tubing. The intake pushrods measured 7.40-inch long, and the exhaust pushrods 7.90-inch.

A special piston dome was designed to match the splayed-valve head's unique combustion chamber shape and valve angles. Piston-to-valve clearance was .125-inch on both the intake and exhaust valves. Compression ratio was 14.5:1—relatively high by conventional road racing standards, but pistons and bearings proved troublefree throughout a long season of racing. The long crankshaft stroke used in the 6.5-liter GTP small-blocks made piston speed a concern, however. The engines reached their horsepower peak at 7200 rpm, and were redlined at 7600 rpm.

The crankshaft counterweights were tapered to clear the main bearing bulkheads and the leading edges were knife-edged.

Katech technicians modified the GTP small-block's aftermarket steel connecting rods to clear the camshaft lobes.

The GTP small-block's forged aluminum pistons required only modest domes to produce a 14.5:1 compression ratio.

Main Bearing Caps

One of the most significant differences between small-block engine cases is the design of the main bearing caps. From 1955 through 1967, all small-block V8s were equipped with two-bolt caps on all five main bearings.

In 1968, high-performance 4.00-inch bore small-blocks were upgraded with four-bolt caps on the three intermediate main bearings (Nos. 2, 3, and 4). The thickness of the main bearing webs was also increased on these four-bolt blocks to provide additional bulkhead strength.

Four-bolt main bearing caps were retained on all 302ci and 350ci small-block V8s until 1971, when certain low-com-

Four-bolt main bearing caps were used on many high-performance small-blocks in the Sixties and Seventies.

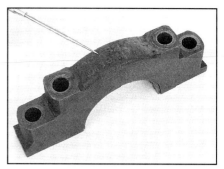

A nodular iron four-bolt main bearing cap can be identified by its "2482" casting number. Nodular iron caps are preferred for heavy-duty use.

pression passenger car engines were again released with two-bolt main caps. 350ci small-blocks installed in Z28 Camaros through 1974, LT-1 and L82 Corvettes through 1980, many late-model Corvettes, and heavy-duty trucks have four-bolt main bearing caps. Four-bolt caps are also installed on second-

BOW TIE TECH 400ci Small-Block

The 400-cubic-inch V8 stands out as a distinctive member of the family of Chevrolet small-block production engines. Although 400ci small-blocks were discontinued after the 1980 model year, this engine remains the subject of intense interest by performance enthusiasts.

The 400ci small-block V8 was introduced in 1970 as a high-torque engine designed to run on low-octane regular fuel. Among the 400ci small-block's unique features were 4.125-inch diameter cylinder bores. Because the 400ci block retained the same bore spacing as other small-block V8s, its cylinder walls were "siamesed," eliminating the water jackets between adjacent bores. The 400ci small-block also used a nodular iron crankshaft with extra-large 2.650-inch diameter main bearing journals and special short connecting rods that measured 5.565-inch between centers (versus 5.70-inch for all other Chevrolet small-block V8s).

The 400ci small-block attracted the interest of budget-conscious engine builders because it offered the possibility of large engine displacement and unusual bore/stroke. The introduction of Bow Tie blocks with siamesed bores has lessened the 400's appeal, however.

Most high-performance small-block components are readily interchange-

Production 400ci small-blocks had 4.125-inch diameter cylinder bores, siamesed cylinder walls, and 2.650-inch main bearings.

able on 400ci blocks. However, the 4.125-inch bore 400ci block requires several specific modifications for high-performance and racing applications. If you intend to build a high-output small-block based on a 400ci engine, the following cautions should be observed:

1. The production 400ci small-block crankshaft is externally balanced with a counterweighted flywheel and torsional damper ("harmonic balancer"). These parts or similar unbalanced parts are usually necessary to achieve final engine balance.

A 3.750-inch stroke production small-block crankshaft can be internally balanced by adding heavy metal to its end counterweights. As a note of

caution, these heavy metal slugs should be installed horizontally (parallel to the crankshaft axis) to prevent centrifugal force from dislodging them.

2. Due to the 400ci small-block's siamesed cylinder walls, six steam holes are drilled in each deck surface between the cylinders to aid water circulation at low engine speeds and to vent steam and air pockets. In production 400ci engines, these holes correspond to matching holes in the head gasket and cylinder heads. These steam holes should be drilled in replacement and high-performance cylinder heads as shown in the accompanying diagram.

A production head gasket from a 400ci small-block makes a suitable

The original straight bolt holes in four-bolt blocks should be plugged before drilling angled outer holes for splayed-bolt main caps.

generation LT1 Corvette V8s and over-the-counter H.O. 350 engine assemblies.

Cylinder blocks for 262, 265, 267, 283, 305, and 307ci engines were not designed to accommodate four-bolt main caps, and

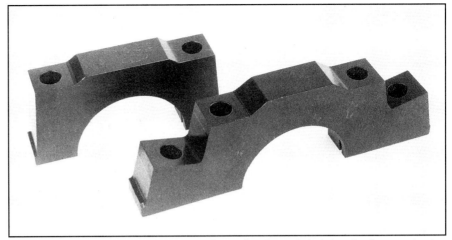

Heavy-duty Chevrolet steel main bearing caps have splayed outer bolts holes. This design anchors the cap to the strongest part of the block. Splayed outer bolts also minimize distortion of the bearing bores by increasing the caps' resistance to "closing up."

A 400ci small-block's externally balanced 3.750-inch stroke crankshaft requires a counterweighted flywheel and damper for proper engine balance.

template for locating the steam holes on the head deck surface. (If the engine will operate primarily at speeds above 3500 rpm, it is not necessary to drill steam holes in the heads, as the increased water circulation will purge the air and steam pockets.)

3. To prevent the head gasket from overhanging the cylinder bores, a large bore gasket must be used. GM heavy-duty head gasket PN 10185054 is recommended for engines with 4.125-inch diameter cylinders. This gasket has solid wire "O"-rings around each cylinder bore, and a compressed thickness of .040-inch. Steam holes should be drilled in the gasket before installation on a 400ci block. This gasket is Teflon-coated, and does not require sealer.

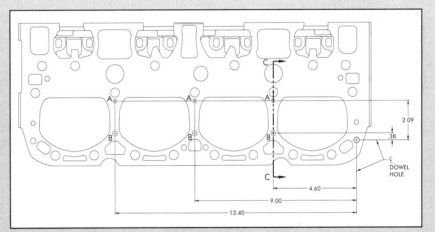

Steam holes should be drilled in replacement cylinder heads before installation on 400ci small-blocks. Locate the holes from the dowel holes as shown.

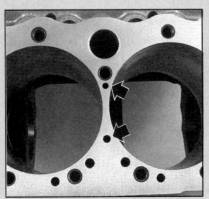

Additional coolant holes in the deck surfaces of 400ci small-blocks aid water circulation and vent steam pockets.

Chevrolet offers raw crankshaft forgings (described in the crankshaft section of this chapter) which can be machined to fit the 400's large diameter main bearing bores. In addition, after-

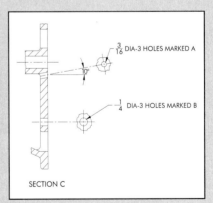

The three ³⁄₁₆-inch diameter holes marked "A" should be drilled at 10-degree angle from vertical.

market engine bearing manufacturers offer extra-thick main bearing inserts that allow the installation of a crankshaft with 2.45-inch diameter main bearing journals in a 400ci block.

TECH SPECS: STEEL MAIN BEARING CAPS (2.45" Journal)

Part Number	Position	Material	Bolts	Outer Angle
14011052	1	1010 steel	2	—
14011072	2, 3, 4	1010 steel	4	12° 30′
10134368[1]	1	8620 steel	4	Straight
10134369[1]	2, 3, 4	8620 steel	4	20°
10134372[2]	5	8620 steel	4	Straight
24502514[3]	1	8620 steel	4	Straight
24502515[3]	2, 3, 4	8620 steel	4	20°
24502516[3]	5	8620 steel	4	Straight

[1]Used on aluminum Bow Tie block PN 10134399 and 10185075
[2]Used on aluminum Bow Tie block PN 10134399 only
[3]Used on race-prepared cast iron Bow Tie blocks PN 24502501, 24502503 and 24502525

do not have additional material in their main bearing bulkheads.

400ci small-blocks were produced with both two-bolt and four-bolt main bearing caps. Four-bolt bearing caps installed on large journal 400ci blocks are *not* interchangeable with caps on medium journal blocks because they have wider bolt spacing to accommodate the 400ci small-block's .200-inch larger diameter main bearing bores.

Two distinct types of four-bolt main bearing caps are available for Chevrolet small-block V8s with 2.45-inch diameter main bearings: parallel bolt and splayed bolt. The most common four-bolt main caps found on production blocks have four parallel ("straight") bolt holes and are made from cast iron.

Block Preparation:
The Hendrick Motorports Method

Heavy-duty Chevrolet components are the foundation of Hendrick Motorsports' stock car racing engines. The list of Bow Tie parts includes the engine block, forged steel crankshaft, high-port aluminum cylinder heads and intake manifold.

The Engine Division of Hendrick Motorsports in Harrisburg, North Carolina, prepares and maintains Chevrolet small-block racing engines for several topflight NASCAR stock car teams. With millions of dollars in prize money and sponsorships on the line, the Hendrick Motorsports staff leaves nothing to chance when preparing an engine for competition. Randy Dorton, manager of the Hendrick Motorsports Engine Division, oversees the preparation of dozens of cast iron Bow Tie blocks for competition.

"We routinely run 5,000 racing miles with a Chevrolet Bow Tie block," Dorton reports. "A Bow Tie block has the strength and integrity to endure tremendous loads if it is prepared and maintained properly. The block is the foundation of any racing engine, so it makes sense to invest the time to make it as reliable as possible.

The main bearing saddles and bulkheads are radiused and the crankcase widened by cutting back the oil pan rails.

"Much of the preparation is really preventive maintenance—double-checking dimensions and taking precautions to prevent future problems," Dorton adds. "However, because Hendrick Motorsports does certain things to a Bow Tie block to prepare it for a NASCAR race does not mean that a sportsman racer has to do the same things for his Saturday night special. Many of the modifications we perform aren't necessary for a racing engine that doesn't face the same severe operating conditions as our motors."

Engine builders can eliminate many of the following steps in engine machining by using a race-prepared Chevrolet Bow Tie block. These "blueprinted" blocks require only honing and decking for many racing applications. However, Hendrick Motorsports' procedures are an excellent guide for

Many high-performance and heavy-duty blocks are equipped with nodular iron caps. These desirable nodular iron mains, which are stronger than gray iron caps, can be identified by the casting number "2482." Semi-finished nodular iron straight-bolt replacement caps are available as PN 3932482.

A nodular iron four-bolt cap can be modified for installation on the front main bearing by machining off its two outer bolt bosses. The main bearing housings *must* be align bored whenever replacement caps are installed.

The second type of four-bolt main bearing cap has splayed ("angled") outer bolt holes. Chevrolet splayed-bolt main caps are available in two materials (1010 and 8620 steel) and with two outer bolt angles (12 degrees and 20 degrees).

Splayed-bolt steel main bearing caps are installed on aluminum Bow Tie small-blocks and race-prepared cast iron Bow Tie blocks. These caps can be retrofitted on other blocks to increase bottom end strength. The angled outer bolts anchor the caps to the strongest part of the block and improve main bearing bulkhead durability under high stress conditions. The splayed outer bolts also reduce distortion of the main bearing bores by increasing the caps' resistance to "closing up."

The main bearing bulkheads must be drilled and tapped for the new outer bolts when splayed-bolt caps are installed on a block originally equipped with production two-bolt or four-bolt main caps. Many engine builders also plug the original straight outer bolt holes on four-bolt blocks during this operation.

Angled outer bolt holes must also be drilled and tapped when installing four-bolt main caps on second-design Bow Tie blocks orginally manufactured with two-bolt mains. Splayed-bolt main bearing caps have semi-finished bearing bores, and must be align bored after they are installed on the block. The caps should be installed with the arrow on the top of the cap pointing toward the front of the block.

A steel two-bolt main bearing cap is available for small-block V8s with 2.45-inch diameter main bearings as PN 14011052. This heavy-duty cap replaces the production grey iron cap installed on the No. 1 main bearing, and eliminates the machining required to modify a nodular iron four-bolt cap to fit the front of the engine case. It will clear most oil pans and windage trays.

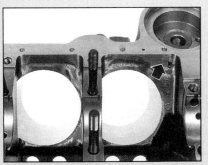

The oil pan rail is removed below the No. 8 cylinder. Studs secure the four-bolt steel main bearing caps.

Hendrick Motorsports drills .090-inch diameter steam holes between the siamesed cylinders in Bow Tie blocks.

preparing other block castings for maximum performance and reliability.

Although Hendrick Motorsports uses both siamesed and non-siamesed Bow Tie blocks in its engine program, Dorton believes that big-bore siamesed blocks complement the performance of Chevrolet 18-degree Bow Tie cylinder heads equipped with large diameter intake and exhaust valves.

"A siamesed-bore Bow Tie block offers a wide range of bore diameters," Dorton comments. "We extend the useful life of a Bow Tie block by juggling crankshaft strokes and cylinder bore diameters to stay right at NASCAR's 358-cubic-inch limit. When a block's cylinder bore diameter is increased by honing or boring the cylinders during an overhaul, we install a crankshaft with a slightly shorter stroke to maintain the same displacement. This strategy will stretch any racer's engine budget."

Inspection

"We visually examine every new block for defects. The only equipment needed is a pair of calipers to take measurements and an assortment of bolts that you can screw into every tapped hole.

"We check the block hardness on the oil pan rail and deck surfaces to make sure that it falls within GM specifications of 197 to 255 Brinell hardness. Then we pressurize the water jackets to 100 psi to check for leaks; porosity is seldom a problem in Bow Tie blocks. Finally, we Magnaflux the block. With a new block, we're just looking for anything unusual. When we inspect a used block for cracks, we pay special attention to the front and rear bulkheads and the outer main cap bolt holes.

"We sonic test the cylinder wall thickness in four locations from the top of each bore to the bottom. I look for a minimum cylinder wall thickness of

.200-inch with a 4.00-inch diameter cylinder bore. In my view, the real purpose of sonic testing is to make sure that none of the cores shifted when the block was cast."

Preparation

"At Hendrick Motorsports, we reference all of the machining dimensions from two points: the centerline of the crankshaft and the location of the rear thrust bearing. All of the major block dimensions are measured in relation to these two reference points.

"Before boring the cylinders, we remove the ribs at the bottoms of the bores with a hand grinder. After the cylinders are bored to size, we offset the boring bar .060-inch and cut reliefs at the bottoms of the cylinders to provide over-stroke clearance for the honing stones. We use a radiused cutter for this operation; any sharp edges in this area can invite cracks in the main bearing bulkheads.

"The lifter bores are machined to accept .875-inch diameter flat tappets, which are used in all NASCAR Winston Cup engines. The lifter bore locations are precisely measured from the camshaft thrust surface on the front face of the block."

Main Bearing Caps

"We outfit our Bow Tie blocks with steel four-bolt main bearing caps. Race-prepared Bow Tie blocks are also

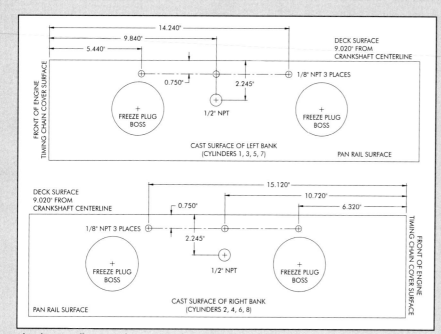

This diagram illustrates the position of the steam holes drilled in siamesed bore Bow Tie blocks to eliminate air pockets under the deck surface.

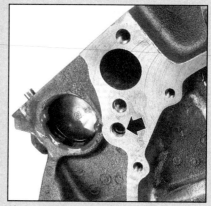

The water pump bypass hole is plugged with a ⅛-inch pipe plug. The soft plugs are pinned and sealed with epoxy.

available with factory-installed four-bolt steel caps.

"Most Bow Tie blocks are machined for a production one-piece rear crankshaft seal. We install a special rear main bearing cap and seal adapter that allows us to use oil pans and crankshafts that require the old-style two-piece seal. Race-prepared Bow Tie blocks already have a rear main bearing cap that uses a two-piece seal and an early-type oil pan.

"We radius the edges of the main bearing saddles when the steel caps are align bored. We also radius the main bearing bulkheads where they meet the cylinder barrels, and machine a large radius where the bulkheads join the oil pan rails. The crankcase is widened by cutting back the oil pan rails almost to the bolt holes. This eliminates the lip above the pan rail that can trap oil. We bolt steel adapter plates to the pan rails that mount a 10-inch wide pan dry sump oil pan, which is the maximum oil pan width allowed by the NASCAR Winston Cup rules.

"We remove the oil pan rail entirely below the No. 8 cylinder, eliminating one of the stock oil pan bolt holes. The oil feed hole in the rear main bearing saddle is radiused to align it with the hole in the bearing insert. We install a rear crankshaft seal adapter on all of our race blocks."

Cooling Modifications

"If you compare our race-prepared block to a new Bow Tie block, you'll see that many of the coolant holes in the deck surfaces have been plugged and resized. The diameter of the coolant holes matches the holes in the head gaskets we use.

"We drill .090-inch diameter steam holes between the siamesed cylinders from the six bosses on the sides of the latest Bow Tie blocks. These holes are .750-inch below the deck surface. Their purpose is to prevent the formation of air pockets under the deck.

"We also drill steam holes in the cylinder heads that correspond to the coolant holes alongside the outside rows of cylinder head bolts. The bosses around the head bolts can trap air; we give this air an escape route through the holes we drill in the cylinder heads. Eliminating air pockets underneath the deck surface significantly improves head gasket reliability in a racing engine.

"We pin the stock brass soft plugs in place, and seal them with epoxy. The water pump bypass hole is plugged with a ⅛-inch pipe plug."

Lubrication System

"The top end of a racing engine generates a lot of debris in the form of metal that wears off valve springs, retainers, and shims. We separate the engine into two separate sumps by sealing off the lifter valley from the crankcase. This prevents valvetrain material from embedding in the camshaft, piston skirts, and cylinder walls.

"The oil drainback holes in the lifter valley are sealed with epoxy, and the oil returning from the cylinder heads is scavenged through a drain hole adjacent to the distributor. We also radius the distributor hole to prevent damage to the "O"-rings on the distributor housing that seal the right-hand lifter gallery.

"A fitting installed in the back of the block is connected to the dry sump pump's scavenge stage with a -10 line. The latest Bow Tie blocks have a boss below the bellhousing flange that simplifies this modification.

"We inspect all of the oil passages for obstructions with a pen light. On a wet sump motor, it's a good idea to radius as many sharp edges in the oil system as possible. Abrasive cord works well for breaking the edges in internal passages."

"We check the grooves in the camshaft bearing bores to make sure they are the proper depth and width. We also enlarge the oil holes from the central oil gallery to the Number 2, 3, and 4 main bearings to ¹¹⁄₃₂-inch diameter. Race-prepared Bow Tie blocks have a 'priority main' oiling system that eliminates the need for these modifications.

"Oil from an external dry sump pump is fed into the front of the center gallery through a -10 line and a ⅜-inch pipe fitting. Chevrolet's new race-prepared

Oil in the lifter valley is scavenged by a -10 line connected to a fitting installed in the rear of the block.

The lifter valley is deburred and the oil drainback holes plugged with epoxy to prevent valvetrain debris from reaching the crankcase.

blocks are drilled and tapped for this oil inlet line."

Honing

"We are constantly refining our block honing procedures at Hendrick Motorsports. Our goal is to simulate the condition of the cylinder bores in the assembled engine as closely as possible during honing.

"We use a two-inch thick steel honing plate that is step-cut to 1.00-inch thick on the outside row of head bolts. We *always* use a new head gasket, and apply anti-seize on the bolt threads and oil on the head bolt washers. The long head bolts are torqued to 70 pounds, and the short bolts to 60 pounds.

"When honing a new block with a Sunnen CK-10 automatic hone, we start with 525 stones (220 grit) and remove approximately .003-inch of material to bring the bore to within .001-inch of its final diameter. Then we switch to 625 stones (280 grit) and hone the bores until they are within .0005-inch of the final size. We finish up with 820 stones (400 grit).

"These are a few of the highlights of our Bow Tie block preparation procedures at Hendrick Motorsports. A Chevrolet Bow Tie block is an excellent foundation for any competition engine. If you pay attention to the details, a Bow Tie block will deliver dependable service for years of racing."

Block Prep Check List

Hendrick Motorsports performs the following inspections and modifications on a new Bow Tie block to prepare it for NASCAR stock car competition. Of course, not every block requires such extensive work, depending on its intended use. You can select the items on this list that apply to your engine project.

- [ ] Hardness test
- [ ] Pressure test for leaks and porosity
- [ ] Magnaflux test for cracks
- [ ] Sonic test for core shift
- [ ] Drill and tap front oil passge (½" drill, ⅜" pipe tap)
- [ ] Drill main oil passage (½" drill)
- [ ] Drill and tap main oil passage plugs (³⁷/₆₄" drill, ⅜" pipe tap)
- [ ] Tap original oil filter holes (¼" pipe tap)
- [ ] Tap water pump hole (⅛" pipe tap)
- [ ] Drill and tap head bolt holes ("U" drill, ⁷/₁₆–14 tap)
- [ ] Drill oil holes in main bearing housing Nos. 2, 3, 4 (⁵/₁₆" drill)
- [ ] Machine bellhousing dowel holes
- [ ] Tap front lifter oil passage holes (¼" pipe tap)
- [ ] Tap dipstick tube—top and bottom (⅛" & ¼" pipe taps)
- [ ] Bottom tap all bolt holes
- [ ] Drill and tap rear oil scavenge hole (³⁷/₆₄" drill, ⅜" tap)
- [ ] Drill and spot face rear of block for scavenge line fitting (⅞" drill)
- [ ] Tap oil hole under rear main cap
- [ ] Plug and drill deck
- [ ] Grind front main oil hole

- [ ] Grind distributor hole for "O" rings
- [ ] Grind angle on rear cam bearing center hole
- [ ] Deburr block and front oil holes for screen kit
- [ ] Notch pan rail for #8 rod
- [ ] Deburr center oil supply and timing chain area
- [ ] Chamfer oil hole in #5 main
- [ ] Grind cam journal oil grooves
- [ ] Machine tappet bores
- [ ] Machine block for steel caps
- [ ] Drill and tap outside main cap bolt holes ("U" drill, ⁷/₁₆–14 tap)
- [ ] Drill and tap four-bolt front main cap outside holes (⁵/₁₆" drill, ⅜–16 tap)
- [ ] Drill steam holes (⅛" drill)
- [ ] Align bore block
- [ ] Align hone block
- [ ] Radius main bearing saddles
- [ ] Align bore cam journals
- [ ] Align hone cam journals
- [ ] Bore block
- [ ] Deck block
- [ ] Chamfer top and bottom of cylinders
- [ ] Hone cylinders
- [ ] Polish tappet bores
- [ ] Replace and pin freeze plugs, use Loctite
- [ ] Drill spark plug cooling holes
- [ ] Check all water cooling holes
- [ ] Spot face all pipe plug holes
- [ ] Final pressure test block

A nodular iron four-bolt main cap can be modified for installation on the front main bearing by machining off its outer bolt bosses. Replacement caps must be align bored.

Race-prepared cast iron Bow Tie and aluminum Bow Tie blocks are outfitted with high-strength 8620 steel main bearing caps. The inner bolt holes are positioned far enough apart to accommodate 2.65-inch (400-type) main bearings. The two-bolt rear main cap used on these blocks incorporates an adapter for a two-piece rear seal and a pre-1986 oil pan. The four-bolt front main bearing cap has ⅜-inch outer bolts that will clear a conventional oil pan.

If main bearing cap studs are used, the threads should be lightly oiled and the ⁷⁄₁₆-inch nuts torqued to 65 ft.-lbs. torque. Torque the nuts on ⅜-inch diameter outer studs to 60 ft.-lbs. On race-prepared and aluminum Bow Tie blocks, the front main bearing cap's ⅜-inch outer bolts should be torqued to 40 ft.-lbs.

Crankshafts

Chevrolet has produced a variety of crankshafts for the small-block V8 during its long production run. Crankshaft variations include:

- Three main bearing journal diameters (2.30, 2.45, and 2.65-inch)
- Two rod journal diameters (2.00 and 2.10-inch)
- Five stroke dimensions (3.00, 3.10, 3.25, 3.48, and 3.75-inch)
- Two rear seal designs (one-piece and two-piece)
- Two flywheel flange bolt patterns (3.00 and 3.58-inch)
- Several iron and steel alloys (1053, 4340, 5140, etc.)

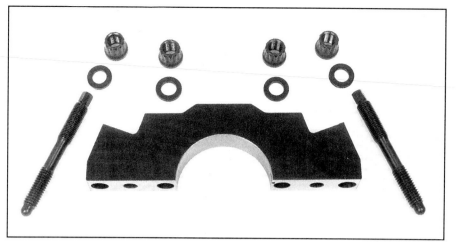

Splayed-bolt steel main bearing caps installed on aluminum and race-prepared Bow Tie blocks use ball-end ⅜-inch outer studs and premium quality 12-point nuts. The outer bolt holes are angled 20 degrees from vertical.

Chevrolet's heavy-duty forged steel 3.48-inch stroke crankshaft (PN 3941184) is nitride heat-treated to improve its fatigue strength.

With so many alternatives, it is essential to match the crankshaft to its related components and the engine's usage.

Production Crankshafts

Several production 3.48-inch stroke steel crankshafts are suitable for high-performance and limited competition applications. All have 2.45-inch diameter main bearing journals and 2.10-inch diameter rod journals.

PN 3941180 is a forged 1053 alloy steel crank designed for a pre-1986 two-piece rear crankshaft seal. A nitride heat-treated version of this same forging is offered as PN 3941184. (Nitride heat treating improves journal hardness and provides greater fatigue strength for high-performance durability.) Both versions use the same "1182" forging ID number. A forged 1053 steel 3.48-inch stroke crankshaft

with a rear flange designed for a one-piece seal is available as PN 14096036.

All 3.750-inch stroke crankshafts originally used in 400ci small-block V8s are cast nodular iron. Note that production 400ci cranks have extra-large 2.650-inch diameter main journals and 2.10-inch diameter rod journals. As outlined in the 400ci small-block section, these crankshafts are externally balanced, and must use counterweighted torsional dampers and flywheels for proper engine balance (unless the crank has been internally balanced by installing heavy metal in the counterweights).

Heavy-Duty Unmachined Crankshafts

Before the introduction of unmachined crankshaft forgings, competition engine builders had few options when selecting

This 3.48-inch stroke forged steel crankshaft (PN 14096036) uses a one-piece rear seal; note its small diameter flywheel flange.

A sharp parting line identifies a cast iron crankshaft (left); a forged steel crankshaft (right) has a wide raised die mark.

A raw crankshaft forging can be ground with large fillets to improve its durability. Hollow rod journals reduce rotating weight.

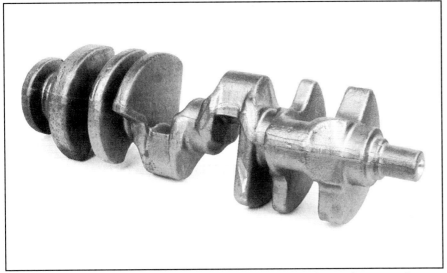

An unmachined Chevrolet small-block crankshaft forging will accommodate strokes ranging from 3.25 to 4.00-inch. The main journals can be ground for 2.65-inch bearings.

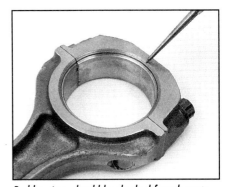

Rod bearings should be checked for adequate clearance when using a custom-ground crankshaft with oversize fillets.

crankshafts. They could either compromise the engine's bore/stroke ratio by using a readily available production crank, or order an expensive billet steel crankshaft. Chevrolet developed unfinished crank forgings to give racers another alternative.

Chevrolet offers a selection of unmachined crankshaft forgings for competition small-blocks. A raw forging gives engine builders the flexibility to tailor the crankshaft stroke and bearing journal diameters to suit a particular class or racing application. The additional material on an unmachined forging also allows crankshaft specialists to grind extra-large fillet radiuses to improve crankshaft durability under the stress of continuous heavy loads. (Bearing inserts should be checked for proper edge clearance with oversized fillet radiuses.)

Advances in metallurgy, design, and manufacturing have produced unfinished forgings that offer superior performance and longevity. Chevrolet unmachined heavy-duty crankshaft forgings are stronger and more versatile than production cranks.

An unmachined version of a production 3.48-inch stroke crankshaft is available as PN 10185100. This crankshaft is forged with S38 micro alloy steel instead of the 1053 steel used in production versions. This raw forging uses a two-piece rear seal, and will accommodate finished stroke dimensions ranging from 3.46-inch to 3.50-inch with 2.100-inch diameter rod journals.

Chevrolet also offers two heavy-duty 4340 steel unmachined crankshaft forgings. These forgings are identical except for their front sections. PN 10051168 has a front snout that can be machined for a conventional small-block torsional damper. PN 24502460 has a larger snout that can be machined to the same dimensions as a big-block Chevrolet V8 (1.60-inch diameter). This larger diameter snout resists cracking caused by the side loads and stresses of driving a dry sump pump and other accessories off of the front of the crankshaft. Small-block crankshafts with big-block snouts are becoming popular in endurance racing applications such as NASCAR stock car and offshore boat competition.

Chevrolet 4340 crankshaft forgings will accommodate finished strokes ranging from 3.25-inch to 4.00-inch. The 2.900-inch diameter main bearing journals can be ground for 2.65-inch (400-type) bearings.

The mechanical properties of 4340 steel are well suited to competition crankshafts. Two characteristics that are important in a crankshaft are the material's *tensile strength* and *fatigue resistance*. Tensile strength is a measure of the metal's ultimate strength before failure—how much force the steel can withstand before it snaps. Fatigue resistance is the material's ability to endure repeated strains without breaking.

The 4340 steel used in Chevrolet unmachined crankshaft forgings has better "hardenability" than the 1053 and 1045 carbon steels that are typically used in production crankshafts. Hardening 4340 steel increases both its tensile strength and its fatigue resistance.

A crankshaft bends and twists with every power pulse. The most frequent cause of crankshaft breakage in racing

Chevrolet small-block raw crankshaft forgings are available with a large front snout (PN 24502460–right) that can be machined to big-block V8 dimensions.

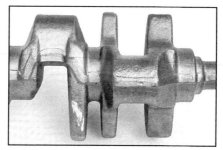

Rod throws are forged in place to eliminate variations in counterweight position. Note the straight forging die marks on this unmachined crankshaft forging.

A competition crankshaft machined from a Chevrolet heavy-duty forging will provide outstanding reliability under severe operating conditions.

Circular counterweights are more effective in balancing the engine assembly than the elliptical counterweights on production cranks.

Specialty crankshaft shops can finish unmachined forgings to customer specifications with a choice of bearing diameter and stroke.

engines is fatigue failure caused by this bending. The load inputs on the connecting rod throws are at a distance from the support of the two adjacent main bearings. Over thousands of cycles, this bending moment can lead to fatigue failure.

All Chevrolet 4340 heavy-duty crankshafts are a "non-twist" design, which means that the four rod journals are forged in place. In contrast, production crankshafts are typically forged flat, and then "twisted" during the manufacturing process to position the front and rear crankshaft throws at 90-degree angles.

Due to manufacturing tolerances, there is always the possibility of some variation in the position of the counterweights in a twisted forging. Ideally the rod throws should be twisted exactly 90 degrees. However, if one end is twisted 87 degrees, for example, the counterweights will not be in the optimum position. The crankshaft can still be machined and balanced, but additional heavy metal is often required. The bearing loads may also be higher due to the compromised counterweight location. Forging all four throws in place eliminates these variations.

The counterweight design of Chevrolet 4340 forgings further reduces bearing loads. Compared to a production crankshaft, the diameter of the counterweights is larger, and the counterweights are circular in shape. Production small-block cranks require elliptical counterweights for piston skirt clearance with specific stroke and connecting rod lengths. Racers have more latitude in their choice of strokes and connecting rod center-to-center lengths. The counterweights' circular shape makes them more effective in balancing the engine because it increases the distance between the counterweight mass and the centerline of the crankshaft. GM Motorsports Technology Group engineers also lightened the unfinished crankshaft forging by reshaping its rod pin arms and eliminating the machining pads that are used for production tooling.

A number of specialty crankshaft shops have the expertise to machine Chevrolet heavy-duty crankshaft forgings. To prepare a raw forging for installation, its rod and main bearing journals must be finish ground, oil holes drilled, the snout ground and slotted, and the flywheel flange trued, drilled, and tapped. Many shops also offer additional services, such as streamlining the counterweights, cross-drilling the main bearing journals, and special heat treating.

Crankshaft Preparation

Production small-block crankshafts should be Magnaflux inspected for cracks before installation. Cast and forged cranks should be carefully deburred to eliminate stress risers. To check crankshaft straightness, support the crankshaft in Vee blocks (or in the cylinder case with front and rear bearings only installed). Set up a dial indicator on the center main journal and slowly rotate the crankshaft. The center main journal should have less than .003-inch runout.

If you regrind a production nodular iron small-block V8 crankshaft, it must be thoroughly polished in a lathe, *turning the crankshaft in the direction of engine rotation.* Polishing the crankshaft in this manner causes any microscopic peaks of metal which are formed when material is torn away during the grinding process to point away from the bearing, and not into the soft overlay. Removing these microscopic "fish scales" by polishing a reground crankshaft while it is turning in its normal direction of rotation is absolutely essential to prevent premature main and rod bearing failure.

The production Chevrolet crankshaft oiling system is suitable for most competition engines. This system provides consistent lubrication at high rpm, and offers better reliability than cross-drilled main bearing journals that feed the rod bearings from the center of the journals.

The GM Motorsports Technology Group has developed a crankshaft modification that is highly recommended for competition small-blocks operated above 7500 rpm for sustained periods. All five main bearing journals should be modified

Cross-drilled main bearings feed oil to the rod bearings regardless of crank position, but may not supply adequate lubrication at high rpm.

The production Chevrolet crankshaft oiling system provides consistent lubrication and is suitable for most competition engines.

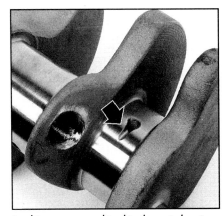

Lead-in grooves machined in the main bearing journals will channel oil to the rod bearing oil feed holes.

by machining lead-in grooves to channel oil into the oil feed holes for the rod bearings. These lead-in grooves should start approximately ½-inch before the rod bearing oil holes (with the crank turning in its normal direction of rotation), tapering to a depth of .125-inch and width of .200-inch.

The final step in preparing a production or heavy-duty crankshaft is to hand polish all journals with #400 grit sandpaper. Cut a strip of sandpaper the same width as the journal and fasten it around the journal with masking tape. Loop a leather or plastic thong once around the sandpaper and polish the journal by rapidly rotating the paper with the thong.

Crankshaft Rear Seal Adapter

As noted earlier, a leak-resistant one-piece rear main bearing seal was intro-

When balancing a crank, install slugs of heavy metal parallel to the crankshaft axis to prevent centrifugal force from dislodging them.

Crankshaft specialists can lighten the rod journals and streamline the counterweights to reduce windage losses.

duced on production Chevrolet small-block V8s at the start of the 1986 model year. The one-piece seal design required corresponding revisions in the engine block, rear main bearing cap, crankshaft, flywheel, and oil pan. Due to these changes, these parts are not interchangeable with 1985 and earlier engines.

Pilot Bearings

The pilot bearing aligns the transmission input shaft with the crankshaft centerline. A worn or misaligned pilot bearing can cause shifting problems and rapid clutch wear.

A heavy-duty needle roller pilot bearing (PN 14061685) is used with Chevrolet 6.2-liter diesel engines. This roller bearing is a direct replacement for the production bronze pilot bushings installed in Chevrolet crankshafts. The roller pilot bearing adds an extra margin of reliability to a high-performance drivetrain.

A production Chevrolet small-block uses a bronze pilot bushing to align the transmission and crankshaft.

A needle roller pilot bearing from a 6.2-liter Chevrolet diesel is a direct replacement for a production bronze pilot bushing.

1986 and newer production Chevrolet small-blocks use a one-piece rear crankshaft seal that bolts to the back of the block.

Crankshafts used in 1986 and newer small-blocks have flywheel flanges designed for one-piece seals (left); 1955-85 crankshafts (right) use two-piece seals.

Chevrolet blocks and rear main bearing caps were revised in 1986 to accommodate a one-piece rear seal and a molded oil pan gasket.

A crankshaft machined for a two-piece seal can be installed in a late-model block with a seal adapter. Center the adapter with a gauge plug.

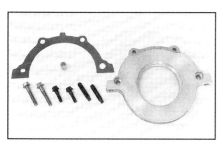

Use Chevrolet adapter PN 10051118 to install a crankshaft designed for a two-piece seal in a block machined for a one-piece seal.

After aligning the seal adapter on the block, drill two holes and install solid dowel pins to hold the adapter in position.

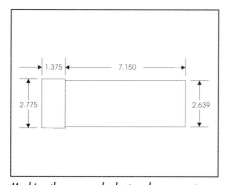

Machine the rear seal adapter plug gauge to the dimensions shown. The plug will align the adapter with the crankshaft centerline.

one-piece seals. The 3.58-inch diameter flywheel flange bolt pattern used on pre-1986 production crankshafts is recommended for high-performance and heavy-duty applications.

The Chevrolet rear crankshaft seal adapter kit contains the following parts:

Qty.	P/N	Description
1	10051119	Retainer—upper crank rear seal
1	10051120	Retainer—lower crank rear seal
2	10051121	Socket head screw
2	10051122	Washer
1	10051123	Bolt/screw retainer
1	10051124	Shouldered screw
2	14080362	Oil pan stud
2	14101030	Upper retainer bolt

Related components not included in the crankshaft seal kit which may be required to complete the engine assembly include the following:

P/N	Description
473424	Two-piece crankshaft seal
14101060	Gasket (adapter to block)
14087077	V8 oil pan (Corvette)
14088505	V8 one-piece oil pan gasket

All heavy-duty Chevrolet Bow Tie small-block V8 cast iron engine blocks manufactured since late 1988 are also machined for a one-piece rear main seal. (Aluminum Bow Tie blocks and race-prepared cast iron Bow Tie blocks use a special rear main bearing cap and adapter that accepts a two-piece rear seal and pre-1986 oil pan.)

A special crankshaft seal adapter (PN 10051118) is available from Chevrolet. This adapter allows pre-1986 crankshafts to be installed in blocks machined for

The inside diameter of the seal adapter must be accurately aligned with the crankshaft centerline for proper oil sealing. The adapter is positioned on the back of the engine block by a hollow dowel. Because the location of this dowel is not held to close tolerances, the seal adapter must be centered when it is first installed. This can be accomplished using a dial indicator or a plug gauge machined to the dimensions shown in the accompanying illustration. In some instances, it may be necessary to remove the hollow dowel in order to align the seal adapter properly.

A block equipped with a rear seal adapter requires a 1986 and later oil pan and a one-piece oil pan gasket.

After the adapter is aligned with the crankshaft centerline, it must be permanently positioned on the block. Drill two holes through the adapter and block and install solid dowel pins. These dowels may be located anywhere on the machined surface of the block flange, but they must not interfere with the flywheel or flywheel flange.

The large outside diameter of this adapter requires a 1986 or later oil pan to complete the conversion. A production oil pan can be modified to increase its capacity, or an aftermarket pan purchased that is compatible with the new gasket design. (Special rear main bearing caps are available from aftermarket sources that allow the use of pre-1986 oil pans on blocks machined for a one-piece rear seal.) The timing chain cover and front seal are unchanged.

Torsional Dampers

A torsional damper ("harmonic balancer") prolongs crankshaft life by controlling harmful torsional vibrations. A crankshaft is not a stiff, solid mass of steel; a crank bends and twists in response to the torque inputs from the piston and rod assemblies. Tests have shown that the crankshaft in a 350ci racing engine can deflect .3-degrees at 8,000 rpm. When the natural frequency of the crankshaft and the frequency of the torque inputs are resonant, the resulting severe vibrations can lead to failure. A torsional damper "quiets" these harmful vibrations.

A broken crankshaft is clear evidence of the destructive power of these torsional vibrations. Not all of the effects are so obvious, however. Torsional crankshaft vibrations can disturb valve timing, damage timing chains and gears, break fan belts, fracture oil pumps, and make transmissions difficult to shift at certain rpm points. These problems can often be cured by installing a more effective torsional damper.

A short, stiff crankshaft is less susceptible to torsional vibrations than a long, flexible crank. Crankshaft stiffness is primarily a function of stroke length and main/rod journal overlap. For example, a 3.00-inch stroke crank is stiffer than a comparable 3.48-inch stroke crank. The short-stroke cranks used in 302ci small-block V8s have a higher natural frequency than the long-stroke crankshafts used in 350ci racing engines. As a result, competition engines equipped with short-stroke crankshafts are not as vulnerable to the ill effects of torsional vibrations.

An engine's operating range also affects its damper requirements. A drag racing engine changes rpm rapidly, minimizing the time that the crankshaft vibrates at its natural frequency. An endurance racing engine, in contrast, may run for several hours with its crankshaft operating close to its critical frequency. The endurance engine has a pressing need for an effective torsional damper, while the drag racing engine may survive dozens of full-power runs without one.

A production small-block 8-inch torsional damper (left) is neutral balanced. A counterweighted damper (right) is used only with an externally balanced 3.75-inch stroke crankshaft.

Elastomer torsional dampers are tuned to specific crankshaft frequencies. Damper PN 3364709 has a malleable iron inertia ring that improves reliability at high rpm.

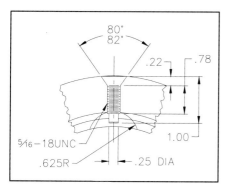

This diagram illustrates the recommended modification for malleable iron torsional dampers installed on competition engines.

Several production Chevrolet torsional dampers are suitable for high-performance small-block V8s. All production Chevrolet torsional dampers are a two-piece elastomer design, with an inner hub that is pressed onto the crank snout and a separate outer inertia ring. The hub and inertia ring are separated by an elastomer (synthetic rubber) sleeve.

Due to variations in engine accessories, two different timing marks have been used to indicate Top Dead Center on Chevrolet production torsional dampers. Dampers produced since 1969 have TDC timing marks that are 8 degrees farther advanced than pre-1969 versions. (Pre-1969 dampers have a timing mark that is two degrees before the keyway centerline; the mark is ten degrees before the keyway centerline on 1969-up dampers.)

These early- and late-style balancers require different timing pointers to correctly indicate TDC. If the timing mark and the timing pointer are mismatched, spark timing will be advanced or retarded from the desired setting, resulting in a

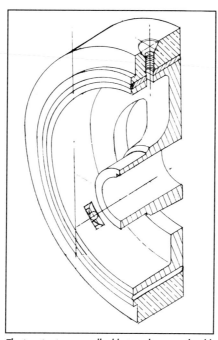

The inertia ring on malleable iron dampers should be pinned through slots in the hub to prevent the ring from moving forward and backward.

loss of performance and possible serious engine damage.

If you are installing a used damper and are unsure whether it is an early- or late-style, the timing mark position should be verified by using a dial indicator or piston stop on the Number One cylinder to accurately determine the damper's Top Dead Center position.

Production Torsional Dampers

Eight-inch diameter torsional dampers are recommended for most high-performance and competition applications. Three different production cast iron 8-inch dampers are available; the width of the damper's outer inertia ring varies according to the original application. PN 3817173 has a thick ($1^{11}/_{16}$-inch wide) inertia ring and the pre-1969 timing mark; it is damper ID #7173. PN 6272224 (ID #2224) is a thick 8-inch damper with the 1969 and later timing mark; this damper was used on 350ci LT-1 and L-82 engines. A thin version with a $1^5/_{16}$-inch wide inertia ring (damper ID #2224, original equipment on 1969 302ci Z-28s) is available as PN 3947708.

Damper PN 6272221 is $6^3/_4$ inches in diameter and is recommended for applications with limited clearance. It is used on many 1969 and newer 305ci and 350ci small-block V8 engines. The timing mark is 10 degrees before the keyway centerline. This damper has been used with

Torsional dampers should be rebalanced after cutting degree marks. Contrasting marks are visible when adjusting ignition timing.

good results on drag racing engines competing in classes that permit the use of cast iron dampers.

As noted earlier, all production 3.750-inch stroke crankshafts used in 400ci small-blocks are externally balanced, and require a counterweighted torsional damper and flywheel for proper engine balance. The recommended 8-inch diameter counterweighted damper for this application is PN 6272225.

Malleable Iron Damper

Chevrolet offers a heavy-duty torsional damper with a malleable iron inertia ring as PN 364709. This 8-inch diameter damper offers an extra margin of safety for high rpm operation, and is highly recommended for all competition small-block V8s that require a neutral balanced damper. It has the late-model timing mark position, and can be identified by the letters "MALL" which are cast in its outer inertia ring.

The hub is balanced separately before the outer ring is pressed on; the damper is then balanced again as a complete assembly. This procedure requires less drilling in the inertia ring. High-temperature rubber is also used in this heavy-duty malleable iron damper to improve its durability under racing conditions.

The damper ring modification shown in the accompanying illustration is recommended for long-stroke small-block

Two versions of the GM/Fluidampr are available for small-block V8s. PN 12341632 is 6.25 inches in diameter and weighs 7.9 pounds; PN 10051170 is 7.25 inches in diameter and weighs 13.9 pounds.

Heavy-duty GM/Fluidamprs dampen harmful crankshaft torsional vibrations with a viscous silicone fluid.

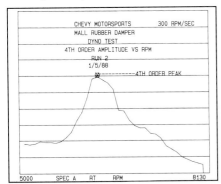
This graph illustrates the vibration-dampening capability of the malleable iron damper, which is tuned for a typical 350ci racing engine.

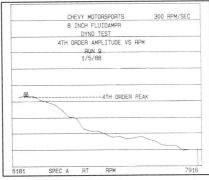
The viscous fluid GM/Fluidampr is not tuned to a specific frequency; its energy absorbing capability increases with engine speed.

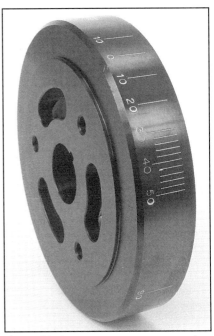
The GM/Fluidampr's contrasting timing marks are easily visible when setting spark advance. The sealed damper housing is laser welded to prevent leaks.

engines that are operated at continuous high speed, such as off-shore marine and NASCAR stock car use. By pinning the inertia ring through the slots in the damper hub as shown, the inertia ring can still move radially in its normal mode of operation, but it is prevented from working its way forward or backward off the hub. *This modification is only recommended for the malleable iron inertia ring damper #364709.*

Many engine builders remachine the outside diameter of the inertia ring and add degree marks. Either procedure requires that the damper be rebalanced before installation. GM balancing specifications call for removal of material from the outer inertia ring with a ½-inch drill to a maximum depth of ¼-inch on a radius of 3.62-inch from the hub centerline. *Warning:* Balance holes of greater diameter or depth may seriously weaken the damper and cause the inertia ring to fail at high engine speed.

GM/Fluidampr®

Chevrolet also markets two viscous fluid GM/Fluidamprs for high-rpm competition engines. PN 12341632 is 6.25 inches in diameter and weighs 7.9 pounds. PN 10051170 is 7.25 inches in diameter and weighs 13.9 pounds.

If damper performance and engine life are the most important considerations, the 7.25-inch diameter GM/Fluidampr is recommended. The 6.25-inch version can be used if weight is important, or if space limitations require a smaller damper. Both Fluidamprs are neutral balanced.

GM does not offer timing pointers for the GM/Fluidamprs. However, a bolt-on timing pointer (PN 12341915) for an 8-inch damper can be modified for a 7.25-inch Fluidampr. Similarly, pointer PN 12341904 (originally designed for a 6.75-inch damper) can be modified for use with the 6.25-inch Fluidampr.

GM/Fluidamprs rely on a viscous silicone fluid to control crankshaft vibrations instead of the elastomer (synthetic rubber) rings used in production dampers. The Fluidampr's inertia ring and fluid are contained in a hermetically sealed housing. The housing is laser welded to ensure a leakproof seal.

Destructive crankshaft vibrations are dampened when the difference in the ro-

tational speeds of the housing and the inertia ring shears the thick silicone fluid. A conventional elastomer damper controls these vibrations by the stretch and rebound of the rubber insert between the hub and the outer inertia ring.

Conventional elastomer dampers are tuned to a specific critical frequency. For example, the heavy-duty malleable iron balancer (PN 364709) described earlier was designed for a NASCAR-style 350ci small-block running at 8000 rpm. The GM/Fluidampr, in contrast, is not tuned to a specific vibration frequency. This is an important advantage in a racing engine

The flywheel flange on 1986 and later production small-block crankshafts was redesigned to accommodate a one-piece rear seal.

A crankshaft used with a one-piece rear seal (left) has a 3.00-inch diameter flywheel flange bolt pattern; a pre-1986 crank designed for two-piece seal (right) has a 3.58-inch diameter bolt circle.

A lightweight nodular iron flywheel with a Corvette pressure plate and clutch disc is suitable for high-performance vehicles.

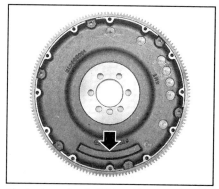

Flywheels used with 1986 and later production small-block crankshafts have a counterweight to produce proper engine balance.

age. A $7/_{16}$-20 x $2\frac{1}{4}$-inch damper bolt (PN 3815933) and washer (PN 14092217) should be used to positively retain the torsional damper on the crankshaft snout.

Flywheels

When building a high-performance small-block, the flywheel (or flexplate) must be matched to the crankshaft flange bolt pattern. Two different flywheel flange bolt patterns have been used on Chevrolet small-block V8 engines. All 1955-85 production crankshafts and all heavy-duty steel cranks have a 3.58-inch diameter bolt pattern. 1986 and later production cranks designed for one-piece rear crankshaft seals have a smaller 3.00-inch diameter flywheel flange bolt pattern. Crankshafts with either bolt pattern are suitable for general high-performance use; however, the pre-1986 3.58-inch pattern is recommended for competition.

All small-block Chevrolet crankshafts use neutral balanced flywheels except the 3.750-inch stroke cranks used in 400ci engines and 1986 and later crankshafts with one-piece rear seals. These crankshafts require flywheels with counterweights to achieve proper balance.

Chevrolet offers a lightweight 15-pound nodular iron neutral-balanced flywheel as PN 14085720; a counterweighted version for late-model crankshafts is available as PN 14088646.

Chevrolet nodular iron flywheels in new condition have been tested at 10,000 rpm engine speeds, and are suitable for most small-block applications. It should be emphasized, however, that overheating a clutch can significantly weaken a flywheel and lower the burst speed at which failure could occur. Although a Chevrolet heavy-duty flywheel is safe for

because any change in the weight of the crankshaft assembly alters its natural harmonic frequency. Unlike a elastomer damper, the energy absorbing capability of the Fluidampr increases with higher engine speed.

A viscous damper is also less affected by heat than an elastomer damper. Changes in the temperature of the rubber ring alter the frequency of an elastomer balancer. Energy absorbed by the viscous fluid in the GM/Fluidampr is transformed into heat, which is dissipated by the housing to the surrounding air.

The Fluidampr has no parts which are subject to wear, and requires no regular maintenance.

The GM/Fluidamper design also eliminates errors in spark timing caused by movement of the inertia ring on an elastomer damper. The Fluidampr housing is marked in two degree increments from 30 to 50 degrees before Top Dead Center to

ensure accurate ignition timing. The housing is also marked at 90-degree intervals to simplify valve adjustments.

Many sanctioning bodies have prohibited the use of stock-type balancers on racing engines because of the possibility of inertia ring failure at high rpm. The Fluidampr meets SEMA 18-1 specifications, and is accepted by many organizations for competition use.

Installation

Regardless of the type of torsional damper used, the damper must fit tightly on the crank snout to effectively control the crankshaft's torsional vibrations. The inside diameter of the damper hub should *not* be honed oversize. Automatic transmission fluid can be used as a lubricant when installing a damper that fits the crankshaft tightly. Special installation tools are available to press the damper onto the crankshaft snout without dam-

Flexplates used with 1986 and newer Chevrolet small-block V8s have a 3.00-inch diameter flywheel flange bolt pattern.

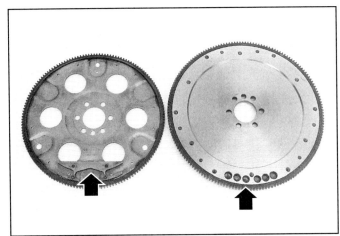

An automatic transmission flexplate (left) for a 1986 and later small-block has a counterweight; always use an "unbalanced" flywheel with a crankshaft with a one-piece rear seal.

TECH SPECS: SMALL-BLOCK V8 MANUAL TRANSMISSION FLYWHEELS

Part Number	Outside Diameter	Year	Crank Flange Bolt Pattern	Clutch Diameter	Starter Ring Gear Teeth	Notes
14085720	12¾"	1955–85	3.58"	10.4"	153	Lightweight nodular iron flywheel; weighs approximately 15 lbs.; for two-piece crank seal.
3986394	14"	1970–80	3.58"	11.0"	168	For externally balanced 400ci small-block V8 only; use with balancer #6272225.
3991469	14"	1955–85	3.58"	10.4, 11.0"	168	For two-piece crank seal.
10105832	14"	1986 up	3.00"	11.0, 11.85"	168	For one-piece crank seal.
14088646	12¾"	1986 up	3.00"	10.4, 11.0"	153	Lightweight nodular iron flywheel; weighs approximately 15 lbs.; for one-piece crank seal.
14088650	12¾"	1986 up	3.00"	10.4"	153	Standard weight flywheel for one-piece crank seal.

TECH SPECS: SMALL-BLOCK V8 AUTOMATIC TRANSMISSION FLEXPLATES

Part Number	Outside Diameter	Year	Crank Flange Bolt Pattern	Converter Bolt Pattern*	Starter Ring Gear Teeth	Notes
471598	14"	1970–85	3.58"	10.75, 11.50"	168	For internally balanced engine with two-piece crank seal.
471578	14"	1970–80	3.58"	10.75, 11.50"	168	For externally balanced 400ci small-block V8 only; use with balancer #6272225.
471529	12¾"	1969–85	3.58"	9.75, 10.75"	153	For internally balanced engine with two-piece crank seal.
10128412	12¾"	1986 up	3.00"	10.75"	153	For one-piece crank seal; used with 5.7L HO engine.
10128413	14"	1986 up	3.00"	11.50"	168	Heavy-duty flexplate with increased thickness for one-piece crank seal.
10128414	14"	1986 up	3.00"	10.75, 11.50"	168	For one-piece crank seal.

*NOTE: Torque converters for TH350 and TH400 transmissions are produced with both 10.75" and 11.50" diameter converter bolt patterns. To identify the correct pattern, measure from the converter center to an attaching bolt hole and then multiply this dimension by 2.

competition use when new, it should be periodically inspected for radial cracks emanating from the flywheel flange bolts holes and for signs of excessive clutch heat. (Some sanctioning bodies prohibit the use of stock-type flywheels in competition. Check the rules regarding flywheel specifications before using a lightweight nodular iron flywheel.)

Chevrolet also offers a variety of flexplates for small-block V8s used with automatic transmissions. Like manual transmission flywheels, these flexplates must be matched to the crankshaft's flywheel flange bolt pattern. Also, small-block V8s with production 3.750-inch stroke crankshafts and crankshafts with one-piece rear main seals require a coun-

terweighted flexplate to produce the proper engine balance. These flexplates are listed in the accompanying chart.

Automatic transmission flexplates used in competition applications should be inspected periodically for signs of stress. Check for cracks around the flywheel flange bolt holes, and inspect the

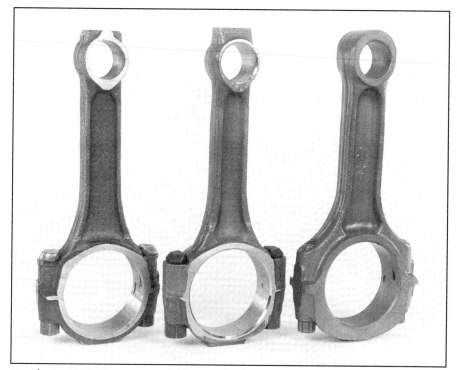

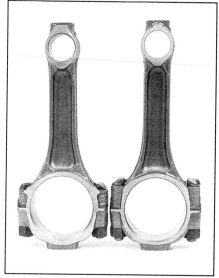

A 400ci small-block rod (left) has shorter bolts and a .135-inch shorter center-to-center length than a standard small-block rod.

A production 1955-67 connecting rod (left) is used with a 2.00-inch diameter rod journal; production 1968-up rod (center) and heavy-duty Bow Tie rod (right) fit 2.10-inch diameter rod journals.

welds that secure the starter ring gear to the flexplate.

Except as noted, all of the heavy-duty flywheels and flexplates described above are 14 inches in overall diameter and have 168-tooth starter ring gears. Chevrolet starter motor PN 1108400 should be used with these 14-inch diameter flywheels and flexplates. In applications that require a 12¾-inch flywheel or flexplate (153-tooth ring gear), starter PN 1108789 is recommended.

Connecting Rods

Chevrolet manufactures production and heavy-duty connecting rods for the small-block V8 to suit a wide range of uses and engine applications.

All production Chevrolet small-block V8 connecting rods have a center-to-center length of 5.700-inch—except the special short rods installed in 400ci small-blocks, which measure 5.565-inch between centers. All Chevy small-block connecting rods use .927-inch diameter wrist pins.

As outlined in the crankshaft section, two different rod journal diameters have been used in Chevrolet small-block V8s. Engines produced from 1955 through 1967 had 2.00-inch diameter rod journals; 1968 and later small-blocks use 2.10-inch rod journals. Pre-1968 small

journal rods have ¹¹⁄₃₂-inch bolts, and are not recommended for severe applications. 1968 and later large journal rods with ⅜-inch bolts are preferred for high-performance use.

A high-performance production connecting rod for 2.100-inch journals is available as PN 14096846. This rod is commonly referred to as the "pink" rod, a reference to its distinctive color code. These high quality rods are forged from 1038 alloy steel, and have ground mating surfaces between the cap and fork. They are also heat treated, shotpeened, and Magnaflux inspected to ensure that they are free of flaws in critical areas. "Pink" rods use pressed wrist pins.

All production connecting rods, bolts and nuts should be inspected before installation. A Rockwell hardness test is generally a reliable indication of whether the bolts will pull up to the proper 45/50 ft.-lb. torque (.006-inch bolt stretch preferred). Production bolts are in the range of 36-40 on the Rockwell "C" scale. Bolts that do not fall within this hardness range should not be used.

Bow Tie Connecting Rods

GM Motorsports Technology Group engineers have developed four heavy-duty Bow Tie connecting rods for competition small-block V8s. These premium quality rods are forged from 4340 alloy

steel that has been vacuum degassed to reduce random impurities in the metal.

Bow Tie connecting rods have been extensively tested by GM's metallurgical department, and have endured over 10 million cycles without failure. Fatigue tests were conducted using big-block rod loads (14,400 pounds in compression and 13,400 pounds in tension). These loads are equivalent to a typical 350ci small-block racing engine running at a sustained 8500 rpm.

Bow Tie small-block connecting rods are offered in two center-to-center lengths. Both versions of the Bow Tie rod are manufactured using dedicated forging dies to minimize reciprocating weight. PN 14011090 is a standard length 5.70-inch rod; PN 14011091 is an extra-long 6.00-inch version. Some engine builders prefer the 6.00-inch rod because its longer center-to-center distance reduces rod angularity, decreases cylinder wall loads, and increases piston dwell time at TDC. A longer connecting rod also allows piston weight to be reduced.

Heavy-duty Bow Tie small-block connecting rods are also available with profiled beams as PN 14011082 (5.70-inch long) and PN 14011083 (6.00-inch). The beam machining operation reduces total rod weight by approximately 50 grams; a typical 5.70-inch long profiled Bow Tie rod weighs 739 grams, with 529 grams on the big end. Profiled Bow Tie rods are also shotpeened to enhance their durability. If you grind or machine the beams, the surface should be shotpeened again.

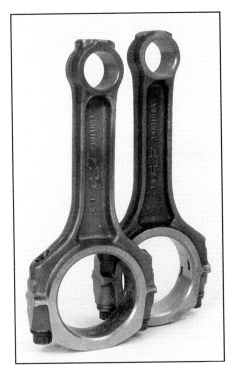

Heavy-duty forged 4340 steel Bow Tie connecting rods are available with 5.70 and 6.00-inch center-to-center lengths.

Bow Tie connecting rods are designed to provide adequate cam and block clearance when used with a 3.50-inch stroke crankshaft. It may be necessary to modify the rods for additional clearance when using longer strokes by relieving the shoulder in the area of the bolt hole. This is not a highly stressed location, so moderate clearancing will not jeopardize the rod's service life.

Bow Tie small-block rods are machined for pressed fit piston pins. If the rods are converted for floating pins, a single .125-inch diameter oil hole should be drilled in the top of the pin bore.

Chevrolet Bow Tie connecting rods are supplied with aircraft quality $^7/_{16}$-inch diameter bolts that thread directly into the rod fork. An enlarged mating surface between the rod and cap and alignment sleeves around the bolt holes positively prevent cap "walk" under racing conditions. This design produces a reasonably lightweight rod and eliminates the stress risers associated with conventional rod bolt head seats.

Bow Tie rod bolts should be lubricated with 30-weight oil during assembly and torqued to 70 ft.-lb. Bolt stretch should be between .005 and .006-inch. Replacement bolts (PN 14011092) and chamfered washers (PN 14011093) are available from Chevrolet.

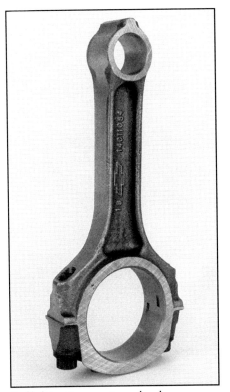

Profiled Bow Tie connecting rods reduce reciprocating weight. The beam machining operation removes 50 grams of metal.

Due to the additional weight of heavy-duty Chevrolet Bow Tie connecting rods, it is essential that the crankshaft be balanced before final assembly.

Pistons

Although all pistons installed in Chevrolet engines are aluminum, they vary considerably in their performance characteristics. Cast aluminum, forged aluminum, and hypereutectic pistons have advantages and disadvantages for different applications.

A cast aluminum piston has a very regular, crystalline grain structure. A cast piston expands uniformly when heated to operating temperature. Most cast pistons also have steel struts that control thermal expansion. Consequently cast aluminum pistons can be installed with relatively tight piston-to-wall clearances without scuffing. (Other factors also affect piston clearance, such as skirt design and rpm.)

Hypereutectic pistons are used in Chevrolet H.O. 350 engine assemblies. The hypereutectic aluminum material contains approximately 16% silicon, compared to the 7% silicon typically found in conventional pistons. Increasing the percentage of silicon produces an extremely hard piston that can withstand

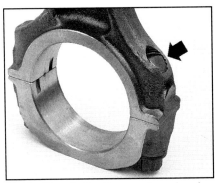

The shoulders of a Bow Tie connecting rod can be ground to increase cam and block clearance when using a long-stroke crankshaft.

Relieve the oil pan rails and the bottoms of the cylinder barrels for connecting rod clearance when using a long-stroke crankshaft.

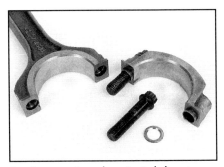

Bow Tie connecting rods use $^7/_{16}$-inch diameter 12-point bolts and chamfered washers. Sleeves align the cap on the rod fork.

high temperatures and pressures. The hypereutectic material also provides superior wear characteristics in the wrist pin hole and ring grooves.

Hypereutectic pistons expand less than conventional cast and forged pistons, and require less piston-to-bore clearance. The tighter clearance reduces blowby and piston rock, which in turn enhances cylinder sealing and oil control. The hypereutectic pistons installed in High Output engine assemblies are also lighter than comparable forgings.

Forged aluminum pistons are preferred over cast pistons in competition applications. The dense grain structure of a forging increases strength and promotes heat

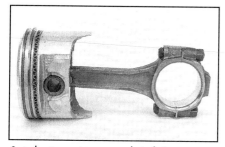
Cast aluminum pistons are relatively inexpensive and will provide quiet, dependable service in a street or mildly modified small-block.

H.O. small-block engines are assembled with hypereutectic (high silicon) pistons. The "reverse dome" piston design yields 9.8:1 compression.

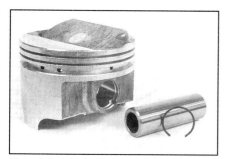
Chevrolet heavy-duty pistons include round wire pin retainers and chamfered wrist pins. Round wire retainers resist pound-out.

A flat-top forged aluminum piston produces a 9.0:1 compression ratio in a 350ci small-block with 76cc combustion chambers.

A 1967-69 Z28 forged aluminum piston produces 11:1 compression in a 302ci small-block with 64cc combustion chambers.

Heavy-duty 12.5:1 compression ratio Chevrolet pistons have asymmetrical domes to fit "right-hand" and "left-hand" cylinders.

transfer away from the piston top. During the forging process, the aluminum's grain structure is formed by the die pattern, improving both the piston's ultimate strength and its fatigue life. Consequently a forged piston is better able to survive the mechanical and thermal stresses in a competition engine than a cast piston.

Compression Ratio

The compression ratio should be a primary consideration when selecting pistons for a high-performance or racing small-block V8. Compression ratio is a function of the cylinder displacement, combustion chamber volume, deck clearance, head gasket thickness, and piston

dome design. Compression ratios that are too high for the octane rating of the available fuel will promote detonation and lead to serious engine damage. (High cylinder pressures that promote detonation are also affected by camshaft timing, ignition advance, cylinder head port design, and other factors.)

The octane rating of commercially available pump gasoline limits high-performance street engines to compression ratios below 10:1. Raising the compression ratio in a modified engine offers a potential performance improvement, but high-octane gasoline and/or octane-improving additives are usually required to prevent detonation. For all-out racing en-

gines, Chevrolet offers heavy-duty domed pistons with a nominal compression ratio of 12.5:1. Engines with such high compression ratios must be operated on high-octane racing fuels exclusively, and should be inspected frequently for evidence of detonation.

Production Pistons

Flat-top forged aluminum pistons originally used in 1971-80 L-82 engines are a good choice for high-performance 350ci engines installed in street rods and similar vehicles. These pistons yield a 9:1 compression ratio when used with cylinder heads with 76cc combustion chambers, and 10.25:1 with 64cc chambers.

Part Number	Engine	Compression Ratio	Head Chamber Volume	Size	Pin Type	ID#	Notes
10104455	350	9.8:1	58cc	Standard	Pressed	10104458 or 14096277	5.7L HO engine assembly; first design with ZZZ ID; hypereutectic (high silicon) aluminum.
10104456	350	9.8:1	58cc	+.001	Pressed	10104459	5.7L HO engine assembly; first design with ZZZ ID; hypereutectic (high silicon) aluminum.
10104457	350	9.8:1	58cc	+.030	Pressed	10104460	5.7L HO engine assembly; first design with ZZZ ID; hypereutectic (high silicon) aluminum.
10181389	350	9.8:1	58cc	Standard	Pressed	10105168 or 10172749	5.7L HO engine assembly; second design with ZZ1, 2, 3 ID; hypereutectic (high silicon) aluminum.
10181390	350	9.8:1	58cc	Standard High Limit	Pressed	10105168 or 10172749	5.7L HO engine assembly; second design with ZZ1, 2, 3 ID; hypereutectic (high silicon) aluminum.
10181392	350	9.8:1	58cc	+.030	Pressed	10105169 or 10181388	5.7L HO engine assembly; second design with ZZ1, 2, 3 ID; hypereutectic (high silicon) aluminum
12520264	350	9.1:1	64cc	Standard	Pressed	10046106 or 14075651 or 14093679	350/300hp service engine.
12520265	350	9.1:1	64cc	+.001	Pressed	N/A	350/300hp service engine.
12520266	350	9.1:1	64cc	+.030	Pressed	N/A	350/300hp service engine with SP ID.
3946876	302	11:1	64cc	Standard	Floating	3927173	1968-69 Z-28.
3946882	302	11:1	64cc	+.030	Floating	3927176	1968-69 Z-28.
3942543	350	11:1	64cc	+.030	Pressed	3942548	1969 L46.
474190	350	9:1	76cc	Standard	Pressed	336747, 464664 or 464692	1971-80 L82; piston OD 3.998–3.999".
474192	350	9:1	76cc	+.030	Pressed	464695	1971-80 L82.
3989051	350	11:1	64cc	+.030	Pressed or floating	3949464	1970 LT-1; requires pin retainer #3946848 and floating rod for floating pin application.

High-compression pistons (11:1 nominal compression ratio with 64cc combustion chambers) are available from Chevrolet for 302ci and 350ci small-blocks. The wrist pin locations and dome designs of these pistons vary to accommodate the different stroke dimensions and cylinder volumes of the two engine displacements. These pistons use production-type $\frac{5}{64}$-inch wide compression rings and $\frac{3}{16}$-inch oil rings. They are machined for either pressed or floating pins as described in the specification chart.

Heavy-Duty Pistons

Chevrolet also offers a wide selection of heavy-duty 12.5:1 forged pistons for 350ci racing engines. These pistons are exceptionally durable in high-speed applications. They are forged from an aircraft alloy aluminum that has superior strength at high temperatures.

Chevrolet heavy-duty pistons use $\frac{1}{16}$-inch wide compression rings that provide an effective cylinder seal at high speeds while reducing internal friction. These pistons are available in standard, +.030-inch, and +.060-inch diameters.

Heavy-duty pistons use round wire pin locks. These locks offer superior resistance to pound-out than other pin retaining systems. The full-floating wrist pins supplied with these pistons are chamfered on both ends to accommodate the wire pin locks. Replacement 1.07-inch OD x .064-inch round wire retainers are available individually as PN 14011033 for overhauls and rebuilds.

TECH SPECS: SMALL-BLOCK V8 HEAVY-DUTY PISTONS

Part Number	Engine	Compression Ratio	Size	Rod Length	ID#	Notes
14011020	350	12.5:1	Standard	5.7"	14011006	For cyl. #2,3,6,7.
14011021	350	12.5:1	Standard	5.7"	14011007	For cyl. #1,4,5,8.
14011022	350	12.5:1	+.030	5.7"	14011008	For cyl. #2,3,6,7.
14011023	350	12.5:1	+.030	5.7"	14011009	For cyl. #1,4,5,8.
14011024	350	12.5:1	+.060	5.7"	14011010	For cyl. #2,3,6,7.
14011025	350	12.5:1	+.060	5.7"	14011011	For cyl. #1,4,5,8.
14011026	350	12.5:1	Standard	6.0"	14011014	For cyl. #2,3,6,7.
14011027	350	12.5:1	Standard	6.0"	14011015	For cyl. #1,4,5,8.
14011028	350	12.5:1	+.030	6.0"	14011016	For cyl. #2,3,6,7.
14011029	350	12.5:1	+.030	6.0"	14011017	For cyl. #1,4,5,8.
14011030	350	12.5:1	+.060	6.0"	14011018	For cyl. #2,3,6,7.
14011031	350	12.5:1	+.060	6.0"	14011019	For cyl. #1,4,5,8.

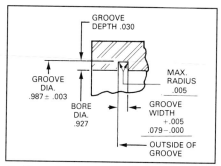

Modify production pistons with floating pins for competition by machining the pin bosses for .072-inch thick Spirolox retainers.

Replacement round wire and Spirolox pin retainers are available from Chevrolet; never reuse retainers when rebuilding an engine.

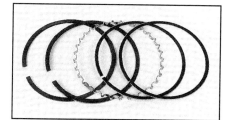

Heavy-duty piston ring sets include moly-faced top and second compression rings and low-tension three-piece oil rings.

Chevrolet racing pistons are available with pin locations to suit both standard 5.70-inch and extra-long 6.00-inch connecting rods. Some competition engine builders prefer long connecting rods because they believe the increased center-to-center length improves the piston/rod geometry and reduces internal friction.

Chevrolet heavy-duty 12.5:1 pistons have asymmetrical piston domes that closely match the combustion chambers in conventional small-block cylinder heads. (Note that these pistons *do not* fit the redesigned combustion chambers in 18-degree and splayed-valve Bow Tie cylinder heads!) Four "right-hand" and four "left-hand" pistons are required for a complete engine set. When installing these pistons, make sure that the domes and valve pockets correspond to the cylinder head layout. (All other Chevrolet forged pistons have "universal" domes and can be installed in any cylinder.)

Piston Preparation

Carefully inspect all new pistons before installation, and smooth all sharp edges on the domes and skirts. When assembling pistons and rods with pressed wrist pins, the small end of the rod should be heated and the pin quickly installed using an assembly fixture. Most automotive machine shops and Chevrolet dealerships are equipped to perform this assembly. There should be a minimum .001-inch press fit (preferably .0012-inch) between the wrist pins and rods to insure that pins will not loosen.

Chevrolet 11:1 compression pistons originally used in 302ci engines are machined for full-floating wrist pins. These pistons use 1.013-inch OD x .042-inch thick Spirolox pin retainers (PN 3946848). These same Spirolox can be used to convert 11:1 compression 1970 350ci LT-1 small-block pistons to floating wrist pins. Modify the connecting rods for floating pins as described in the engine building chapter.

Production and service replacement wrist pins used with floating pin retainers must have machined flat ends (except pins designed for round wire retainers). When using production-type pistons with floating pins in competition, the pin bosses should be regrooved to accommodate .072-inch thick Spirolox retainers (PN 366219). After machining the grooves, grind or turn the wrist pins to length to obtain the recommended zero to .005-inch wrist pin end clearance. *Wrist pin retainers should never be reused after a high-performance engine has been run and disassembled.*

Pistons should be checked for adequate valve-to-piston clearance by pre-assembling one piston and rod with the other engine components (camshaft, crankshaft, cylinder heads, rocker arms, etc.) you intend to use. Measure the piston-to-valve clearance by laying small strips of clay across the valve notches in the piston dome and then turning the crankshaft at least two complete revolutions. Disassemble the engine and measure the minimum thickness of the clay where the valves have left impressions.

The absolute minimum piston-to-valve clearance required to prevent engine damage is .045-inch, measured with the recommended valve lash. This minimum piston-to-valve clearance assumes that the engine will never operate in valve float. For drag racing, road racing, and similar forms of motorsports, it is essential to provide more than the minimum piston-to-valve clearance to allow for occasional valve float. The generally accepted minimum clearances for these applications are .080-inch for the intake valves and .100-inch for the exhausts.

Piston Rings

Production Corvette piston ring sets are a good choice for all small-block pistons machined for 5/64-inch wide compression rings and 3/16-inch oil rings. These sets include moly-filled, radiused face compression rings manufactured from high strength iron. They are offered in both standard and oversize diameters for a variety of cylinder bore sizes.

Chevrolet also offers racing piston ring sets with $\frac{1}{16}$-inch moly-filled compression rings and low-tension $\frac{3}{16}$-inch oil rings for heavy-duty 12.5:1 compression pistons. These sets are available in 4.005-inch, 4.035-inch, and 4.065-inch diameters. The engine builder must file the rings to provide the desired end gap.

Always measure the piston ring end gaps with each ring square in its respective cylinder bore. If the end gaps are under the minimum recommended size (.020-inch top, .016-inch second, .016-inch oil), the end gaps must be filed to prevent ring scuffing.

The GM Motorsports Technology Group recommends a smooth cylinder wall finish, using 400 grit stones for the final hone as described in the engine building chapter. Modern ring manufacturing techniques virtually eliminate the need for a lengthy break-in time to seat the rings; rough bore finishes are simply not necessary to seat the rings. A smooth cylinder bore finish on initial build results in a significant power increase due to decreased engine internal friction.

Cylinder Heads

A large part of the Chevrolet small-block's success in motorsports is due to its efficient and effective cylinder head design. Small-block cylinder head castings have been continuously refined and updated to reflect advances in airflow and combustion technology. From the famous "Power Pack" and "fuel injection" heads of the Fifties and Sixties to the "turbo" and "Bow Tie" designs of the Seventies, Eighties, and Nineties, the small-block V8 has set the pace in cylinder head development for two-valve racing engines.

Chevrolet high-performance and heavy-duty cylinder heads are offered in both cast iron and aluminum to cover the entire spectrum of engine applications. Cylinder head choices for the small-block V8 range from replacement castings for street and limited competition use to special Bow Tie designs for maximum-effort racing engines.

Production Cast Iron Heads

The chief difference between currently available cast iron replacement high-performance cylinder heads is their combustion chamber volumes. PN 3987376 has a nominal chamber volume of 64cc, while PN 464045 has larger 76cc chambers. The choice between these castings

should hinge on the desired compression ratio and the octane rating of the available gasoline. Small-chamber heads were original equipment on various 302, 327, and 350ci engines produced in the late Sixties with 10.0:1 to 11.0:1 compression ratios. Large chamber castings were typically used throughout the Seventies on small-blocks with 9.0:1 compression.

These heads are suitable for high-performance street and some limited competition engines when intake manifold heat and low-speed throttle response are desir-

able. These service replacement cylinder heads are machined for 2.02-inch diameter intake valves and 1.60-inch diameter exhaust valves. Both assemblies include screw-in $\frac{3}{8}$-inch diameter rocker arm studs and pushrod guideplates.

Cylinder heads on many production small-block V8s were redesigned in 1987 with fast-burn combustion chambers and raised rocker cover rails. These cast iron cylinder heads feature revised combustion chambers with centrally located spark plugs. Starting the flame front closer to the

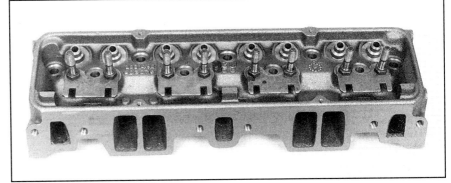

Production cast iron cylinder heads are available with 64cc and 76cc combustion chambers. Heads include pushrod guideplates and $\frac{3}{8}$-inch studs.

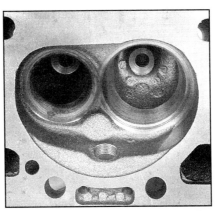

Early-model Z28/LT-1 cast iron cylinder head has 64cc combustion chambers machined for 2.02/1.60-inch valves.

High-performance service replacement cylinder heads are equipped with screw-in rocker arm studs and hardened pushrod guideplates.

The angle of the two middle bolt holes was changed from 90 degrees to 73 degrees on 1987 and newer production cast iron cylinder heads.

The center bolt holes on high-performance intake manifolds must be machined to match the 73-degree bolt angle on a late-model head (left).

Part Number	Description	Casting Number	Material/Weight (lbs.)	Port Volume Int./Exh (cc)	Combustion Chamber Volume	Valve Diameter Int./Exh. (in.)	Spark Plugs	Heat Risers	Notes
10185086	H.O. 350 head assembly	10088113	Aluminum/19.0	163/NA	58	1.94/1.50	Angled	No	Assembly w/springs, valves, studs and guideplates.
3987376	Service replacement	3991492	Cast iron	157/NA	64	2.02/1.60	Straight	Yes	Screw-in studs, pushrod guideplates.
464045	Service replacement	462624	Cast iron	161/NA	76	2.02/1.60	Straight	Yes	Screw-in studs, pushrod guideplates.
10134392	Bow Tie	14011034	Cast iron/42.5	184/55	64	2.02/1.60	Angled	No	Off-highway cast iron head.
10051167	Phase 6 Bow Tie	14011049	Aluminum/19.5	175/59	59	2.02/1.60	Angled	No	Standard port location, includes valve seats and guides.
14011049	Phase 6 Bow Tie (bare)	14011049	Aluminum	180/NA	55	N/A	Angled	No	No seats, guides or pushrod holes.
10051101	Raised Runner Bow Tie	10051101	Aluminum/19.0	197/65	54	N/A	Angled	No	Intake ports .200" higher than standard location; no seats, guides, or pushrod holes.
10134352	Low-Port 18°	10134352	Aluminum/23.0	223/80	44	N/A	Angled	No	18° valve angle; no seats, guides.
10134363	High-Port 18°	10134363	Aluminum/24.5	210/80	45	N/A	Angled	No	18° valve angle; no seats, guides; 4.060–4.125" bore recommended.
10134364	High-Port 18°	10134363	Aluminum/24.5	210/80	44	N/A	Angled	No	18° valve angle; no seats, guides; 4.000–4.060" bore recommended.
24502482	CNC-ported Bow Tie High-Port 18°	10134363	Aluminum/22.0	250/95	50	2.15/1.625	Angled	No	Fully ported with seats and guides.
10185040	Splayed-valve	10185040	Aluminum/24.0	260/NA	45	N/A	Angled	No	Splayed-valve design.

center of the chamber speeds up the combustion process and produces a more uniform burn rate in the cylinder. Combustion chamber volume was reduced to 58cc in these fast-burn cylinder heads; redesigned sump-head pistons maintained a compression ratio that was compatible with unleaded pump gasoline.

Late-model production cylinder heads also have raised rocker cover rails and redesigned valve covers to improve oil sealing. Raising the rocker cover rail places the valve cover gasket above the drainback oil level and prevents oil from saturating the gasket. The cylinder head's valve cover gasket surface is machined for a more consistent seal, and shields on the inside of the production valve cover protect the gasket from oil splash. The rocker covers are attached to the cylinder heads by four bolts piloted through the top of the rocker covers, and internal flanges distribute the clamping loads over the entire sealing area.

The angle of the two middle intake manifold bolts was changed from 90 degrees to 73 degrees on 1987 and newer production cast iron cylinder heads. Before installing a high-performance intake manifold on these heads, the manifold's center bolt holes must be drilled and spotfaced to match this 73-degree angle. (Wedge-shaped spacers available from aftermarket suppliers can also be used to adapt intake manifolds to late-model cylinder heads with 73-degree center bolts.) All Chevrolet Bow Tie intake manifolds will fit 1986 and older production cast iron heads and all Bow Tie cast iron heads without modifying the middle manifold bolt holes.

H.O. 350 Aluminum Cylinder Head PN 10185018

Aluminum small-block cylinder heads were introduced on production 350ci Corvette engines in mid-1986. In 1988, this casting was updated with raised "D"-shaped exhaust ports. These revised aluminum heads were specified for the H.O. 350 engine assembly introduced in 1989.

The H.O. aluminum cylinder head assembly includes valves, valve springs, screw-in studs, and pushrod guideplates.

The H.O. cylinder head's lightweight retainers enhance reliability at high rpm.

High-performance H.O. aluminum cylinder heads are available as PN 10185086. This complete assembly includes valves, heavy-duty chrome silicon valve springs, lightweight retainers, ³⁄₈-inch screw-in rocker studs, and pushrod guideplates. H.O. heads offer excellent performance at reasonable cost for high-performance street engines. However, they are not designed to withstand the stress of all-out racing. The H.O. aluminum head is an affordable alternative for street rods, bracket racers, and other emission-exempt applications.

H.O. aluminum cylinder head assemblies are based on brand new Corvette light alloy castings (casting #10088113). The aluminum head's design features include D-shaped exhaust ports that enhance the flow of burned gases, high-velocity intake runners that provide crisp throttle response, and centrally located spark plugs that improve overall combustion efficiency.

A pair of aluminum cylinder heads weighs approximately 50 pounds less than comparable cast iron cylinder heads. (A bare aluminum casting, less valves and springs, weighs 19 pounds versus 44 pounds for a bare cast iron head). This reduction in total engine weight can noticeably improve handling, acceleration, and fuel economy.

The H.O. cylinder head's angled spark plugs improve combustion efficiency.

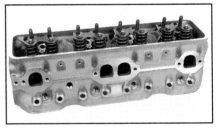

The D-shaped exhaust ports in Corvette and H.O. aluminum heads are .100-inch higher than the ports in production cast iron heads.

The H.O. head's 58cc combustion chambers have radiused seat inserts and angled spark plug holes for ³⁄₄-inch reach gasketed plugs.

BOW TIE TIPS — H.O. Head Installation

The following related components are recommended when installing H.O. aluminum cylinder heads:

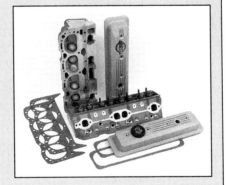

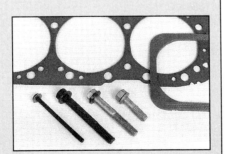

Part No.	Description
10046197	Stamped steel rocker cover, left hand
14091636	Stamped steel rocker cover, right hand
10055781	Magnesium Corvette valve cover, left hand
10055782	Magnesium Corvette valve cover, right hand
10229162	Corvette screw-in oil filler cap
12341960	Chrome screw-in oil filler cap
12338092	Valve cover hold-down bolts (8 required)
14094717	Hold-down bolt washers (8 required)
14088793	Hold-down bolt gaskets (8 required)
14088564	Neoprene rocker cover gasket
14088948	Composition head gasket, .051" thick
12338045	Long head bolt with washer (14 required)
14088946	Medium head bolt with washer (4 required)
14088947	Short head bolt with washer (16 required)

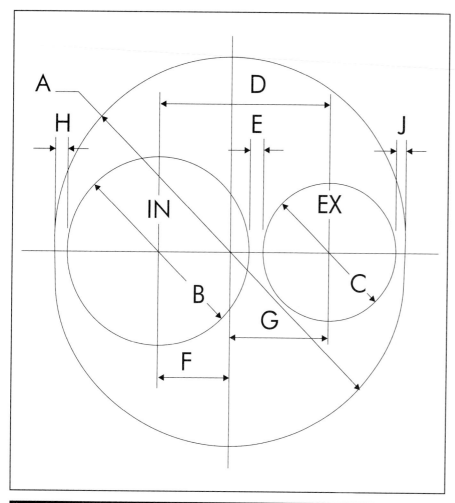

TECH SPECS:
SMALL-BLOCK V8 CYLINDER HEAD VALVE POSITIONS

P/N	A	B	C	D	E	F	G	H	J
10134392	4.030	2.02	1.60	1.86	.050	.850	1.01	—	—
14011049	4.030	2.10	1.62	1.91	.050	.850	1.06	.115	.141
10134352	4.125	2.15	1.62	1.935	.050	.805	1.13	.183	.123
10134363	4.125	2.20	1.62	1.955	.045	.825	1.13	.138	.123

This chart shows the valve spacing for Chevrolet Bow Tie heads. "H" and "J" are the clearance between the valve head and cylinder wall at a specified bore diameter ("A").

The head uses ¾-inch reach gasketed spark plugs with ⅝-inch hex heads. AC FR5LS, 904, or MR43LTS spark plugs are recommended for street use. If a colder spark plug heat range is required, use FR3LS or FR2LS.

The pushrod guideplates installed on aluminum H.O. cylinder heads are designed for self-aligning production rocker arms (PN 10089648). These rail-type rocker arms have guides that center the rocker tip on the valve stem; consequently the pushrod guideplates are *not* hardened. If you install any other type of rocker arm (including old-style produc-

tion rockers without aligning guides), hardened pushrod guideplates (PN 14011051) should be substituted.

H.O. aluminum cylinder heads do not have heat riser passages because modern electronic fuel injection systems provide extra mixture enrichment during engine warm-up. Carbureted engines equipped with aluminum H.O. cylinder heads may require a longer warm-up period due to the lack of manifold heat to operate a mechanical choke stove.

A composition head gasket with stainless steel fire rings should be used with aluminum heads to prevent galvanic ac-

tion between the head and a cast iron engine block. Production Corvette composition head gaskets (PN 14088948) are recommended. These gaskets have a compressed thickness of .051-inch and stainless steel compression rings. Extra-long cylinder head bolts with washers are required to complete the Corvette aluminum cylinder head assembly; see the accompanying list for part numbers.

The aluminum H.O. cylinder head has a raised rocker arm rail to prevent valve cover gasket oil leaks. This revised rocker rail design requires late-model rocker covers with four central bolt holes. Magnesium Corvette rocker covers and stamped steel rocker covers are available for aluminum heads.

The H.O. cylinder head's exhaust port exits are approximately .100-inch higher than production cast iron heads; exhaust manifolds and aftermarket headers may require modification to maximize airflow. Also, the spark plugs must be checked for adequate exhaust manifold or header clearance. Both ends of the head are machined for alternator, power steering, air conditioning compressor, and accessory mounts.

Cast Iron Bow Tie Head
PN 10134392

Chevrolet developed the cast iron Bow Tie cylinder head (PN 10134392) to meet the need for a cast iron cylinder head with better port flow performance than a production casting for off-highway use. The cast iron Bow Tie head incorporates numerous improvements over both production cylinder heads and the heavy-duty designs that preceded it.

Two versions of the cast iron Bow Tie cylinder head have been produced. Phase 1 castings have a raised parting line between the exhaust manifold flanges; Phase 2 heads can be identified by their redesigned outer water jacket wall with flat, machined surfaces between the exhaust manifold flanges. The manifold heat riser passages are deleted in Phase 2 Bow Tie heads to produce a cool, dense intake charge. The area around the tapped water temperature sensor hole is also machined flat on the Phase 2 head. However, there is no significant difference in airflow between the two versions because the intake and exhaust ports are identical in Phase 1 and Phase 2 castings.

The Bow Tie cylinder head's intake runners are recontoured with a higher roof and floor than conventional small-block heads. The intake port volume of the cast iron Bow Tie head is approximately 184cc, in contrast to the 160cc runners which are typical of replacement service heads. In unmodified form, the cast iron Bow Tie head will flow more air than any production cast iron small-block head. Extra-thick port wall sections allow the runners to be enlarged to increase their flow capacity.

The Bow Tie head's redesigned intake tract and increased valve bowl volume combine with a carefully designed cross-sectional area to develop high inlet flow velocities that enhance low-speed torque output. The large valve bowl volume provides the cylinder with air and fuel as soon as the valve opens. It also serves as a storage area to accept the fuel charge after the valve closes; this feature maintains the incoming charge's momentum toward the intake valve. The intake port's high short-turn radius produces a gradual turn that reduces turbulence and presents the incoming column of air to the entire valve head. This approach significantly increases the Bow Tie head's airflow potential over "line of sight" intake port designs.

The exhaust port is also designed to enhance airflow. The flange opening was reduced by raising the port floor and short-turn radius .060-inch. This revision has a stabilizing effect on the flow through the port at low valve lifts, but the reduced cross-section does not restrict flow at higher lifts.

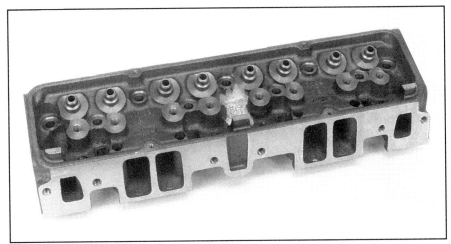

Chevrolet's affordable heavy-duty cast iron Bow Tie cylinder head (PN 10134392) offers better airflow than any production cast iron head.

The Bow Tie head's exhaust ports have raised floors to stabilize flow at low valve lifts. Angled spark plugs enhance combustion efficiency.

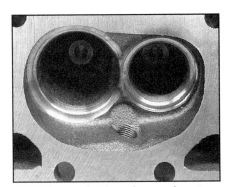

The combustion chamber volume in Phase 2 cast iron Bow Tie heads is 64cc's. The seats are machined for 2.02/1.60-inch valves.

The Phase 2 Bow Tie head has a revised combustion chamber design with a true volume of 64cc's. The quench areas beneath the spark plugs are filled to increase compression. The intake valve seats are machined for 2.02-inch diameter valves; the 1.60-inch exhaust valve seats are induction hardened.

TECH SPECS: SMALL-BLOCK V8 VALVES AND SEATS

| Part Number | Valves (in.)[1] | | | | | | Valve Seat Inserts (in.) | | | |
| | Intake | | | Exhaust | | | Intake | | Exhaust | |
	Dia.	Length	Margin	Dia.	Length	Margin	Dia.	Depth	Dia.	Depth
10134392	2.02[3]	4.94	.025	1.600[4]	4.94	.045	Not applicable			
10051167	2.02[3]	4.94	.025	1.600[4]	4.94	.045	2.10	.312	1.65	.312
10051101[2]	2.10	5.15	.065	1.600	5.15	.100	2.10	.312	1.65	.312
10134352[2]	2.15	5.35	.065	1.625	5.35	.100	2.20	.312	1.65	.312
10134363[2]	2.20	5.45	.065	1.625	5.45	.100	2.25	.312	1.65	.312
10134364[2]	2.15	5.45	.065	1.625	5.45	.100	2.20	.312	1.65	.312
24502482	2.15	5.45	.065	1.625	5.45	.100	2.25	.312	1.68	.312
10185040[2]	2.20	5.70	.065	1.650	5.70	.100	2.25	.312	1.68	3.75

[1]Note: These are recommended valve specifications—all Bow Tie cylinder heads are supplied without valves.
[2]Not supplied with valve seat inserts.
[3]P/N 3849814
[4]P/N 3849818

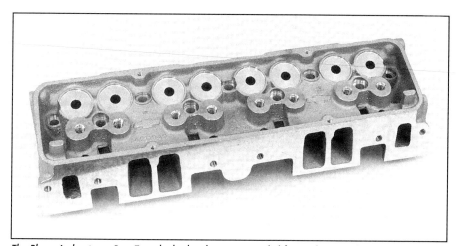

The Phase 6 aluminum Bow Tie cylinder head is recommended for applications that require production intake port locations and valve angles.

The Phase 6 Bow Tie cylinder head has 59cc combustion chambers; material was added above the spark plugs and between the valves.

Use pushrod guideplate PN 14011051 (right) with production and Bow Tie aluminum cylinder heads to provide proper rocker arm alignment.

The cast iron Bow Tie head has angled spark plug holes that position the plug gaps near the exhaust valves. Reliefs in the combustion chambers allow the spark plug threads to break cleanly through the chamber wall. The spark plug location reduces plug shrouding with high-dome pistons and improves access to the plugs with headers. The spark plug holes are machined for 3/8-inch reach tapered seat spark plugs with 5/8-inch hex heads.

All cast iron Bow Tie heads have a revised water jacket design that improves the casting's integrity. Water passages under the valve spring seats were eliminated to accommodate large diameter springs. The valve spring pockets are machined for 1.50-inch diameter springs.

The rocker stud bosses are tapped for screw-in studs, but studs and pushrod guideplates are not included. Use 3/8-inch rocker studs (PN 397416) or 7/16-inch diameter studs (PN 3921912). The larger 7/16-inch big-block rocker studs are recommended to improve valvetrain reliability; these studs require aftermarket rocker arms. Hardened pushrod guide-

plates (PN 3973418) for 5/16-inch diameter pushrods should be used with cast iron Bow Tie heads.

Aluminum Bow Tie Cylinder Head PN 14011049 and 10051167

An aluminum version of the Bow Tie cylinder head was introduced in 1980. An aluminum competition cylinder head offers several significant advantages over cast iron. Aluminum is significantly lighter, and much easier to modify and repair. The aluminum Bow Tie cylinder head's stock port volumes and airflow performance are comparable to a highly modified cast iron head, and it is more reliable in endurance racing applications.

The aluminum Bow Tie head has been continuously upgraded and improved since its introduction. Six distinct versions, or "phases", have been released. All six share the same 14011049 casting number, which is located under the valve cover between two rocker stud bosses.

Among the various "049" aluminum Bow Tie heads, the "Phase 6" version has

the highest performance potential. This head is recommended for applications that require a heavy-duty aluminum head that retains the production 23-degree valve angle and stock intake port locations. This head also uses production-type stud-mounted rocker arms and pushrod guideplates.

The Phase 6 Bow Tie head can be identified by its 59cc combustion chambers and distinctive "D"-shaped exhaust port exits. Two versions of the Phase 6 aluminum Bow Tie cylinder head are available. PN 14011049 is a fully machined bare head casting without seats, guides, and pushrod clearance holes. PN 10051167 has iron valve guides and valve seat inserts for 2.02-inch diameter intake valves and 1.60-inch exhausts.

The aluminum Bow Tie head has a one-piece water jacket, a design that does not require gluing or handling of the water jacket cores during manufacture. This allows more freedom in sand section strength and requires fewer sand bridges for continuity of the water jacket cores. Due to this smaller water jacket, the ports in aluminum heads have fewer restrictions than the ports in cast iron versions.

The aluminum Bow Tie head has no water passages between the roofs of its intake ports and the spring pockets. This feature allows the spring seats to be machined for large diameter valve springs, and the port roof to be raised.

The Phase 6 Bow Tie head has a high-efficiency combustion chamber design that it shares with the "raised runner" cylinder head described later in this chapter. This chamber promotes turbulence in the cylinders, thereby enhancing combustion and suppressing detonation. The combustion chamber volume in the Phase 6 head is approximately 59cc; Phases 1 through 5 had conventional production-type 64cc chambers.

The combustion chamber volume was reduced in the Phase 6 casting by adding material above the spark plug and between the valve seats. This reduction in chamber volume allows competition engine builders to achieve high compression ratios with smaller piston dome volumes.

The spark plug holes are .050-inch lower in Phase 6 heads to eliminate residual threads in the combustion chambers when the plug holes are tapped. The spark plug holes in Phase 6 aluminum heads are machined to accommodate both gasketed (Champion N series or equivalent) and

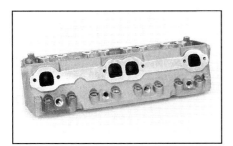

The Phase 6 Bow Tie cylinder head has "D"-shaped exhaust ports and a continuous bar between the exhaust manifold flanges.

Phase 6 heads are machined for both gasketed and tapered seat plugs. The head bolt bosses are spotfaced for 3/4-inch washers.

Pushrod guideplates for aluminum cylinder heads are stamped "05." Big-block 7/16-inch rocker arm studs are recommended.

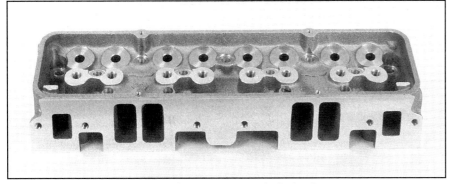

The intake ports in a "raised runner" aluminum Bow Tie cylinder head (PN 10051101) are .200-inch higher than the production location.

The difference in the intake port location in a raised runner aluminum Bow Tie head (left) and a Phase 6 head (right) is significant.

tapered seat (BN series or equivalent) plugs. Tapered seat plugs are easier to "index" for proper clearance between the electrodes and piston dome. After repeated torquings, however, the tapered seats may gall the head's plug sealing surfaces. Anti-seize thread lubricant can minimize this wear.

The exhaust manifold flange is moved outward .125-inch on the Phase 6 head to increase the length of the exhaust port and to improve exhaust flow. The exhaust port exits have a "D" shape that first appeared on the Phase 5 casting. The exhaust manifold bolt holes are located on the port centerline in Phase 6 castings, and the tapped hole for a production water temperature sending unit is deleted. The boss for the sending unit is retained in the water jacket, however, and it can be drilled and tapped as necessary.

The diameter of the bolt columns in Chevrolet heavy-duty aluminum heads was increased to improve head gasket clamping. The head bolt bosses on Phase 6 heads are spotfaced for 3/4-inch diameter head bolt washers (PN 10051155). The Phase 6 aluminum head's deck surface and combustion chamber walls are a minimum of .400-inch thick to withstand high cylinder pressures.

Valve machining in the aluminum Bow Tie head closely follows production di-

mensions. The exhaust valves, however, are moved .050-inch away from the intake valves to accommodate 2.100/1.650-inch diameter valves. The exhaust rocker arm studs are also relocated to compensate for this revised valve location. Special pushrod guideplates (PN 14011051) *must* be installed on all aluminum Bow Tie cylinder heads to establish the correct valvetrain geometry. These guideplates can be identified by the stamped numbers "05."

The valve spring pads are raised .200-inch to accommodate extra-long valves. Both the intake and exhaust rocker arm studs in Phase 6 heads are moved .058-inch toward the intake flange to optimize the valvetrain geometry with .100-inch longer-than-stock valves.

The pushrod holes are deleted in Phase 6 Bow Tie heads to allow the intake ports to be widened without welding when aftermarket offset rocker arms are used. Valve guides installed in Bow Tie aluminum heads are shouldered to prevent movement; replacement guides are available as PN 14011048.

Raised Runner Aluminum Bow Tie Cylinder Head
PN 10051101

The introduction of heavy-duty "raised runner" Bow Tie aluminum cyl-

inder heads (PN 10051101) in 1986 marked a dramatic advance in small-block cylinder head technology. The raised runner casting was developed to provide a significant improvement in the reliability and performance of competition small-block V8s.

The 10051101 casting was the first heavy-duty small-block cylinder head with a higher intake runner location than conventional small-block V8 cylinder heads. This change in intake port position required a new intake manifold and revised valvetrain layout to complete the assembly. The combustion chamber was also revised to improve engine efficiency. Due to these extensive design changes, the raised runner Bow Tie cylinder head is not a "bolt-on" replacement for production-type small-block castings.

Raised runner cylinder heads have been replaced by the later "high-port" 18-degree cylinder heads in most maximum-effort racing engines. However, raised runner heads are still a good choice for racing classes that require a conventional 23-degree valve angle and stud-mounted rocker arms.

The most apparent change in the raised runner Bow Tie head is the location of the intake ports, which is .200-inch higher than the stock port position. This higher

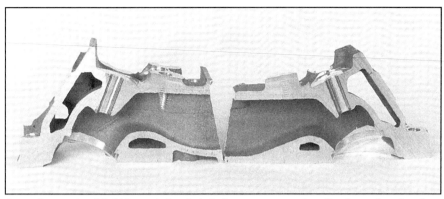

A raised runner head (left) has a thicker deck, higher port entry, and a taller short-side radius than a Phase 6 casting (right).

The rocker cover rail on a raised runner head (right) is .300-inch higher than a production head to improve gasket sealing.

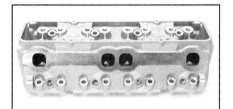

The exhaust manifold flange bolts are not drilled in raised runner heads to allow widening the ports without bolt hole interference.

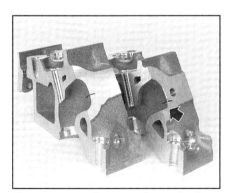

The casting parting line in raised runner heads was relocated near the center of the exhaust port (left) to allow a larger radius.

inlet entry improves the fuel/air mixture's approach to the valve bowl and promotes more efficient cylinder filling. This airflow improvement was achieved without increasing the cross-sectional area of the intake runners, so the velocity of the intake charge remains high.

The 54cc combustion chambers in raised runner cylinder heads promote efficient combustion and suppress detonation.

Pushrod holes are deleted in raised runner heads to allow the intake ports to be widened. Holes must be machined to provide clearance.

The shape of the intake runners is also revised in the "101" small-block cylinder head. The "long wall" of each inlet port (the side adjacent to the exhaust valve) is moved back .125-inch to open up the port and to direct the incoming air/fuel mixture into the valve bowl uniformly around the valve head. The minimum port wall thickness of the raised runner casting is .240-inch (.300 inch over the intake runner roof) to provide sufficient material for a cylinder head porter to substantially increase the port size if required. Intake pushrod clearance holes are not drilled to allow widening of the intake runners without welding.

The rocker cover rail is raised .300-inch to accommodate the raised runner cylinder head's higher intake port location. The intake flange gasket surface is stepped above the ports, similar to a big-block V8 cylinder head. These changes improve valve cover and intake manifold gasket sealing.

Chevrolet offers a single four-barrel aluminum Bow Tie intake manifold (PN 10051103) that is specifically designed for raised runner cylinder heads. This manifold's runners are .200-inch higher than conventional small-block manifolds to align properly with the raised cylinder head ports. This manifold is described in the intake manifold section.

The raised runner cylinder head's exhaust ports are also designed to enhance high-rpm performance. In previous heavy-duty cylinder heads, the parting line between the top and bottom halves of the head casting was near the bottom of the exhaust port exits, limiting the radius at the bottom corners of the ports to .200-inch. This parting line is relocated to the center of the ports on the raised runner head, and the corner radiuses are enlarged to .500-inch. This revision reduces the cross-sectional area of the port to increase flow velocity. It also allows an experienced head porting specialist to raise the port exits even higher without welding.

The heavy-duty "101" cylinder head has a revised combustion chamber design that improves combustion efficiency and suppresses detonation. The reduced combustion chamber volume permits high compression ratios with a relatively small piston dome. Material added between the valve seats and above the spark plug produces a noticeably peaked roof. Machining pads are located in the quench area beneath the plugs to eliminate dead spots in the chamber roof. This revised combustion chamber design requires pistons with compatible dome shapes. *Piston dome clearance must be checked before final assembly.*

The spark plug holes are machined for .708-inch reach tapered seat plugs with

Aftermarket rocker arms with offset pushrod seats provide additional pushrod clearance with widened intake ports.

⅝-inch hex heads (BN and S series or equivalent). These small diameter plugs improve wrench access with racing exhaust systems.

The minimum deck thickness of the raised runner head casting is .600-inch. This extra-thick deck enhances durability and permits extensive milling to reduce combustion chamber volumes. Raised runner cylinder heads are supplied without valve seats and guides to allow competition engine builders to install their preferred components. The increased height of the 101 head's valve bowls and the higher spring seat location require valves that are .100-inch longer than stock.

The raised runner head requires special pushrod guideplates (PN 14011051). This guideplate can be identified by the stamped numbers "05." The rocker arm stud holes are moved .040-inch toward the intake manifold flange to compensate for the increase in valve stem length. The rocker stud bosses are also substantially enlarged and strengthened to improve durability with high valve spring loads. Heavy-duty ⁷⁄₁₆-inch diameter big-block V8 rocker studs (PN 3921912) are recommended for racing use. These large diameter studs require aftermarket rocker arms.

18-Degree Bow Tie Cylinder Heads PN 10134352, 10134363, 10134364

The introduction of 18-degree Bow Tie cylinder heads was a dramatic advance in Chevrolet small-block engine technology. Compared to conventional small-block V8 designs, 18-degree Bow Tie heads have radically raised intake runners, revised valve angles, relocated valve centerlines, smaller combustion chambers, and more efficient exhaust ports. These cylinder heads are the best choice for a maximum-effort competition engine with in-line valves.

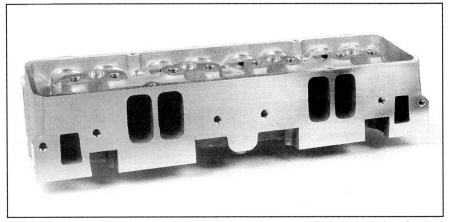

The intake runners in high-port aluminum Bow Tie heads are 1.220-inch above the deck surface; low-port versions are .650-inch above the deck.

A comparison between a high-port head (bottom) and a Phase 6 Bow Tie casting (top) spotlights the 18-degree head's radically revised port location.

The family of Chevrolet 18-degree aluminum Bow Tie cylinder heads was introduced in 1989. Castings have been continuously updated to keep pace with the demands of competition. Three different versions are currently available for small-block Chevrolet V8 engines:

10134352	Low-port aluminum Bow Tie cylinder head
10134363	High-port aluminum Bow Tie cylinder head (recommended for 4.060-inch and larger cylinder bores)
10134364	High-port aluminum Bow Tie cylinder head (recommended for under 4.060-inch cylinder bores)

The chief difference between high-port and low-port 18-degree heads is the location of the intake runners. The distance from the runner floors to the deck surface in low-port heads is .650-inch; the entrances in high-port versions are 1.220-inch above the deck. For comparison, the ports in a conventional Bow Tie aluminum head (PN 14011049) are .250-inch above the deck.

The high-port and low-port head designs were developed for different applications. Low-port castings are recommended for carbureted engines with lim-

An 18-degree small-block head (right) is taller than a Phase 6 casting (left). The 18-degree head has a 5-degree intake manifold flange angle; the Phase 6 head has a 10-degree angle.

ited hood clearance. They may also be legal in some restricted racing classes. High-port heads are recommended when hood clearance is not a consideration, and when the rules permit non-production cylinder head designs.

The two high-port heads are based on the same casting (#10134363). The major differences between them are the locations of the inlet valve guides and the machining for the valve seats. The valve centerlines in the "big bore" head (PN 10134363) are 1.955-inch apart; the valves are 1.935-inch apart in the "small-bore" version (PN 10134364). This change in valve spacing accommodates the larger valve diameters made possible by bigger cylinder bores.

18-Degree Valve Angle

The "18-degree" designation refers to the angle of the valves relative to the deck surface. All other production and heavy-duty heads for small-block Chevrolet V8s have a valve angle of 23 degrees. The shallower 18-degree valve angle of these Bow Tie heads is in keeping with the trend toward more upright valves in wedge-head racing engines.

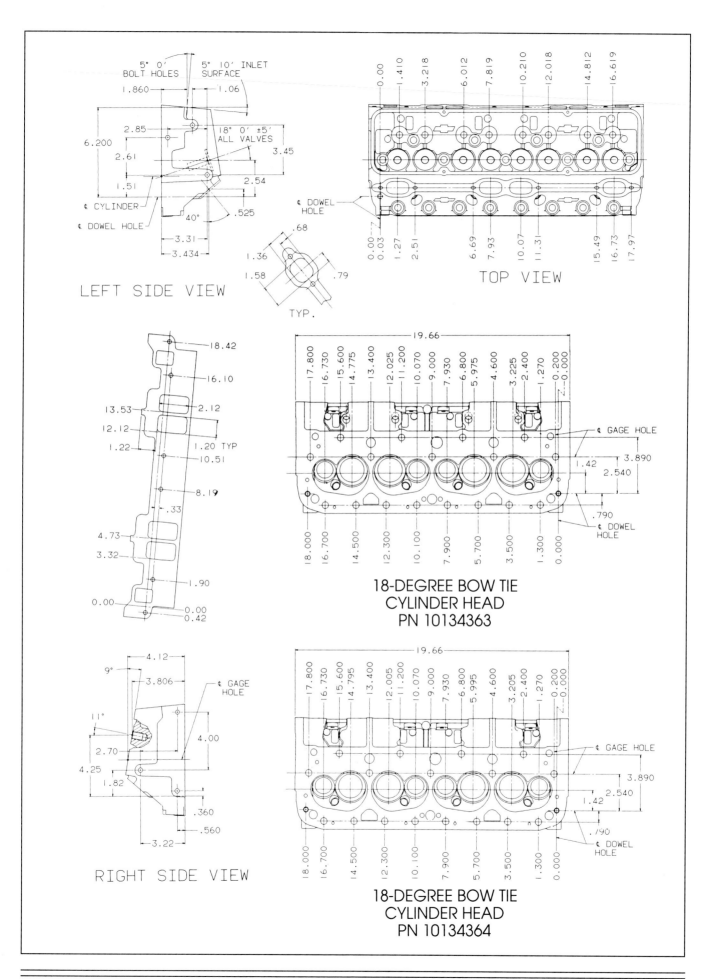

LEFT SIDE VIEW

TOP VIEW

18-DEGREE BOW TIE
CYLINDER HEAD
PN 10134363

RIGHT SIDE VIEW

18-DEGREE BOW TIE
CYLINDER HEAD
PN 10134364

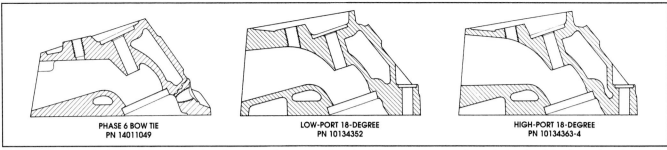

PHASE 6 BOW TIE
PN 14011049

LOW-PORT 18-DEGREE
PN 10134352

HIGH-PORT 18-DEGREE
PN 10134363-4

Chevrolet Bow Tie cylinder heads have several intake port configurations. Note the differences in runner shape, the height of the short-side radius, and the depth of the valve bowls in Phase 6, low-port 18-degree, and high-port 18-degree heads.

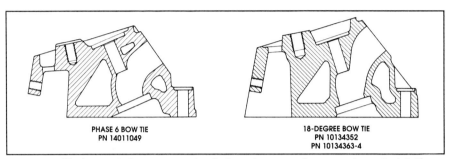

PHASE 6 BOW TIE
PN 14011049

18-DEGREE BOW TIE
PN 10134352
PN 10134363-4

Low-port and high-port 18-degree Bow Tie heads share the same exhaust port design (right). The port exit is .550-inch higher than a Phase 6 exhaust (left).

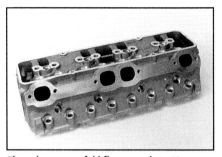

The exhaust manifold flange angle is 40 degrees on high-port and low-port heads.

The valves' location is as important as their angle, however. The intake and exhaust valves in 18-degree cylinder heads are positioned on the cylinder bore centerline. This seemingly minor change produces a substantial improvement in the total airflow potential.

The valves in conventional 23-degree Chevy heads are positioned .275-inch from the cylinder bore centerline. This location ultimately limits the engine's breathing ability because the valve heads are shrouded by the combustion chamber and cylinder walls as they approach maximum lift. Shifting the valves to the bore centerline reduces this shrouding.

The valves are also moved laterally in the 18-degree heads to enhance intake flow. The exhaust valves are shifted toward the cylinder wall to provide room for larger intakes. The intake valves are in turn moved toward the center of the cylinder bores to unshroud the valve heads at high lift.

The problems of valve shrouding and cylinder wall interference effectively limit conventional 23-degree heads to a maximum intake valve diameter of 2.100-inch. The new 18-degree heads, in contrast, can take advantage of the additional airflow offered by intake valves up to 2.200-inch in diameter (depending on bore size).

Relocating the valves to the bore centerline measurably improved the airflow

capability of the 18-degree head. The intake port shape is essentially a cast version of the runners in a well-prepared racing head. However, most of the gains in the 18-degree head's intake airflow are the result of installing larger valves, not from improvements in the design of the intake port.

High-Port Intake Runners

The 18-degree Bow Tie cylinder heads' raised intake runners are a striking departure from previous small-block castings. Changing the valve angle from 23 to 18 degrees without repositioning the ports would have forced the incoming fuel/air charge to make an abrupt turn on its way to the valve bowl; raising the ports restored the proper runner/valve relationship.

The high-port intake runner typically flows more air at high valve lifts than the low-port design. The difference between the two ports becomes significant at valve lifts above .600-inch. The high-port runner has a more direct "line of sight" path, which typically enhances high-lift flow. Both designs have excellent flow at low valve lifts due to their tall short-side radiuses and deep valve bowls.

The angle of the intake manifold flange was also revised to accommodate the relocated intake runners. Conventional small-block heads are machined at a 10-degree angle on the manifold face; 18-degree heads are machined at a 5-degree angle.

Three single four-barrel Bow Tie intake manifolds are available for high-port 18-degree heads. Chevrolet does not offer an intake manifold specifically for low-port versions. However, a standard Bow Tie intake (PN 10051103) can be modified to fit 18-degree low-port heads by machining the intake flange. Refer to the small-block intake manifold section for details on this modification.

The angle of the rocker cover rails was also changed from 17 degrees to 9 degrees. The gasket sealing surfaces are fully machined to prevent rocker cover oil leaks. The rocker cover flange has a standard small-block bolt pattern.

Exhaust Port

The 18-degree head's reshaped and redesigned exhaust port yields an improvement in flow over conventional heads. The exhaust ports are raised .550-inch and widened .240-inch at the manifold flange. The port's high short-side radius provides a smooth, gradual transition from the valve bowl to the header pipe, minimizing turbulence in the runner.

The angle of the exhaust manifold flange was changed from 35 degrees to 40 degrees on 18-degree Bow Tie heads. This revision smoothes the flow of burned gases at the junction between the ports and the primary header pipes.

Combustion Chamber

Chevrolet 18-degree cylinder heads feature small, efficient combustion

An 18-degree valve angle produces a shallow combustion chamber and allows the use of large diameter valves to increase airflow.

18-degree Bow Tie cylinder heads have efficient combustion chambers. Spark plug position, chamber depth, and valve location differ in Phase 6 (left) and 18-degree (right) heads.

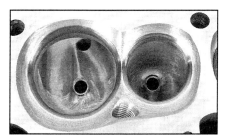

Magnesium bronze valve guides are recommended for 18-degree heads. Shape the guide bosses to smooth the flow of air.

Piston domes and valve reliefs must match the 18-degree cylinder head's chamber shape and valve positions (right).

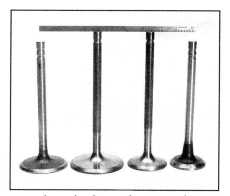

An 18-degree head's raised runners and increased overall height require 5.450-inch long valves (5.350-inch for low-port heads).

chambers. Changing the valve angle from 23 to 18 degrees was an essential step in creating a shallow combustion chamber. Reducing the valve angle in a wedge-type cylinder head forces the incoming air/fuel mixture to make a sharper turn from the port entrance to the valve seat. GM Motorsports Technology Group engineers evaluated head designs with valve angles ranging from 23 degrees to 10 degrees. An 18-degree valve angle proved to be a good compromise between chamber design and intake port performance.

The change to an 18-degree valve angle allowed GM engineers to reduce the small-block's combustion chamber volume significantly. A typical combustion chamber in an 18-degree head holds 45cc's, in contrast to the 64cc chambers used in conventional Bow Tie castings. The 18-degree heads' shallow combustion chambers and on-center valves allow engine builders to achieve high compression ratios with small piston domes.

The 18-degree Bow Tie cylinder heads' optimized valve locations allow the use of larger valves than conventional 23-degree small-block heads. Of course,

the valve diameters and overall lengths that will produce the best performance depend on each engine's specifications and usage. Recommended valve sizes for engines with 4.060-inch and smaller cylinder bores are 2.125-inch intake valves and 1.620-inch exhaust valves. Engines with 4.125-inch cylinders can benefit from the increased flow of 2.150-inch intake valves. Larger intake valves can be installed (up to 2.20-inch diameter, depending on bore size).

The raised runner roofs in all 18-degree Bow Tie heads (both low-port and high-port) require valves with extra-long stems. An overall valve length of 5.450-inch (.500-inch longer-than-stock) is suitable for most high-port applications; 5.350-inch long valves are recommended for low-port heads. This stem length will produce a 2.00-inch valve spring installed height with most racing valvetrain components. Minor adjustments in valve spring installed height can be achieved with different stem lengths, retainers, and spring shims.

Chevrolet 18-degree cylinder heads are sold without valve guides. Magnesium

bronze guides (2.125-inch long x .500-inch diameter) are suitable for most racing applications. These guides are compatible with titanium and stainless steel valves. When porting 18-degree heads, do not remove the bosses around the valve guides; shape the bosses to smooth the flow of air around the guides.

The 18-degree heads' .600-inch thick deck surface and generous combustion chamber walls provide plenty of material for enlarging or reducing the final chamber volume. If it is necessary to mill the cylinder head deck surface to reduce the combustion chamber volume, the head should be machined flat, not angle-milled. Angle milling an 18-degree head can impair airflow by moving the valves away from the cylinder bore centerline, thereby increasing valve shrouding. It is not necessary to notch or grind "eyebrows" in the tops of the cylinder bores as is a common practice with 23-degree Chevrolet heads.

Valve reliefs in racing pistons must be machined to match the 18-degree cylinder head's revised valve locations. Custom pistons for 18-degree cylinder heads

Raised exhaust ports in the 18-degree Bow Tie small-block head (right) provide a 15 percent improvement in airflow over previous designs.

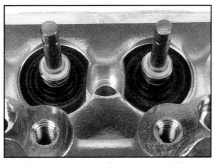

Modify the spring seats for the two middle exhaust valve springs to clear the center head bolt or stud.

Use a 12-point bolt or stud nut between the middle exhaust ports. Install the adjacent valve springs after torquing the head fasteners.

The two bolt holes between the intake runners are drilled for ⅜-inch studs in a high-port head. Special "step-down" studs must be used in these holes.

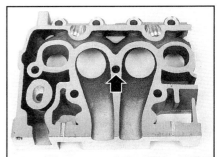

This cutaway of an early 18-degree Bow Tie casting reveals the small cross-sectional area around the head bolt column between the intake ports with a clearance hole for a ⁷⁄₁₆-inch head bolt. The change to a ¹³⁄₃₂-inch diameter hole for a ⅜-inch head bolt and the elimination of the bolt sleeve increases this cross-sectional area by 40 percent.

are available from several aftermarket manufacturers.

Spark Plugs

The 18-degree head's revised spark plug location also contributes to the efficiency of the new combustion chamber design. Compared to conventional heads, the plugs are moved .350-inch closer to the center of the cylinder bore and shifted toward the top of the combustion chambers. Engines equipped with 18-degree cylinder heads typically require less spark advance (32 to 34 degrees BTDC) because the centrally located spark plugs enhance flame travel across the cylinders.

The revised plug location also improves spark plug access, and protects the spark plug boots and wires from heat damage caused by header pipes. The spark plug holes in 18-degree cylinder heads are machined for .708-inch reach tapered seat spark plugs with ⅝-inch hex heads (Champion S series, formerly BL series, or equivalent) and ¾-inch reach gasketed seat, ⅝-inch hex head plugs (C series). Spark plug heat range will depend on the particular engine characteristics; a

57 heat range is a good starting point for most naturally aspirated small-block racing engines.

Valvetrain

The factory-machined valve spring seats in 18-degree cylinder heads are 1.640-inch diameter. Hardened spring seat cups or spring locators should be installed under the valve springs to protect the aluminum head. The spring seats for the two center exhaust valves must be modified to clear the center head bolt (or stud). Before final assembly, check for adequate clearance between the head stud and nut (or head bolt) and the valve spring and spring seat.

When using large-diameter valve springs on 18-degree heads, install the cylinder heads on the engine without the two center exhaust valve springs. This will provide wrench clearance for the center head bolts. Then install the remaining valve springs after the head bolts are torqued.

All 18-degree small-block heads require aftermarket shaft-mounted rocker arms. Pushrod clearance holes were

drilled in all early production 18-degree Bow Tie cylinder heads. Intake pushrod holes were eliminated in later versions of head PN 10134364 to allow cylinder head specialists to drill holes to suit their particular applications.

Head Studs and Bolts

The heights of the head bolt columns in 18-degree cylinder heads differ from conventional Chevrolet heads. As a result, production head bolts and most "off-the-shelf" head stud kits cannot be used with 18-degree Bow Tie heads. Special stud kits for 18-degree heads are available from aftermarket suppliers. See the head bolt column length chart on page 68 for specific dimensions.

Twelve-point nuts and small-diameter washers must be used with 18-degree Bow Tie heads to fit the .875-inch diameter head bolt counterbores. (Some early production 18-degree heads had .780-inch counterbores.) Chevrolet 12-point nuts (PN 14044866) and hardened washers (PN 10051155, .750-inch OD x .456-inch ID) are recommended. The large diameter washers and 6-point nuts

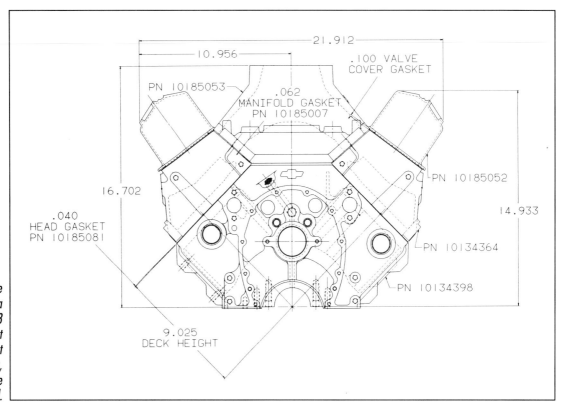

This diagram shows the overall dimensions of a small-block Chevrolet V8 equipped with high-port 18-degree heads, cast aluminum rocker covers, and a Bow Tie intake manifold.

supplied with many stud kits will not clear the head bolt counterbores in 18-degree cylinder heads.

Special head studs must be used in the two bolt holes between the intake ports on high-port heads. The diameter of these holes is $^{15}/_{32}$-inch; the other bolt holes are $^{13}/_{32}$-inch diameter. Special "step-down" head studs with $^{7}/_{16}$-14 threads on the block end, $^{3}/_{8}$-inch shanks, and $^{3}/_{8}$-24 nut threads should be used in these holes. When torqued to 70 ft.-lbs., these high-strength $^{3}/_{8}$-inch studs produce the same clamping load on the deck surface as conventional $^{7}/_{16}$-inch studs.

It is a common porting procedure to insert steel sleeves in the head bolt holes between the intake ports, and then grind back the port walls until the sleeves are exposed. However, this modification can weaken the head bolt column and create a stress riser where the sleeve breaks out into the port. GM Motorsports Technology Group engineers recommend that sleeves *not* be installed and material *not* be removed from the common wall between the siamesed intake runners when porting Bow Tie heads.

Elimination of the head bolt sleeve and the change to a $^{13}/_{32}$-inch head bolt clearance hole increases the cross-sectional area of the material between port and head bolt hole by approximately 40 percent. If the port and valve bowl are widened, material should be removed from the "long wall" next to the exhaust valve.

BOW TIE TECH — Trans-Am Champion

At the conclusion of the 1993 racing season, Chevrolet had won the SCCA Trans-Am manufacturer's championship 13 times in the popular road racing series' 28-year history—including a streak of four straight titles from 1990 to 1993. Teammates Scott Sharp and Jack Baldwin drove Buz McCall's American Equipment Racing Z28 Camaros to the Trans-Am driver's championship in 1991, 1992, and 1993. Their title-winning Z28 Camaros were powered by 310ci Chevrolet V8s

Camaro driver Scott Sharp won SCCA Trans-Am championships in 1991 and 1993.

Katech's championship-winning Trans-Am small-blocks produced over 600 horsepower from 310 cubic inches.

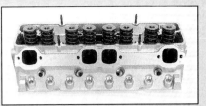

Katech machinists ported the Bow Tie cylinder head's exhaust runners with distinctive square exits.

The piston domes mirrored the shape of the combustion chambers. A relatively small dome produced a 13.5:1 compression ratio with the Bow Tie heads' small 42cc combustion chambers.

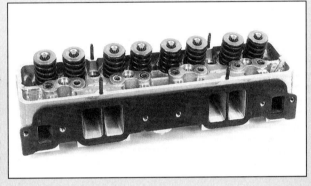

Low-port Chevrolet 18-degree Bow Tie aluminum cylinder heads (PN 10134352) were the centerpiece of the Trans-Am engine development program.

The 3.00-inch stroke crankshaft's rod throws were drilled to reduce the assembly's rotating weight. Lead-in grooves in the main bearing journals channeled oil to the rod bearing oil feed holes.

equipped with a full complement of Bow Tie components.

Katech, Inc. in Mt. Clemens, Michigan, assembled the 610hp small-block V8s that powered the AER Camaros. Katech's machinists bored the cylinders in the Camaros' cast iron Chevrolet Bow Tie blocks (PN 10051183) to 4.055-inch diameter. The steel crankshafts had 3.00-inch strokes.

"Our engine building philosophy has been the same since we built our first road racing motor," said Katech General Manager Warren Frieze. "A driver needs torque to pull the car out of the corners, and enough power to run the straightaways. We don't aim for outrageous engine speed; 8,000 rpm is the top. Limiting the rpm improves engine reliability, and that's what usually wins races."

The Trans-Am engines were testbeds for Chevrolet's low-port 18-degree Bow Tie aluminum cylinder heads (PN 10134352) in 1991. The bare Bow Tie castings were fully ported before being outfitted with titanium valves and stainless steel rocker arms. The shallow 42cc combustion chambers produced a 13.5:1 compression ratio with custom-made pistons. Aftermarket steel connecting rods completed the internal engine assembly. With a 6.30-inch center-to-center distance, these rods were significantly longer than production small-block rods' 5.70-inch center-to-center length. The rod length/stroke ratio was 2.1:1.

The induction system was straightforward, in keeping with the requirements of the SCCA rulebook. A 750cfm Holley four-barrel carburetor was installed on a Chevrolet Bow Tie aluminum intake manifold (PN 10051103). Katech technicians machined the intake manifold to match the cylinder head's 5-degree flange angle. A GM electronic distributor (PN 14044871) sparked the championship-winning Chevrolets.

A 750cfm four-barrel carburetor was installed on a Chevrolet Bow Tie single-plane intake manifold (PN 10051103). The manifold was machined to match the cylinder heads' 5-degree flange angle.

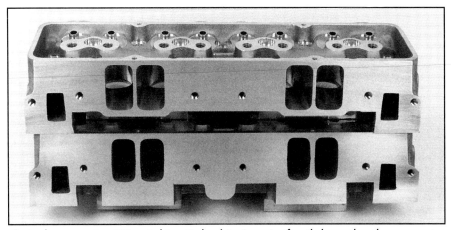

The intake runners in a CNC-ported Bow Tie head (top) are significantly larger than the passages in an unported casting. The modified ports meet NASCAR specifications for height and location.

Race-Prepared 18-Degree Cylinder Heads
PN 24502482

Chevrolet CNC-ported cylinder heads simplify engine building by eliminating the tedious work of modifying heads by hand for competition. These fully ported high-port Bow Tie cylinder heads are virtually ready to assemble.

The CNC-ported heads are based on Chevrolet 18-degree high-port castings (PN 10134364). Race-ready cylinder heads are designed for professional racing venues such as NASCAR's Winston Cup series. They are also suitable for various drag racing and road racing classes.

BOW TIE TIPS Keeping Cool

The small-block Chevrolet's port layout positions two exhaust valves side by side in the center of the cylinder head. The heat produced by the flow of exhaust gases through these adjacent ports is a potential source of trouble in endurance racing engines. Localized "hot spots" can cause premature head gasket failure.

GM Motorsports Technology Group engineers instrumented two 18-degree high-port Bow Tie cylinder heads installed on a racing engine to provide accurate information on cylinder head operating temperatures. Thermocouples were installed next to the exhaust valves, and the temperatures of the cylinder head material measured during a series of dyno tests.

These baseline tests revealed that the cylinder head temperature between the two center exhaust valves was approximately 250 degrees higher than the temperatures near the exhaust valves on the ends of the cylinder head. The evidence of this high temperature can often be seen in the discoloration that occurs in the head gasket between the two center cylinders in a competition small-block V8.

The cylinder head temperature between the two center exhaust valves can be reduced approximately 125 degrees by drilling a .090-inch diameter coolant passage between the valves. There are

Connect the water inlet lines directly to fittings at the water pump outlets. GM MTG engineers recommend a -4 coolant line.

two ways to circulate coolant through this passage. Both methods have proven effective.

In the method shown in Figure 1, an external line carries coolant from the water pump directly to the cooling passage. A sleeve made from brass tubing is inserted through the cylinder head's water jacket to route coolant into the two intersecting water passages drilled between the center exhaust valves. After circulating through the drilled passages, the coolant returns to the cylinder head's water jacket.

The system shown in Figure 2 requires no external plumbing. The large core hole in the cylinder head's deck surface between the two middle combustion chambers is plugged with an aluminum pipe plug. Two intersecting coolant passages are drilled from the outside of the cylinder head, and then plugged as shown. The plug in the deck surface is also drilled to route water from the block through the intersecting passages. The pressure of the water pump forces coolant from the block through this passage.

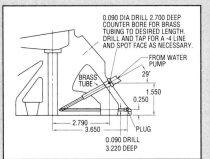

Figure 1: To improve cooling between the two center exhaust valves in an 18-degree high-port Bow Tie cylinder head, drill two intersecting .090-inch cooling holes as shown. Counter-bore the angled upper hole for a brass tubing sleeve. Drill and tap the outer water jacket wall of the cylinder head for a -4 male fitting and spot face as necessary. Braze a small brass tube to the end of the -4 fitting and insert the tube into the counterbored hole.

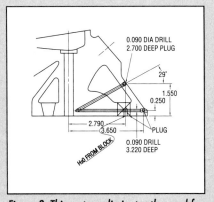

Figure 2: This system eliminates the need for external coolant lines. Water enters the intersecting .090-inch diameter cooling holes from the block. Plug and drill the core hole in the cylinder head deck surface.

Sophisticated multi-axis CNC (Computer Numerical Control) equipment is used to machine the complex three-dimensional runner and combustion chamber shapes. GM Motorsports Technology Group engineers worked with leading airflow experts to develop port and combustion chamber designs that would produce competitive power levels.

The ports are configured for engines in the range of 350 cubic inches, and the runners' cross-sectional areas have been optimized for 2.150/1.620-inch diameter valves. The ports meet NASCAR specifications for size and location. Tests have shown that polishing the runners does not significantly improve airflow.

The CNC-ported cylinder heads' combustion chambers are machined to fit 4.100-inch and larger cylinder bores. Compared to the as-cast combustion chamber shape, the CNC heads' chambers are relieved on the intake valve side to enhance airflow. The deck surface is then milled .050-inch to produce a 50cc chamber volume.

Interlocking ductile iron intake valve seats (2.250-inch OD x .312-inch) and beryllium-copper exhaust seats (1.680-inch OD x .312-inch) are installed in Chevrolet CNC-ported heads. These valve seat materials are compatible with stainless steel and titanium valves. The seats are machined for 2.150-inch diameter intake valves and 1.620-inch diameter exhausts.

Profiled seat cutters are available from Serdi to service CNC cylinder heads. Use cutter #H1N1 to machine the intake seats. The exhaust seat requires two cutters: Use #H1X1 for the seat and top angles, and H1X2 for the radius under the seat.

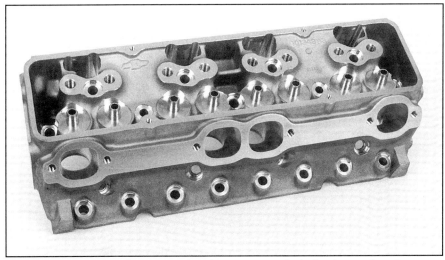

The exhaust ports in Chevrolet CNC-ported 18-degree Bow Tie cylinder heads are enlarged to complement the increased intake airflow.

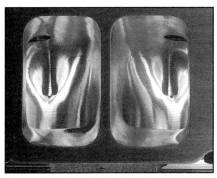

The ports and combustion chambers in Chevrolet CNC-ported aluminum Bow Tie small-block competition cylinder heads (PN 24502482) are ported with precision computer-controlled equipment. The runner shapes and valve sizes are optimized for 358-cubic-inch NASCAR racing engines.

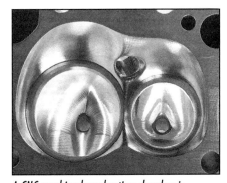

A CNC-machined combustion chamber is opened up to fit a 4.100-inch or larger cylinder bore. The chamber wall is laid back on the intake side of the chamber to enhance flow. The interlocking valve seats are finish-ground, and the deck is milled to produce a 50cc chamber volume.

CNC-Ported Bow Tie Head

BOW TIE SPECS

Part Number	24502482
Material:	Aluminum alloy
Combustion Chamber Volume:	50cc
Valve Spacing:	1.935-inch between valve centerlines
Intake Valve Seats:	Ductile iron, 2.250-inch OD x .312-inch deep
Exhaust Valve Seats:	Beryllium-copper, 1.680-inch OD x .312-inch deep
Recommended Valve Specifications:	
Diameter:	2.150-inch intake/1.620-inch exhaust
Back Angle:	12-degree intake/25-degree exhaust
Overall Length:	5.450-inch
Valve Guides:	Bronze, 11/32-inch ID
Valve Springs:	1.550-inch diameter with cups
Spark Plugs:	.709-inch reach tapered seat, 5/8-inch hex ("S" series) or 3/4-inch reach gasketed seat, 5/8 hex head ("C" series)
Rocker Arms:	Aftermarket shaft-mounted, .550-inch offset intake rockers with flat tappet lifters or .450-inch offset with .150-inch offset roller lifters.
Recommended Components:	
PN 10185053	Bow Tie intake manifold
PN 10185064	Bow Tie rocker cover
PN 10185054	Head Gasket
PN 10185007	Intake manifold gasket set

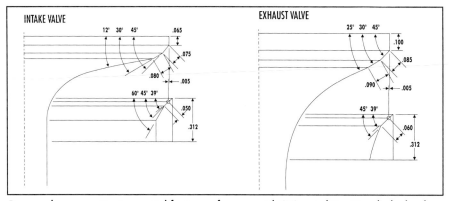

Proper valve preparation is essential for top performance with CNC-ported Bow Tie cylinder heads. These diagrams show the GM Motorsports Technology Group's recommendations for intake and exhaust valves.

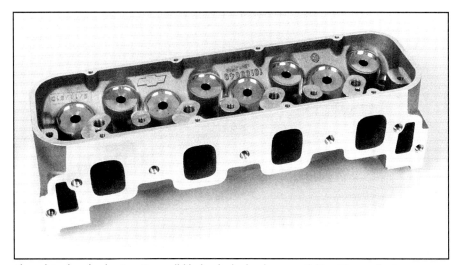

Chevrolet splayed-valve Bow Tie small-block cylinder heads are available with ports for large displacement engines as PN 10185040. A splayed-valve casting with downsized runners for 300-350ci engines is offered as PN 24502517.

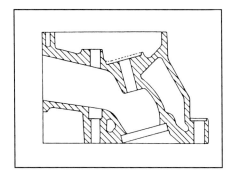

The splayed-valve head's symmetrical intake ports have counterbored head bolt holes in the floors of the runners.

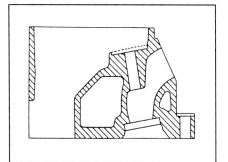

The raised exhaust port's long, gradual turn minimizes turbulence in the runner and speeds the flow of burned gases.

Bronze valve guides (¹¹⁄₃₂-inch ID) are installed in ported Bow Tie heads. The guides are already honed to provide adequate stem-to-guide clearance for most competition valves.

The recommended overall valve length is 5.450-inch (.500-inch longer than stock). This valve length typically yields a 1.950-inch valve spring installed height, depending on the spring retainer used. The recommended back angles for the intake and exhaust valves are 12 and 25-degrees respectively. The valve spring pads are machined for 1.550-inch diameter springs with spring cups.

Like all 18-degree small-block heads, ported versions require aftermarket shaft-mounted rocker arms. Pushrod clearance holes are machined for .450-inch offset intake rockers (when using a .150-inch offset roller lifter) or .550-inch offset when using a flat tappet lifter.

GM MTG engineers recommend that ported heads be modified for endurance racing applications by drilling coolant passages between the center exhaust valves (see sidebar on page 62).

Splayed-Valve Bow Tie Heads PN 10185040 and 24502517

Chevrolet's splayed-valve small-block V8 cylinder heads were inspired by the symmetrical port Bow Tie big-block cylinder heads developed for Pro Stock competition. Splayed-valve small-block V8 heads offer potential improvements in airflow, combustion efficiency, and engine performance over conventional small-block heads with in-line valves.

Splayed-valve cylinder heads are recommended for unlimited racing classes that allow non-production cylinder heads. Their advanced intake port design yields a five percent improvement in flow over an 18-degree high-port Bow Tie cylinder head with in-line valves, and the exhaust flow is equivalent. The .240-inch thick port walls provide ample material for cylinder head porters seeking further gains in airflow.

Valve Angles

Like a big-block Chevrolet V8 cylinder head, the valves in a splayed-valve small-block head are inclined in *two* axes relative to the cylinder bore centerline. The intake valves are angled 16 degrees to the deck surface, and tilted inward ("splayed") four degrees. The exhaust valve angle is 11 degrees, with a four-degree inward tilt.

These compound valve angles offer several advantages over in-line valves. The valve heads move away from the cylinder walls as the valves open, unshrouding the valves at maximum lift. The splayed-valve arrangement also minimizes the compromises between port design and combustion chamber shape. Consequently the splayed-valve head's shallow, heart-shaped combustion chambers enhance combustion efficiency.

Intake Ports

Splayed-valve small-block heads have symmetrical intake and exhaust ports; unlike a conventional small-block head, there are no "right-hand" and "left-hand" ports. In an in-line valve head, each pair of siamesed intake ports is sandwiched

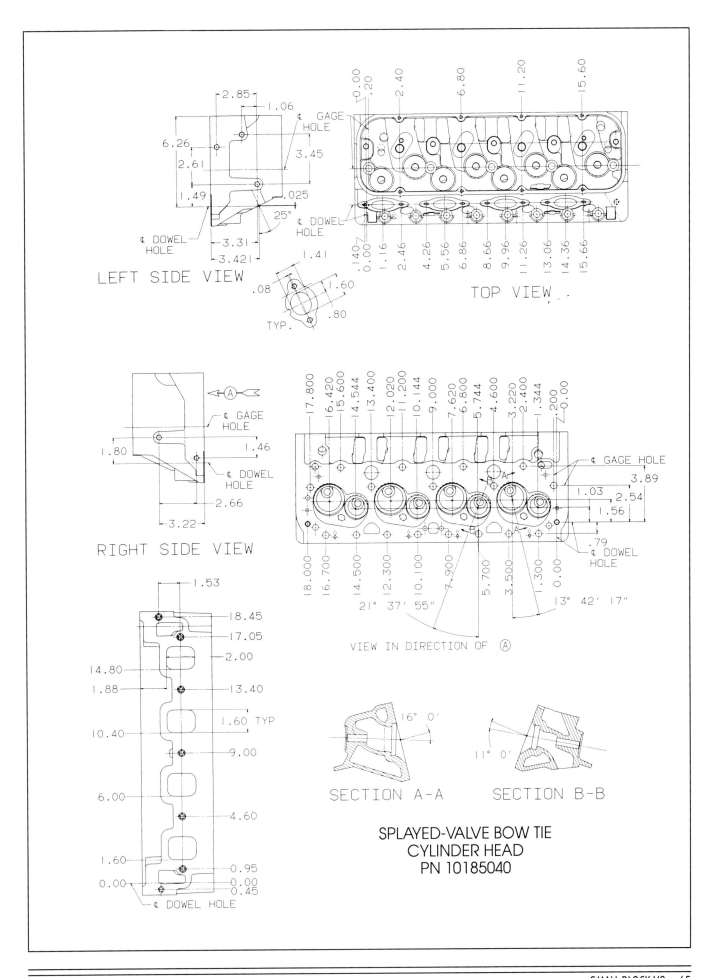

LEFT SIDE VIEW

TOP VIEW

RIGHT SIDE VIEW

VIEW IN DIRECTION OF (A)

SECTION A-A   SECTION B-B

SPLAYED-VALVE BOW TIE
CYLINDER HEAD
PN 10185040

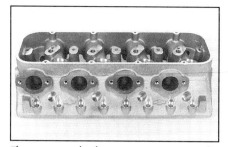

The symmetrical exhaust ports require special header flanges. Centrally located spark plugs reduce spark advance requirements and improve plug access.

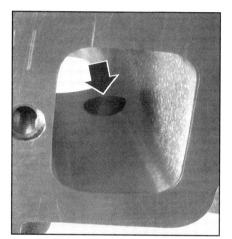

Holes in the intake runner roofs provide access to socket head capscrews in the runner floors. These capscrews replace the top four head bolts on each cylinder bank.

The 45cc heart-shaped combustion chambers have centrally located spark plugs. Splayed-valve cylinder heads are supplied without valve seats and valve guides.

Dowel holes accurately locate the rocker mounting bar on its bosses. The mounting bar fasteners seal the head bolt access holes in the tops of the intake ports.

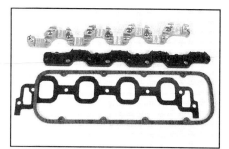

Accessory components for splayed-valve V8 heads include rocker mounting bars (PN 10185041), intake manifold gaskets (PN 10185042), and rocker cover gaskets (PN 10185043).

Splayed-valve cylinder heads require aftermarket shaft-mounted rocker arms. This system eliminates pushrod guideplates.

between two pushrods. The splayed-valve head's symmetrical port layout eliminates this shortcoming, and allows the intake ports to have a more constant cross-sectional area.

Splayed-valve Bow Tie cylinder head PN 10185040 is specifically designed for large-displacement engines. These high-flow heads make it practical to build competitive 400ci (and larger) small-block Chevy V8s with 4.125-inch to 4.155-inch cylinder bores. A splayed-valve head with downsized intake runners is available as PN 24502517 for 300 to 350ci engines with 4.00-inch to 4.060-inch cylinder bores.

The intake valve centerlines differ in the two versions, with intakes in small-bore heads shifted .050-inch closer to the exhaust valves. The diameter of the intake valve seat pockets is 2.250-inch in both heads; however, the recommended valve diameter is 2.200-inch in the large-port heads and 2.150-inch for the smaller version. The recommended exhaust valve diameter for both heads

is 1.625-inch. Recommended valve length is 5.70-inch.

The splayed-valve small-block's symmetrical intake ports pass directly over the top row of cylinder head bolts. Threaded holes in the roofs of the intake runners provide access to socket-head cap screws that replace the top four head bolts on each cylinder bank. After tightening these short head bolts, a rocker arm mounting bar is bolted to the threaded access holes to seal the intake runners. Dowel pins precisely locate this rocker mounting bar on its bosses. The holes for the socket head capscrews and rocker mounting bar bolts have a negligible effect on intake airflow.

Combustion Chamber
The splayed-valve head's nominal combustion chamber volume is 45cc, although the actual volume will depend on the valves and valve seats installed by the engine builder. The centrally located spark plug holes are machined for .709-inch reach plugs with tapered seats (Champion S series or equivalent). Holes

drilled in the splayed valve V8 head's deck surface circulate coolant around the spark plug bosses.

Splayed-valve small-block cylinder heads require aftermarket shaft-mounted rocker arms. Chevrolet offers a rocker arm mounting bar for splayed-valve heads as PN 10185041. This mounting bar can be used on both big-bore and small-bore heads; however, the intake rockers on small-port heads should be shimmed .050 toward the exhaust rockers to center the rocker tips on the intake valve stems.

Chevrolet also offers several related components to complete a splayed-valve cylinder head conversion: intake manifold gasket set (PN 10185042); steel-reinforced cork rocker cover gasket set (PN 10185043); and cast aluminum rocker covers (PN 10185045).

Splayed-valve heads require specific valvetrain hardware, including aftermarket shaft-mounted rocker arms and custom-made pushrods. The conversion to splayed-valve heads also requires special pistons, a fabricated intake manifold, modified headers, rocker covers, and a camshaft with lobes ground to match the revised port layout.

Head Gaskets

Chevrolet offers shim and composition-type head gaskets in a variety of thicknesses for the small-block V8. Steel shim gaskets are recommended only for cast iron cylinder heads, while composition gaskets can be used with both iron and aluminum heads.

When selecting head gaskets for a small-block V8, it is important to use gaskets that will produce the desired piston-to-head clearance with the engine's piston deck height. The *minimum* acceptable piston-to-head clearance (gasket thickness plus deck clearance) in an engine equipped with steel connecting rods is .035-inch. This figure must be increased when high engine speeds are anticipated, when piston-to-cylinder wall clearance is increased, or when aluminum connecting rods are used.

The head gasket should not overhang the cylinder bores, a condition that can cause preignition. This is especially important on small-block V8s with 4.125-inch diameter and larger cylinders. Also, steam holes must be drilled in some heavy-duty head gaskets when they are installed on production 400ci blocks, as described in the block section.

BOW TIE TIPS: Head Gasket Help

Head gaskets must endure extreme heat, pressure, and temperature in a competition small-block. GM Motorsports Technology Group engineers have conducted extensive durability tests to evaluate head gaskets for Chevrolet 18-degree cylinder heads. As a result of these tests, plus feedback from racing teams, the GM MTG recommends PN 10185054 (4.166-inch bore, also available as Fel-Pro #1003) or Fel-Pro #1034 (4.200-inch bore) head gaskets for use with 18-degree Chevrolet Bow Tie cylinder heads.

Both recommended head gaskets have steel wire fire rings; in the latest versions, the wire is pre-flattened to reduce marking (brinnelling) of the cylinder head deck surface. Both gaskets also have a revised coolant hole pattern to reduce coolant temperature between the center cylinders.

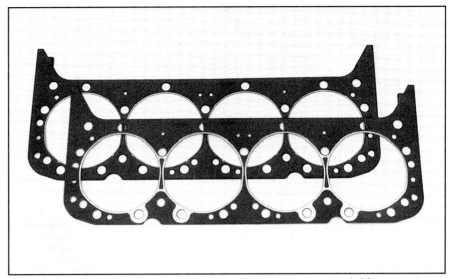

Heavy-duty composition cylinder head gaskets (PN 10185054) are recommended for competition small-block V8s. These Teflon-coated gaskets have integral "O"-rings.

Head gasket choices for Chevrolet small-block V8s include the following:

Part Number	Description
3830711	Production steel shim head gasket with raised beads around cylinder bores and water passages. Recommended for stock and mildly modified engines with 4.00-inch cylinder bores. Compressed thickness is .026-inch.
10105117	Composition head gasket with stainless steel faces. Recommended for stock, mildly modified, and all marine engines with 4.00-inch cylinder bores. Compressed thickness is .028-inch.
14088948	Composition gasket recommended for Corvette and H.O. aluminum cylinder heads; can also be used with iron heads. Compressed thickness is .051-inch.
10185054	This heavy-duty blue Teflon-coated composition gasket has solid wire "O"-rings around each cylinder bore. This gasket is highly recommended for competition engines. Fits bore sizes from 4.00 to 4.125-inch. Gasket has no steam holes, but holes may be drilled to match production 400ci blocks. Compressed thickness is approximately .040-inch.

Steel shim head gaskets should be installed with a commercial head gasket sealer. High-compression engines may benefit from using aluminum paint as a sealer, which improves heat transfer and simplifies clean-up during engine disassembly. Composition head gaskets should be installed without sealer.

Steel shim gaskets do not require retorquing. Most composition gaskets (except PN 10185054) should be retorqued (either hot or cold) after the engine is first warmed up. Follow the bolt torquing sequence shown in the diagram on page 68 when installing or retorquing small-block V8 head gaskets.

Head Bolts and Studs

Chevrolet small-block V8s use 17 fasteners per bank to attach the cylinder head to the block. Many competition engine builders prefer head studs over bolts. Studs reduce wear and tear on the block threads during frequent rebuilds, and produce more consistent torque readings. However, studs can make it more difficult to remove and replace cylinder heads, and to gap piston rings in the cylinder bores.

The height of the head bolt columns is different in various Bow Tie cylinder heads. Production head bolts and many "universal" head stud kits cannot be used with 18-degree and splayed-valve cylinder heads. Refer to the head bolt column chart on page 68 when ordering studs for your application.

The latest 18-degree high-port Bow Tie heads use special $\frac{3}{8}$-inch diameter head studs between the intake ports, as described on page 60 in the cylinder head section. You must use four $\frac{7}{16}$ x $\frac{3}{8}$-inch "stepped" head studs when installing late-model 18-degree Bow Tie heads.

A cylinder head stud kit for small-block engines is available from Chevrolet as PN

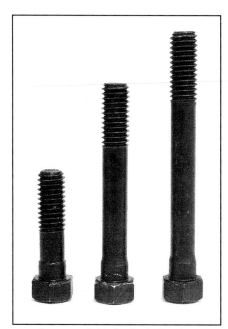

A production small-block cylinder head requires eight short head bolts, two medium bolts, and seven long bolts.

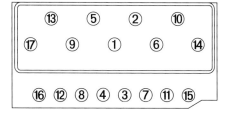

Follow this sequence when torquing head bolts or studs on a small-block V8. Most composition head gaskets should be retorqued.

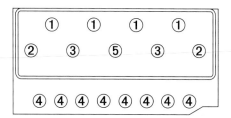

The height of the head bolt columns is different in various cylinder heads. Use the chart below to find the column height for specific heads.

Head studs prevent damage to the cylinder block threads during rebuilds.

TECH SPECS: SMALL-BLOCK V8 CYLINDER HEAD BOLT BOSS HEIGHTS

P/N	1	2	3	4	5
3987376	3.06	2.32	2.96	1.01	2.96
10185086	3.03	2.29	2.93	0.98	2.93
10134392	3.06	2.32	3.02	1.01	3.02
14011049	3.06	2.32	3.00	1.12	3.00
10134352	3.60	2.60	3.36	1.12	3.10
10134363	3.60	2.60	3.36	1.12	3.10
10185040	0.91	2.96	2.96	1.12	2.96

12-point nuts (right) provide more wrench clearance than conventional 6-point nuts.

A heavy-duty 2.05-inch stainless intake valve (right) has a flat face.

14014408. This kit can be used with conventional cast iron and aluminum cylinder heads only (Phase 6 and raised runner Bow Tie). It contains a total of 34 studs, with sixteen $7/_{16}$-14 x 2.69-inch studs (available individually as PN 14011035), fourteen $7/_{16}$-14 x 4.73-inch studs (PN 14011036), and four $7/_{16}$-14 x 3.99-inch studs (PN 14011037). Nuts and washers must be ordered separately; use 34 hardened steel washers (PN 14011040, .45-inch ID x .778-inch OD) and 34 hex nuts (PN 3942410).

If you are using studs with Phase 6 or 18-degree aluminum Bow Tie cylinder heads, you must use .45-inch ID x .750-inch OD hardened washers (PN 10051155) and special 12-point nuts (PN 14044866) to fit the head bolt counterbores. These 12-point nuts, which are manufactured from 4037 steel and 100% Magnaflux inspected, are recommended for all applications with limited wrench clearance.

Cylinder head bolts and studs should be tightened in the sequence shown in the accompanying diagram. Bolt threads that penetrate the block's water jacket should be coated with sealant during assembly. (Most Bow Tie blocks have blind-tapped head bolt holes that do not break into the water jacket. Head bolts should be lubricated with oil in these instances.)

Tighten head bolts to 65 ft.-lbs. torque. If studs are used, lightly oil the studs' fine threads before torquing the nuts. Tighten the nuts to 65 ft.-lbs. on the long studs and 60 ft.-lbs. on the short studs.

Valves

Chevrolet offers two swirl polished intake valves for production-type cylinder heads. The first is a standard 2.02-inch diameter valve (PN 3849814). For extreme high loads, Chevrolet also offers a 2.05-inch diameter stainless steel intake valve (PN 366285). This valve has a flat face to maximize compression and a 10-degree angle on the back of the head to enhance airflow. The cylinder head valve seats must be reworked before installing 2.05-inch diameter intake valves.

A high-performance standard length 1.60-inch diameter exhaust valve for small-block V8s is available as PN 3849818. This valve is swirl polished and has an aluminized face.

The unused portion of the valve seat on the underside of the valve head should be removed with a 20-degree cut. "Backcutting" the intake and exhaust valves in this manner narrows the valve faces to match the seats in the cylinder head and increases airflow.

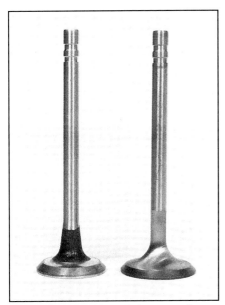

High-performance 1.60-inch diameter exhaust valve PN 3849818 (right) is swirl-polished and has an aluminized face.

Production valves can be "back cut" to improve flow. Grind the unused portion of the valve seat at a 20-degree angle.

All Chevrolet aluminum Bow Tie cylinder heads require extra-long valves; see the small-block valves and seats chart on page 51 in the cylinder head section for valve length recommendations. Valves with longer-than-stock stems are available from aftermarket suppliers.

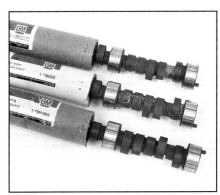

Chevrolet offers a variety of hydraulic flat tappet, hydraulic roller, and mechanical tappet camshafts for small-block V8s.

Phase 6 Bow Tie cylinder heads (PN 14011049 and 10051167) can be modified to use stock length valves by machining the valve spring seats .100-inch. Note that this modification limits how high the intake runner roofs can be raised when the heads are ported.

TECH SPECS: SMALL-BLOCK V8 CAMSHAFTS

Part Number	Description	Crankshaft Duration @ Lash Point, Int./Exh., (degrees)	Crankshaft Duration @ .050" Tappet Lift, Int./Exh., (degrees)	Maximum Lift w/1.5:1 Rocker Ratio, Int./Exh., (inches)	Valve Lash, Int./Exh., (inches)	Lobe Centerlines (degrees)	Notes
14093643	Hydraulic roller tappet	294/294	202/206	.403/.415	——	115	1987 350ci Corvette and IROC-Z Camaro.
10134334	Hydraulic roller tappet	336/336	235/235	.480/.480	——	114	5.7L HO engine asm. cam; use with spring #10134358; for ZZZ through ZZ2 engines.
10185071	Hydraulic roller tappet	N/A	208/221	.474/.510	——	112	5.7L HO 350 ZZ3 engine.
14088843	Hydraulic flat tappet	294/294	202/206	.403/.415	——	115	1983-86 305ci Z28 and L69 Camaro.
3863151	Hydraulic flat tappet	320/320	221/221	.447/.447	——	114	1965-67 Corvette and Chevy II L-79 cam; excellent power and torque, ID #3863152.
3896962	Hydraulic flat tappet	312/312	222/222	.450/.460	——	114	1969-81 L-46 and L-82 Corvette cam; moderate torque, excellent power, ID #3896964.
3972178	Mechanical flat tappet	300/312	242/254	.435/.455	.024/.030	116	1970-71 Corvette and Camaro LT-1 cam; good all-around street mechanical cam, ID #3972182.
3927140	Mechanical flat tappet	316/323	256/268	.469/.483	.024/.026	112	First design racing cam; good short track cam for small V8; use with spring #3927142; ID #33927141.
3965754	Mechanical flat tappet	318/327	262/273	.488/.509	.024/.026	112	Second design racing cam; good short track and road racing cam for 350ci and larger V8; use with spring #330585; ID #3965751.
24502476	Hydraulic flat tappet	N/A	212/222	.435/.460	——	N/A	350/300hp special performance engine #12355345.

An "edge orifice" hydraulic lifter (PN 5231585 –left) supplies less oil to the top end than a "piddle valve" lifter (PN 5232695–right).

Hydraulic roller tappets eliminate the sliding friction of conventional lifters and allow higher lift velocity.

A stamped steel guide retainer bolted to the lifter valley aligns the hydraulic roller tappets on the cam lobes.

Camshafts

Chevrolet offers several mechanical tappet, hydraulic flat tappet, and hydraulic roller lifter camshafts that are suitable for street, high-performance and limited competition uses. The chart on page 69 summarizes the timing and valve lift specifications for Chevrolet small-block V8 performance profiles, and indicates recommended applications.

Flat valve lifters can be made more compatible with the camshaft lobes by polishing the lifter bottom with #600 grit sandpaper before installation. Good used lifters that retain some crown or convex curvature across the bottom are generally satisfactory for reuse when installed on the same camshaft lobe.

Before installing new tappets in an aluminum block, deburr or sand off any sharp edges in the grooves around the

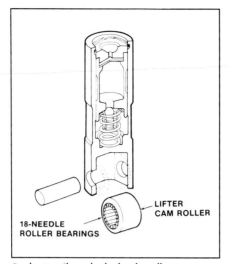

Production Chevrolet hydraulic roller tappets are .630-inch taller than standard small-block flat hydraulic and mechanical lifters.

Most 1987 and later production small-block V8s are equipped with hydraulic roller tappets, which require special block machining.

lifter bodies. These edges can gall and wear the aluminum lifter bores rapidly.

Refer to the engine building section for camshaft installation information.

Hydraulic Lifters

Production hydraulic lifters (PN 5232720) are recommended for all high-performance Chevrolet hydraulic flat tappet camshafts. For normal use, the rocker adjusting nuts should be tightened ½ to ¾ turn after all valvetrain lash is taken up. If all new valvetrain parts are being installed, the lifters should be readjusted after 1,000 to 2,000 miles to compensate for run-in wear.

Higher engine operating speeds can often be attained by "zero-lashing" Chevrolet hydraulic lifters. This requires idling a thoroughly warmed up engine and backing off each rocker arm adjusting nut until an audible clicking is heard.

Tighten the adjusting nut until the clicking just stops, and then turn the nut ⅛ turn tighter. Repeat this operation for each valve until all lifters have been set to "zero lash."

Mechanical Lifters

Two Chevrolet production mechanical (solid) valve lifters are available. PN 5232695 is similar in appearance to a hydraulic tappet. Its overhead oil metering is controlled by an internal inertia flapper valve, sometimes called a "piddle valve."

A second mechanical lifter is offered as PN 5231585. This lifter was original equipment in several high-performance small-block V8s produced from 1959-69. This lifter meters oil to the top end of the engine on the basis of the clearance between the lifter body and the block's lifter bore; it is commonly referred to as an "edge orifice" lifter.

An edge orifice lifter has several desirable features that are not available with the piddle valve design. The edge orifice lifter effects a 10 to 20 percent reduction in the total oil circulation rate. Because this lifter limits the flow of oil to the top end of the engine, it can be beneficial in engines equipped with dry sump oiling and engines with limited oil pan capacity. Due to the reduction in oil reaching the rocker arms, edge orifice lifters should be used only with roller bearing rockers.

Hydraulic Roller Lifters

Chevy's high-performance valvetrain innovations for small-block V8s includes a new generation of hydraulic roller camshafts. These cams use hydraulic roller lifters to reduce friction, maintain valve lash, and produce faster valve action. From a performance perspective, the chief advantage of a roller lifter is the higher lift velocity it allows.

Hydraulic roller tappets were introduced in production Chevrolet small-block V8 engines at the start of the 1987 model year. Tests conducted during development of the low-friction hydraulic roller tappets showed a 3.5 percent improvement in fuel economy and a five horsepower increase in engine output over comparable flat tappets. Hydraulic roller lifters require zero maintenance in normal service.

Roller tappets must be properly oriented on the cam lobes with their roller axis parallel to the camshaft axis. A guideplate aligns each pair of adjacent tappets. The lifter guides are held in place by a guide retainer attached to bosses in the block's lifter valley. A camshaft thrust plate located behind the timing chain sprocket absorbs thrust loads and centers the cam lobes under the roller lifters.

Production Chevrolet hydraulic roller valve lifters have a steel roller bearing assembly that rotates on 18 needle bearings, eliminating the sliding friction of a conventional tappet. Hydraulic roller tappets are .630-inch taller than standard small-block mechanical and hydraulic flat lifters; the pushrod length was shortened .630-inch to compensate for the longer lifters. The lifter bores in production cylinder blocks were also lengthened to accommodate the longer roller tappet assemblies. Due to these design changes, production hydraulic roller lifters cannot be used in pre-1987 engines because these blocks do not have the special machining and guide retainer bosses required.

The contact stress on the cam lobe is greater with a roller lifter than a conventional flat tappet due to the roller's smaller contact area. GM engineers upgraded the camshaft material from cast iron to steel to handle this higher stress. Chevrolet hydraulic roller steel cams are machined from solid, high carbon bar stock, and induction hardened to a Rockwell hardness of 60 Rc to ensure strength.

Pushrods

The demands on the pushrods have escalated dramatically as competition engine builders have turned to harsher camshaft profiles and stiffer valve springs in their search for improved performance. The pushrod is a critical link in an overhead valve engine like the small-block V8.

Chevrolet heavy-duty pushrods are available in two materials. Pushrods made from 1010 mild steel are suitable for high-performance street cars, power boats, street

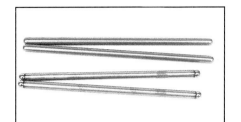

Pushrods for standard flat hydraulic and solid lifters are .630-inch longer than the pushrods used with hydraulic roller lifters.

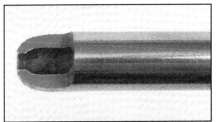

Chevrolet heavy-duty pushrods have a one-piece design that eliminates problems caused by loose or misaligned tip inserts.

BOW TIE SPECS: Pushrod Performance

This chart compares the performance of 1010 and 4130 steel heavy-duty Chevrolet pushrods. Both pushrods are $\frac{5}{16}$-inch in diameter.

Part Number	Material	Stiffness (lbs./in.)	Bending Force (lbs.)
10134309	4130	200,000	4,765
366277	1010	148,722	2,947

rods, and limited competition applications. Premium quality pushrods made from 4130 chrome moly steel are recommended for maximum-effort racing engines.

Heavy-duty pushrods are case hardened for use with pushrod guideplates. They can be used with all conventional hydraulic and mechanical flat tappets and most aftermarket roller lifters. They *cannot* be used with hydraulic roller lifters installed in 1987 and later small-block V8 engines; these lifters require pushrods that are .630-inch shorter than the pushrods used with flat tappets.

One-piece heavy-duty 1010 and 4130 steel pushrods offer significant improvements in reliability and performance over

production pushrods. Compared to the discontinued "blue tip" Chevy pushrods, the stiffness of the $\frac{5}{16}$-inch 4130 small-block pushrod was increased by almost 50,000 pounds per inch. The force required to bend the pushrod also increased by more than 1,800 pounds.

Tests conducted by GM Motorsports Technology Group engineers have shown that increasing pushrod stiffness improves valvetrain stability. At extreme engine speeds, a pushrod begins to act like a spring, compressing and stretching as the valve opens and closes.

Strain gauge tests have shown that the pushrod is actually in tension as the valve approaches its maximum lift and the lifter goes over the nose of the cam lobe. A stiff

TECH SPECS: SMALL-BLOCK V8 PUSHRODS

Part Number	Description	Material	Diameter	Length	Wall Thickness	Notes
14044874	Intake/Exhaust	1010 steel	$\frac{5}{16}$"	Standard	.075"	Stock length version of heavy-duty pushrod; replaces discontinued "blue tip" pushrod; recommended for high-performance street engines.
366277	Intake/Exhaust	1010 steel	$\frac{5}{16}$"	+.100"	.075"	Extra-long version of heavy-duty pushrod; recommended for high-performance and limited competition engines with high-lift cams and/or extra-long valves.
10134309	Intake/Exhaust	4130 chrome moly steel	$\frac{5}{16}$"	+.100"	.080"	Premium quality pushrod for maximum effort racing engines; one-piece design; 35% stiffer than pushrod #366277.

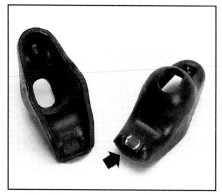

Guided rocker arms were introduced in 1988. These rockers have "rails" that align the rocker tip on the end of the valve stem.

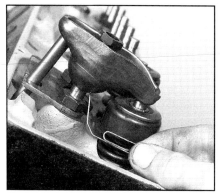

Check the clearance between the rocker arms and studs at maximum valve lift with a paper clip gauge after installing a high-lift cam.

Grooved rocker arm pivot balls will improve the reliability of stamped steel rocker arms installed on high-performance engines.

pushrod stabilizes a racing valvetrain by minimizing this undesirable deflection. The extra stiffness provided by increasing a pushrod's wall thickness more than compensates for the few additional grams of weight.

Valvetrain geometry also has a major impact on the reliability and performance of a high-performance Chevrolet. Heavy-duty pushrods for small-block V8 engines are available in both standard and extra-long lengths. Engines with high-lift

camshafts and/or extra-long valve stems often require pushrods that are .100-inch longer than stock (7.796-inch overall length) to restore the valvetrain geometry. When the pushrod length is correct, the rocker arm and valve stem will be at a 90-degree angle when the valve is at one-third of its maximum lift.

Rocker Arms

Before the small-block Chevrolet debuted in the mid-Fifties, most overhead valve engines were saddled with heavy, complex shaft-mounted rocker arms. The small-block's system of individual stud-mounted rockers was a performance breakthrough. It was simple, lightweight, reliable, inexpensive, and effective. Generations of enthusiasts have learned that the small-block's valvetrain is also easy to modify for improved performance. With only minor refinements, the same basic valvetrain design has proven itself in production motors and high-speed racing engines.

Production Chevrolet small-block rocker arms have a nominal ratio of 1.5:1. A rocker arm assembly consists of a stamped steel rocker arm, a pivot ball, and an adjusting nut.

Guided rocker arms were introduced on production small-blocks in 1988. These rockers have stamped guides, or "rails," that align the rocker tips on the valve stems. These lip guides prevent the rocker arm from skewing as it opens and closes the valve. Self-centering guided rocker arms do not require close-tolerance guideplates or pushrod guide holes in the cylinder head. These rail-type rockers can be used in blocks designed for both flat and hydraulic roller camshafts.

Because of the many advantages of the guided rocker arm design, early-style

BOW TIE TIPS — Guideplate Guidance

H.O. and Corvette aluminum cylinder head assemblies are designed to use late-model guided rocker arms. These heads are equipped with mild steel pushrod guideplates (PN 10111771). If flat-tip (non-guided) rocker arms are installed on H.O. aluminum cylinder heads, the pushrods and guideplates will wear excessively.

To avoid possible engine damage, the rocker arms and guideplates must be matched. Replacement guided rocker arms should be used when installing aluminum H.O. heads with their original guideplates. Alternatively, early-style flat rocker arms can be used if *hardened* pushrod guideplates (PN 14011051) are

installed on the aluminum heads. Hardened guideplates for aluminum cylinder heads are stamped "05."

The following rocker arms and guideplates are used with the H.O. and Corvette aluminum heads:

Part Number	Description
10089648	Rocker arm, guided (replaces flat-tip rocker #3974290)
10111771	Pushrod guideplate, wide slots, for guided rockers
14011051	Pushrod guideplate, for aluminum heads, hardened, with narrow slots for flat-tip rockers

Guides on self-aligning rocker arms center the rocker arm on the valve stem tip.

Hardened pushrod guideplates are required when using early-style non-guided rocker arms with flat tips.

rocker arms with flat tips have been discontinued. Replacement guided rocker arms for small-block V8s are available as PN 10089648.

The clearance between the rocker arms and studs should always be checked before final assembly when installing a high-lift camshaft. This can be done by inserting a gauge made from a wire paper clip between the rocker arm slot and rocker stud when the valve is at maximum lift. If the clearance is insufficient, elongate the rocker arm slot with a small grinder. Ball-type rocker arms with extra-long slots are also available from aftermarket sources.

Production rocker arm adjusting nuts (PN 3744341) are recommended for Chevrolet rockers. The adjusting nuts must have enough preload torque to prevent them from loosening while the engine is running. Any nuts with insufficient preload should be discarded.

Significant changes in valve lash may be experienced when new valvetrain components are first run-in. Valve lash should be checked and adjusted frequently until it stabilizes. New rocker arms and balls should be observed closely for overheating and excessive wear during break-in.

If it is necessary to change a rocker and ball, always install a good used rocker arm assembly. If good used rockers and balls are not available, move an intake rocker and ball over to replace a burned exhaust rocker arm. Then install the new components on an intake valve, which runs cooler. Always keep usable rocker arms and balls together during engine disassembly and rebuild.

Several aftermarket manufacturers offer grooved rocker balls that resist galling with high valve spring loads. 1970 and later die-cast aluminum rocker covers have cast drippers over the rocker fulcrums to improve rocker ball lubrication.

BOW TIE TIPS — Unequal Rocker Ratios

Competition engine builders often install rocker arms with different ratios on the intake and exhaust valves of small-block V8s. GM MTG engineers have discovered that using higher rocker arm ratios on the four "corner" cylinders (#1, 2, 7, and 8) can improve the performance of a competition engine equipped with a single four-barrel intake manifold. These high-ratio rockers apparently compensate for the differences in intake manifold runner length between the four middle cylinders and the four cylinders on the ends of the block.

A series of rocker arm ratio tests was conducted on a Chevrolet 358ci small-block V8 built to NASCAR specifications. The engine was equipped with Chevrolet high-port 18-degree cylinder heads and a Bow Tie single four-barrel intake manifold. The engine was initially equipped with 1.65:1 ratio rocker arms on the intake valves and 1.6:1 rocker arms on the exhaust valves.

In the first test, 1.7:1 ratio rocker arms were installed on the intake valves on the four corner cylinders (#1, 2, 7, and 8). This produced an increase of four horsepower at 7600 rpm as shown in the accompanying chart. Power increased again when 1.65:1 ratio rockers were installed on the exhaust valves on these outside cylinders. However, horsepower decreased when higher ratio rocker arms were tested on the four

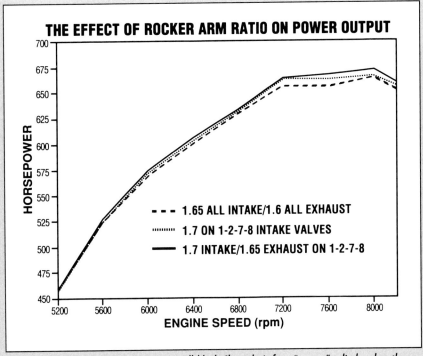

THE EFFECT OF ROCKER ARM RATIO ON POWER OUTPUT

- - - 1.65 ALL INTAKE/1.6 ALL EXHAUST
········· 1.7 ON 1-2-7-8 INTAKE VALVES
—— 1.7 INTAKE/1.65 EXHAUST ON 1-2-7-8

Increasing the rocker arm ratios on a small-block Chevrolet's four "corner" cylinders has the potential to improve performance.

middle cylinders (#3, 4, 5, and 6). Repeating this series of tests on other development engines produced similar results. (Of course, not every racing engine will respond positively to unequal rocker arm ratios due to differences in individual components and operating conditions.)

Raising the rocker arm ratio increases both maximum valve lift and effective duration. Before duplicating this test on a competition engine, make sure that the higher valve lift and longer duration will not cause problems with valve spring coil bind, retainer-to-guide clearance, and piston-to-valve clearance.

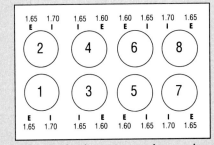

The unequal rocker arm ratios shown in this diagram produced more horsepower than a conventional combination of 1.65:1 intake rockers and 1.6:1 exhaust rockers.

Aftermarket roller bearing rocker arms with large diameter trunions are recommended for endurance racing applications.

Splayed-valve and 18-degree Bow Tie cylinder heads are designed to use aftermarket shaft-mounted rocker arms. Offset rocker arms provide additional pushrod clearance with widened intake ports.

Check the spring retainer, seal, and rocker arm clearance on a competition small-block V8.

Small-block V8 valve springs (left to right): PN 3911068 production spring; PN 3927142 high-performance spring; PN 330585 dual valve spring; PN 366282 dual spring with damper.

Roller Rocker Arms

Many Chevrolet Bow Tie cylinder heads are designed to use aftermarket rocker arm systems. Shaft-mounted rockers are required on 18-degree and splayed-valve cylinder heads. Stud-mounted needle roller rocker arms are recommended for maximum-effort racing engines equipped with other Bow Tie cylinder heads (cast iron, aluminum 049, and raised runner castings). Hardened adjusting nuts and 7/16-inch diameter big-block V8 rocker studs (PN 3921912) should be used whenever possible with stud-mounted roller rockers.

Needle roller rocker arms typically lower the engine oil temperature and require less lubrication than ball-type rockers. Rocker arms should be inspected frequently for signs of fatigue, and must be checked for adequate spring, retainer, and stud clearance during assembly. Rocker arm studs should be Magnaflux inspected to ensure their quality.

Increasing the rocker arm ratio on high-performance and competition small-block V8s can often improve engine performance. High-ratio rocker arms can be installed on the intake valves, on the exhaust valves, or in both positions. The degree of improvement will vary, however, depending primarily on the camshaft profile and cylinder head airflow. A particular combination should be dyno or track tested with higher ratio rocker arms in each position separately, and then together to find the most effective ratios.

Although high-ratio rockers may offer a performance gain, they also impart higher loads to the rest of the valvetrain. These higher loads can cause valvetrain malfunctions, reduce durability, and contribute to premature valve float.

Valve Lash

Engine failures are frequently caused by problems in the valvetrain. It is essential that the valve lash not change during a racing event. If the valve lash increases significantly for any reason, valve springs and valves cannot reasonably be expected to survive. Failure of either component can seriously damage an engine.

Valve lash adjustments should be made with the engine hot whenever possible. If this is impractical, a determination of the lash change during warm-up should be made and allowed for when the lash is set cold. Valve lash may increase or decrease during warm-up depending on whether cast iron or aluminum cylinder heads are used.

Due to thermal expansion of aluminum blocks, there is considerable valve lash change between cold and hot engine conditions. Valves should be lashed cold .010-inch tighter than the recommended running lash and then readjusted after the engine reaches operating temperature.

Valve Springs

Valve springs are among the most highly stressed components in a high-performance engine. It is essential that the valve springs have sufficient pressure to control valve motion at the intended engine speeds. The springs must also have adequate travel to prevent the coils from stacking solid ("coil binding") at maximum valve lift.

Chevrolet has developed five different valve springs that are suitable for high-performance and competition small-block V8 engines. The accompanying chart summarizes Chevrolet valve spring specifications.

Part Number	Description	Outside Diameter	Pressure @ Installed Ht.	Solid Height	Pounds Per Inch	Retainer Part Number	Valve Seal Kit	Notes
3911068	Single w/ damper	1.241"	80# @ 1.70"	1.15"	267	14003974	10132715	Production spring used with special high-performance 350/300hp engine.
3927142	Single w/ damper	1.273"	110# @ 1.70"	1.16"	358	14003974	10132715	Use with camshaft #3927140 and all high-performance production cams to extend rpm range.
10134358	Single w/ damper	1.273"	110# @ 1.70"	1.16"	356	14003974	10132715	Chrome silicon steel; used with 10185086 aluminum head assembly; orange color code.
330585	Dual	1.379"	140# @ 1.75"	1.15"	325	330586	10132715	Use with camshaft #3927140, 3965754 and all moderate lift racing cams.
366282	Dual w/ damper	1.525"	128# @ 1.70"	1.26"	406	366254	Aftermarket	Use with high-lift mushroom or roller tappet racing cams (.625" lift).
10168425	Single	1.300"	85# @ 1.78"	1.26"	373	10168424	N/A	1992-93 LT1 production Corvette engine.

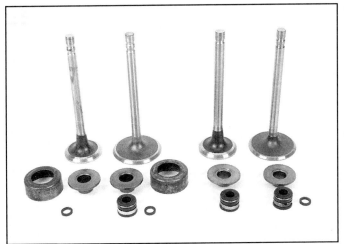

ZZ3 H.O. 350 engine assemblies use lightweight valve spring retainers (right) and valve stem seals that eliminate the need for oil shields.

Chrome silicon valve springs are installed on H.O. aluminum heads. These springs are recommended for high-performance engines.

PN 10134358 is the best choice for a high-performance street small-block. GM engineers designed this spring specifically for the H.O. 350 engine assembly. It is wound from chrome silicon wire, a material commonly used in competition valve springs because it improves the spring's ability to maintain its rated load over time. This heavy-duty small-block spring is a single coil design with a flat wire damper. It is painted bright orange to distinguish it from production versions.

This spring is installed on the latest ZZ3 version of the H.O. 350 engine with a lightweight retainer (PN 10045007) that

has half the mass of the previous design. Earlier H.O. engines can be updated by installing this retainer along with valve seals (PN 460483) and spacers (PN 10185066). Discard the valve spring oil shields when making this conversion.

PN 3911068 is a production valve spring and damper originally installed on many 302ci and 350ci small-blocks. It can be used with all Chevrolet hydraulic flat lifter cams and street high-performance mechanical lifter cams. Production "O"-ring valve stem seals (PN 12511890) and steel retainers (PN 14003974) are recommended for this spring. Chevrolet hardened valve stem locks (PN 3947770) should be used in all high-performance applications. These locks are color-coded copper.

PN 3927142 was originally designed to complement the Z28 off-highway racing cam (PN 3927140), but this spring can also be used to extend the rpm range of all Chevrolet mechanical tappet street performance cams. It increases the seat pressure by approximately 30 pounds over a production valve spring, and does not require machining the cylinder head's spring pockets.

PN 330585 is a dual-coil valve spring designed for moderate lift racing cams, including Chevrolet camshafts PN 3927140 and 3965754. This spring can also be used to extend the rpm range of street high-performance mechanical cams, and it is suitable for production rocker arms at engine speeds up to 7000 rpm. It requires aluminum retainer PN

Link-type timing chains are used on most production small-blocks; a heavy-duty Chevrolet double roller timing set (right) is recommended for high-speed operation. Timing set PN 12341093 includes a chain, an iron cam sprocket, and a steel crankshaft sprocket.

A special camshaft sprocket is required to clear the thrust plate installed on the front of the block when using a hydraulic roller camshaft.

330586. (Note: Aluminum retainers must be inspected frequently for wear. They are not recommended for street engines.) Spring seats and valve guides on production cylinder heads must be machined to accommodate this spring's 1.379-inch outside diameter.

PN 366282 is a dual-coil valve spring designed for competition engines equipped with high-lift camshafts. It should be used with lightweight titanium retainer PN 366254 and aftermarket valve stem seals. Due to this spring's high pressure, new flat tappet camshafts should be broken in for at least ½ hour running time with only the outer coils installed. This spring has an outside diameter of 1.550-inch. It is recommended for installation only on Bow Tie cylinder heads, which have enough material in the spring pockets to accommodate large diameter valve springs.

In all installations where high-lift camshafts and heavy-duty springs, retainers, and valve stem seals are used, all parts should be checked carefully for adequate clearance. Make a temporary assembly of the complete valvetrain on the engine and check for possible interference between the spring retainer and seal at maximum valve lift, bottoming of the inner, outer, and damper coils at maximum lift, and possible interference between the rocker arm and valve spring retainer. Any of these conditions will result in very short engine life if not corrected before final assembly!

Aftermarket flat tappet and roller lifter camshafts may require different valve springs and related components. The camshaft manufacturer's recommendations should be followed in these instances.

Timing Sets

Production Chevrolet small-block aluminum/nylon camshaft sprockets and link-type timing chains are used with good results by many engine builders. However, for sustained high-speed durability and extended life, the GM Motorsports Technology Group recommends a double-roller timing chain and sprocket set. A heavy-duty roller timing set is available as PN 12341093. This kit includes a double-roller chain (PN 3735411), an iron camshaft sprocket (PN 3735412), and a steel crankshaft sprocket (PN 3735413). Aftermarket belt-type timing sets are also suitable for many competition applications.

1987 and newer production engines equipped with hydraulic roller camshafts use a camshaft thrust plate to control camshaft movement. This thrust plate bolts to the front of the engine block behind the camshaft sprocket, and requires a special camshaft sprocket to clear its attaching bolts. First-design H.O. 350 engine assemblies used a heavy-duty single-roller timing chain set with the correct camshaft sprocket for hydraulic roller applications. This timing set con-

sists of camshaft sprocket PN 14096262, crankshaft sprocket PN 14088784, and timing chain PN 14088783.

Always verify that there is adequate clearance between the timing set and the front of the block. This is especially important on late-model production and Bow Tie blocks with oil galleries that extend to the front face of the block. It may be necessary to relieve the oil gallery bosses for clearance when using double-row timing chains or aftermarket camshaft belt drives.

As noted in the camshaft section, changes in camshaft phasing can be achieved by installing offset cam dowel bushings in the camshaft timing sprocket. The cam bushing should be staked in place to prevent it from turning or falling out after installation.

When using roller lifters, the cam should be prevented from moving forward or backward in the block. Late-model blocks have provisions for a camshaft thrust plate. However, this method of limiting camshaft movement cannot be used with most aftermarket racing camshafts and timing sets. Needle roller thrust bearings are recommended to control camshaft movement in competition engines equipped with roller lifters.

Suitable bearings to prevent forward cam thrust are available from many aftermarket camshaft manufacturers. A plate should be brazed to the timing chain

A thrust plate limits forward cam movement with hydraulic roller camshafts. The No. 1 cam journal is machined to fit the plate.

Install a needle thrust bearing between the cam sprocket and block to restrict cam movement with aftermarket roller lifters.

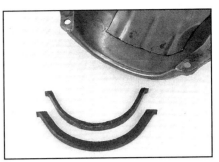

1955-75 oil pans use a thin front cover seal (top); 1976-85 pans require a thick seal. 1986-up pans use a one-piece molded gasket.

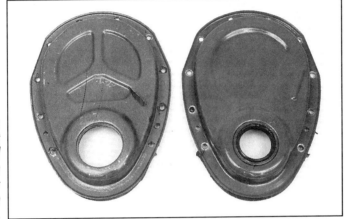

The timing pointer on an early-style front cover (left) is welded in position; a late-model cover (right) uses a bolt-on timing pointer.

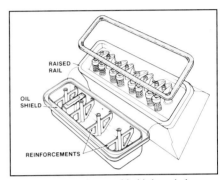

Rocker covers with central hold-down bolts were introduced in 1987. This design uses a captured neoprene gasket to prevent oil leaks.

cover or other reinforcement provided. A Chevrolet heavy-duty aluminum water pump has a boss on the bottom of the casting that can be drilled and tapped for a stop bolt to limit camshaft movement.

Camshaft rear thrust control is normally provided by the cam sprocket rubbing against the block face. Although this method of thrust control is satisfactory for most flat tappet camshafts, needle thrust bearings are preferred when using roller lifter camshafts.

A needle thrust bearing should be installed between the camshaft sprocket and the block face to control rearward cam thrust. A suitable needle bearing can be assembled using two Torrington thrust races (#TRA-3244) and one Torrington thrust bearing (#NTA-3244). These parts are available from bearing suppliers and speed equipment manufacturers. The rear surface of the cam sprocket must be machined in a lathe to accommodate the thickness of the two races and the thrust bearing. Timing sets that are already machined for a roller thrust bearing are also available from aftermarket sources.

Front Covers

A chrome plated timing chain cover stamped with the Chevrolet Bow Tie em-

blem is available for small-block V8s as PN 12342088. This cover includes a production oil seal (PN 10111769).

Two different oil pan/timing cover seals have been used on Chevrolet small-block V8s. Early-model engines (1955-75) used a thin ¼-inch seal; later small-blocks (1976-85) require a ⅜-inch thick seal. The thickness of the pan seal depends on the year of the timing cover and oil pan, not the year of the block.

All late-model covers (including the chromed cover described above) use the thick seal. If you are unsure which seal to use, measure from the oil pan rail gasket to the bottom of the seal surface. Early-model pans measure approximately 2¼-inch; late-model pans are 2⅜-inch.

In 1986, production small-block Chevrolet V8s were converted to a one-piece neoprene oil pan gasket that replaced the previous four-piece gasket and seal set. The chromed timing chain cover described above can be used with 1986 and later oil pans.

Two chromed front timing cover pointers are available for the small-block V8. PN 12341904 should be used with 6.75-inch diameter torsional dampers; PN 12341915 is designed for 8-inch diameter dampers. *These bolt-on pointers should*

be used only with 1969 and later dampers. Earlier dampers have a different timing mark location, as described in the section on torsional dampers. Use of these pointers with pre-'69 dampers will result in incorrect spark timing. Early-style dampers can be modified for use with these pointers by relocating the TDC mark on the outer ring.

Rocker Covers

Four different rocker cover bolt patterns have been used on Chevrolet small-block cylinder heads. Small-block V8s produced in 1955-58 had four hold-down bolts on the rocker cover flange. The two bolts on the intake side were ½-inch closer together than the bolts on the exhaust side. In 1959, the hold-down bolts on the intake side of the rocker covers were relocated directly across from the bolts on the exhaust side. This bolt pattern was used continuously through 1986 on production cylinder heads. All Bow Tie cylinder heads with in-line valves also use this rocker cover bolt pattern.

A new rocker cover design with four central hold-down bolts was introduced in 1987 on production cylinder heads. The rocker cover rails were raised to move the gasket above the oil drainback level, thereby reducing the possibility of leaks. Internal flanges were added to the rocker covers to distribute the clamping load over the entire sealing area, and a new neoprene gasket was introduced.

Splayed-valve Bow Tie cylinder heads have a unique rocker cover bolt pattern. Special cast aluminum rocker covers (PN 10185045) and gaskets (PN 10185043) are available for this cylinder head.

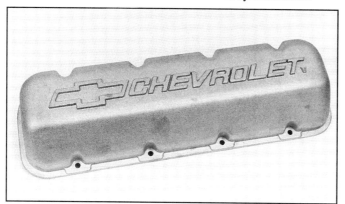

Splayed-valve Bow Tie cylinder heads have a unique rocker cover pattern. Use cast rocker cover PN 10185045 with these heads.

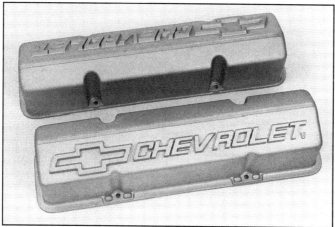

Cast aluminum Bow Tie rocker covers for competition small-block V8s are available as PN 10185064. These covers are designed to clear racing valvetrains.

BOW TIE TIPS
Corvette Covers

Corvette magnesium rocker covers PN 10055781 (left) and PN 10055782 (right) can be installed on 1987 and newer production cylinder heads with central hold-down bolts. This conversion requires eight hold-down bolts (PN 12338092), eight washers (PN 14094717), eight bolt gaskets (PN 14088793), and two rocker cover gaskets (PN 14088564). The right-hand Corvette cover has an oil filler hole; use screw-in filler cap PN 14100672.

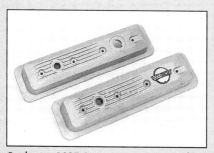

Production 1987 Corvette magnesium rocker covers can be installed on late-model cylinder heads with four central hold-down bolts.

Magnesium rocker covers give a "high tech" look to a small-block. Covers can be painted to match the engine.

Cast Rocker Covers

Cast aluminum Bow Tie rocker covers (PN 10185064) are recommended for competition small-block V8s. These covers provide increased clearance for competition valvetrains, and their rigid structure prevents oil leaks. The "kick-out" on the intake manifold side will clear aftermarket rocker arms and stud girdles without machining. The outer bolt holes are reinforced to distribute clamping loads evenly on the rocker cover gasket, and integral gasket retainers hold the gasket in position.

The Bow Tie rocker cover's flat upper surface provides a convenient location for mounting custom breathers and vent tubes. Extra-thick bosses on the underside provide additional material for threaded fittings. These covers do not have holes for oil fillers or PCV valves.

Cast aluminum Bow Tie rocker covers fit all conventional Chevrolet cylinder heads (including 18-degree designs) with hold-down bolts on the rocker cover rails. The covers are taller than production stamped covers (4.0-inch overall height), and may not clear power brake boosters and engine-mounted accessories in some applications. The covers have .100-inch thick walls, and weigh less than 3 pounds each.

A plain version of this rocker cover without the Bow Tie and Chevrolet name is available as PN 24502466. This cover has additional material on its underside to allow engine builders to mill a custom logo on the top of the cover.

Stamped Rocker Covers

Stamped steel Bow Tie rocker covers are available for small-block cylinder heads with hold-down bolts on the rocker cover rail. The Bow Tie logo and the Chevrolet name are deeply embossed on the top of these heavy gauge covers. Each cover has a single hole that can be used for an oil filler plug, breather, or PCV valve.

Stamped Bow Tie rocker covers are available in two heights. Tall versions offer additional clearance for rocker stud girdles and racing valvetrains. Shorter production height versions will clear alternators, air conditioning compressors, master cylinders, and other underhood components. Both tall and short Bow Tie rocker covers are available with baffles that prevent oil from being pulled into the breathers. (These baffles will not clear rocker stud girdles.)

Plain steel covers are designed for racers and competition engine builders. These unplated covers make it easy to weld on breather tubes and fittings. They can also be painted to match the engine.

A chrome-plated rocker cover with the Bow Tie emblem outlined in red is available for 1987 and newer production cylinder heads as PN 12355350. This cover has central hold-down bolts and a breather baffle.

Chevrolet offers an assortment of related rocker cover components. Spring bar retainers prevent oil leaks by spreading the clamping force over a wide area. These bars are specifically designed to fit the flange width on stamped Bow Tie rocker covers. Grommets and push-in oil caps are available to complete the installation.

The following are part numbers and applications for small-block V8 rocker covers and components:

Part No.	Description
10134316	Tall Bow Tie cover, plain steel without baffle
10185045	Cast aluminum Bow Tie cover, splayed valve-head
10185064	Cast aluminum Bow Tie cover
24502466	Cast aluminum cover, plain top
12341002	Tall Bow Tie cover, chromed steel without baffle
12341003	Production height Bow Tie cover, chromed steel with baffle
12341004	Tall Bow Tie cover, chromed steel with baffle
12341969	Production height cover, plain top, chromed steel with baffle
12341972	Tall rocker cover, plain top, chromed steel with baffle
12355350	Production height cover, ribbed with red Bow Tie emblem, four central hold-down bolts, chromed steel with baffle

Related components:

3894337	Rubber grommet for Bow Tie covers
6421868	Push-in oil cap and breather, not chromed
14082321	Spring bar retainer, plain steel
14044820	Spring bar retainer, chromed
3933964	Gasket, for rocker covers with outer hold-down bolts
14088564	Gasket, for rocker covers with central hold-down bolts
10185043	Gasket, for splayed-valve cylinder heads

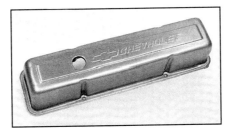

Plain steel Chevrolet Bow Tie rocker covers can be customized by welding on breather tubes and fittings for vent lines.

Bow Tie rocker covers are available with baffles to prevent oil from being pulled into the breathers. Baffles will not clear stud girdles.

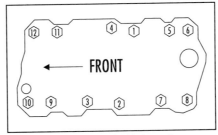

Tighten the intake manifold bolts in the sequence shown. The recommended bolt torque for small-block V8s is 30 ft.-lbs.

Intake Manifolds

An intake manifold is more than a simple conduit that carries the mixture of fuel and air from the carburetor to the combustion chambers. Its design and construction significantly impacts the engine's performance.

Chevrolet offers aluminum intake manifolds for applications ranging from street rods to NASCAR stock cars. In general, dual-plane Bow Tie manifolds are suitable for street performance and limited competition uses. The dual-plane design enhances low-speed and mid-range torque, and most castings have provisions for chokes, accessory brackets, and emission-control equipment. In contrast, single-plane Bow Tie intakes are intended exclusively for racing. Their short runners and open plenums are tai-

Chrome plated Bow Tie rocker covers are available for 1987-up production cylinder heads with four central hold-down bolts.

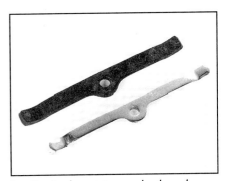

Install spring bar retainers under the rocker cover bolts to spread out the clamping load and prevent oil leaks.

A low-profile aluminum L82 Quadrajet intake manifold (PN 14004377) can be used on vehicles with limited hood clearance.

lored for high-rpm engines, and the castings do not incorporate emission controls, choke stoves, and other street equipment.

Engineers at the GM Motorsports Technology Group have developed an array of intake manifolds to complement specific cylinder head designs (standard runner, raised runner, high-port, etc.). Refer to the intake manifold specifications chart on page 80 to determine the best manifold for your small-block V8.

Aluminum Quadrajet Manifold PN 14004377

1979-80 L-82 engines were equipped with aluminum Quadrajet manifold PN 14004377. This manifold is a good choice for moderate performance street engines and restricted racing classes that require production intake systems. It is a dual-plane design with a divided plenum that produces good low and mid-range torque with a Quadrajet-type spread-bore carburetor. This low-profile manifold will fit under Corvette hoods and is recommended for other applications with limited clearance.

ZZ2 High Rise Intake Manifold PN 10185024

This manifold is an updated version of Chevy's famous high-rise 1967-71 Z28/LT-1 intake manifold. Like its predecessors, this lightweight aluminum intake

manifold mounts a standard-flange Holley four-barrel. Its overall height is 4.5-inch from the end rails to the carburetor mounting flange.

There are several significant differences between this manifold and the original Z28 casting, however. This manifold does not have an oil filler tube, and its choke stove mounting holes are not drilled and tapped. The upper edges of the manifold gasket flanges are chamfered to clear the raised rocker cover rails on late-model aluminum cylinder heads.

Mounting bosses have been added for air conditioning compressor brackets and other accessories.

Porting is unnecessary for most high-performance uses, but the manifold runners should be matched to the intake manifold gasket and cylinder head ports for peak performance. The plenum divider can be machined to a depth not greater than one inch below the carburetor mounting flange if an increase in top-end power is desirable (although low-speed torque will be reduced).

TECH SPECS: SMALL-BLOCK V8 INTAKE MANIFOLDS

Part Number	Description	Type	Carburetor	Application	Features	Notes
14007377	Production	Dual-plane	Spread-bore (Quadrajet)	Street performance, restricted racing classes	EGR, choke stove, heat riser	Low profile, fits vehicles with restricted hood clearance (Corvette, etc.)
10185024	ZZ2 H.O. 350 (high rise)	Dual-plane	Standard flange (Holley)	Street performance, moderate competition	Heat riser	Updated version of Z28/LT-1 intake. Overall height from end rails to carburetor flange is 4.5 inches.
10185063	ZZ3 H.O. 350 (low profile)	Dual-plane	Spread-bore (Quadrajet) and standard flange (Holley)	Street performance, moderate competition	Dual-pattern carburetor flange, EGR, hot air choke, heat riser	Produces same power as high-rise ZZ2 manifold, but provides ½-inch more hood clearance. Overall height from end rails to carburetor flange is 4.0-inch.
14096011	Cast iron high rise	Dual-plane	Spread-bore (Quadrajet) and standard flange (Holley)	Street performance, marine, restricted racing classes	Dual-pattern carburetor flange, heat riser	Cast iron version of Z28 intake.
14096241	Cast iron high rise	Dual-plane	Spread-bore (Quadrajet) and standard flange (Holley)	Street performance, marine, restricted racing classes	Dual-pattern carburetor flange, heat riser	Cast iron version of Z28 intake; middle bolt holes drilled at 73° angle for 1987-up production cast iron cylinder heads.
10051102	Standard runner Bow Tie	Single-plane	Standard flange (Holley)	Moderate competition	Air gap under runners, no heat riser	Use with standard port aluminum Bow Tie cylinder heads #14011049 and #10051167 and cast iron Bow Tie cylinder head #10134392.
10051103	Raised runner Bow Tie	Single-plane	Standard flange (Holley)	Maximum competition	Air gap under runners, no heat riser	Runners are raised .200-inch to match ports in raised runner cylinder head #10051101. Can be modified for low-port 18-degree head #10134352 by machining intake flanges to 5-degree angle.
10185053	High-port 18-degree Bow Tie	Single-plane	Standard flange (Holley)	Maximum competition, high rpm	Air gap under runners, no heat riser	Overall height is 6.75 inches. Use with high-port 18-degree heads #10134363-4 and 24502482.
24502487	High-port 18-degree Bow Tie	Single-plane	Standard flange (Holley)	Maximum competition, high rpm	Air gap under runners, no heat riser	"Line of sight" runners. Use with high-port 18-degree heads #10134363-4 and 24502482. Casting number 10185053.
24502481	High-port 18-degree Bow Tie	Single-plane	Standard flange (Holley)	Maximum competition, short track and road racing	Air gap under runners, no heat riser. Has bosses for auxiliary coolant lines.	Smaller runners than 10185053 to enhance mid-range torque. Use with high-port 18-degree heads #10134363-4 and 24502482.

The stock carburetor for the original Z28/LT-1 manifold was a 780cfm Holley four-barrel, but any standard flange carburetor from 390 to 850cfm airflow can be mounted. A 600 to 830cfm Holley carburetor with mechanically operated secondaries and dual accelerator pumps will perform well with this manifold. If a richer or leaner fuel mixture is desired, change all four jets up or down in size.

ZZ3 H.O. 350 Intake Manifold PN 10185063

This aluminum intake manifold was developed for the ZZ3 H.O. 350 engine assembly. Dyno tests have shown that it produces the same horsepower as a conventional high-rise manifold, but its low-profile design provides ½-inch more hood clearance (overall height from the end rails to the center of the carburetor flange is 4.0-inch.)

The dual-pattern carburetor flange is machined for standard flange Holley and Quadrajet spread-bore four-barrels. The casting also has mounting bosses for late-model accessory brackets, exhaust gas recirculation (EGR), and an integral hot air choke. The manifold flanges are chamfered to clear the raised rocker cover rails on late-model aluminum small-block cylinder heads.

If a mechanical choke is not required, use choke stove block-off plate PN 14094792, gasket PN 14096848, and bolts PN 3930347 (2 required). If EGR is not required, use block-off plate PN 6269414, gasket PN 14031369, and bolts PN 3930347 (2 required).

This manifold also has provisions to mount a heat shield (PN 6271071) underneath the exhaust cross-over to prevent coking when EGR is used. Use four rivets (PN 3959544) to attach the heat shield.

Cast Iron High Rise Intake Manifolds PN 14096011 and 14096241

Chevrolet offers a cast iron version of the Z-28/LT-1 intake manifold as PN 14096011. A similar casting for 1987 and

BOW TIE TIPS A New Angle

In 1987 the angle of the two middle intake manifold bolts was changed from 90 degrees to 73 degrees on production cast iron cylinder heads. Before installing a high-performance intake manifold on these heads, the manifold's center bolt holes must be drilled and spot-faced to match this 73-degree angle. (Wedge-shaped spacers available from aftermarket suppliers can also be used to adapt intake manifolds to late-model cylinder heads with 73-degree center bolts.)

BOW TIE TIPS Better Breathing

Intake manifold runners should be carefully matched to the intake manifold gasket and cylinder head ports for peak performance. Lightly radius the runner entries in the plenum with an abrasive cartridge roll to remove casting flash.

The performance of a small-block racing engine equipped with a single-plane Bow Tie intake manifold can often be improved by installing a spacer between the carburetor and the manifold mounting flange. A two-inch spacer is recommended for all applications if hood clearance is sufficient.

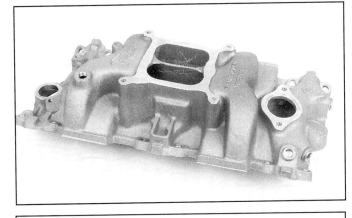

Aluminum intake manifold PN 10185024 is an updated version of the classic Z28/LT-1 high-rise intake.

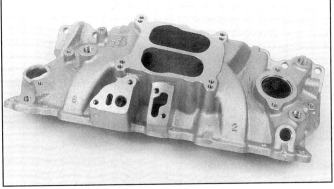

The ZZ3 low-profile aluminum intake manifold (PN 10185063) has a dual-pattern carburetor flange and provisions for emissions controls.

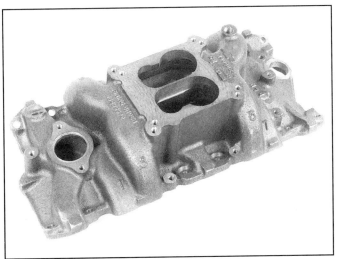

High-rise intake manifolds PN 14096241 and 14096011 are recommended for restricted racing classes that require cast iron intakes.

newer production cast iron heads with 73-degree angle center bolt holes is available as PN 14096241.

This manifold has the same design as the high-rise aluminum intake, and its carburetor pad is machined for both standard flange Holley four-barrels and spread-bore Quadrajets. This manifold is less expensive than an aluminum intake, and is ideal for performance enthusiasts building a small-block on a tight budget. It is highly recommended for many "street stock" oval track classes that require a cast iron intake. Cast iron is also preferred for many marine applications because it is less susceptible to corrosion damage than aluminum. This manifold weighs approximately 41 pounds; its aluminum counterpart weighs 13 pounds.

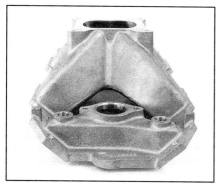

Single-plane Bow Tie aluminum manifolds have air gaps under their runners to isolate the intake charge from engine heat.

Bow Tie intake manifold PN 24502481 has reduced runner cross-sections to enhance torque and bosses for auxiliary coolant lines.

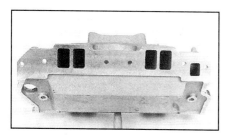

Bow Tie intake manifolds PN 10185053, 24502481, and 24502487 fit the 18-degree high-port cylinder head's unique bolt pattern.

Standard Runner Bow Tie Manifold PN 10051102

This single four-barrel competition Bow Tie intake manifold is recommended for cast iron and aluminum Bow Tie cylinder heads with standard port locations. The cross-sectional area of its runners complements the intake ports in cast iron Bow Tie cylinder heads (PN 10134392) and Phase 6 aluminum cylinder heads (PN 14011049 and 10051167). The carburetor flange is drilled for a standard flange Holley.

This manifold's single-plane design enhances high-rpm horsepower, while its curved runners boost mid-range torque. The runner entries are radiused to minimize turbulence in the plenum and to promote uniform fuel distribution to all eight cylinders. An air gap beneath the runners isolates the intake charge from engine heat.

When matching this manifold's runners to the cylinder head ports, use Mr. Gasket intake gasket #102, Fel-Pro #1205 or 1206, or an equivalent gasket. Align the gasket openings with the tops of the intake runners, and remove material from the bottom of the runners. Then match the cylinder head ports to the same gasket to ensure proper port alignment.

Raised Runner Bow Tie Intake Manifold PN 10051103

Chevrolet heavy-duty "raised runner" Bow Tie aluminum cylinder heads (PN 10051101) have intake runners that are .200-inch higher than standard small-block heads. This revised port location requires an intake manifold with corresponding raised runners to maintain proper port/manifold alignment. Bow Tie intake manifold PN 10051103 is recommended for all small-block engines equipped with raised runner cylinder heads. It shares many of its design features with the standard runner Bow Tie intake manifold described previously.

18-Degree High-Port Intake Manifolds PN 10185053, 24502481 and 24502487

The GM Motorsports Technology Group developed three single-plane Bow

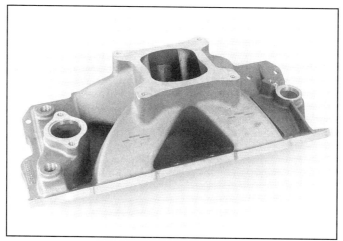

Chevrolet single-plane aluminum intake manifolds are recommended for use with Bow Tie cylinder heads. PN 10051102 fits cast iron and aluminum heads with standard port locations.

Bow Tie intake PN 10185053 was developed for 358ci small-blocks equipped with 18-degree high-port cylinder heads. The high-port intake manifold's runners are an extension of the cylinder head ports. Its overall height is 6.75-inch.

Tie aluminum intake manifolds specifically designed for competition small-blocks equipped with high-port 18-degree cylinder heads.

PN 10185053 is the original intake manifold for high-port 18-degree heads. Introduced in 1991, this casting eliminated the spacers and expensive modifications that were previously required to adapt a conventional intake manifold to high-port heads. It was the first Bow Tie manifold designed to fit the high-port heads' unique five-degree intake flange angle. This manifold is 6.75-inch tall, measuring from the front end gasket surface to the top of the carburetor pad.

Bow Tie manifold PN 24502487 uses the same casting (and the same casting number) as manifold PN 10185053. The differences between the two are readily apparent, however. Manifold #24502487 has a square plenum opening, while #10185053 has a more oval-shaped opening. Approximately .100-inch of aluminum was added under the runners and to the outer walls of the four middle runners on the "287" manifold (last three digits of the part number) to provide more raw

BOW TIE TECH — Manifold Modification

This simple modification can enhance the performance of a competition small-block V8 equipped with a Chevrolet high-port Bow Tie intake manifold (PN 10135053).

GM Motorsports Technology Group engineers modified two Bow Tie intake manifolds by removing .100-inch and .200-inch of material respectively from the inside walls of the runners that feed the four middle cylinders (#3, 4, 5, and 6) as shown in the illustration. These modified manifolds were then dyno tested on two different engines. The results were compared with a standard ported-and-polished Bow Tie intake manifold and a popular aftermarket competition intake manifold.

Removing material from the manifold runners significantly improved the

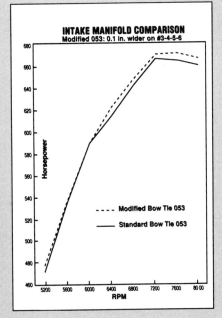

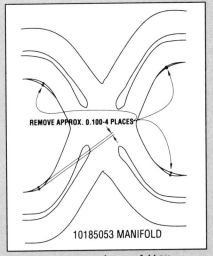

High-port Bow Tie intake manifold PN 10185053 can be modified to improve a racing small-block V8's mid-range power by removing .100-inch of material from the inside walls of the runners that feed the four middle cylinders.

performance of both engines. As shown in the accompanying graph, the most significant gains were produced in the engine's mid-range rpm. Subsequent tests have shown that removing .100-inch of material generally produces the best results.

BOW TIE TECH — Low-Port 18-Degree Intake

Low-port and high-port 18-degree Bow Tie cylinder heads have a 5-degree intake manifold flange angle. This change from the small-block V8's traditional 10-degree flange angle provides additional clearance for racing rocker arms and pushrods.

Chevrolet offers three Bow Tie intake manifolds for high-port 18-degree heads, but does not produce an intake manifold specifically for low-port versions. However, a standard Bow Tie intake manifold (PN 10051103) can be modified to fit low-port 18-degree cylinder heads. The manifold flanges must be machined to match the heads' five-degree flange angle as shown in the accompanying diagram.

On Chevrolet blueprints, the manifold flange angle is measured relative to the cylinder bore centerlines. When measuring the flange angle from the end gasket sealing surface, the flange should be remachined from a 35-degree angle to 40 degrees. The manifold bolt holes must also be enlarged and spotfaced to allow the intake bolts to tighten squarely against the manifold flange.

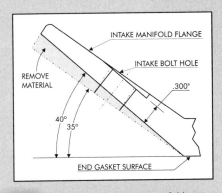

A conventional Bow Tie intake manifold (PN 10051103) can be modified to fit low-port 18-degree cylinder heads by machining its intake gasket surfaces to match the head's five-degree intake flange angle. The angles shown are measured from the end gasket sealing surface.

material for porting. The runners in the "287" manifold provide a more direct "line of sight" path from the plenum to the cylinder head ports to enhance high-rpm horsepower. Bosses were also added at the rear of the manifold to facilitate the installation of auxiliary cylinder head coolant lines.

Bow Tie intake PN 24502481 (which is both its part number and casting number) combines design elements from two previous manifold designs: Its base is derived from PN 10185053 and its top from the original "raised runner" intake PN 10051103. This manifold's runners have a smaller cross-sectional area than the ports in the "053" manifold to enhance low-speed and mid-range torque. Recommended applications for this manifold include short-track oval engines as well as small-displacement road racing (Trans-Am) and drag racing (Super Stock, Competition, etc.) motors.

The original "053" high-port Bow Tie intake was engineered for 358ci NASCAR engines. In general, the smaller runner sizes in the "281" manifold should improve performance in the 7000 rpm range, while the larger runners of the "053" and "287" intake are designed for higher engine speeds. Of course, engine displacement, cylinder head preparation, camshaft profile, and related components also play important roles in determining an engine's optimum operating range.

Fuel System

Chevrolet offers a heavy-duty mechanical fuel pump for small-block V8 engines as PN 6415325. This high-capacity pump has a removable lower housing that can be rotated to position the inlet and outlet fittings as required by the chassis and plumbing. This pump uses a standard fuel pump pushrod (PN 3704817).

An electric fuel pump should be used whenever possible to boost (or replace) the engine's mechanical fuel pump. A late-model in-tank electric pump such as PN 25116279 (included with the H.O. 350 Camaro performance package described later in this chapter) has sufficient capacity for a high-performance small-block V8. This pump produces 14 psi pressure, and has a built-in check valve to prevent reverse flow. It should be used with a fuel pressure regulator for carbureted engines; adjust the regulator to provide 6 psi fuel pressure at the carburetor.

A fuel pressure gauge should be installed between the fuel filter and carburetor. A minimum fuel pressure of at least 4 psi should be maintained at maximum engine speed with a wide open throttle. Fuel lines should be formed from neoprene rubber, steel tubing, or braided steel. *Never* use copper tubing, which will eventually crack from engine vibration.

Heavy-duty Chevrolet mechanical fuel pump PN 6415325 has a removable lower housing that can be rotated to reposition the fuel line fittings.

Install a paper element fuel filter between the fuel pump and carburetor. Discard production sintered bronze carburetor filters.

When installing a Holley four-barrel carburetor, the production sintered bronze fuel filters located inside the fuel inlet nuts should be removed and discarded. Install a single large paper element replaceable filter (PN 854619) between the fuel pump and carburetor. The fuel pressure drop through the sintered bronze filters cannot be detected because they are located after any fuel pressure gauge connection. Clogged fuel filters are frequently responsible for engine failures and poor performance.

Carburetor heat shields are available from Chevrolet for Holley four-barrel carburetors (PN 3969835) and Quadrajet carburetors (PN 3969837). These shields should be installed between the carburetor and the manifold flange to isolate the fuel in the carburetor float bowls from engine heat. A carburetor heat shield can be especially effective in curing fuel percolation problems.

A low-restriction foam or paper element air cleaner should always be used to diffuse the air entering the carburetor.

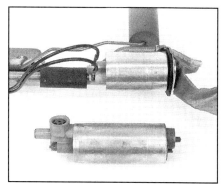

A high-volume in-line electric fuel pump such as PN 25116279 can augment or replace a mechanical fuel pump.

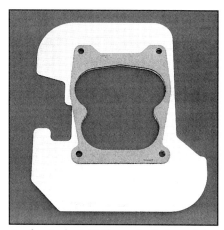

A carburetor heat shield can solve fuel percolation problems. Shields are available for Holley and Quadrajet carburetors.

BOW TIE TIPS **Gasket Guide**

The following gasket sets are available for Chevrolet small-block V8 intake manifolds (2 gaskets per set):

10147994	For production and standard runner heads
10185042	For splayed valve cylinder head #10185040
10185007	For high-port 18-degree cylinder heads #10134363-4 and 24502482

The fuel mixture distribution can be upset if no diffuser is used, causing poor power and misfiring at high engine speeds. A 14-inch diameter open element chromed air cleaner assembly for single four-barrel carburetors is available from Chevrolet as PN 12341859. This air cleaner assembly is supplied with a three-inch tall filter element (PN 6421746, AC #A212CW). A taller four-inch element is available as PN 8997189 (AC #A697C).

Lubrication System

The information in this section applies specifically to the Chevrolet small-block V8. Refer to the chapter on lubrication systems for general information on oil system requirements, wet sump and dry sump design, oil filters, and oil recommendations.

When properly assembled and installed in a vehicle with the correct oil pan, pump, coolers and filters, the Chevrolet small-block V8 is remarkably free of failures caused by inadequate lubrication. Diagrams of the basic engine lubrication system are shown on page 86.

The production small-block oiling system is suitable for high-performance and most moderate competition uses. Several Bow Tie blocks are available with "priority main" oiling systems and front-inlet main oil galleries for maximum-effort racing applications. See the cylinder block section in this chapter for information on these race-prepared blocks.

Oil Pump

Two high-performance oil pumps are available for the small-block Chevrolet V8. The production Z28/LT-l oil pump (PN 3848907) has 1.20-inch long gears. A high-volume, high-pressure version with 1.50-inch long gears is available as PN 14044872.

Both pumps are supplied without pickups and screens, which must be ordered separately to suit the particular oil pan configuration. Oil pump pickups should always be tack-welded or brazed to the pump body. This will prevent the pickup from vibrating loose when the engine is running. (Remove the oil pressure regulating spring before brazing to prevent heat damage.)

The production small-block V8 oil pump intermediate driveshaft (PN 3998287) is attached to the oil pump with a plastic retaining sleeve (PN 3764554). The sleeve should be replaced whenever the pump and driveshaft are disassembled for service. Shafts with steel couplers are available from aftermarket suppliers; if you are using an all-steel shaft, make sure that the coupler is securely pinned to the shaft. Also note that 400ci small-blocks require pump shafts with a reduced diameter to prevent possible interference caused by the block's 2.65-inch diameter main bearings.

Oil pressure is regulated by a bypass spring located in the oil pump cover. The production high-performance spring (PN 3848911, color coded with a white stripe) will usually produce 65-70 psi oil pressure even with a remote oil filter and cooler. Any oil pressure above 65 psi at operating speeds is usually sufficient for high-performance use. (A general rule of thumb is that a racing engine requires 10 psi oil pressure for every 1,000 rpm. Using this formula, an engine that runs 7,000 rpm needs approximately 70 psi oil pressure.) Inadequate oil pressure can result in bearing failures and engine damage.

H.O. Air Cleaner

1983-86 Camaros equipped with 305ci L69 engines had dual snorkel air cleaners with cold air ducts as original equipment. This "ram air" system improved performance by supplying cool outside air to the carburetor.

The L69 air cleaner assembly is included with the H.O. 350 performance package for 1982-87 Camaros (PN 10185077). It can be adapted to other vehicles equipped with Quadrajet carburetors for improved off-highway performance. The duct inlets should be mounted behind the grille.

The components of the L69 cold air intake package include:

Part Number	Description
25043641	Air cleaner assembly
14070917	Left-hand duct
14070918	Right-hand duct
14073299	Left-hand hose
14083990	Right-hand hose
14048874	Stud
25512090	Wing nut
469506	Hot air tube
3970070	Fresh air elbow

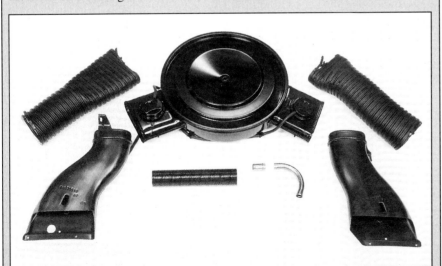

A dual snorkel air cleaner assembly originally used on L69 Camaros can be adapted to other vehicles. This "ram air" system ducts cool outside air to the carburetor inlet.

A high-volume oil pump (PN 14044872—right) has .300-inch longer gears than a production small-block oil pump.

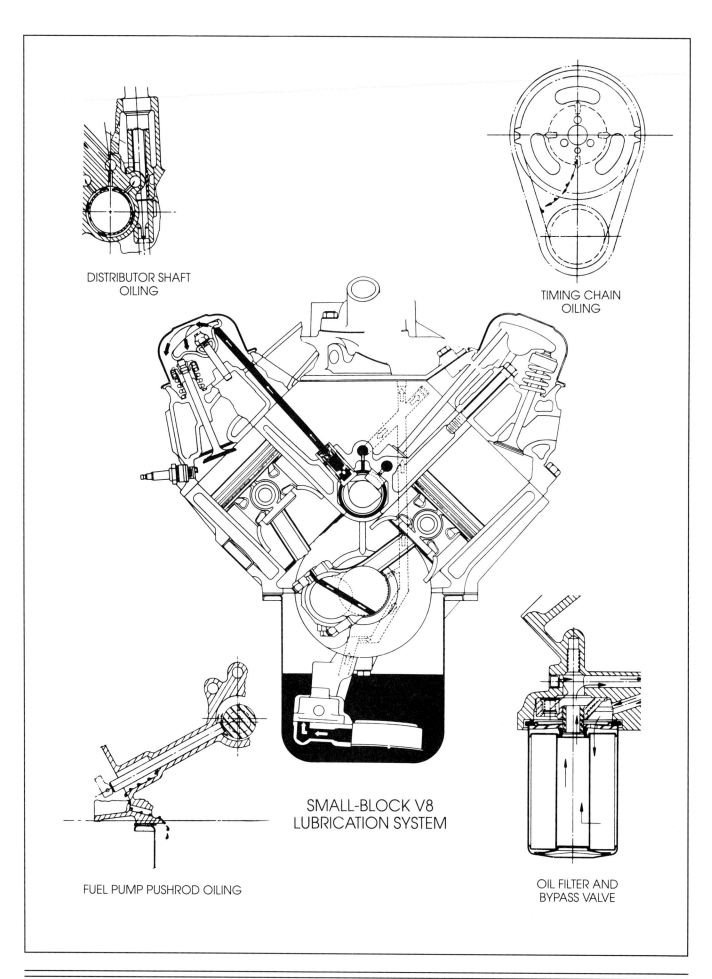

DISTRIBUTOR SHAFT
OILING

TIMING CHAIN
OILING

SMALL-BLOCK V8
LUBRICATION SYSTEM

FUEL PUMP PUSHROD OILING

OIL FILTER AND
BYPASS VALVE

If the oil pressure is insufficient, the pump bypass spring can be shimmed to increase oil pressure by inserting small washers or a Holley carburetor jet inside the bypass piston. Be careful not to use so many spacers that the bypass piston will not uncover the bypass port in the oil pump cover. If the bypass port is blocked by the piston, very high cold oil pressure may blow out the oil filter seal or cause excessive distributor wear due to high loading.

Oil Pan

When selecting an oil pan for a small-block Chevrolet V8, the pan must be compatible with the block's rear crankshaft seal and the dipstick location.

Three different oil pans designs have been used on production Chevrolet small-block V8 engines. Pre-1980 blocks have the oil dipstick on the left-hand (driver's) side. Blocks produced from 1980-85

Extended pickups for deep oil pans should be braced to prevent damage caused by engine vibration. Braze or tack-weld the pickup.

Production oil pump intermediate driveshafts use plastic couplings; all-steel shafts are available from aftermarket suppliers.

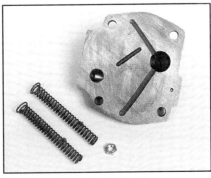

A pressure relief spring in the oil pump cover regulates oil pressure. Install shims or washers to increase the oil pressure.

have dipsticks on the right-hand (passenger's) side. Regardless of the dipstick location, all oil pans for pre-1986 engines are designed to fit rear main bearing caps with two-piece crankshaft seals.

A one-piece rear crankshaft seal design was introduced on production small-block V8 engines at the start of the 1986 model year. This one-piece seal replaced the two-piece seal design used previously. This change required a revised oil pan design to fit a new rear seal retainer that is bolted to the back of the engine block. A one-piece formed neoprene oil pan gasket replaced the four-piece gasket set used on pre-1986 production engines. 1986 and newer oil pans have right-hand dipsticks.

Cast iron Bow Tie blocks have provisions for both right-hand and left-hand oil

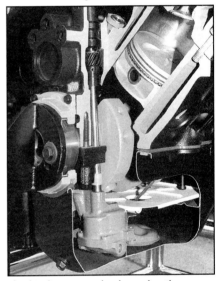

The distributor gear also drives the oil pump. Check the length of the intermediate oil pump driveshaft before final assembly.

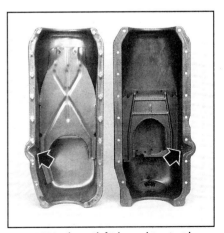

A pre-1980 oil pan (left) has a driver's side dipstick; later pans have a passenger's side dipstick (right). The pan must match the block.

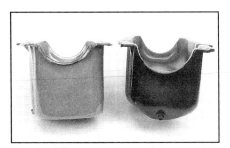

Note the difference in the size of the rear oil pan seal on a pre-1986 oil pan (left) and a 1986 and later oil pan (right).

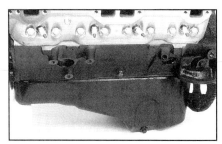

Five-quart oil pan PN 10110837 for 1986-up small-blocks will clear the front crossmember in a Camaro or Chevelle chassis.

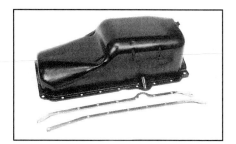

Six-quart Corvette oil pan PN 10055765 for 1986-up small-blocks has an elongated sump. Late-model pans use pan rail reinforcements.

A windage tray separates the oil in the sump from the rapidly spinning crankshaft assembly. The tray mounts on extended main cap studs.

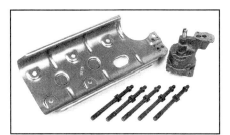

Curved windage tray PN 3927136 is used with Z28/LT-1 oil pans with left-hand dipsticks. This tray requires five mounting studs.

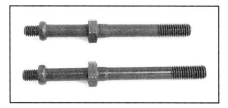

1955-67 blocks use 5¼-inch long windage tray mounting studs (PN 3872718); 1968-up blocks require 5⅝-inch long studs (PN 14087508).

dipsticks; however, dipstick holes are not drilled in cast iron Bow Tie blocks. Aluminum blocks have provisions only for left-hand dipsticks.

If you are using crankshaft adapter PN 10051188 to convert a block originally machined for a one-piece rear seal to a two-piece seal, you must use an oil pan and gasket designed for 1986 and newer engines. The exceptions to this rule are aluminum Bow Tie blocks and race-prepared cast iron Bow Tie blocks (PN 24502501 and 24502503); these blocks have special rear main bearing caps that use a pre-1986 oil pan.

Chevrolet offers an oil pan with six-quart capacity (including filter) for small-block V8s as PN 359942. This pan was original equipment on 1963-65 and 1969-71 high-performance Corvettes. It features internal baffling and an elongated sump (which may not clear undercarriage components in other chassis). This pan has a left-hand dipstick, and is designed for 1985 and earlier blocks with two-piece rear seals.

Five-quart oil pan PN 465220 offers more chassis clearance, and should be used in applications where the Corvette pan will not fit. This production Z28/L-82 oil pan also has internal baffling, and has proven satisfactory in competition use. It has a left-hand dipstick, and is designed for pre-1986 blocks with two-piece rear seals.

There are two good oil pan choices for 1986 and newer blocks with one-piece rear seals. PN 10055765 is a late-model Corvette six-quart pan. PN 10110837 is a five-quart version that will clear the front frame crossmember in Camaros, Chevelles, and similar chassis. (This pan is original equipment on H.O. 350 engine assemblies.) Both of these pans have right-hand dipsticks and fit blocks with one-piece rear seals. They should be installed with oil pan rail reinforcements PN 14088501 (left-hand) and 14088502

(right-hand). These pans can be used as cores to fabricate custom oil pans for competition engines.

Overfilling a wet sump oil pan to increase its oil capacity is not recommended. Adding oil beyond the pan's designed capacity may cause the lubricant to overheat and the oil pressure to fluctuate if the oil is aerated by the spinning crankshaft assembly.

A magnetic oil drain plug (PN 23011420) is inexpensive insurance for any high-performance engine. It will collect and hold small particles of engine debris until they can be removed during oil changes. Close inspection of the metal chips can also reveal internal engine problems before they reach a critical stage.

Windage Trays

The purpose of an oil splash shield ("windage tray") is to retard aeration of the engine lubricant by separating the oil in the pan from the rapidly spinning crank-

A late-model Corvette oil-to-water cooler will reduce normal oil operating temperature ten percent. Faster warm-ups are a bonus.

The Corvette heat exchanger is sandwiched between the oil filter pad and the filter. Coolant circulates from the block's drain plugs.

An HEI distributor from an H.O. 350 engine has a high-performance spark curve and conventional mechanical/vacuum advance.

shaft assembly. A windage tray can also improve internal oil control and prevent oil slosh on rapid braking. Chevrolet windage trays are installed on special main cap bolts with extended mounting studs.

Chevrolet offers two sheetmetal windage trays for small-block V8s. PN 3927136 is a semi-circular tray with a cut-out for a left-hand dipstick; this tray can be used with oil pan PN 465220. PN 10147830 is a flat tray designed for late-model Corvette oil pan PN 10147830. It requires a right-hand oil dipstick.

Both small-block windage trays require special mounting studs that replace several main cap bolts. The curved tray requires five studs; the flat tray uses three. 1955-67 blocks with small journal main bearings use 5¼-inch long studs (PN 3872718); 1968 and later engines with medium and large main bearing journals use 5⅝-inch long studs (PN 14087508). When installing a windage tray on a 400ci small-block, it is necessary to elongate the tray's mounting holes to compensate for the wider spacing of the 400 block's main bearing bolts.

When installing a windage tray, always make sure there is sufficient clearance between the tray and the connecting rods. This is especially important when using a long-stroke crankshaft or aftermarket connecting rods.

Oil Cooler

An oil cooler may be necessary in some applications to maintain the desired oil temperature. If a remote-mounted oil filter is used, it should be plumbed so the oil is filtered before it is returned to the engine to prevent contamination of the engine bearings. The remote filter adapter should be designed to use a non-bypassing filter. Check the adapter to make sure

that the upper cavity of the block's oil filter pad is completely sealed to eliminate partial bypassing.

An oil cooler with its inlet and outlet fittings on opposite ends is preferred. This design minimizes restrictions and pressure loss as the oil flows through the cooler core. Oil cooler lines should have a minimum inside diameter of ½-inch in all installations.

An oil cooler is a good addition to any high-performance small-block. An oil-to-water cooler was optional on late-model Corvettes. This Corvette oil cooler assembly (PN 14084369) circulates engine coolant through a heat exchanger mounted between the block's oil filter pad and the oil filter element. The benefits of this system include faster engine warm-up, more consistent oil temperatures, and a reduction in normal oil operating temperature of approximately ten percent. This cooler assembly requires an adapter (PN 14088848), gasket (PN 326100), seal (PN 14015353), and connector (PN 3853870). For coolant lines, use 1985-86 Corvette service parts.

Ignition System

Distributors are interchangeable between small-block and standard height big-block Chevrolet V8s. Chevrolet small-block V8 engines produced through 1974 were equipped with conventional breaker point distributors. In 1969 production distributors were converted to aluminum housings, except for Corvette models which retained a cast iron mechanical tach drive distributor until 1975.

HEI Distributor

The Chevrolet high energy ignition (HEI) introduced in 1975 is a transistor-

ized ignition with special heavy-duty temperature-resistant plug wires and boots. The HEI system is an excellent choice for street high-performance and moderate competition uses. However, the HEI distributor's physical size may interfere with other underhood components when space is limited.

The HEI distributor assembly (PN 1103436) included with the H.O. 350 engine assembly is recommended for most high-performance applications. This distributor has conventional centrifugal and vacuum advance mechanisms, and its spark curve is suitable for most emissions-exempt engines.

An HEI ignition system requires a 12-volt power supply for proper operation. In racing installations, the HEI should be connected directly to the battery through a high-quality ignition switch as shown in the ignition chapter. If you are installing an HEI ignition in an early-model vehicle originally equipped with a point-type ignition, be sure to remove or bypass the resistor in the wiring harness to ensure the HEI receives a full 12 volts.

Electronic Distributors
PN 10134355 and 10093387

Chevrolet markets two heavy-duty distributors for competition small-block V8s. PN 10134355 features a cast aluminum housing, a hardened shaft, and a ground and hardened centrifugal advance cam. This distributor has a high-output magnetic pickup to trigger a heavy-duty ignition amplifier (PN 10037378), and uses a standard small diameter V8 distributor cap. It does not have a mechanical tach drive, but it can be used with several GM electronic tachometers (PN 10038474, 10185001, and 10185002). This distributor and related components

Heavy-duty distributors, ignitions, and coils are available for Chevrolet V8s. Distributors are interchangeable between small-block and short-deck big-block engines.

The ignition advance curve can be tailored with springs and bushings included with Chevrolet electronic distributors.

Distributor Oiling

Electronic distributor PN 10093387 has provisions to seal the distributor hole in the engine block's right-hand lifter oil gallery. The shaft housing is grooved for two Viton "O"-rings which are supplied with the distributor. Installing these "O"-rings will increase oil pressure and improve the engine's internal oil control by sealing the distributor hole in the lifter oil gallery. A .030" bleed hole at the housing base sprays pressurized oil onto the distributor and camshaft gears to reduce wear.

The engine block *must* be modified to use this feature; do not install the "O"-rings unless the block has been modified. Refer to the accompanying illustration for required modifications. (If the "O"-rings are not installed, the oil pressure will be the same as if a standard distributor was used.)

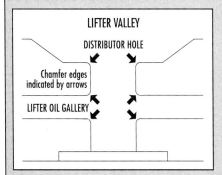

Chamfer the upper and lower edges of the distributor hole in the block when using a distributor with "O"-ring seals.

An oil bleed hole in the billet distributor's housing lubricates the distributor and camshaft gears.

are described in detail in the ignition system chapter.

Electronic distributor PN 10093387 is machined from a solid billet of aluminum to eliminate porosity and casting flaws. The polished and heat-treated steel shaft is .500-inch in diameter to reduce flex at high rpm. The shaft turns in a precision ball bearing at the top of the distributor housing and a sintered bushing at the bottom. These low-friction bearings ensure stable spark timing beyond 10,000 rpm.

The billet distributor's molded Rynite glass-reinforced base features an integral steel reinforcing plate. The distributor cap can be retained with either spring clips or socket head cap screws.

The centrifugal advance weights are mounted on chrome moly steel pins to prevent bending at high rpm. The weights glide on nylon bushings, responding quickly to changes in engine speed. The centrifugal advance cam is welded to the distributor shaft for durability. An assortment of springs and advance limit bushings is included with the billet electronic distributor. These can be used to tailor the ignition advance curve to suit virtually any high-performance application.

The billet distributor housing shaft has an adjustable slip collar that can be repositioned to compensate for changes in the height of the intake manifold's distributor pad. This feature allows the camshaft gear and distributor gears to be properly aligned regardless of modifications made to the block, cylinder heads, or manifold.

The electronic distributor's high-output magnetic pickup never needs adjusting. The trigger plugs directly into GM Performance Parts wiring harnesses (PN 10039932 and 10037377) with a reliable Weatherpack connector. A strain relief on the pickup wire eliminates chafing and kinking. The reluctor (trigger wheel) is plated to prevent corrosion. The magnetic trigger can be used to control a heavy-duty electronic ignition (PN 10037378).

Spark Plug Wires

A solid core spark plug wire kit for the small-block V8 is available as PN 12043789. This kit includes stainless steel wire conductors with high temperature silicon insulation. Its 90-degree spark plug terminals are suitable for most small-block V8 installations.

This plug wire set is designed for socket-type distributor caps, and cannot be used with HEI distributors. Also, because this is a solid conductor wire, it generates electrical (RF) interference that can disrupt the operation of onboard computers, rev limiters, pit radios, and other electronic devices.

A high-quality RF-suppression spark plug wire set is available as PN 10037375. This wire set has Monel solid core wires that reduce current loss and minimize interference with electronic devices. The wire resistance is less than 150 ohms per foot. Thick 8mm insulation prevents cross-firing and arcing. The extra-long leads can be cut to size for custom installations. Distributor terminals for socket-type distributor caps are included with this wire set.

Starters

The diameter of the flywheel determines which heavy-duty starter should be installed on a small-block V8. Flywheels with two different diameters are used on Chevrolet small-block V8 engines. Large flywheels are 14 inches in diameter, and have 168 teeth on the starter ring gear. Small diameter flywheels are 12¾-inch in diameter, and have starter ring gears with 153 teeth.

This difference in flywheel diameter requires two distinct starter housings. Starter noses used with large diameter flywheels have two offset bolt holes; the bolt holes in starters for small flywheels are parallel to the back of the block. Most, but not all, Chevrolet small-blocks are drilled for both types of starters.

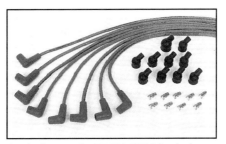

Spark plug wire kit PN 12043789 has high temperature silicone boots and stainless steel solid conductor wire.

Many starter problems can be cured by using a production brace to support the motor and reduce the load on the starter nose.

Two heavy-duty starters are available for Chevrolet small-block V8 engines. (Note that small-block starter motors are interchangeable with big-block V8 and many V6/90 engines.) Starter PN 1108789 is used with 12¾-inch diameter flywheels and flexplates; PN 1108400 is for 14-inch diameter flywheels.

These starters can be converted to fit a different diameter flywheel by installing the appropriate starter nose. Starter nose PN 1968122 is used with 12¾-inch diameter flywheels; its bolt holes are

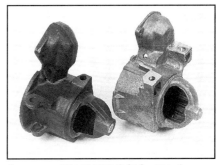

Starter nose PN 1984098 (left) for 14-inch flywheels has offset bolt holes; PN 1968122 for 12¾-inch flywheels has straight across bolts.

Use heavy-duty starter motor PN 1109789 with 12¾-inch diameter flywheels and flexplates with 153 teeth on the ring gear.

straight across. PN 1984098 is used with 14-inch diameter flywheels; its bolt holes are offset.

Chevrolet starter motors use special shouldered bolts that register the starter on the block. These bolts are PN 14097278 (⅜-16 x 4²¹⁄₆₄) and PN 14097279 (⅜-16 x 1²⁷⁄₃₂).

Many starter problems can be traced to inadequate support for the starter motor. Starter brace PN 354353 will reduce the load on the starter nose.

Gear Reduction Starter

BOW TIE TIPS

A lightweight starter (PN 10455702) was introduced on 1988 Corvettes. This starter has an internal gear reduction and weighs just over 10 pounds—approximately nine pounds less than a conventional starter. It also offers additional clearance for competition oil pans and chassis components, and is used by many front-running Chevrolet stock car teams. This starter fits a 12¾-inch diameter flywheel.

Installing an aluminum water pump (PN 14011012) is an easy way to reduce engine weight. This casting has short mounting legs.

Aluminum small-block V8 water pumps have high-flow cast iron rotors, ¾-inch shafts, and heavy-duty bearings.

Some late-model production water pumps used with serpentine accessory drive systems have a reverse-rotation impeller.

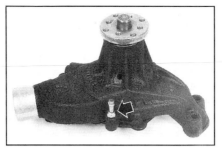

A boss on the bottom of the aluminum water pump can be drilled and tapped for a cam stop bolt to limit forward camshaft movement.

Machine the reinforcing ribs on the snout of an aluminum water pump for clearance when using a small diameter cog-type pulley.

Cast iron water pump PN 10048917 is installed on H.O. 350 engines. It has long mounting legs and a standard rotation impeller.

Deep-groove pulleys and captured dual drive belts (PN 9433722) can be used without an alternator or idler pulley.

Cooling System

A lightweight aluminum water pump for the small-block Chevrolet is available as PN 14011012. This heavy-duty water pump has a ¾-inch shaft, a reinforced snout, a high-flow cast iron rotor, and 1.50-inch diameter bearings. The housing has a boss under the snout that can be drilled and tapped for a cam stop bolt to limit forward camshaft movement when using roller lifters.

The small-block aluminum water pump has short mounting legs as used on all pre-1969 engines and 1969-82 Corvettes. Water pump spacers are available from speed shops and aftermarket manufacturers if long mounting legs are required for a particular installation. A service replacement bearing and shaft assembly for this pump is available as PN 908101.

Two production cast iron pumps are suitable for high-performance engines. PN 10048921 was used on 1971-82 Cor-vettes, and has short mounting legs. A version with long mounting legs is PN 10048917; this pump is installed on H.O. 350 engine assemblies. Both pumps have heavy-duty ¾-inch shafts; the end of the shaft on PN 10048917 is reduced to ⅝-inch to fit production pulleys.

Deep-groove pulleys are recommended for high-performance engines to prevent belt loss at high engine speeds. A 6¾-inch diameter two-groove crankshaft pulley for short water pumps is available as PN 3858533. The corresponding two-groove 7⅛-inch diameter water pump pulley is listed as PN 3770245. (This pulley has a ⅝-inch diameter shaft hole, and must be modified for use with a ¾-inch shaft aluminum water pump.) A special "captured" ⅜ x 34-inch fan belt (PN 9433722) can be used with these crankshaft and water pump pulleys without an alternator or idler pulley.

Exhaust System

Early-model Corvette "ram's horn" cast iron manifolds with 2½-inch diameter outlets are an excellent choice when tubular headers cannot be used. These Corvette components are popular in racing classes which require the use of cast iron exhaust manifolds. (Note that Corvette manifolds will not fit Chevelle and Camaro chassis without frame modifications.) A dual exhaust system with low-

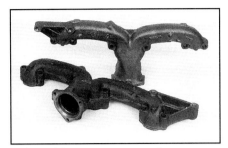

Early-model Corvette cast iron exhaust manifolds with 2½-inch diameter outlets are popular in restricted racing classes.

IROC-Z Camaro exhaust manifolds have 2¼-inch outlets instead of the 1⅞-inch outlets found on most late-model manifolds.

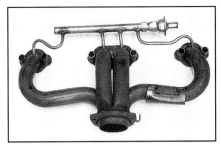

Late-model Corvette stainless steel tubular exhaust manifolds can be adapted to street rods and other emission-exempt vehicles.

restriction Corvette mufflers and a 2-inch diameter cross-over pipe ahead of the mufflers will perform quite well on high-performance small-blocks that are not subject to emission regulations.

Three "ram's horn" manifolds are available. Two are left-hand (driver's side) manifolds: PN 3797901 has a generator mount on the side of the casting; PN 3846563 has a generator mount on the end. PN 3814970 is right-hand manifold with a generator mount on the side of the casting.

GM Motorsports Technology Group engineers developed a low-restriction exhaust system specifically for 1982-87 Camaros as part of the emission-legal H.O. 350 performance package. IROC-Z Camaro cast iron exhaust manifolds with 2¼-inch outlets were selected for this conversion kit. These manifolds (PN 14094063–left and PN 14094064–right) have higher airflow potential than the manifolds with 1⅞-inch outlets originally installed on many production Chevrolet engines. They will also clear the raised rocker cover rails on H.O. 350 aluminum cylinder heads.

The H.O. 350 performance package exhaust system for 1982-87 Camaros also includes dual catalytic converters, a specially designed Y-shaped intermediate pipe, a large diameter tailpipe, and a low-restriction muffler. See the H.O. 350 section in this chapter for more information.

1986-90 Corvettes were equipped with stainless tubular exhaust manifolds which are suitable for engine swaps, street rods, and other non-stock small-block V8 installations. PN 14087511 (left) and PN 10055734 (right) are two typical small-block tubular exhaust manifolds that can be adapted to many chassis.

A small-block racing engine should be equipped with a well designed and carefully constructed header exhaust system whenever a non-production exhaust sys-

tem is legal. The exact pipe diameter and length that will produce the best engine performance depends on several factors, including engine displacement, operating rpm range, camshaft profile, induction

system, and cylinder head selection. The chassis configuration must also be considered when designing a tubular header system. Exhaust systems may also require mufflers to meet noise regulations.

"Street Legal" Exhaust System

Stainless steel headers for 1985-92 Camaros are available as components of the GM Performance Parts "Street Legal" Performance Packages. (These packages are legal for street use in 49 states; they are legal in California only for racing vehicles which may never be driven on public highways.)

The SLP headers use a "Tri-Y" design that substantially increases torque and horsepower from 1500 to 5500 rpm. 1⅝-inch diameter primary tubes join two cylinders on each bank; the pairs of primary pipes from each side of the engine are then routed to a single 3-inch diameter outlet. This system can provide superior performance over a wider range of engine speeds than conventional "4-into-1" headers.

SLP headers for Camaros are manufactured from mandrel-bent 409 stainless steel tubing. This alloy has twice the corrosion resistance of mild steel, and it is able to withstand high temperatures without cracking. The SLP exhaust system features all stainless steel components from the catalytic converter back. The system includes a 3-inch diameter stainless steel tailpipe and a low-restriction stainless steel muffler.

This exhaust system produces up to a 10 horsepower increase, depending on application. For additional information and part numbers, see the GM Performance Parts catalog.

GM Performance Parts SLP headers for 1985-92 Camaros use a "Tri-Y" design that boosts low-speed and mid-range torque.

The SLP exhaust system includes a low-restriction stainless steel muffler and a 3-inch diameter tailpipe.

Competition exhaust systems must maximize engine output while meeting the noise regulations imposed by many sanctioning bodies.

Headers with 1⅝ or 1¾-inch diameter primary pipes are recommended for most emission-exempt street performance applications.

For street performance and limited competition applications, primary pipe dimensions of 1⅝ or 1¾-inch OD x 30 inches long feeding 3¼ to 3½-inch collectors have proven successful. Large displacement and high-rpm engines typically respond well to 1⅞ to 2⅛-inch primary tubes, measuring 32 to 34 inches in length with 3½ to 4½-inch tailpipes.

Some Chevrolet engine builders have found improved performance with "step headers." This header design uses primary pipes that grow progressively larger in diameter. For example, the primary tubes may be 1⅞-inch diameter at the exhaust ports, increasing to 2-inch and 2⅛-inch diameter downstream. "Cross-over" pipes that connect the header collectors of the two cylinder banks have also produced positive results in many instances.

H.O. 350 Camaro Performance Package

GM Motorsports Technology Group engineers developed an emission-legal conversion kit to install a High Output 5.7-liter (350ci) small-block V8 in a 1982-87 Camaro originally equipped with an LG4 or L69 305ci V8 engine and a 700R4 automatic transmission. This coordinated package of components significantly improves vehicle performance while retaining all required emission controls.

During development of the H.O. 350 Camaro performance package, a prototype H.O. 350 engine equipped with a computer-controlled Quadrajet carburetor and all emission controls required for this application produced 308 horsepower (at 5000 rpm) and 365 lb.-ft. torque (at 3500 rpm). A 1987 Camaro test vehicle equipped with the H.O. 350 performance package ran a quarter-mile elapsed time of 13.83 seconds at 98 mph.

The H.O. 350 performance package retains all required emission equipment for 1982-87 Camaros originally equipped with an LG4 or L69 305ci V8 engine and a 700R4 automatic transmission.

A dual-snorkel air cleaner and flexible ducts supply cool air to the engine.

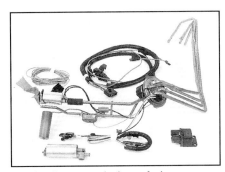

A high-volume in-tank electric fuel pump replaces the standard Camaro pump. A regulator reduces the fuel pressure to 6 psi.

A replacement servo piston, pressure regulator spring, and boost valve improve the 700R4 transmission's shift firmness.

The H.O. 350 performance package includes a replacement Engine Control Module with a specially programmed PROM chip.

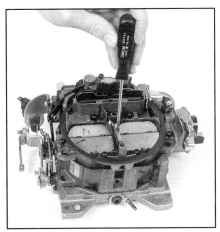

The H.O. 350 performance package retains the LG4/L69 computer-controlled Quadrajet carburetor. New secondary metering rods are supplied with the conversion kit.

When all components are installed as specified in the instruction manual, the H.O. 350 conversion meets emission requirements under EPA Memorandum 1A for operation in 49 states (excluding California). The conversion is also legal for sale and use in California under California Air Resources Board Exemption Order #D-278.

Note that the *entire* H.O. 350 conversion package must be installed exactly as described in the manual to comply with emissions regulations. Also note that this conversion is certified *only* for the specific year models, engines, and transmissions listed above.

The H.O. 350 conversion is designed for "do-it-yourself" installation. A comprehensive instruction manual is included. Minor welding is required to install the exhaust system.

The H.O. Camaro conversion is a coordinated package of components that work together to improve vehicle performance. The heart of the Camaro conversion is the H.O. 350 Chevrolet small-block V8 (PN

A low-restriction exhaust system with high-flow exhaust manifolds, dual catalytic converters, Y-shaped intermediate pipe, large diameter single tailpipe, and a transverse muffler improves performance.

10185072) described earlier in this chapter. The other major components include:

Air Cleaner. A "ram air" system channels cool air to a dual-snorkel air cleaner through flexible ducts.

Fuel Pump. A high-volume in-tank electric pump meets the H.O. engine's fuel requirements. The pump kit includes vent lines, a sending unit, and a wiring harness. An adjustable external regulator controls fuel pressure.

Exhaust System. The H.O. 350 performance package includes a low-restriction exhaust system with dual catalytic converters, high-flow exhaust manifolds

with 2¼-inch outlets, a single 3-inch diameter tailpipe, and a transverse muffler.

Calibration. The kit includes an engine control module (ECM), specially programmed PROM chips, a coolant fan switch, an electronic spark control (ESC) module, and Quadrajet secondary metering rods.

Transmission. A pressure regulator spring, boost valve, and servo assembly improve the 700R4 automatic transmission's shift firmness.

Rear Control Arms. Rear axle control arms with high-durometer (50K) bushings reduce wheel hop under acceleration. ⌐

TECH SPECS: CAST IRON BLOCK BOLT TORQUE AND LUBRICANT RECOMMENDATIONS

	Torque	Lubricant
Main Bearing Cap:		
Inner Bolt ($^7/_{16}$")	70 ft.-lbs.	Molykote
Outer Bolt ($^7/_{16}$")	65	Molykote
Inner Stud ($^7/_{16}$")	65	Oil
Outer Stud ($^3/_8$")	60	Oil
Outer Bolt ($^3/_8$")	40	Oil
Connecting Rod Bolt ($^3/_8$")	45-50 ft.-lbs. (.006" stretch preferred)	Oil
Bow Tie Connecting Rod Bolt ($^7/_{16}$")	70 ft.-lbs. (.005-.006" stretch preferred)	Oil
Cylinder Head Bolt	65 ft.-lbs.	Sealant (Use oil in blind-tapped bolt holes in Bow Tie blocks)
Rocker Arm Stud:		
Cast Iron Head	50	Sealant
Aluminum Head	50	Oil
Camshaft Sprocket	20	Oil
Intake Manifold, Iron Head	30	Oil
Flywheel	60	Oil
Bellhousing	25	Oil
Spark Plugs:		
Conventional Gasket, Iron Head	25	Dry
Conventional Gasket, Alum. Head	25	Anti-seize
Tapered Seat, Iron Head	15	Dry
Tapered Seat, Alum. Head	15	Anti-seize
Exhaust Manifold	25	Anti-seize
Oil Pan Bolt	165 in.-lbs.	Oil
Front Cover Bolt	75 in.-lbs.	Oil
Rocker Cover	25 in.-lbs.	Oil

TECH SPECS: ALUMINUM BLOCK BOLT TORQUE AND LUBRICANT RECOMMENDATIONS

	Torque	Lubricant
Main Bearing:		
Inner Stud ($^7/_{16}$")	65 ft.-lbs.	Oil
Outer Stud ($^3/_8$")	60	Oil
Outer Bolt ($^3/_8$")	40	Oil
Bow Tie Connecting Rod Bolt ($^7/_{16}$")	70 ft.-lbs. (.005-.006" stretch preferred)	Oil
Head Studs—$^7/_{16}$" NF Thread:		
Long	65	Oil
Short	60	Oil
Rocker Arm Stud	50	Oil
Camshaft Sprocket	20	Oil
Intake Manifold, Alum. Head	25	Anti-Seize
Flywheel	60	Oil
Bell Housing	25	Anti-Seize
Spark Plugs:		
Conventional Gasket, Alum. Head	25	Anti-seize
Tapered Seat, Alum. Head	15	Anti-seize
Exhaust Manifold	20	Anti-seize
Oil Pan Bolt	165 in.-lbs.	Anti-seize
Front Cover Bolt	75 in.-lbs.	Anti-seize
Rocker Cover	25 in.-lbs.	Anti-seize

TECH SPECS: RECOMMENDED SPECIFICATIONS FOR HIGH-PERFORMANCE SMALL-BLOCK V8

Firing Order	1-8-4-3-6-5-7-2
Spark Advance	Maximum of 40-44 (32-34 degrees w/18°heads)
Maximum Oil Temp	270 degrees in oil pan
Minimum Fuel Pressure	4-5 psi at maximum engine speed
Piston to Bore	.006-.007" measured at centerline of wrist pin hole perpendicular to pin for Chevrolet forged piston; .002-.003" for cast pistons. Follow manufacturer's recommendations for other pistons. Finish bores with 400 grit stones or equivalent.
Minimum Piston Ring End Gap	Top .018"; 2nd .016"; Oil Rails .016"
Wrist Pin	.0006-.0008" in piston. (.0005-.0008" in bushed rod for floating pin. 0-.005" end play preferred)
Rod Bearing	.002-.0025"; side clearance .010-.020"
Main Bearing	.002-.003", minimum preferred; .005-.007" end play
Piston to Cylinder Head	.035" minimum
Valve Lash	As specified by camshaft manufacturer. See text for recommended lash for Chevrolet camshafts.
Valve to Piston Clearance	.045" exhaust and intake at running valve lash . NOTE: These are absolute minimum clearances for an engine running below the valvetrain limiting speed. More clearance must be allowed for engines operating at valvetrain limiting speed; allow .080" intake and .100" exhaust valve clearance for high rpm engines.
Valve to Guide	Inlet .0018" and Exhaust .0025" minimum for racing

NOTES:

Chevrolet Big-Block V8

454ci Mark IV

The Chevrolet big-block has flexed its muscles in street machines, Can-Am road racers, NASCAR stock cars, Pro Stock drag racers, offshore powerboats, modified oval track cars, and truck pulls. With its innovative splayed-valve cylinder heads, rugged block design, and trouble-free oiling system, the big-block V8 has rightfully earned its reputation as an extremely powerful and dependable engine.

The Chevrolet big-block V8 is the engine of choice for applications that demand maximum horsepower and rock-solid reliability. A direct descendent of the famous Mark II "Mystery Motor" of 1963, the Mark IV big-block debuted in 1965. The Chevrolet big-block V8 was revised and updated in 1991, and rechristened the Gen V.

The big-block Chevrolet V8 has been produced in displacements ranging from 366 to 502 cubic inches. Production versions of the big-block V8 were offered in a wide variety of Chevrolet vehicles in the late Sixties and early Seventies, including Corvettes, Chevelles, Novas, Camaros, and full-size passenger cars. Currently the Gen V version is available in light- and medium-duty Chevrolet trucks, and in over-the-counter high-performance engine assemblies.

An assortment of special service packages and heavy-duty components has also been developed for the big-block Chevrolet. The big-block's high-performance pedigree includes linerless aluminum blocks that allowed displacements up to 510ci and heavy-duty Bow Tie blocks that have given engine builders the hardware to assemble behemoth 600+ cubic inch powerplants. Advances in cylinder

- Bigger Is Better
- An Irresistible Force in Racing
- Splayed-Valve Innovations
- Gen V: The New Generation

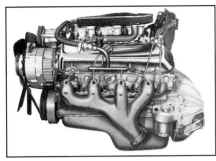

The musclecar era reached its zenith with the advent of the big-block Chevrolet V8. Induction systems ranged from Quadrajet and Holley single four-barrels to the Corvette's triple two-barrel carburetors.

Restorers have rediscovered the appeal of Chevy's biggest V8. Big-blocks were available in models ranging from Novas to Monte Carlos.

The big-block Chevrolet V8 is a winner on water, too. This supercharged Chevy powered a championship-winning Grand Prix hydroplane.

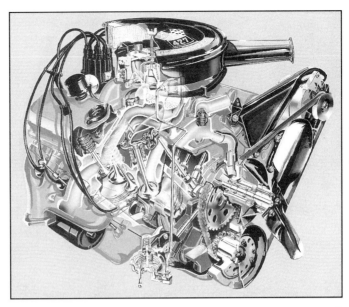

The Chevrolet big-block V8 opened a new avenue to performance with its free-breathing cylinder heads and rugged construction. Introduced in 1965 with a displacement of 396 cubic inches, the big-block grew to a 510ci behemoth in the early Seventies.

The most exotic big-block to reach the streets was the all-aluminum 1969 427ci ZL-1. The limited-production ZL-1 weighed 496 pounds and produced over 650 horsepower.

The big-block Chevrolet has become an irresistible force in racing. A 500-cubic-inch Pro Stock big-block produces over 1150 horsepower.

head technology have bolstered the big-block's airflow to meet the demands of constantly increasing cylinder volumes and higher operating speeds.

The specifications and procedures in this chapter are intended primarily to aid Chevrolet enthusiasts in preparing the big-block V8 engine for "off-highway"

and emission-exempt applications. This information applies to road racing, oval track competition, drag racing, heavy-duty marine use, off-road racing, and

No engine can match the visual impact of a polished and plated big-block Chevy. The Rat motor is a mainstay of street machining.

Big-blocks are fun in the dirt, too. SODA champion Jack Flannery makes tracks up Pikes Peak with his big-block Chevrolet pickup.

tractor pulls. Due to the diversity of sanctioning bodies' rules and the special demands of various types of motorsports, an engine may require specific preparation procedures and accessories not covered in this manual. These specifications and recommendations are intended as general guidelines that have been tested and proven by leading competitors.

Many of the points discussed in this chapter apply specifically to the big-block V8. For additional information on engine building procedures, valvetrain geometry, ignition systems, and lubrication requirements, refer to the chapters on these topics.

Big-Block V8 Interchangeability

The basic architecture of the big-block Chevrolet V8 has been unchanged since its introduction in 1965. Many major and minor components are readily interchangeable among the millions of big-block Chevy V8s that have been produced. There are, however, several significant differences between various production engines.

The internal dimensions and design features of big-block V8 engines are summarized in the accompanying chart. Chevrolet also offers heavy-duty Bow Tie engine blocks and components that have never been installed in production vehicles. Technical details on these

TECH SPECS: BIG-BLOCK V8 FEATURES

Engine Displacement (ci)	Model Year	Bore (in.)	Stroke (in.)	Block Material	Main Bearing Caps
396	1965-69	4.094	3.76	Cast iron	2 Bolt Low Perf. 4 Bolt High Perf.
402	1970-72	4.125	3.76	Cast iron	2 Bolt LP 4 Bolt, 1970 only HP
427	1966-69	4.250	3.76	Cast iron	2 Bolt LP 4 Bolt HP
454	1970-94*	4.250	4.00	Cast iron	2 Bolt LP 4 Bolt HP
427	1969	4.250	3.76	Alum. w/ liners	4 Bolt
430	1969	4.440	3.47	Alum. w/ liners	4 Bolt
465	1970-71	4.440	3.76	Alum. w/ liners	4 Bolt
495	1970-71	4.440	4.00	Alum. w/ liners	4 Bolt
495	1972	4.440	4.00	Alum., no liners	4 Bolt
502 (Gen V)	1992-94	4.446	4.00	Cast iron	4 Bolt
510	1972	4.500	4.00	Alum., no liners	4 Bolt
	*Gen V introduced 1991 model year.				

heavy-duty parts are included throughout this chapter.

Gen V Big-Block

The arrival of a second-generation big-block in 1991 marked the first significant revision in the basic design of the big-block Chevrolet V8. The substantial changes warranted a new designation to differentiate the updated engine from its Mark IV predecessor. The revised big-block was named "Gen V."

The Gen V big-block retains all of the Mark IV's external dimensions. The block height, cylinder bore centers, and lifter bore locations are identical in the two engines. Bosses for motor mounts and accessory brackets are also unchanged, making the Gen V a bolt-in replacement for most early-model big-blocks. The Gen V block does not have provisions for a mechanical fuel pump, however; an electric pump can be substituted in most installations.

Although the second-generation big-block shares its major dimensions and many internal components with its predecessor, numerous revisions made it more reliable and more oiltight than the Mark IV big-block. In production versions, a new cast nodular iron crankshaft was introduced with rolled fillets for increased strength. Hypereutectic (high silicon) aluminum pistons with low-friction skirts and rings reduced reciprocating weight.

Most of the revisions in the Gen V design were aimed at improving reliability and eliminating sources of potential oil leaks. A one-piece rear crankshaft seal replaced the two-piece lip seal used on the Mark IV. This change to a one-piece seal required a redesigned crank-

Electronic fuel injection and rigid cast aluminum covers identified the new Gen V 454ci L19 big-block introduced in 1991.

 **Mark IV vs. Gen V**

The following are the chief differences between the Mark IV (1965-1990) and Gen V (1991-up) versions of the Chevrolet big-block V8:

	Mark IV	Gen V
Rear Seal	2 piece	1 piece*
Main Oil Gallery Location	Oil pan rail	Camshaft tunnel
Mechanical Fuel Pump	Yes	No
Adjustable Valvetrain	Yes	No
Rocker Covers	Stamped steel	Cast aluminum
*2 piece seal in race-prepared Gen V.		

The Chevrolet big-block was updated in 1991 with a redesigned block, a new crankshaft design, and a one-piece rear seal. The revised big-block was christened the Gen V.

All Gen V Chevrolet big-blocks (except race-prepared Bow Tie) use a one-piece rear crankshaft seal. The oil filter pad is flush with the oil pan rail; the filter element spins onto a threaded connector. The water jacket plugs are located in raised bosses, and the 1.625-inch diameter soft plugs are interchangeable with small-block V8 and V6/90 Chevrolets. Raised numerals on the outside of the case identify the engine displacement; Bow Tie blocks are identified by the Bow Tie logo.

shaft flywheel flange, rear main bearing cap, and oil pan. Consequently these components are not interchangeable between Mark IV and Gen V engines. However, many other components, including intake manifolds, water pumps, camshafts, and distributors are interchangeable between the two versions.

Although the crankshaft's flywheel flange bolt pattern was unchanged in the Gen V big-block, the revised crankshaft balance required a special counterweighted flywheel (or flexplate) for proper engine balance. Second-generation big-blocks do not use the same flywheels and flexplates as externally balanced first-generation 454ci Mark IV V8s. Flywheels are also not interchangeable between second-generation cast iron and forged steel cranks. (See the flywheel section for more information.)

The Gen V's cast aluminum rocker covers with captured gaskets and screwin filler caps replaced the stamped steel covers used on Mark IV versions. The new block also introduced integral oil cooler connections that eliminated the seals, gaskets, and adapters formerly required for oil cooler plumbing.

Another significant difference between Mark IV and Gen V big-blocks is the location and size of the coolant passages in the cylinder block deck surfaces. Mark IV cylinder heads should not be installed on production Gen V blocks because coolant may leak into the lifter valley. However, Mark IV cylinder heads can be used with Bow Tie Gen V blocks, which have smaller holes in their decks.

The Gen V big-block's lubrication system was updated by relocating the main oil gallery from the driver's side oil pan rail to the camshaft tunnel. This change reduced the possibility of oil leaks.

The Gen V's valvetrain was revised to ensure consistent quality. Shouldered bolts replaced the threaded rocker arm studs used on previous big-blocks. This nonadjustable system eliminated assembly line variations in lash that were possible with the old design. (Instructions for converting Gen V heads to adjustable rocker arms for high-performance camshafts are included in this chapter.)

Production and heavy-duty Gen V Bow Tie big-block engine cases are machined with similar tooling. As a result, Gen V Bow Tie big-blocks incorporate many features of the revised engine design. Heavy-duty Gen V Bow Tie blocks have the same external appearance, one-piece rear crankshaft seal, and revised oiling system as production cases.

Bow Tie versions of the Gen V big-block differ from production blocks in several important areas. Bow Tie blocks have siamesed cylinder walls, extra-thick deck surfaces with blind tapped head bolt holes, and machined main bearing bulkheads with four-bolt bearing caps.

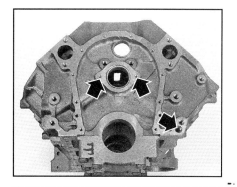

A comparison between a Mark IV block (top) and a Gen V version (bottom) spotlights several significant changes. The main oil gallery was relocated from the oil pan rail to the camshaft tunnel. The bolt holes and pad for a camshaft thrust plate are rotated 90-degrees to accommodate the new oil gallery position. The bolt pattern for the timing chain cover is the same on both blocks, but the cover itself has been changed on Gen V blocks to accept a one-piece oil pan gasket. The Gen V block's front bulkhead is moved forward to improve coolant flow around the No. 1 cylinder. Water pumps are interchangeable between the old and new blocks. (Production big-blocks with serpentine belt systems use reverse-rotation water pumps.)

All Mark IV big-blocks use a two-piece rear crankshaft seal (top); Gen V blocks use a one-piece seal. The rear main cap and bulkhead were redesigned to accommodate this new seal. The Gen V engine has two tapped holes for external oil cooler connections. Oil is routed out of the block through the rear hole, and returned through the front hole.

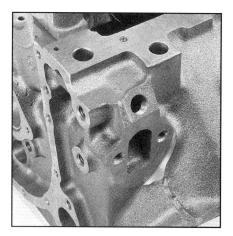

A Mark IV block (top) has provisions for a mechanical fuel pump. This mounting pad is deleted on a Gen V block (bottom).

Block Selection

Selecting the right engine block for the intended application is an important step in preparing a high-output big-block V8. Differences in cylinder bore diameter, cylinder wall thickness, main cap design, rear seal type, and deck height are some of the factors that should be considered. The following is a summary of the differences between Chevrolet big-block V8s.

Cylinder Bores

For optimum performance and durability, the cylinder walls should be as thick as possible to minimize bore distortion and to reduce the risk of failure under severe loads.

Production blocks have thinner cylinder walls than heavy-duty Bow Tie castings. Production blocks are therefore lighter, but they are not as durable as heavy-duty castings under the stress of competition.

The largest cylinder bore diameter currently available in a production Chevrolet big-block truck engine is 4.250-inch, while 8.2-liter (502ci) marine and High Output engines are produced with 4.466-inch cylinder bores. A

production block's comparatively thin cylinder walls limit how far the cylinders can be overbored—an especially important consideration when preparing a used block for competition.

In most instances, production blocks can be safely overbored .060-inch for street and moderate competition uses if the block does not have significant core shift. Boring a production block more than .060-inch is not recommended.

All Bow Tie big-blocks and production 8.2-liter (502ci) Gen V blocks have "siamesed" cylinder walls without water passages between adjacent cylinder barrels. Siamesed cylinder walls allow larger bore diameters than cylinder barrels with coolant passages between them. For example, the cylinders in a cast iron Gen V Bow Tie big-block with siamesed cylinders can be safely bored to 4.600-inch diameter, while a non-siamesed version is limited to a maximum recommended bore diameter of 4.310-inch. Siamesed cylinder walls allow an engine builder to build an engine with more displacement

than would be possible within the limitations of a non-siamesed cylinder block.

Main Bearing Caps

Three types of main bearing caps are available on Chevrolet big-block V8s: two-bolt, parallel four-bolt, and splayed four-bolt.

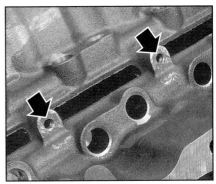

The Gen V big-block's lubrication system is similar to the oiling system in an aluminum ZL-1 block. Holes drilled through bosses in the lifter valley carry oil from the main gallery to passages leading to the main bearing saddles.

The main bearing bulkheads in Gen V 8.2-liter marine and H.O. engine assemblies (top) are cast to provide clearance for an automatic hone. The Gen V Bow Tie block has thicker, fully machined main bearing bulkheads. All Gen V big-blocks are equipped with four-bolt main bearing caps.

The water passages between cylinders are eliminated in a siamesed bore block. A Gen V Bow Tie block can be safely bored to 4.600-inch.

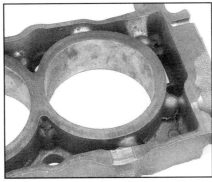

Gen V Bow Tie blocks have blind-tapped head bolt holes. The bolt holes do not penetrate the water jacket, eliminating the possibility of coolant seepage around the threads.

A non-siamesed block has coolant passages between the cylinder barrels. This design enhances cooling but limits the bore diameter.

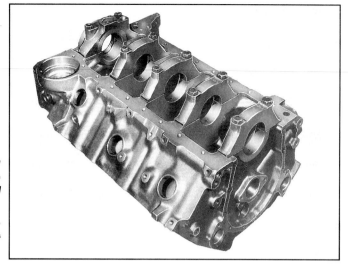

Two-bolt main bearing caps were installed on standard Mark IV big-blocks. These caps are suitable for street engines.

A Mark IV big-block's rear main bearing cap and crankshaft are machined for a two-piece rear seal.

High-performance Mark IV blocks were equipped with four-bolt main bearing caps. Four-bolt caps are preferred over two-bolt versions for racing and severe service applications.

The Gen V block and rear main bearing cap are designed for a one-piece rear seal. Crankshafts are not interchangeable with Mark IV versions.

Two-bolt cast iron main bearing caps were installed on standard production Mark IV engines. They are suitable for street and high-performance usage.

Four-bolt gray cast iron main bearing caps are used on all five main bearings on high-performance and Bow Tie Mark IV blocks, and all Gen V blocks. These caps have four parallel ("straight") bolt holes. The four-bolt caps' increased clamping force reduces bearing cap movement under high loads.

Four-bolt steel main bearing caps are available only on "race-prepared" Gen V Bow Tie blocks. The steel caps for the three middle main bearings (Nos. 2, 3, and 4) have splayed outer bolt holes. These angled outer bolts anchor the cap to the strongest part of the block structure to reduce cap movement and minimize bearing bore distortion.

Rear Seal

Production Chevrolet Mark IV big-block V8 engines produced from 1965 through 1990 used a two-piece rear crankshaft seal. In 1991, a leak-resistant one-piece rear was introduced on the Gen V big-block. This new seal design required revisions in the crankshaft flywheel flange, rear main bearing cap, block, oil pan, and flywheel. Consequently these components are not interchangeable with production engines manufactured before 1991.

Crankshafts that use one-piece rear oil seals have the same flywheel flange bolt pattern as pre-1991 cranks designed for two-piece seals (3.58-inch bolt circle). However, flywheels and flexplates are *not* interchangeable between Mark IV and Gen V big-blocks due to differences in the crankshaft balance that were made to accommodate a one-piece rear seal.

Deck Height

Chevrolet big-block V8s have been produced with two block heights. The "short" version, which measures 9.80-inch from the crankshaft centerline to the deck surfaces, is used in passenger cars, light-duty trucks, and all high-performance applications. The "tall" block measures 10.20-inch from the crank centerline to the decks, and is used most frequently in heavy-duty trucks. Mark IV and Gen V Bow Tie blocks are also available in tall-deck versions.

A short-deck big-block allows the use of lightweight piston and connecting rod assemblies, which are preferred for most racing applications. A tall-deck block, on the other hand, is suited to large displacement engines that require long-stroke crankshafts. The additional height of the tall-deck block permits the use of longer connecting rods, which reduce rod angularity problems associated with extremely long crankshaft strokes.

The short-deck and tall-deck versions of the big-block V8 are essentially identical except for this difference in block height. Major components such as crankshafts, cylinder heads, and camshafts are interchangeable between the two blocks. However, intake manifolds and distributors designed for the short version will not

The Gen V's crankshaft flywheel flange and oil pan were redesigned to accommodate a one-piece rear seal.

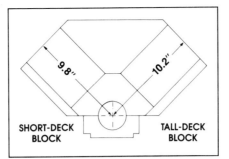

A tall-deck (heavy-duty truck) block is .400-inch taller than a short-deck (passenger car) version.

A high-performance Mark IV block has tapped holes for oil cooler fittings. Note the "HI PERF PASS" casting marks.

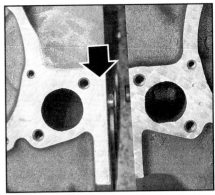

A tall-deck big-block (left) can be identified by the additional material above the water pump bolt holes.

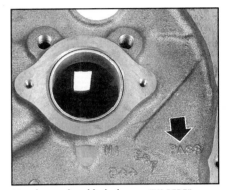

Most heavy-duty blocks have a "HI PERF" designation cast in the front of the block. "PASS" indicates a short-deck block.

fit tall blocks. Intake manifold spacers are available from several aftermarket sources to adapt manifolds designed for passenger car blocks to tall-deck blocks. Aftermarket pistons and/or rods are required when building a big-block V8 with a non-standard crankshaft stroke.

High-Performance Blocks

High-performance Mark IV big-blocks can be identified by two threaded oil cooler outlets located directly above the oil filter pad. The tops of the cylinder bores are relieved to unshroud the intake valves, and the designation "HI PERF" appears on the front of the block below the camshaft bearing.

Bow Tie blocks can be identified by the Bow Tie emblem that appears on the sides of both Mark IV and Gen V block castings.

Clutch Pivot

Production Gen V and early Gen V Bow Tie engine blocks do not have bosses for clutch linkage pivot balls. Late-model Gen V Bow Tie blocks have pivot ball mounts above the oil filter pad. The oil filter bosses on these blocks also have threaded outlets to simplify the installation of external oil coolers and dry sump systems.

Fuel Pump

All Mark IV big-blocks have provisions to mount a mechanical fuel pump. The mechanical fuel pump boss is eliminated on Gen V blocks.

Engine Assemblies

Chevrolet offers several partial and complete engine assemblies that are excellent starting points for big-block pro-

jects. The chief advantage of purchasing an engine assembly is that all components are new, eliminating the uncertainty and cost of reconditioning used parts.

7.4-liter (454ci) H.O. Engine Assembly PN 10185058

The H.O. 454 is the successor to the legendary Mark IV LS-6 engine assembly. Like the LS-6, the H.O. 454 is a force to be reckoned with. During development of the H.O. 454, a prototype engine equipped with a 750cfm Holley four-barrel carburetor, aftermarket headers, and low-restriction mufflers produced 426 horsepower and 467 lb.-ft. of torque.

The H.O. 454 uses a non-siamesed bore Gen V block. Its features include a leak-resistant one-piece rear crankshaft seal, relocated oil passages, a redesigned oil filter pad with integral oil cooler connections, and cast aluminum rocker covers. The H.O. block has four-bolt main bearing caps. It does not have provisions for a mechanical fuel pump.

The H.O. 454 is completely assembled, less ignition, spark plug wires, carbure-

tor, and exhaust manifolds. A water pump, torsional damper, and automatic transmission flexplate are included. The engine is fire-tested and final balanced at the factory.

The H.O. 454 is equipped with a high-rise aluminum four-barrel intake manifold and high-performance rectangular port cylinder heads. These cast iron heads have open-style combustion chambers and 2.19/1.88-inch diameter valves. The H.O. 454's rigid cast aluminum covers and screw-in oil filler cap resist oil leaks.

The crankshaft assembly includes a 4.00-inch stroke forged steel crankshaft and forged 4340 steel connecting rods with $7/16$-inch bolts. The forged aluminum pistons yield a nominal compression ratio of 8.75:1.

The H.O. 454 utilizes a hydraulic lifter camshaft (PN 10185060) which has .510-inch valve lift and 224 degrees duration (at .050-inch tappet lift). This high-performance profile is ground on an intake lobe centerline of 109 degrees with 116-degree lobe centers. The H.O. engine uses a non-adjustable "net lash" valvetrain and $3/8$-inch diameter pushrods.

BOW TIE SPECS
H.O. 454 Big-Block V8

Part Number:	10185058
Displacement:	7.4-liter (454 cubic inches)
Horsepower:	425 @ 5250 rpm
Bore/Stroke:	4.250" x 4.00"
Compression Ratio:	8.75:1
Engine Block:	Cast iron with four-bolt main bearing caps, non-siamesed bore
Crankshaft:	Forged 1053 steel with one-piece rear seal (#14096983)
Connecting Rods:	Forged 4340 steel, 7/16" bolts, shotpeened (#10198922)
Pistons:	Forged aluminum (#14097018)
Camshaft:	Hydraulic flat tappet (#10185060)
Valve Lift (Intake/Exhaust):	.510"/.510"
Duration (Intake/Exhaust):	224/224 degrees at .050" tappet lift
Cylinder Heads:	Cast iron rectangular port, 118cc open combustion chambers (#14096801)
Valve Diameter (Intake/Exhaust):	2.19"/1.88"
Rocker Arm Ratio:	1.7:1
Timing Chain:	Single roller
Intake Manifold:	Aluminum high-rise, for Holley four-barrel
Oil Pan:	6 quart with windage tray
Oil Pressure (Normal):	40psi @ 2000 rpm
Fuel Pressure Required:	5 to 8.5 psi
Spark Plugs:	MR43T
Spark Timing:	36 degrees total advance at 3600 rpm (with vacuum advance line disconnected and plugged)
Fuel requirement:	Premium unleaded 92 octane (R+M/2)
Maximum Recommended Engine Speed:	5500 rpm

The H.O. 454 engine assembly includes a high-rise aluminum intake manifold, cast aluminum rocker covers, high-performance cylinder heads, and a .510-inch lift hydraulic cam.

The H.O. 502 is Chevy's biggest big-block. This massive motor produces an irresistible 515 lb.-ft. of torque at 3500 rpm.

The H.O. 502 has 4.466-inch cylinder bores. Forged aluminum pistons yield an 8.75:1 compression ratio.

The H.O. 454 engine assembly includes a six-quart oil pan. When installing an H.O. big-block in a Chevelle, Camaro, or similar chassis, the pan and oil pump pickup must be modified to clear the front crossmember. Four-quart oil pans for these applications are not available for the H.O. 454.

The 454ci H.O. engine assembly includes a 14-inch diameter automatic transmission flexplate with dual bolt patterns (PN 10185034). For manual transmission applications, a 14-inch diameter flywheel drilled for an 11-inch clutch is available as PN 14096987. Due to differences in crankshaft counterweights, this flywheel should be used *only* with the

forged steel crankshafts installed in H.O. 454 and H.O. 502 engine assemblies.

A fitted block for the H.O. engine assembly is available as PN 12508097. This assembly includes the block, pistons, and piston rings only.

8.2-liter (502ci) H.O. Engine Assembly PN 10185085

The H.O. 502 engine assembly is Chevrolet's biggest big-block. This high-torque engine offers exceptional performance in an over-the-counter package for off-highway applications. During development of the H.O. 502 assembly, a prototype engine equipped with a 750cfm

The H.O. 502 partial engine assembly includes a siamesed bore block, steel crankshaft, forged rods and pistons, and a torsional damper.

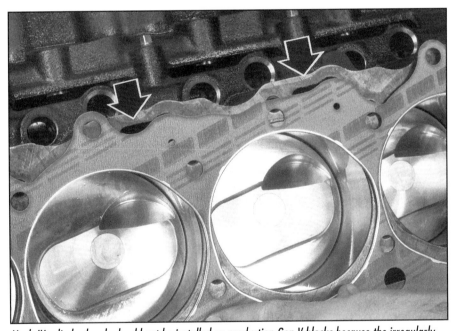

Mark IV cylinder heads should not be installed on production Gen V blocks because the irregularly shaped core holes in the Gen V's decks may allow coolant to leak into the lifter valley. Mark IV heads can be installed on Gen V Bow Tie blocks, which have smaller holes in the decks.

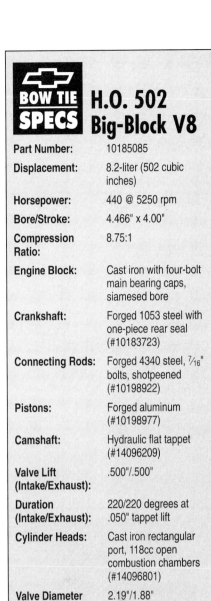

BOW TIE SPECS	H.O. 502 Big-Block V8
Part Number:	10185085
Displacement:	8.2-liter (502 cubic inches)
Horsepower:	440 @ 5250 rpm
Bore/Stroke:	4.466" x 4.00"
Compression Ratio:	8.75:1
Engine Block:	Cast iron with four-bolt main bearing caps, siamesed bore
Crankshaft:	Forged 1053 steel with one-piece rear seal (#10183723)
Connecting Rods:	Forged 4340 steel, $7/16$" bolts, shotpeened (#10198922)
Pistons:	Forged aluminum (#10198977)
Camshaft:	Hydraulic flat tappet (#14096209)
Valve Lift (Intake/Exhaust):	.500"/.500"
Duration (Intake/Exhaust):	220/220 degrees at .050" tappet lift
Cylinder Heads:	Cast iron rectangular port, 118cc open combustion chambers (#14096801)
Valve Diameter (Intake/Exhaust):	2.19"/1.88"
Rocker Arm Ratio:	1.7:1
Timing Chain:	Single roller
Intake Manifold:	Aluminum high-rise, for Holley four-barrel
Oil Pan:	6 quart with windage tray
Oil Pressure (Normal):	40psi @ 2000 rpm
Fuel Pressure Required:	5 to 8.5psi
Spark Plugs:	MR43T
Spark Timing:	36 degrees total advance at 3600 rpm (with vacuum advance line disconnected and plugged)
Fuel requirement:	Premium unleaded 92 octane (R+M/2)
Maximum Recommended Engine Speed:	5500 rpm

Holley four-barrel carburetor, aftermarket headers (2-inch x 30-inch primaries) and low-restriction mufflers produced 440 horsepower (at 5250 rpm) and 515 lb.-ft. of torque (at 3500 rpm).

Like the H.O. 454 engine, High Output 502 engines are completely assembled (less ignition, spark plug wires, carburetor, and exhaust manifolds) using brand new, premium quality components. The H.O. 502 assembly includes a water pump, torsional damper, and automatic transmission flexplate. All H.O. engines are fire-tested and final balanced at the factory to ensure their quality.

The H.O. 502 is based on the Gen V cast iron short-deck marine block with four-bolt main bearing caps. This block has 4.466-inch diameter siamesed cylinder bores and blind-tapped head bolts. It is otherwise identical to the H.O. 454 block, and has the same features as other Gen V engines. It requires a counter-weighted flywheel or flexplate.

	Mark IV Bow Tie Big-Block (Short-Deck)	Mark IV Bow Tie Big-Block (Tall-Deck)	Gen V Bow Tie Big-Block (Short-Deck)	Gen V Bow Tie Big-Block (Tall-Deck)	Gen V Bow Tie Big-Block (Short-Deck)	Gen V Bow Tie Big-Block (Tall-Deck)
Part Number	10051106	14044808	10185049	10134367	24502500	24502502
Block Material	Cast Iron	Cast Iron	Cast Iron	Cast Iron	Cast Iron	Cast Iron
Cylinder Wall Type	Siamesed	Siamesed	Siamesed	Siamesed	Siamesed	Siamesed
Cylinder Deck Height	9.800"	10.200"	9.800"	10.200"	9.800+"	10.200+"
Cylinder Bore Range	4.250–4.560"	4.250–4.560"	4.250–4.600"	4.250–4.600"	4.125–4.600"	4.250–4.600"
Bearing Cap Bolts	4	4	4	4	4	4
Cap Bolt Orientation	Straight	Straight	Straight	Straight	Splayed 20°	Splayed 20°
Bearing Cap Type	Cast Iron	Cast Iron	Cast Iron	Cast Iron	8620 steel	8620 steel
Crankshaft Journal Diameter	2.75"	2.75"	2.75"	2.75"	2.75"	2.75"
Oil Sump Type	Wet	Wet	Wet	Wet	Wet	Wet
Crankshaft Seal Type	2 piece	2 piece	1 piece	1 piece	2 piece	2 piece
Design Max. Stroke	4.250"	4.250"	4.600"	4.600"	4.600"	4.600"
Weight (lbs. —bare)	269	269	269	272	270	270
Notes	Has fuel pump boss, Mark IV style oiling and two-piece rear seal.	Has fuel pump boss, Mark IV style oiling and two-piece rear seal.	No fuel pump boss.	No fuel pump boss.	Race-prepared machining, valley head bolt bosses, enlarged main oil gallery, uses Mark IV oil pan.	Race-prepared machining, valley head bolt bosses, enlarged main oil gallery, uses Mark IV oil pan.

The H.O. 502 partial engine assembly includes a torsional damper and front cover, but does not include a camshaft and timing set.

The H.O. 502 uses the same crankshaft assembly (except pistons), cylinder heads, and intake manifold as the H.O. 454 described previously. However, the H.O. 502 uses a specific hydraulic lifter camshaft (PN 14096209) with .500-inch valve lift and 220 degrees duration (at .050-inch tappet lift). This profile is ground on an intake lobe centerline of 114 degrees with 115-degree lobe centers. Like all Gen V big-blocks, the H.O. 502 has a non-adjustable valvetrain.

H.O. 502 Partial Engine Assembly PN 10185059

This "long block" includes the block, crankshaft, connecting rods, pistons, rings, oil pan, oil pump, windage tray, torsional damper, front cover, and flexplate. It does *not* include a camshaft, timing set, cylinder heads, intake manifold, or ignition system.

The H.O. 502 partial engine assembly requires Gen V (1991-up) cylinder heads. Earlier Mark IV heads will bolt onto the block, but there is a high potential for water leaks because of changes in the location of coolant holes in the Gen V's deck surfaces.

High-performance rectangular port cast iron cylinder head assemblies (PN 14096801) are recommended for the H.O. 502 partial engine assembly. They have open-style 118cc combustion chambers that yield a compression ratio of 8.75:1 when installed on a H.O. 502 partial assembly. These cylinder head assemblies include valves and springs; a bare head without valves and springs is available as PN 14096802.

Composition head gaskets (PN 14097001) are recommended for the 502 partial engine assembly. This gasket has a compressed thickness of .040-inch, and fits bores up to 4.500-inch in diameter.

Engine Blocks

Chevrolet offers a variety of production and heavy-duty engine blocks that are suitable for high-performance and competition applications. The following overview highlights their features.

Production Blocks

Bare big-block engine cases are available in both Mark IV and Gen V versions. PN 10069285 is a production high-performance passenger car 427/454 short-deck block (9.80-inch from crank centerline to decks). This block has four-bolt main bearing caps and semi-finished 4.250-inch cylinder bores; the cylinders must be honed to final bore diameter. It has non-siamesed cylinder walls, and provisions for a mechanical fuel pump.

A Mark IV Bow Tie block has siamesed cylinder walls with a 5.060-inch maximum barrel diameter. A Bow Tie logo on the side of the block identifies this heavy-duty cylinder case.

A precision deck plate is required to properly locate the cylinder bore centers when machining a Mark IV Bow Tie block.

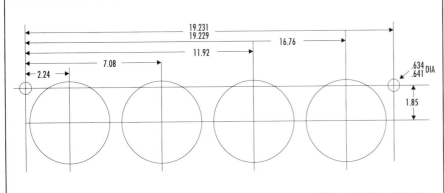

Use the dowel-to-cylinder bore dimensions shown above to position the cylinder bores accurately in a Mark IV Bow Tie block with semi-finished cylinders.

The tall-deck version of the Mark IV Bow Tie big-block (PN 14044404) has a raised oil passage above the front cover.

The cylinders in Mark IV Bow Tie blocks are rough-bored to 4.250-inch diameter. Valve notches at the tops of the bores are deleted.

Cover the oil drainback holes in a big-block's lifter valley with screen to prevent debris from reaching the crankcase. Screens can be bolted or epoxied in place.

A bare Gen V block with 4.466-inch cylinder bores is available as PN 14096817. This short-deck block is used in H.O. 502 partial and complete engine assemblies. It has four-bolt main bearing caps and siamesed cylinder walls. This block has no mechanical fuel pump boss.

Bow Tie Blocks

Heavy-duty Bow Tie blocks are produced in both Mark IV and Gen V configurations, with both short-deck and tall-deck block heights. "Race-prepared" Gen V Bow Tie blocks are also available.

Mark IV Bow Tie Blocks

10051106	Short-Deck Mark IV Bow Tie Block
14044808	Tall-Deck Mark IV Bow Tie Block

Chevrolet offers two heavy-duty cast iron Mark IV Bow Tie blocks specifically for off-highway applications. PN 10051106 is a heavy-duty version of the short-deck (9.80-inch) production Corvette/passenger car block. This block was originally developed for Pro Stock drag racing, offshore boat racing, and similar applications that require 500-cubic-inch engine displacements.

PN 14044808 is a heavy-duty version of the tall-deck (10.20-inch) Mark IV truck block; it is ideal for large displacement competition engines that require long-stroke crankshafts.

Both the short and tall versions of the Bow Tie big-block offer significant advantages over production engine cases. Their cylinder walls are "siamesed," with no water passages between adjacent cylinders. The maximum core diameter of the cylinders in the Mark IV Bow Tie

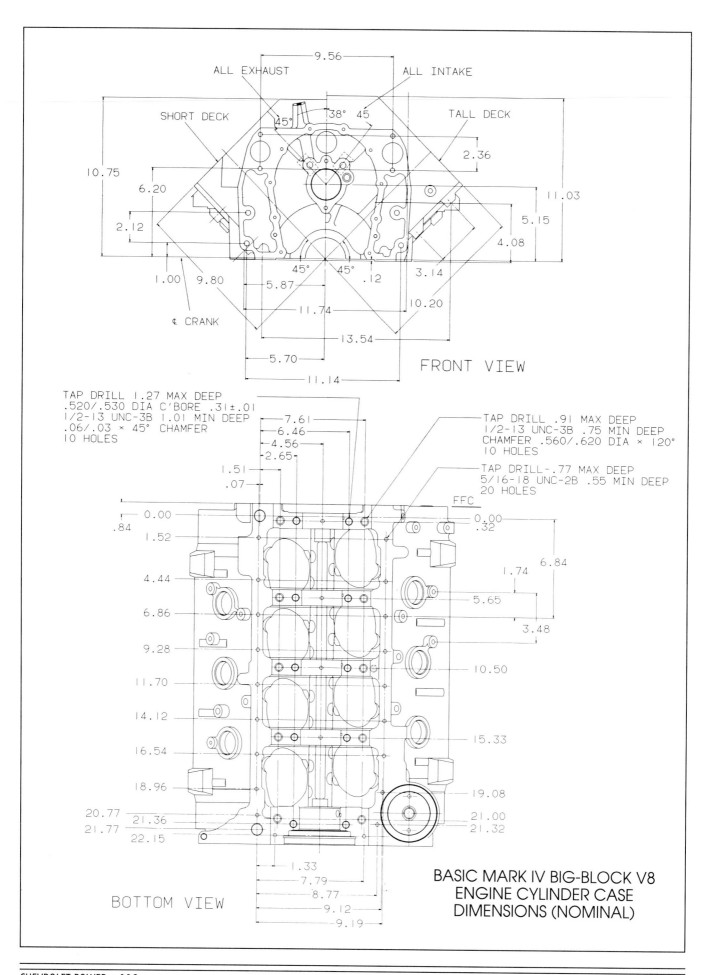

FRONT VIEW

ALL EXHAUST   ALL INTAKE

SHORT DECK   TALL DECK

9.56

45°   38°   45

2.36

10.75

6.20

11.03

2.12

5.15

4.08

45°   45°   .12

3.14

1.00   9.80

5.87

10.20

¢ CRANK

11.74

13.54

5.70

11.14

TAP DRILL 1.27 MAX DEEP
.520/.530 DIA C'BORE .31±.01
1/2-13 UNC-3B 1.01 MIN DEEP
.06/.03 × 45° CHAMFER
10 HOLES

TAP DRILL .91 MAX DEEP
1/2-13 UNC-3B .75 MIN DEEP
CHAMFER .560/.620 DIA × 120°
10 HOLES

TAP DRILL -.77 MAX DEEP
5/16-18 UNC-2B .55 MIN DEEP
20 HOLES

7.61

6.46

4.56

2.65

1.51

.07

FFC

0.00

0.00

.84

.32

1.52

1.74

6.84

4.44

5.65

6.86

3.48

9.28

10.50

11.70

14.12

15.33

16.54

18.96

19.08

20.77

21.00

21.36

21.32

21.77

22.15

1.33

7.79

BOTTOM VIEW

8.77

9.12

9.19

BASIC MARK IV BIG-BLOCK V8
ENGINE CYLINDER CASE
DIMENSIONS (NOMINAL)

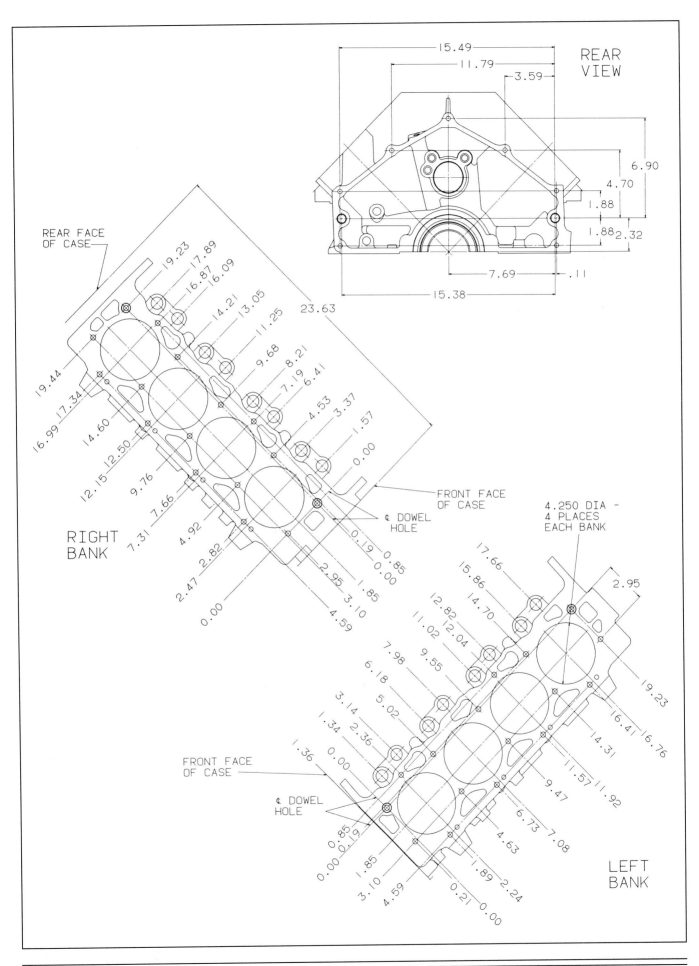

REAR VIEW

15.49
11.79
3.59
6.90
4.70
1.88
1.88 2.32
7.69
.11
15.38

REAR FACE OF CASE

19.23
17.89
16.87
16.09
14.21
13.05
11.25
23.63
9.68
8.21
7.19
6.41
4.53
3.37
1.57
0.00

19.44
16.99 17.34
14.60
12.15 12.50
9.76
7.66
7.31
4.92
2.47 2.82
0.00

FRONT FACE OF CASE

¢ DOWEL HOLE

0.19 0.85
0.00
2.95 1.85
3.10
4.59

RIGHT BANK

4.250 DIA – 4 PLACES EACH BANK

2.95

17.66
15.86
14.70
12.82
12.04
11.02
7.98
9.55
6.18
5.02
3.14
2.36
1.34

19.23
16.41 16.76
14.31
11.57 11.92
9.47
6.73
7.08
4.63

1.36
0.00

FRONT FACE OF CASE

¢ DOWEL HOLE

0.85
0.19
0.00
1.85
3.10
4.59
1.89 2.24
0.21 0.00

LEFT BANK

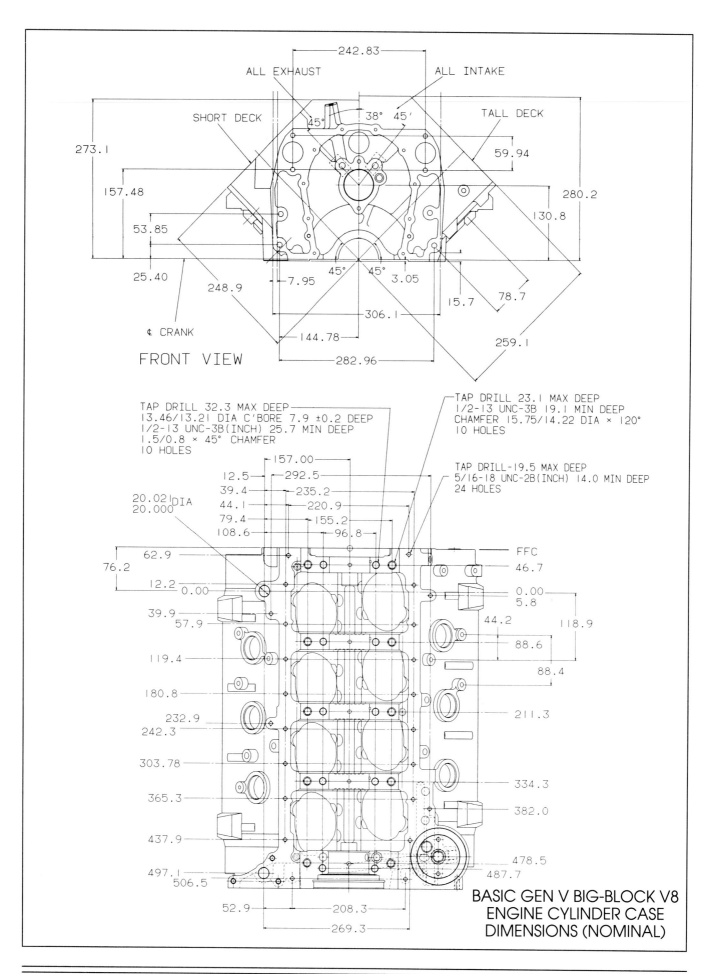

ALL EXHAUST   ALL INTAKE

242.83

SHORT DECK   45°   38° 45°   TALL DECK

273.1   59.94

157.48   280.2

53.85   130.8

25.40   45° 45° 3.05

248.9   7.95   15.7   78.7

¢ CRANK   144.78   259.1

306.1

FRONT VIEW   282.96

TAP DRILL 32.3 MAX DEEP
13.46/13.21 DIA C'BORE 7.9 ±0.2 DEEP
1/2-13 UNC-3B(INCH) 25.7 MIN DEEP
1.5/0.8 × 45° CHAMFER
10 HOLES

TAP DRILL 23.1 MAX DEEP
1/2-13 UNC-3B 19.1 MIN DEEP
CHAMFER 15.75/14.22 DIA × 120°
10 HOLES

157.00

12.5   292.5
39.4   235.2
44.1   220.9
79.4   155.2
108.6   96.8

TAP DRILL-19.5 MAX DEEP
5/16-18 UNC-2B(INCH) 14.0 MIN DEEP
24 HOLES

20.021 DIA
20.000

62.9   FFC
76.2   46.7
12.2 0.00   0.00
                    5.8
39.9
57.9   44.2   118.9
119.4   88.6
180.8   88.4
232.9   211.3
242.3
303.78   334.3
365.3   382.0
437.9
497.1   478.5
506.5   487.7

52.9   208.3

269.3

**BASIC GEN V BIG-BLOCK V8
ENGINE CYLINDER CASE
DIMENSIONS (NOMINAL)**

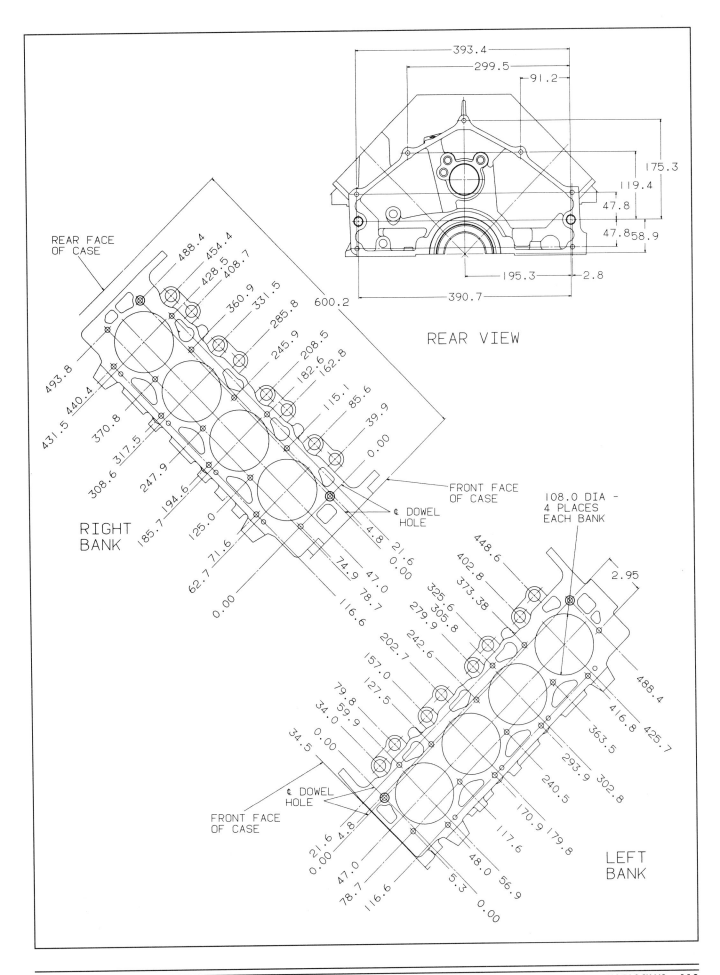

REAR FACE
OF CASE

488.4
454.4
428.5
408.7
360.9
331.5
285.8
245.9
208.5
182.6
162.8
115.1
85.6
39.9
0.00

600.2

493.8
440.4
431.5
370.8
317.5
308.6
247.9
185.7 194.6
125.0
62.7 71.6
0.00

RIGHT
BANK

FRONT FACE
OF CASE

¢ DOWEL
HOLE

4.8
21.6
0.00
74.9
47.0
78.7
116.6

393.4
299.5
91.2
175.3
119.4
47.8
47.8 58.9
195.3 2.8
390.7

REAR VIEW

108.0 DIA –
4 PLACES
EACH BANK

2.95

448.6
402.8
373.38
325.6
305.8
279.9
242.6
202.7
157.0
127.5
79.8
59.9
34.0
34.5
0.00

488.4
416.8 425.7
363.5
293.9 302.8
240.5
170.9 179.8
117.6

¢ DOWEL
HOLE

FRONT FACE
OF CASE

21.6 4.8
0.00
47.0
78.7
116.6

48.0 56.9
5.3 0.00

LEFT
BANK

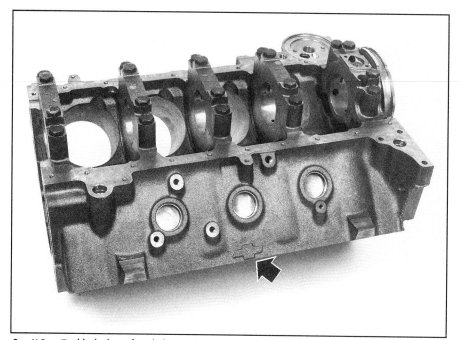

Gen V Bow Tie blocks have four-bolt main bearing caps, siamesed cylinders, reinforced decks, and fully machined main bearing bulkheads. The Bow Tie logo identifies this heavy-duty cylinder case.

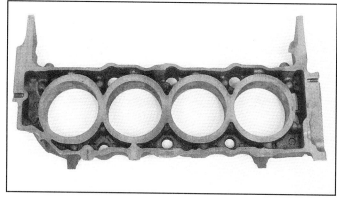

A cross-section of a Gen V Bow Tie block reveals its siamesed cylinder walls and elliptical cylinder barrels. The head bolt bosses around the cylinders are blind tapped.

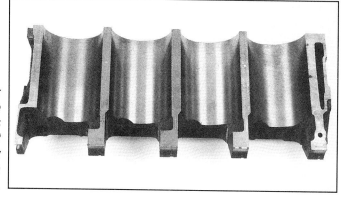

Siamesed cylinder walls eliminate the water passages between adjacent cylinders to allow larger bore diameters.

blocks is 5.060-inch. This permits an engine builder to safely bore the cylinders in a heavy-duty Bow Tie block to 4.560-inch diameter. The deck surfaces are reinforced to improve head gasket sealing, and the head bolt holes are blind tapped. The rear main bearing bolt bosses and cylinder barrels are reinforced to improve bottom end strength, and four-bolt main bearing caps are standard.

Mark IV Bow Tie big-blocks are manufactured with semi-finished 4.250-inch diameter cylinders. A fixture is required to properly locate the bore centers when machining a Mark IV Bow Tie block for competition. If you are using a Bow Tie case as the basis for a big-block engine project, make sure that your machinist has the necessary equipment and expertise to prepare these blocks properly.

Gen V Bow Tie Blocks

| 10185049 | Short-Deck Gen V Bow Tie Block |
| 10134367 | Tall-Deck Gen V Bow Tie Block |

Cast iron Gen V Bow Tie blocks are engineered for maximum-effort racing engines. PN 10185049 is a "short-deck" (passenger car) block with a 9.80-inch crankshaft centerline-to-deck dimension. A "tall-deck" version with a 10.20-inch block height is available as PN 10134367.

Gen V Bow Tie blocks have four-bolt ductile iron main bearing caps with straight outer bolt holes. Production service or aftermarket semi-finished Mark IV caps for the No. 1, 2, 3, and 4 main bearings can also be installed on a Gen V block if bolts or studs designed for Mark IV caps are used.

Cylinder Walls

Like Mark IV Bow Tie big-blocks, Gen V Bow Tie blocks have extra-thick cylinder walls with no water passages between adjacent cylinders. These siamesed cylinder walls allow larger bore diameters than blocks with water between the cylinders.

The Gen V Bow Tie block's cylinders are bored to 4.250-inch diameter at the factory, leaving a minimum wall thickness of .500-inch. The maximum recommended bore diameter is 4.600-inch; at this size, the cylinder walls will be .325-inch thick on the major and minor thrust axes. The cylinder barrels are slightly oval-shaped to ensure consistent wall thicknesses for all cylinders.

Decks

The cored openings in the Gen V Bow Tie block's deck surfaces differ from the holes in both Mark IV and production Gen V blocks. Production Gen V blocks have irregularly shaped core holes in the deck surfaces; these openings are small and round in Bow Tie blocks. These smaller openings in the deck surfaces improve the integrity of the head gasket seal under high cylinder pressures and reinforce the tops of the cylinder bores to reduce distortion. Competition engine builders can block or resize these round holes by installing threaded plugs.

Gen V blocks have additional holes at the front of the cylinder case. These passages are vent holes that allow gas to escape during the casting process. If these holes are not plugged, water entering the block from the water pump can "short circuit" the cooling system by bypassing the block and cylinder head coolant jackets and returning directly to the radiator.

Gen V Bow Tie blocks have larger lifter bosses than production versions. The lifter bores can be enlarged or relocated.

These vent holes should be blocked on both deck surfaces to force the coolant to circulate through the engine. Gen V head gaskets do not have coolant holes in this position, and will effectively block the passages. See the head gasket section in this chapter for additional information on recommended cooling system modifications.

All head bolt holes in the Gen V Bow Tie block are blind-tapped. Sealant is unnecessary on the head bolt threads because the holes do not penetrate the water jacket. Lightly lubricate the threads to produce accurate torque readings when tightening the head bolts.

Lifter Bosses

The lifter bosses in Gen V Bow Tie blocks are larger than the bosses in Mark IV Bow Tie and production Gen V blocks. These oversize bosses allow engine builders to install larger diameter lifters after boring out the tappet bores. The lifters can also be relocated to optimize valvetrain geometry by offset boring the lifter holes.

Lubrication System

One of the major differences between Mark IV and Gen V big-blocks is the oiling system. The main oil gallery in Mark IV blocks is located above the driver's side oil pan rail. This oil gallery location prevents the installation of main bearing caps with splayed outer bolts. There is also a possibility of breaking into the Mark IV's oil passages when machining clearance for long-stroke cranks and when boring the cylinders.

The main oil gallery in all Gen V blocks is located alongside the camshaft tunnel. This oil gallery location allows engine builders to install splayed-bolt main bearing caps and to machine the oil pan rails for crankshaft clearance without the risk of breaking into the main oil passage.

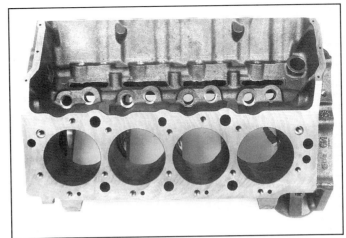

A Gen V Bow Tie block has small round coolant holes in its deck surfaces. The size of these openings is reduced in Bow Tie blocks to strengthen the decks.

A production Gen V block has irregularly shaped holes in its decks. Compare the sizes of the holes and lifter bosses in this casting with the Bow Tie block above.

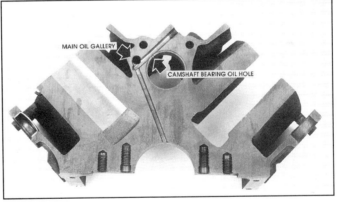

The Gen V block's priority main oiling system supplies oil directly to the main bearings. The oil hole in the cam bearing must be aligned with the feed hole in the block.

All Gen V big-blocks have a "priority main" oiling system. Drilled passages carry oil directly to the main bearings from the main oil gallery located next to the camshaft tunnel.

Oil is supplied to the camshaft bearings in a Gen V big-block through passages drilled from the lifter valley. These passages intersect the cam bearing bore tangentially, opening an oval "window" approximately ½-inch long and ¼-inch wide. *When installing camshaft bearings in a Gen V block, the oil hole in the camshaft bearing must be aligned with this opening.* The oil hole in the bearing

insert should be at the 2 o'clock position when viewed from the front of the block.

The main oil gallery in a Gen V Bow Tie block is the same size (⁷⁄₁₆-inch diameter) and in the same position as the main oil gallery in a production Gen V block. Material was added to the Bow Tie casting to allow engine builders to enlarge this passage. However, if the diameter of the main gallery is increased, its centerline must be relocated to prevent breaking into the lifter bores.

The Gen V Bow Tie block has provisions for a dry sump oil inlet line. The oil passage at the rear of the block above the

Gen V Bow Tie blocks have provisions for a dry sump oil inlet line. Drill out the oil passage at the rear of the block.

Tap the oil inlet and install a ½-inch NPT fitting. Connect the inlet line to the pressure stage of an external oil pump.

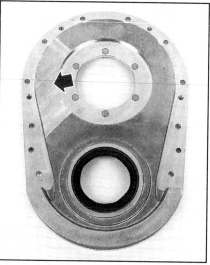

Aftermarket belt camshaft drive covers may require machining for clearance when installed on a Gen V Bow Tie block.

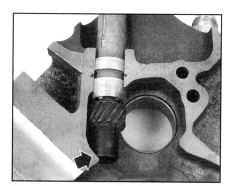

It may be necessary to chamfer the bottom of the distributor gear or grind the cylinder barrel for clearance.

The front cover cavity is shallower in a Gen V block than in a production block. Check the camshaft drive for clearance in this area.

Tall-Deck Block

The tall-deck cast iron Gen V Bow Tie big-block has a 10.20-inch crankshaft centerline-to-deck dimension—.400-inch taller than the short-deck version. This additional block height allows an engine builder to reduce connecting rod angularity by installing extra-long rods. It also provides more flexibility in piston design by reducing interference between the wrist pin and ring pack.

The tall-deck Gen V Bow Tie block can be identified by an additional oil passage above the timing chain cover. This passage provides a convenient source of pressurized oil to lubricate turbochargers.

Race-Prepared Bow Tie Blocks

| 24502500 | Short-Deck Race-Prepared Gen V Bow Tie Big-Block (4.125" Bore) |
| 24502502 | Tall-Deck Race-Prepared Gen V Bow Tie Big-Block (4.250" Bore) |

Two race-prepared Gen V Bow Tie big-blocks are available from Chevrolet. These "blueprinted" blocks are precision machined to exacting tolerances. The cylinders are bored slightly undersize to leave enough material to allow final honing to a standard bore diameter. The main oil galleries are enlarged to 9/16-inch diameter. Race-prepared blocks are virtually ready to assemble after honing, decking (as required), and cleaning. Features of the race-ready big-blocks include:

Steel Main Bearing Caps

Race-prepared Bow Tie big-blocks are outfitted with 8620 steel four-bolt main bearing caps. Unlike production big-

---

bellhousing flange can be drilled out to the main oil gallery and threaded for a ½-inch NPT pipe fitting. Oil from the pressure stage of the dry sump oil pump can be pumped directly into the main oil gallery through this hole.

All Gen V blocks have integral connections for an external oil cooler. Oil is routed out of the block through the rear hole, and returns from the cooler through the front hole.

Distributor Clearance

Material was added to the bottom of the cylinder barrels in Gen V Bow Tie blocks to increase their strength and to accommodate large cylinder bore diameters. In some instances, the bottom of the No. 8 cylinder barrel may interfere with the distributor gear. (This is not a problem in production Gen V blocks, which have smaller cylinder barrels.) Any interference can be easily corrected by chamfering the bottom of the distributor gear or grinding additional clearance in the block.

Some racing distributors have "O"-rings on the distributor shaft that seal the passenger's side lifter oil gallery. These "O"-rings may not effectively seal the distributor hole in big-block V8s due to

the size of the camshaft tunnel. This can be checked by pre-assembling the engine and verifying the position of the "O"-rings in relation to the distributor hole. The position of the distributor in the block can be adjusted if necessary by machining the distributor pad on the intake manifold (to lower the distributor) or adding spacers between the distributor and manifold (to raise the distributor).

Front Cover

The front cover cavity in front of the No. 1 cylinder is .300-inch shallower in a Gen V Bow Tie block than the cavity in a production Gen V block. This change improves coolant flow around the No. 1 cylinder in the Bow Tie block, which has larger cylinder barrels than a production casting. Clearance for the camshaft drive (timing chain) should be checked in this area. Both production and aftermarket chain drives were used to establish the depth of this cavity; however, you should make sure that there is at least 1/16-inch clearance between the block and the drive you are using. If an aftermarket belt-type timing system is installed on a Gen V Bow Tie block, the back of the aluminum cover must be machined for clearance.

Mark IV blocks originally manufactured with two-bolt main bearing caps can be upgraded with replacement four-bolt caps.

Gen V Bow Tie blocks have fully machined main bearing bulkheads; production versions have thinner cast bulkheads.

High-performance crankshafts have cross-drilled main bearing journals to ensure a constant oil supply for the rod bearings.

block caps with four parallel bolts, the steel main caps' outer bolts angle outward at 20 degrees. Premium quality studs and 12-point nuts retain the steel caps. The rear main bearing cap is similar to the Mark IV design; it uses a two-piece rear seal and fits a Mark IV-type oil pan.

Head Bolt Bosses

Eight inner head bolt bosses were added to the lifter valley to enhance head gasket sealing in severe duty applications (supercharged, turbocharged, nitrous oxide injection, etc.). Chevrolet Bow Tie and many aftermarket competition cylinder heads have provisions for these additional head fasteners.

Maximized Deck Height

The block deck heights are maximized on both short-deck and tall-deck versions by removing the minimum amount of material required to "clean up" the deck surfaces. This typically results in an increase in block height of approximately .025 to .050-inch over a production block.

Main Bearing Caps

All high-performance and Bow Tie Mark IV big-block engine cases are manufactured with four-bolt main bearing caps. Replacement semi-finished cast iron four-bolt caps for main bearings Nos. 1-4 are available as PN 14015334. A replacement rear main bearing cap for Mark IV engines is PN 14103156.

The ends of these replacement caps must be cut to register the cap correctly on the main bearing bulkheads, and the oil groove in the replacement rear main cap must be machined. It is mandatory that the main bearing housings be align bored when installing replacement caps.

Production Gen V big-blocks use an "O"-ring seal (PN 6264902) between the rear main cap and block.

Main bearing bolts are not interchangeable between Mark IV and Gen V blocks

	Mark IV	Gen V
Outer Bolt	½-13 x 2.60" PN 3859927	½-13 x 2.78" PN 10106460
Inner Bolt	½-13 x 3.34" PN 3909834	½-13 x 3.52" PN 10106461

due to differences in the heights of the main caps as shown in the chart above.

Crankshafts

Chevrolet offers several forged steel crankshafts for Mark IV and Gen V big-block V8s that are suitable for high-performance and competition use.

Two stroke dimensions have been used in production Chevrolet big-blocks. All 366, 396, 402 and 427ci engines use 3.76-inch stroke crankshafts; 454 and 502ci big-blocks use 4.00-inch stroke cranks. All big-block crankshafts share the same bearing journal diameters: 2.75-inch mains and 2.20-inch rods.

High-performance Mark IV big-block crankshafts are nitride heat treated to increase their journal hardness and to provide improved fatigue strength. Nitrided crankshafts should not be ground for extra bearing clearance because this procedure removes the case hardened surface. Oversize bearings should be used with nitrided crankshafts that require additional oil clearance.

Chevrolet forged steel crankshafts for Mark IV big-blocks use two-piece rear seals; 3.76-inch and 4.00-inch strokes are available.

High-performance Mark IV big-block crankshafts also have cross-drilled main bearing journals. This feature provides a constant supply of oil to the rod bearing regardless of crankshaft position.

All 4.00-inch stroke big-block Chevrolet crankshafts are *externally* balanced. In order to achieve proper engine balance, a portion of the counterweight mass is included in both the torsional damper and flywheel on 454 and 502ci Chevrolet V8s. The correct counterweighted damper and flywheel *must* be used with externally balanced 4.00-inch stroke crankshafts to prevent engine damage. However, flywheels and flexplates are *not* interchangeable between 4.00-inch stroke Mark IV and Gen V crankshafts; see the flywheel section for additional information.

Specialty machine shops can internally balance a 4.00-inch stroke big-block crankshaft by installing slugs of "heavy metal" in the crankshaft counterweights. These heavy metal slugs should be installed parallel to the crankshaft axis to prevent centrifugal force from dislodging them at high engine speeds. Following this procedure, a non-counterweighted damper and flywheel should be installed.

Mark IV Crankshafts

Mark IV big-block crankshafts are machined for two-piece rear seals. They can be installed in Gen V blocks by using a

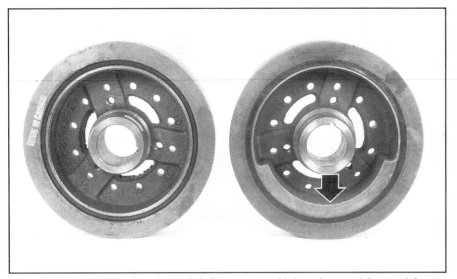

Internally balanced 3.76-inch stroke crankshafts use a neutral-balanced torsional damper (left); externally balanced 4.00-inch stroke cranks require a counterweighted damper (right).

Torsional dampers must be balanced after truing the outer inertia ring or engraving degree marks for ignition timing.

The GM/Fluidampr for externally balanced 4.00-inch stroke Mark IV crankshafts uses viscous fluid to control crankshaft vibrations.

crankshaft seal adapter. An adapter is not required to install a Mark IV crankshaft in a race-prepared Gen V Bow Tie block.

PN 3967811 is a 3.76-inch stroke, forged steel crankshaft used in high-performance 427ci big-blocks. It is internally balanced, and can be identified by the forging number "7115."

PN 3963523 is a 4.00-inch stroke forged 1053 steel Mark IV crankshaft. This crank was installed in the discontinued LS-6 and LS-7 engine assemblies, and can be identified by forging number "3520" or "7416."

Gen V Crankshafts

All Gen V big-block crankshafts use a one-piece rear seal. They cannot be installed in Mark IV or race-prepared Gen

V Bow Tie blocks, which have rear main caps designed for two-piece seals.

PN 14096983 is a 4.00-inch stroke forged 1053 steel crankshaft used in 454 H.O. engine assemblies. PN 10183723 is a similar 4.00-inch stroke crankshaft, balanced for use in 502 H.O. engines. Both of these cranks are externally balanced, and have the same "14097044" forging ID number.

A 3.76-inch stroke Gen V crankshaft is available as PN 10114186. This forged 1053 steel cranks is used in 1991-up 427ci truck engines.

Torsional Dampers

The torsional damper requirements of a high-performance engine vary with its duty cycle. Engines used in drag racing and short track competition frequently

operate without torsional dampers (sometimes called "harmonic balancers") with no apparent ill effects. In these engines' duty cycles, the engine rpm changes frequently and rapidly. This reduces the length of time that the crankshaft vibrates at its natural frequency and diminishes the need for a torsional damper.

Engines used in endurance racing and high-performance marine applications typically operate at a much slower rate of change in engine speed. This increases the length of time that the crankshaft may operate near its natural frequency, and may require a torsional damper to prevent crankshaft breakage due to high torsional vibrations. (See the "Torsional Damper" section on page 37 for more information on the effects of torsional vibrations on high-performance engines.)

A big-block Chevrolet V8's torsional damper and crankshaft must be properly matched to achieve proper engine balance. Chevrolet Mark IV crankshafts with 3.76-inch strokes are internally balanced, and use a neutral-balanced damper; 4.00-inch stroke Mark IV crankshafts and all Gen V crankshafts (regardless of stroke) are externally balanced, and must use a counterweighted damper (unless the crank has been internally balanced with heavy metal).

Production Torsional Dampers

Chevrolet offers three heavy-duty 8-inch diameter torsional dampers for big-block V8 engines. PN 3879623 is a neutral balanced damper designed to be used with all internally balanced Mark IV big-blocks. This damper was original equipment on 1967-69 427ci engines.

PN 14097024 was designed for LS-6 and LS-7 454ci engine assemblies. This counterweighted damper can be used with 4.00-inch stroke externally balanced Mark IV crankshafts.

Gen V 454 and 502ci engines use torsional damper PN 14097023. This damper is used *only* with forged steel Gen V crankshafts. Nodular iron 4.00-inch stroke Gen V cranks require torsional damper PN 10101160.

Production big-block torsional dampers are marked for Top Dead Center only. Many engine builders prefer to true up the outer ring and add degree marks. Either procedure requires that the damper be rebalanced before installation. Chevrolet balancing specifications call for removal of material from the outer inertia ring with

Contrasting degree marks on the GM/Fluidampr are easy to see with a timing light. The housing is hermetically sealed.

a ½-inch drill to a maximum depth of ¼-inch on a radius of 3.62-inch from the hub centerline. *Warning:* Balance holes of greater diameter or depth may seriously weaken the damper and cause the inertia ring to fail at high engine speed.

GM/Fluidampr®

Chevrolet also offers an 8-inch GM/Fluidampr for externally balanced Mark IV big-blocks as PN 10051171. This counterweighted damper uses a thick, viscous fluid instead of an elastomer ring to control crankshaft vibrations. The Fluidampr's inertia ring and viscous fluid are contained in a hermetically sealed housing. The difference in rotational speed between the housing and the inertia ring dampens crankshaft vibrations by shearing the silicone fluid. (In a conventional damper, vibrations are controlled by the stretch and rebound of the rubber elastomer ring between the hub and inertia ring.)

The Fluidampr torsional damper offers several benefits for high-performance big-block V8s. Unlike a simple hub (which has no inertia ring, and therefore no vibration damping capability), the Fluidampr will extend crankshaft, main bearing, and timing chain life. Errors in ignition timing caused by movement of the outer inertia ring on a conventional damper are eliminated. This damper also

Flywheels used with externally balanced crankshafts must have a counterweight to produce proper engine balance.

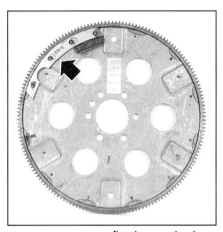

Automatic transmission flexplates used with 4.00-inch stroke crankshafts also require a counterweight for correct balance.

meets the safety specifications of many racing organizations which prohibit the use of stock-type cast iron balancers on competition engines.

Unlike conventional elastomer dampers, viscous dampers are not tuned to a specific vibration frequency. This is an important consideration in a racing engine because any change in the weight of the engine's reciprocating assembly alters the natural harmonic frequency. The Fluidampr requires no maintenance.

Installation

Regardless of the type of torsional damper you select for your big-block, the damper must fit tightly on the crank snout to effectively control the crankshaft's torsional vibrations. The inside diameter of the hub should not be honed oversize; automatic transmission fluid can be used as a lubricant when installing a damper that fits the crankshaft tightly. A ½-20 x 1¼-inch damper bolt (PN 9419218) and

Flexplate PN 10185034 for 4.00-inch stroke Gen V forged steel crankshafts has a dual torque converter pattern.

Lightweight nodular iron flywheels are available for internally and externally balanced big-block V8s.

washer (PN 3864814) should be used to positively retain the harmonic balancer on the crankshaft snout.

Flywheels

Like torsional dampers, big-block Chevrolet flywheels must be correctly matched to the crankshaft to produce proper engine balance. All big-block crankshafts have a 3.58-inch diameter flywheel flange bolt pattern. Although Mark IV and Gen V flywheels appear to be interchangeable, they are balanced differently, and should be used only with the engine and crankshaft for which they were designed.

Flywheel and flexplate selection for Mark IV big-blocks is straightforward. Internally balanced 3.76-inch stroke cranks used in 396, 402, and 427ci engines require neutral balanced flywheels. The 4.00-inch stroke cranks used in 454ci Mark IV engines are externally balanced,

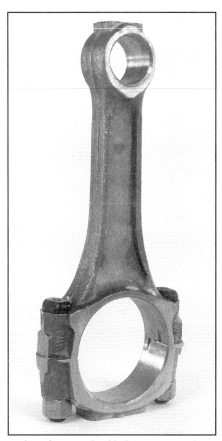

High-performance big-block connecting rods with ⁷⁄₁₆-inch bolts are produced for pressed and floating piston pins.

and require counterweighted flywheels and flexplates.

All Gen V crankshafts use unbalanced flywheels and flexplates. However, the crankshaft *material* also affects engine balance in Gen V big-blocks. Different flywheels are required depending on whether the crankshaft is forged steel or cast nodular iron. Flywheels and flexplates for Gen V and Mark IV big-blocks are listed in the specifications chart.

Two lightweight 15-pound nodular iron flywheels are available for Mark IV big-blocks. Chevrolet nodular iron flywheels in new condition have been tested at 10,000 rpm engine speeds, and are suitable for many high-performance applications. It should be emphasized, however, that overheating a clutch can significantly weaken a flywheel and lower the burst speed at which failure could occur. Although a Chevrolet heavy-duty flywheel is safe for competition use when new, it should be periodically inspected for radial cracks emanating from the flywheel flange bolts holes and for signs of excessive clutch heat. (Some sanctioning bodies prohibit the use of stock-type flywheels in competition. Check the rules regarding flywheel specifications before using a nodular iron flywheel.)

Except as noted in the chart, all heavy-duty flywheels and flexplates are 14 inches in overall diameter and have 168-tooth starter ring gears. Chevrolet starter motor PN 1108400 should be used with these 14-inch diameter flywheels and flexplates. In applications that require a 12³⁄₄-inch flywheel (153-tooth ring gear), starter PN 1108789 is recommended.

Connecting Rods

Chevrolet has developed a variety of connecting rods for the big-block V8 to suit different applications. Connecting rods are interchangeable between Mark IV and Gen V big-blocks. All big-block rods have a center-to-center length of 6.135-inch, and a bearing bore diameter of 2.3247/2.3252-inch.

Most standard performance and some early-model high-performance big-blocks were originally equipped with connecting rods with ³⁄₈-inch bolts. These rods are suitable for moderate-duty use in pleasure boats, tow vehicles, and limited competition classes. Rod bolts and nuts should be inspected frequently and replaced at every engine overhaul. High-strength alloy ³⁄₈-inch bolts are available from aftermarket sources.

TECH SPECS: BIG-BLOCK V8 MANUAL TRANSMISSION FLYWHEELS

Part Number	Outside Diameter	Year	Crank Flange Bolt Pattern	Clutch Diameter	Starter Ring Gear Teeth	Notes
14085720	12³⁄₄"	1965–69	3.58"	10.4"	153	Lightweight nodular iron flywheel; weighs approximately 15 lbs.; for internally balanced Mark IV only.
3963537	12³⁄₄"	1970–90	3.58"	10.4"	153	Lightweight nodular iron flywheel; weighs approximately 15 lbs.; for externally balanced 454ci Mark IV only.
3991469	14"	1965–69	3.58"	11.0"	168	For internally balanced Mark IV only.
3993827	14"	1970-90	3.58"	11.0"	168	For externally balanced 454ci Mark IV only.
14096987	14"	1991 up	3.58"	11.0"	168	For externally balanced H.O. 454, H.O. 502 Gen V engines with 4.00" stroke steel crankshaft only.
10101169	14"	1991 up	3.58"	11.0"	168	For Gen V with 4.00" stroke nodular iron crankshaft only.

TECH SPECS: BIG-BLOCK V8 AUTOMATIC TRANSMISSION FLEXPLATES

Part Number	Outside Diameter	Year	Crank Flange Bolt Pattern	Starter Ring Gear Teeth	Notes
471597	14"	1965–69	3.58"	168	For internally balanced Mark IV only.
14001992	14"	1970–90	3.58"	168	For externally balanced 454ci Mark IV only.
10185034	14"	1991 up	3.58"	168	For externally balanced Gen V H.O. 454 and H.O. 502 with forged steel crankshaft only.
10185035	14"	1991 up	3.58"	168	For externally balanced 454ci Gen V with cast iron crankshaft only.

Connecting rods with $\frac{7}{16}$-inch bolts are strongly recommended for severe service and high-performance use. Chevrolet offers two connecting rods that are suitable for competition engines. PN 10198922 (white color code) is a pressed-pin rod originally installed in LS-6/LS-7 and H.O. 454 and H.O. 502 engine assemblies. This rod is forged from 4340 alloy steel, Magnaflux inspected, and shotpeened. It is supplied with $\frac{7}{16}$-20 heavy-duty bolts with knurled shanks. (Replacement bolts are available as PN 14096148; nuts are PN 3942410). Recommended bolt torque is 73 ft.-lbs.

A second Chevrolet big-block connecting rod with $\frac{7}{16}$-inch bolts is designed for full-floating pins and available as PN 3969804 (green color code). This rod is also forged from 4340 alloy steel, Magnaflux inspected, and shotpeened. This rod is equipped with special boron steel bolts that are 100 percent Magnaflux inspected and shotpeened. These fasteners are of exceptionally high quality, and generally do not require replacement during rebuilds. (Individual bolts are offered

as PN 3969864. Corresponding 12-point 6304 alloy steel nuts are PN 340289.) Recommended torque for boron bolts is 67 to 73 ft.-lbs., or .009-inch bolt stretch.

Refer to the engine blueprinting chapter for recommendations on connecting rod preparation for competition engines.

Pistons

Forged aluminum pistons are preferred over cast pistons in heavy-duty applications. The dense grain structure of a forging increases strength and promotes heat transfer away from the piston top. During the forging process, the aluminum's grain structure is formed by the die pattern, improving both the piston's ultimate strength and its fatigue life. Consequently a forged piston is better able to survive the mechanical and thermal stresses in a competition engine than a cast piston.

Compression Ratio

Due to differences in the combustion chamber volumes of big-block V8 cylinder heads, heavy-duty Chevrolet pistons

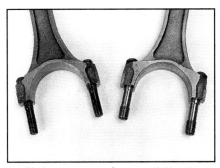

Big-block connecting rods are available with $\frac{3}{8}$-inch (left) and $\frac{7}{16}$-inch bolts (right). Larger bolts are recommended for racing.

Premium quality boron steel $\frac{7}{16}$-inch rod bolts are standard in big-block connecting rods machined for floating pins.

TECH SPECS: BIG-BLOCK V8 HIGH-PERFORMANCE PISTONS

Part Number	Engine	Compression Ratio	Size	Dome Type	Pin Type	ID#	Notes
14097018	454	8.75:1	Standard	N/A	Pressed	10185058	Use with Gen V 454 HO engine.
12509000	454	8.75:1	+.030	N/A	Pressed	10185058	Use with Gen V 454 HO engine.
10198977	502	8.75:1	Standard	N/A	Pressed	N/A	Use with all 502 (8.2L) engines (compression based on 118 cc head).
10198996	502	8.75:1	+.030	N/A	Pressed	N/A	Use with all 502 (8.2L) engines (compression based on 118 cc head).
3959105	427	12.25:1	Standard	Open	Floating	3947886 or 3959108	68-69 L-88 and ZL-1. Use pin retainer #3942423.
3976013	454	11:1	Standard	Closed	Pressed	3963550 or 3976031	1970 LS-6; produces 10:1 compression ratio with open chamber head.
3976014	454	12.25:1	Standard	Open	Pressed	3963551 or 3976032	1970 LS-7
3976018	454	12.25:1	+.001 (Std. high limit)	Open	Pressed	3976036	1970 LS-7
6262976	454	9:1	Standard	Closed	Pressed	3994031, 3999295, 6262972 or 6269362-3	1971 LS-6
6262977	454	9:1	+.001 (Std. high limit)	Closed	Pressed	3994032, 6262973 or 6269364	1971 LS-6
6262979	454	9:1	+.030	Closed	Pressed	3994034, 6262975 or 6269366	1971 LS-6

High-compression big-block pistons must match the combustion chamber design. The piston on the left is designed for a closed combustion chamber; the piston on the right fits an open chamber.

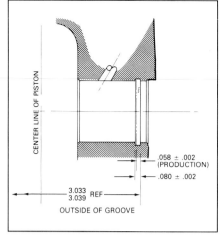

Modify 427ci L-88/ZL-1 pistons (PN 3959105) to use .072-inch pin retainers by widening the grooves in the pin bosses.

Big-block Chevrolet forged pistons (left to right): PN 6262976 9:1 closed chamber 454ci; PN 3976013 11:1 closed chamber 454ci; PN 3959105 12.25:1 open chamber 427ci.

Piston valve pockets must be deepened if there is less than .080/.100-inch valve clearance.

will yield different compression ratios depending on the cylinder heads used.

Flat-top pistons can be used with both closed and open combustion chambers. Similarly, pistons designed for closed-type chambers can also be used with open chamber heads if a reduction in the actual compression ratio is desired. However, open chamber pistons must *never* be used with closed chamber heads because the piston domes will hit the heads.

For example, Chevrolet piston PN 3976013 was originally installed in closed chamber LS-6 big-blocks to produce an 11:1 compression ratio. When used with open chamber heads, this same piston yields a 10.2:1 compression ratio.

The compression ratio should be a primary consideration when selecting pistons for a high-performance or racing big-block V8. Compression ratio is a function of the cylinder displacement,

combustion chamber volume, deck clearance, head gasket thickness, and piston dome design. Compression ratios that are too high for the octane rating of the available fuel will promote detonation and lead to engine damage. (High cylinder pressures that promote detonation are also affected by camshaft timing, ignition advance, port design, and other factors.)

The octane rating of commercially available pump gasoline limits high-performance street engines to compression ratios below 10:1. Raising the compression ratio in a modified engine offers a potential performance improvement, but high-octane gasoline and/or octane-improving additives are usually required to prevent detonation. For all-out racing engines, Chevrolet offers heavy-duty domed pistons with a nominal compression ratio of 12.25:1. Engines with such high compression ratios must be operated on high-octane racing fuels exclusively,

and should be inspected frequently for evidence of detonation.

Piston Preparation

All Chevrolet big-block pistons listed in the accompanying chart are manufactured from forged aluminum and are machined for pressed piston pins. The only exception is the 427ci L-88/ZL-1 piston (PN 3959105), which is machined for full-floating pins and .055-inch thick Spirolox pin retainers. These pistons should be modified to use .072-inch retainers (PN 3964238) for competition engines. The thicker retainers are more resistant to being pushed out of their grooves.

Heavy-duty Spirolox pin retainers should also be used when converting pressed-pin pistons to full-floating wrist pins. Production and service wrist pins must have machined flat ends for use with floating pin retainers (except pins designed for round wire retainers). After

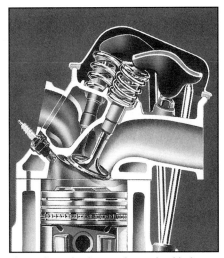

The intake and exhaust valves in big-block heads are inclined in two axes.

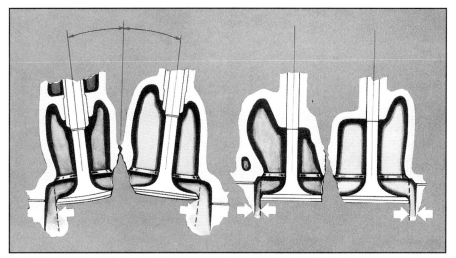

A big-block V8's splayed valves (left) move away from the cylinder walls as lift increases; in-line valves (right) remain shrouded.

machining the retainer grooves, grind or turn the wrist pins to produce zero to .005-inch wrist pin end play. *Wrist pin retainers should never be reused after the engine has been run and disassembled.*

The recommended piston-to-cylinder wall clearance for Chevrolet forged aluminum pistons is .0065/.0075-inch, measured perpendicular to the piston pin at the centerline of the wrist pin hole. Follow the manufacturer's recommendations when installing aftermarket pistons.

Piston Rings

Chevrolet heavy-duty piston ring sets include high-strength iron, moly-filled, radius-faced 1/16-inch wide top and second rings with three-piece 3/16-inch oil rings. Oversize ring sets are available for 4.250-inch cylinder bores (+.030 PN 3993830; +.060 PN 3993831). These rings must be filed to obtain the recommended end gaps (.018-inch top, .016-inch second and oil). In all cases, end gaps should be measured when installing new rings.

The ring sets used in H.O. 454 and H.O. 502 engine assemblies have barrel-faced moly top rings, tapered-face moly second rings, and low-tension oil rings.

The GM Motorsports Technology Group recommends a smooth cylinder wall finish, using 400 grit stones for the final hone as described in the engine building chapter. Modern ring manufacturing techniques virtually eliminate the need for a lengthy break-in time to seat the rings; rough bore finishes are simply not necessary to seat the rings. A smooth cylinder bore finish on initial build results in a significant power increase due to decreased engine internal friction.

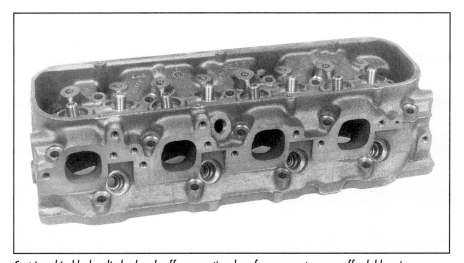

Cast iron big-block cylinder heads offer exceptional performamce at a very affordable price. Rectangular port heads are available for Mark IV and Gen V engines. Heads are supplied bare, without valves, rocker arm studs or pushrod guideplates.

Cylinder Heads

Certainly much of the success of the Chevrolet big-block V8 can be attributed to the engine's innovative splayed-valve layout. This design inclines the intake and exhaust valves in two planes to provide exceptional airflow potential. In production Mark IV and Gen V cylinder heads, the intake valve angle is 26 degrees (relative to the cylinder bore centerline) and the exhaust valve angle is 17 degrees. Both valves also have a four degree "tilt" toward the center of the cylinder.

The big-block V8's compound valve angle moves the valve heads away from the combustion chamber and cylinder walls as lift increases. The unshrouded intake and exhaust valves contribute to the big-block's breathing ability.

The valves in Chevrolet big-block V8s are actuated by stud-mounted rocker arms. This lightweight, rugged valvetrain design provides outstanding performance and reliability at high rpm.

Chevrolet has produced a variety of cylinder head castings for the big-block V8. These heads differ in material (cast iron and aluminum), intake port shape (round, oval and rectangular), and combustion chamber design (closed and open).

For maximum performance, aluminum heads are preferred over cast iron because of their lighter weight and ease of modification. Large rectangular intake ports produce higher airflow than the smaller oval runners, giving them the advantage in competition applications. Open combustion chambers unshroud the valves at high lifts, improving engine performance over closed chamber designs.

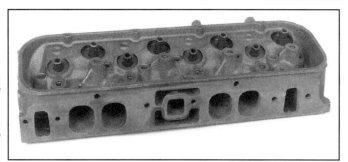

Light-duty big-block truck engines use heads with round intake ports to boost low-speed and mid-range torque output.

Oval port cylinder heads are common on standard performance big-blocks. These heads perform well on the street.

A "symmetrical port" Bow Tie aluminum cylinder head was also developed specifically for maximum-effort Chevrolet big-block racing engines. This head is a marked departure from all previous big-block cylinder heads. Its features are described later in this section.

Cylinder Head Interchangeability

Cylinder heads are not readily interchangeable between Mark IV and Gen V production big-blocks due to differences in the two engines' coolant passages. Although Mark IV heads will bolt onto a Gen V production block, there is a high potential for water leaks because of changes in the size and location of the coolant holes in the Gen V's decks.

Gen V Bow Tie blocks have smaller cored holes in their decks than production

TECH SPECS: BIG-BLOCK V8 CYLINDER HEADS

Part Number	Description	Casting Number	Material/ Weight (lbs.)	Combustion Chamber Type/ Volume(cc)	Valve Diameter Int./Exh. (inches)	Port Volume Int./Exh. (cc)	Exhaust Port	Notes
10140633	Service replacement Mk. IV	3964291	Cast iron	Closed/108cc	2.19/1.72	325/NA	Square	Do not use with open chamber pistons; originally produced 1965-71.
6260482	Service replacement Mk. IV	6272990 or 14096188	Cast iron	Open/118cc	2.19/1.88	325/NA	Square	Used on LS-6 and LS-7; open or closed chamber pistons; originally produced 1968-71.
14096802	Service replacement Gen V	14097088	Cast iron	Open/118cc	2.19/1.88	325/NA	Square	Use with Gen V big-block engine #10185058-59; bare casting.
14096801	Service replacement Gen V	14097088	Cast iron	Open/118cc	2.19/1.88	325/NA	Square	Use with Gen V big-block engine #10185058-59; complete with springs and valves.
3919838	Service replacement Mk. IV	3919842	Aluminum	Closed/107cc	2.19/1.84	325/NA	Round	Do not use with open chamber pistons.
14011076	Service replacement Mk. IV	14011077	Aluminum/ 27.0	Open/114cc	2.19/1.88	290/103	D-shaped with vane	Standard port locations; referred to as "C-port" head.
14044862	Bow Tie Mk. IV	14044861	Aluminum/ 28.5	Open/112cc	2.19/1.88	358/126	Rectangular with vane	Raised intake and exhaust runners, special combustion chambers, "W-port" head.
14044861	Bow Tie Mk. IV (bare)	14044861	Aluminum/ 27.5	Open/112cc	N/A	358/126	Rectangular with vane	No seats and guides.
10051128	Symmetrical port Bow Tie Mk. IV Unmachined	10051128	Aluminum/ 31.5	Semi-open/ 68cc	N/A	404/158	Round	Evenly spaced intake runners, raised exhaust ports; Pro Stock head; no seats and guides.
10051129	Symmetrical port Bow Tie Mk. IV	10051129	Aluminum	Semi-open/ 72cc	N/A	N/A	Round	Raw casting.

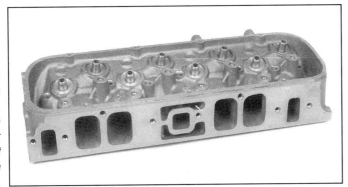

High-performance big-block heads have rectangular ports. These heads are recommended for large displacement and high-rpm engines.

Match the cylinder head ports to the intake manifold runners for maximum performance.

Gen V blocks. These smaller passages permit the installation of Mark IV cylinder heads on Gen V Bow Tie blocks without the risk of coolant leaks. Refer to the head gasket section of this chapter for gasket recommendations when making this conversion.

Cast Iron Cylinder Heads

Cylinder heads used on big-block truck engines have round intake runners, while passenger car big-block cylinder heads generally have oval intake ports. These heads' relatively small intake runners maintain high flow velocities at low and moderate engine speeds. Their closed and semi-open combustion chambers provide adequate breathing with the camshaft profiles used in street and mild performance applications.

High-performance cast iron cylinder heads have large, rectangular intake runners, and offer exceptional performance at an affordable price. Mark IV rectangular port heads are available with closed (108cc) combustion chambers as PN 10140633, and with open (118cc) chambers as PN 6260482. Both heads are supplied without valves, springs, rocker studs, and pushrod guideplates.

A rectangular port cast iron cylinder head assembly is available for Gen V big-blocks as PN 14096801. This assembly, which is used on H.O. 454 and H.O. 502 engines, includes valves, springs, and retainers. (Bare Gen V heads without springs and valves are available as PN 14096802.) This head has open-style 118cc combustion chambers that produce 8.75:1 compression on an H.O. 502 short block.

An appealing cylinder head alternative for high-torque Gen V engines is to install 2.19-inch intake valves and 1.88-inch exhaust valves in production cast iron oval port cylinder heads (PN 10101137). These heads have high-velocity intake runners and closed combustion chambers that yield 9.8:1 compression on an H.O.

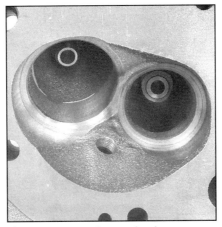

The 118cc open combustion chamber in cylinder head PN 6260482 is machined for 2.19-inch intake valves and 1.88-inch exhausts.

"HI PERF" casting mark under the rocker cover identifies a high-performance rectangular port big-block cylinder head.

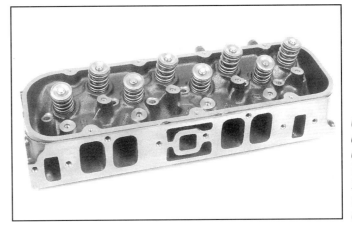

Gen V H.O. cast iron cylinder head assembly PN 14096801 includes 2.19/1.88-inch valves, dual springs, and retainers.

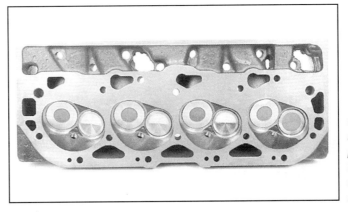

Gen V cylinder heads have coolant passages that match the cored openings in a Gen V block's deck surface.

Aluminum cylinder head PN 3919838 has 107cc closed combustion chambers. This head cannot be used with open chamber pistons.

The open combustion chambers in aluminum cylinder head PN 14011076 have seat inserts for 2.19/1.88-inch diameter valves.

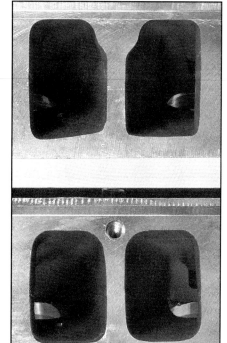

The intake port entrances in the Bow Tie cylinder head (top) are .100-inch higher than the runners in a production head (bottom).

Aluminum cylinder head PN 3919838 was originally installed on high-performance Mark IV engines in 1965-69.

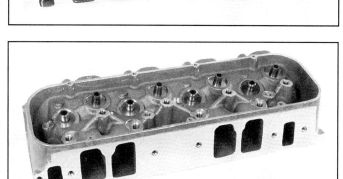

Aluminum Bow Tie cylinder head PN 14044861-2 has a higher performance potential than any production big-block head.

"C"-port exhausts in aluminum cylinder head PN 14011076 offer improved airflow over round ports in early aluminum heads.

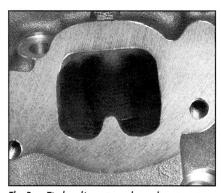

The Bow Tie head's rectangular exhaust port exits are .750-inch higher than the ports in production big-block heads.

502 partial engine assembly. GM Motorsports Technology Group engineers recommend this oval port/big-valve cylinder head combination for street performance and bracket racing applications with a 5500 rpm maximum engine speed.

Production Aluminum Cylinder Heads

Aluminum cylinder heads for Chevrolet big-block V8s range from service replacement castings for production engines to purpose-built designs for competition motors.

PN 3919838 is a closed chamber (106.8cc) aluminum head originally installed on 1965-69 396 and 427ci engines. Because of advances in cylinder head technology incorporated in later castings, this head is recommended only for restoration projects that require original components.

PN 14011076 is frequently referred to as a "C" port casting because of its distinctive exhaust port shape. The "C" is formed by material added to the floor of the exhaust port and a "vane" in the center of the runner. Raising the runner floor smoothed the flow of exhaust gases from the valve bowl, while the vane prevented the formation of negative pressure in the exhaust runner and inhibited reverse flow. These revisions produced a 25 percent increase in exhaust airflow over the round ports in early-model heads.

The intake runners of the "076" head were also revised to improve their airflow potential. Material added to the floor of the intake ports raised the short side radius and produced a smoother transition from the runner to the valve bowl. The floor of the runner was also canted to match the intake valve angle, eliminating a hollow behind the intake valve seats found on earlier aluminum cylinder heads.

The "076" C-port aluminum cylinder head retains the Mark IV's standard

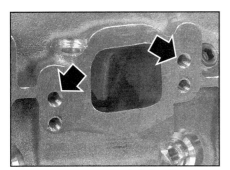

In a pre-1992 Bow Tie head, drill and tap additional exhaust mounting holes or redrill the header flanges to raise the primary pipes.

Use modified pushrod guideplates and .200-inch longer intake pushrods with Bow Tie heads for correct valvetrain geometry.

The Bow Tie cylinder head has 112cc open combustion chambers and seat inserts for 2.19/1.88-inch valves.

Pushrod guideplates must be ground to fit the raised intake runners in Bow Tie big-block cylinder heads.

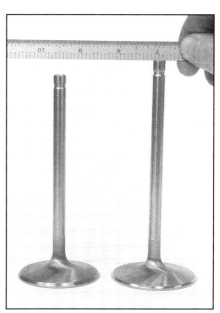

The raised runners in Bow Tie head PN 14044861-2 require aftermarket intake valves with .200-inch longer stems.

Relieve Bow Tie heads to clear the guideplates, or space the guideplates upward with washers and extra-long aftermarket rocker arm studs.

intake and exhaust port locations. It is recommended for mildly modified engines, truck and tractor pull motors, marine usage, and other applications where high torque output at low and moderate engine speeds is desirable.

Aluminum Bow Tie Cylinder Head PN 14044861-2

A revised heavy-duty big-block aluminum cylinder head was introduced in 1984 as PN 14044862. A fully machined version without seats and guides was released as PN 14044861. The Bow Tie cylinder head casting incorporated advances in airflow technology developed by leading competition engine builders and cylinder head specialists.

The intake runner entrances are .100-inch higher than the standard port location. The ports are raised an additional .100-inch immediately downstream from the head/manifold junction—a total change of .200-inch in the intake runner location compared to the ports in production big-block cylinder heads.

The short-side radius of the intake port was also raised to provide a more efficient approach to the intake valve. These changes account for an increase in runner volume of approximately 68cc over the

ports in a production big-block aluminum cylinder head. The Bow Tie cylinder head's larger intake ports are sized to produce a significant increase in horsepower and torque at high engine speeds, especially on large displacement engines.

The Bow Tie head's exhaust ports were revised to improve their airflow capacity. The port exits are raised .750-inch above the standard location. The port vanes introduced on the "C" port head were retained, but the exhaust port exits are rectangular in shape. The exhaust runners' high short side radius substantially reduces turbulence in the ports.

The Bow Tie head's revised exhaust port location may require modifications to headers and exhaust systems. This can be accomplished in pre-1992 heads by drilling additional holes in the header flange, or by drilling and tapping the cylinder head's exhaust manifold flange.

The Bow Tie head also has a revised combustion chamber with a volume of approximately 112cc. Although the Bow Tie chamber is similar to the production open chamber design, there are several important differences. Material was added to the quench area between the intake and exhaust valves to decrease chamber volume. Also, the combustion

chamber walls adjacent to the intake and exhaust valves are not relieved. These changes may require modifications to standard piston domes for adequate clearance, depending on the dome profile and the piston-to-head clearance.

Bow Tie cylinder head PN 14044862 is supplied with valve guides and seat inserts for 2.19-inch diameter intake valves and 1.88-inch diameter exhaust valves. Due to the Bow Tie head's higher intake port location, valves with .200-inch longer-than-stock stems are recommended. These extra-long valves are available from aftermarket sources. Stock length valves can be installed in Bow Tie heads if the valve spring seats are machined .200-inch deeper into the cylinder head. The roofs of the intake runners should not be raised when porting

Chevrolet developed the symmetrical port Bow Tie head (PN 10051128) specifically for 500ci Pro Stock drag racing engines.

The round exhaust ports in a symmetrical port head (top) are .400-inch higher than the runners in a Bow Tie head (bottom).

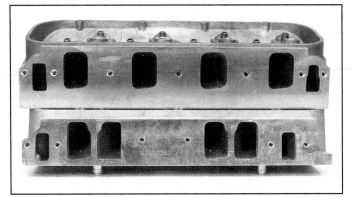

A conventional heavy-duty Bow Tie cylinder head (PN 14044862–bottom) has two pairs of siamesed intake ports; the symmetrical port head (PN 10051128) has four equally spaced runners.

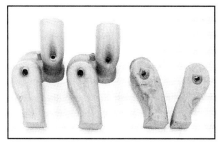

Conventional heads have "long" and "short" intake runners (right); a symmetrical port head has four identical runners (left).

the heads if you have machined the valve spring pockets deeper.

The Bow Tie big-block head has reinforced rocker stud bosses that are designed to resist cracking when high-pressure valve springs are used. Before installing the pushrod guideplates, the area around the rocker stud bosses must be relieved with a hand grinder or the guideplates ground to fit.

The rocker cover rails on Bow Tie big-block heads are raised .250-inch to improve gasket sealing with the higher intake port location. The rocker cover bolt pattern is the same as on production cylinder heads, allowing the use of standard Chevrolet rocker covers.

Symmetrical Port Bow Tie Head

A new heavy-duty aluminum Bow Tie cylinder head was released for the Chevrolet big-block V8 in 1987 as PN 10051128. This head was developed in cooperation with leading Chevrolet Pro Stock engine builders, and was designed for maximum-effort competition engines displacing 500 cubic inches. Although this new casting incorporates several noteworthy features, its most striking characteristic is four equally spaced, symmetrical intake runners.

Unlike other big-block cylinder heads, the symmetrical runner Bow Tie head is not machined on production tooling. This allowed greater freedom in the design and engineering of the cylinder head for racing applications.

The symmetrical port design requires significant revisions in related engine components. Pistons, valvetrain, intake manifold, exhaust headers, spark plugs, and gaskets all have to be changed or fabricated. Due to these extensive changes, the symmetrical port Bow Tie cylinder head it is not a "bolt-on" replacement for production heads.

This head's most significant departure from conventional big-block castings is its intake port configuration. Production heads have two distinct intake runners—a long "dog leg" port (cylinders #1, 4, 5, and 8) and a short, direct port (cylinders #2, 3, 6 and 7). This port layout is necessitated by the big-block V8's head bolt pattern. One byproduct of this dual-port design is a measurable difference in the airflow capacity, camshaft requirements, and spark plug heat range for the cylinders served by long and short intake ports. A primary objective of the symmetrical port layout was to equalize the airflow between all eight cylinders.

Two runners are located directly above the head bolt holes in the symmetrical port Bow Tie head. Short socket-head capscrews replace the conventional hex-head bolts in these locations. AN plugs with "O"-ring seals (Parker 8HP50N-5 or equivalent) provide access to these capscrews, which are recessed in the intake runner floors. Because all four intake runners can be machined for plugs, it is possible to drill and tap the block's deck surfaces for additional head bolts on the intake manifold side of cylinders 2, 3, 6, and 7. This modification provides six head bolts around every cylinder, significantly improving head gasket sealing with high compression ratios.

The inlet runners of the symmetrical port head are raised .750-inch higher than the ports in a conventional Bow Tie head to provide a more direct "line of sight" path to the intake valve. The port floors are also moved upward and the valve angles revised to improve the efficiency of the intake port. The intake runner volume is approximately 404cc, depending on the final valve and seat configuration chosen by the engine builder. This runner

BOW TIE TIPS — Head Bolt Help

The following head bolt hardware is recommended for big-block V8 engines equipped with symmetrical port Bow Tie cylinder heads:

Qty.	Description
4	3/8 NC x 1.5" Allen head bolt
4	7/16 NC x 1.5" Allen head bolt
8	7/16 NC x 2" Allen head bolt
2	7/16 NC x 4.25" Allen head bolt
10	7/16 NC x 4.5" Allen head bolt
8	7/16 NC x 5.5" Allen head bolt
28	Washer, 7/16 x .75" O.D. (PN 10051155)
4	Washer, 7/16 x .625" O.D. (PN 14011093)
4	Washer, 3/8" AN

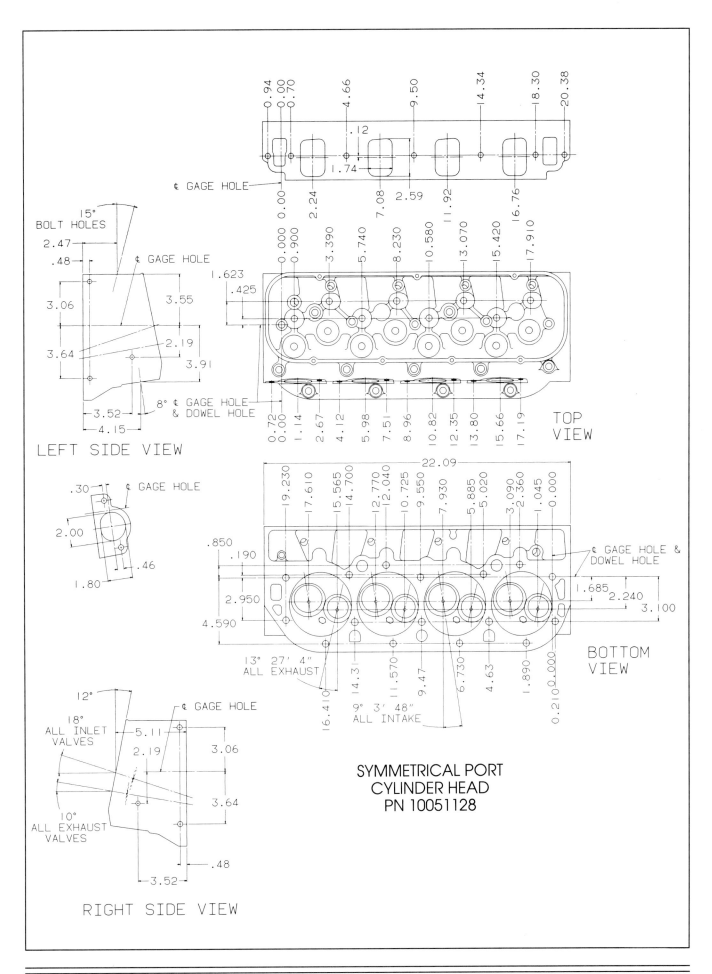

0.94
0.00
0.70
4.66
9.50
14.34
18.30
20.38

.12

¢ GAGE HOLE

1.74

0.00
2.24
7.08
2.59
11.92
16.76

15°
BOLT HOLES

2.47
.48

¢ GAGE HOLE

0.000
0.900
3.390
5.740
8.230
10.580
13.070
15.420
17.910

1.623
.425

3.06
3.55

3.64
2.19
3.91

3.52
4.15

8° ¢ GAGE HOLE
& DOWEL HOLE

LEFT SIDE VIEW

0.72
0.00
1.14
2.67
4.12
5.98
7.51
8.96
10.82
12.35
13.80
15.66
17.19

TOP VIEW

.30
¢ GAGE HOLE

2.00

.46

1.80

22.09

19.230
17.610
15.565
14.700
12.770
12.040
10.725
9.550
7.930
5.885
5.020
3.090
2.360
1.045
0.000

.850
.190

¢ GAGE HOLE &
DOWEL HOLE

2.950

1.685
2.240

4.590

3.100

13° 27' 4"
ALL EXHAUST

16.410
14.31
11.570
9.47
6.730
4.63
1.890

0.210
0.000

9° 3' 48"
ALL INTAKE

BOTTOM VIEW

12°

18°
ALL INLET
VALVES

¢ GAGE HOLE

5.11

2.19

3.06

3.64

10°
ALL EXHAUST
VALVES

.48

3.52

SYMMETRICAL PORT
CYLINDER HEAD
PN 10051128

RIGHT SIDE VIEW

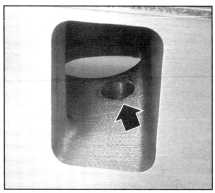

Socket head capscrews in the floors of the intake ports replace standard head bolts. These holes have a negligible effect on airflow.

Holes in the roofs of the intake runners provide access to the capscrew head bolts. AN plugs with "O"-rings seal the ports.

A big-block's decks can be drilled and tapped in two locations for additional head bolts when using symmetrical port heads.

The 68cc combustion chambers in a symmetrical port head (right) are shallower than the chambers in a Bow Tie head (left).

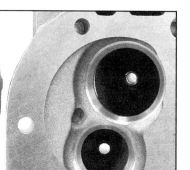

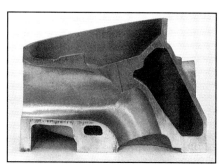

The raised runners in the symmetrical port Bow Tie head provide a direct "line-of-sight" path to the intake valves.

Rework the combustion chambers in symmetrical port heads as shown to improve intake and exhaust flow.

The symmetrical port head's raised intake and exhaust runners require valves that are .800-inch longer than production valves.

size was selected to provide optimum performance on a 500-cubic-inch drag racing engine. The minimum port wall thickness of the symmetrical port Bow Tie head is .240-inch, providing material for cylinder head porters to make extensive modifications without welding.

The ports require only minimal preparation work before installation. An abrasive cartridge roll should be used to lightly polish and blend the runners. The short-side radiuses and the valve bowls should not be enlarged or recontoured; modifying these areas generally results in a loss of airflow and reduced engine performance throughout the rpm range.

The combustion chamber is a shallow, semi-open design with a volume of approximately 68cc. This revised chamber allows an engine builder to achieve high compression ratios with a relatively small piston dome. The quench area extends between the intake and exhaust valves. The chamber shape also provides maximum material for head porting specialists to shape for various piston configurations. The minimum wall thickness of the combustion chamber and deck surface is .600-inch. The symmetrical port Bow Tie head is supplied without valve seats and guides, allowing competition engine builders to install their preferred components for specific applications.

Valve angles were also revised in the symmetrical port head. The intake valve angle is 18 degrees (versus 26 degrees in other big-block heads), and the exhaust valve angle is 10 degrees (versus 17 degrees in conventional heads). The compound angle of both valves was reduced from 4 to 2.5 degrees. These changes increase valve clearance, and make it possible to install large diameter valves. The intake valve is positioned in line with the bore centerline at .500-inch lift to minimize cylinder wall shrouding.

The symmetrical port Bow Tie head's raised runners and deep valve bowls require valves that are .800-inch longer than production big-block heads, and .600-inch longer than Bow Tie heads. These extra-long valves are available from aftermarket sources.

Spark plugs are centrally located in the symmetrical port head's revised combustion chambers to suppress detonation and to improve flame travel across the cylinder. The plug holes are machined for tapered seat ⅝-inch plugs with .708-inch reach. Spark plugs are readily available in a variety of heat ranges.

The symmetrical port big-block head's exhaust port exits are .400-inch higher than the ports in a Bow Tie big-block head, and 1.150-inch higher than the

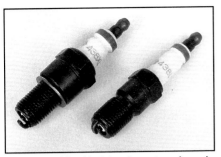

Conventional big-block heads use ¾-inch reach gasketed plugs (left); the symmetrical port head's spark plug holes are machined for ⅝-inch hex-head, .708-inch reach tapered seat plugs (right).

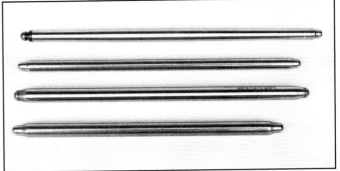

Exhaust pushrods for Bow Tie heads can be used as intake pushrods with symmetrical port heads.

Shaft-mounted rocker arms are recommended for symmetrical port heads. Offset rockers increase pushrod clearance.

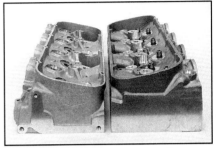

The rocker cover rail on a symmetrical port head (right) is .625-inch higher than a conventional Bow Tie head.

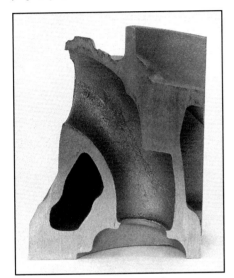

The exhaust port in a symmetrical port Bow Tie head has a deep valve bowl and a smooth, gradual turn to the exit.

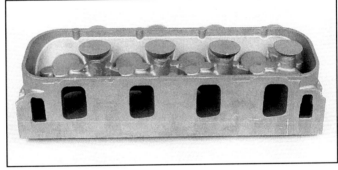

The unmachined version of the symmetrical port head (PN 10051129) is cast from 355-T6 aluminum.

ports in production big-block castings. The exhaust port's deep valve bowl and smooth, gradual turn enhances exhaust gas flow. The symmetrical port head retains the standard big-block exhaust port spacing and flange bolt pattern, but its higher port location requires custom-made headers to cleaar most chassis.

The overall height of the symmetrical port Bow Tie head is .625-inch taller than conventional big-block cylinder heads. The symmetrical port head retains the standard Chevrolet big-block rocker cover bolt pattern.

Pushrod length must also be adjusted to compensate for the symmetrical port cylinder head's greater overall height and revised valve geometry. Chevrolet sells heavy-duty pushrods only for conventional Bow Tie heads; however, an exhaust pushrod for an "862" Bow Tie head can be used as an intake pushrod with a "128" symmetrical port head.

Custom-made pushrods for symmetrical port heads are available from aftermarket sources. The following are typical pushrod dimensions for big-block Chevrolet heads:

Cylinder Head	14044862	10051128
Intake Pushrod Part Number	10134306	N/A
Intake Pushrod Length	8.285"	9.100"
Exhaust Pushrod Part Number	10134305	N/A
Exhaust Pushrod Length	9.256"	10.0"

The rocker arm ratio of the symmetrical port Bow Tie head was raised by increasing the distance from the rocker stud hole to the valve stem by .200-inch. This change increased the nominal rocker ratio from 1.7:1 to 1.8:1. Conventional stud-mounted rocker arms cannot be installed on symmetrical port cylinder heads; however, aftermarket shaft-mounted rocker systems are available with ratios ranging from 1.5:1 to 2.0:1. The rocker stud bosses must be machined flat to allow the rocker arm mounting bar to bolt to the head without binding.

Since most competition engine builders prefer to fabricate an intake manifold to suit a particular application, Chevrolet does not offer cast aluminum intake manifolds to fit the symmetrical port head's unique port layout and manifold bolt pattern. Tunnel ram manifolds fabricated from sheet aluminum are very popular in Pro Stock drag racing. This design allows the engine builder to vary runner length and plenum volume to suit various engines. Intake manifold gaskets for symmetrical port heads must also be made by the engine builder. Rocker covers and gaskets are interchangeable with other big-block heads.

The unfinished combustion chambers in a raw casting are not machined for valve seat inserts or spark plugs.

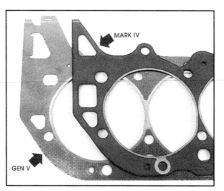

Mark IV and Gen V head gaskets are not interchangeable due to differences in the location and size of the coolant transfer holes.

Mark IV head gaskets may allow coolant to leak into the lifter valley if used with Gen V cylinder heads.

A Mark IV head gasket (left) leaves the passage at the end of the cylinder head open; a Gen V head gasket (right) blocks this passage.

An unmachined version of the symmetrical port Bow Tie head is available as PN 10051129. This raw casting is intended primarily for engine builders and cylinder head specialists who want to make extensive modifications to the combustion chambers and ports. It should be emphasized that considerable expertise and equipment are required to produce a finished head from a raw casting. It is a job that should be attempted only by experienced machinists.

There are several differences between the machined and unfinished versions of the symmetrical port big-block cylinder head. Raw castings have slightly smaller intake runners and the squish areas located beneath the spark plugs are smaller. Fully machined and unfinished heads are produced with different alloys. Machined heads are made from 356-T6 aluminum, while raw heads are manufactured with 355-T6 alloy aluminum. Consequently raw castings have a higher percentage of magnesium and copper than finished heads, and less zinc and silicon. This change in material increases the hardness of unmachined symmetrical port heads, and makes them easier to weld than finished versions.

Head Gaskets

Chevrolet offers a variety of head gaskets for Mark IV and Gen V big-block V8s. As noted earlier, there are significant differences in the cored holes in the deck surfaces of Mark IV and Gen V blocks. Consequently the head gaskets must be selected for the specific block and cylinder heads being used.

Head Gasket Interchangeability

The locations and sizes of the coolant passages in the deck surfaces differ in Mark IV and Gen V blocks. Mark IV cylinder heads should not be installed on production Gen V blocks because coolant may leak into the lifter valley. However, both Mark IV and Gen V cylinder heads can be used with Gen V Bow Tie blocks, which have smaller holes in their decks.

There are also differences in the sizes and locations of coolant passages in the cylinder heads and head gaskets used with Mark IV and Gen V big-blocks. The Gen V head gasket blocks the large coolant passage at the end of the head; a Mark IV gasket leaves this passage open.

Mark IV head gaskets can be used on a Gen V block *if* the coolant passages in the front of the decks are plugged. These passages are vent holes that allow gas to escape during the casting process. If the holes are not plugged, water entering the block from the water pump can "short circuit" the cooling system by bypassing the block and cylinder head coolant jackets and returning directly to the radiator.

These vent holes should be blocked on both deck surfaces to force the coolant to circulate through the Gen V block. Gen V head gaskets do not have coolant holes in this position, and will effectively block the passages. (Production Gen V head gaskets plug the top holes in both the front and the rear of the block, which changes the coolant flow from the routing in a Mark IV. To make the coolant flow from the block to the head as in a Mark IV engine, the top rear holes should be punched open in the head gaskets on both banks.) The vent holes can also be plugged by reaming the cast holes to ¾-inch diameter and inserting soft plugs. Use a length of ⅝-inch diameter bar stock to drive the plugs into the block so they are flush with (or below) the deck surfaces.

Gasket Selection

The gasket's compressed thickness, its bore size, and the cylinder head material should all be considered when selecting a head gasket. Steel shim gaskets are recommended only for cast iron cylinder heads, while composition gaskets can be used with both iron and aluminum heads.

When selecting head gaskets for a big-block V8, it is important to use gaskets that will produce the desired piston-to-head clearance with the engine's piston deck height. The *minimum* acceptable piston-to-head clearance (gasket thickness plus deck clearance) in an engine equipped with steel connecting rods is .035-inch. This figure must be increased

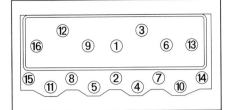

Follow this torquing sequence when installing or retorquing big-block V8 head gaskets.

when high engine speeds are anticipated, when piston-to-cylinder wall clearance is increased, or when aluminum connecting rods are used.

The head gasket should not overhang the cylinder bores, a condition that can cause preignition. This is especially important on engines with oversize bores.

Mark IV Head Gaskets

PN 14015351 This beaded steel gasket has a compressed thickness of .022-inch. It was originally used on LS-6 engines, and is recommended for Mark IV engines with 4.25-inch cylinder bores.

PN 10126768 This composition head gasket is recommended for use with Chevrolet aluminum cylinder heads on Mark IV big-blocks with 4.250-inch cylinders. It has a .039-inch compressed thickness, and was originally used with LS-7 engines.

PN 10159507 Similar to PN 10126768, for 4.40-inch cylinder bores.

Gen V Head Gaskets

PN 14097000 This composition head gasket is used with H.O. 454 engine assemblies. It has a .027-inch compressed thickness, and is recommended for Gen V big-blocks with 4.250-inch cylinder bores.

PN 14097001 Used with H.O. 502 engines, this composition gasket has a compressed thickness of .040-inch, and fits cylinder bores up to 4.500-inch in diameter.

Aftermarket dead soft copper head gaskets are recommended for Bow Tie blocks with cylinders that have been bored to 4.500-inch or larger for Pro Stock and similar maximum-effort racing applications. The block's deck surfaces should be machined for steel "O"-rings to seal the copper head gaskets. An alternative sealing solution for big-bore big-blocks is Fel-Pro composition head gasket (PN 1093), or equivalent. This

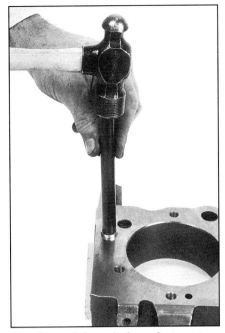

Plug the vent holes in the front of a Gen V Bow Tie block with ¾-inch soft plugs when using Mark IV head gaskets.

gasket has a 4.620-inch gasket bore, .051-inch nominal compressed thickness, and a compressed volume of 13.9cc. If additional head bolts are used, the gasket must be modified by punching holes for the extra fasteners.

Installation

Steel shim head gaskets should be installed with a commercial head gasket sealer. High-compression engines may benefit by using aluminum paint as a sealer, which improves heat transfer and simplifies clean-up during engine disassembly. Composition head gaskets should be installed without sealer.

Steel shim gaskets do not require retorquing. Most composition gaskets should be retorqued (either hot or cold) after the engine is first warmed up. Follow the bolt torquing sequence shown in the accompanying diagram when installing or retorquing big-block V8 head gaskets.

Head Bolts and Studs

Chevrolet big-block V8s use 16 fasteners per bank to attach the cylinder head to the block. Many competition engine builders prefer head studs over bolts because studs reduce wear and tear on the block threads during frequent rebuilds, and produce more consistent torque readings. However, studs can make it more difficult to remove and replace cylinder heads, and to gap piston rings in the bores.

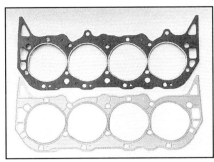

Composition head gaskets (top) can be used with iron and aluminum heads; use steel shim gaskets (bottom) only with cast iron heads.

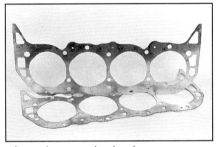

Aftermarket copper head gaskets are recommended for Bow Tie blocks with 4.500-inch diameter and larger cylinder bores.

The height of the head bolt columns is different in various Bow Tie cylinder heads. Production head bolts and many "universal" head stud kits cannot be used with "862" Bow Tie and symmetrical port Bow Tie cylinder heads. Refer to the head bolt column chart when ordering studs for your application.

Engines equipped with production cast iron and aluminum heads use 24 ⁷⁄₁₆-14 x 4.06-inch bolts (PN 10141204) and eight ⁷⁄₁₆-14 x 2.08-inch bolts (PN 10141205). When installing Bow Tie aluminum head PN 14044861-2, use eight ⁷⁄₁₆-14 x 5.25-inch bolts (PN 12337919) in the holes adjacent to the raised exhaust ports.

Engines equipped with symmetrical port Bow Tie head PN 10051128 require four ⁷⁄₁₆-14 capscrews for the head bolts holes which are underneath the intake runners. (A total of eight capscrews are needed if the block has been modified for six bolts around each cylinder bore.) Aftermarket head bolt studs are required for the symmetrical port Bow Tie head due to the increased height of this casting.

Hardened head bolt washers (PN 3899696) should be used with all aluminum cylinder heads. When installing aluminum cylinder heads on cast iron blocks, be sure to plug the cylinder head stud holes on the underside of two intake ports on each head. These holes are used

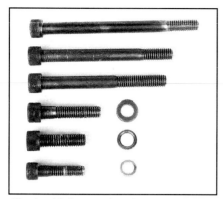

Allen head bolts or studs with 12-point nuts are recommended for symmetrical port Bow Tie heads to provide wrench clearance.

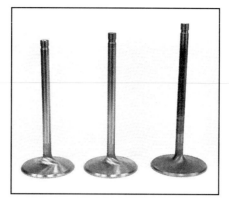

Bow Tie heads use .200-inch longer valves (center) than production heads; symmetrical port heads use .800-inch longer valves (right).

only with aluminum cylinder blocks to provide additional head clamping.

Cylinder head studs for big-block V8 engines are also available from Chevrolet. An engine assembly requires 32 studs, with 24 $\frac{7}{16}$-14 x 5.14-inch studs (PN 330861) and eight $\frac{7}{16}$-14 x 3.13-inch studs (PN 330862). Use 32 hardened steel washers (PN 38999696) and 32 hex nuts (PN 3942410—1038 steel). Twelve-point nuts are also available for limited clearance applications as PN 14044866; these nuts are made from 4037 steel, and are Magnaflux inspected. Stud kits are not available from Chevrolet for Bow Tie and symmetrical port cylinder heads; they can be obtained from aftermarket sources.

Head bolt threads that penetrate the block's water jacket should be coated with sealant during assembly. (Most Bow Tie blocks have blind-tapped head bolt holes that do not break into the water jacket. Head bolts should be lubricated with oil in these instances.) All head bolts should be tightened to 70 ft.-lbs. torque. If studs are used in place of bolts, the stud threads should be lightly oiled and the nuts tightened to 65 ft.-lbs.

Allen head bolts or studs can be used with symmetrical port cylinder heads. However, the fasteners must clear the bottom of the rocker arm mounting bars. With Allen bolts and hardened washers, there is typically less than .100-inch

clearance between the bolt heads and the mounting bars. This tight clearance leaves little margin for error in the length of a head stud. Wrench clearance is also limited in several locations; studs require 12-point nuts to provide room for a socket. Allen bolts neatly solve this problem of restricted wrench room.

Valves

Chevrolet offers both standard replacement and high-performance valves for enthusiasts who want to improve their big-block's performance. All production big-block valves have $\frac{3}{8}$-inch diameter stems. A heavy-duty 2.19-inch diameter intake valve with a hard chrome plated stem is available as PN 3969815, and a 2.30-inch version is PN 3879618. Enlarging the diameter generally improves airflow and thereby increases engine performance. However, 2.30-inch intake valves were never used in production cylinder heads, so the seats must be reworked to match the valve diameter.

Both valves have standard length valve stems. The valve spring pockets in Bow Tie aluminum cylinder heads (PN 14044861-2) must be machined .200-inch deeper for these valves.

Most high-performance big-block heads require 1.88-inch diameter exhaust valves. These valves are available as PN

TECH SPECS: BIG-BLOCK V8 CYLINDER HEAD BOLT BOSS HEIGHTS

P/N	1	2	3	4	5	6
14011076	3.30"	2.88"	3.30"	3.30"	1.26"	2.88"
14044861-2	3.30"	2.88"	3.30"	4.30"	1.26"	3.30"
10051128	0.62"	3.88"	3.88"	4.75"	1.25"	3.36"

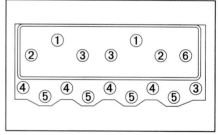

The height of the head bolt columns is different in various big-block cylinder head castings. Refer to the chart above to find the column height for specific heads when selecting head bolts or studs. Make sure that the fasteners have adequate thread engagement in the block.

TECH SPECS: VALVES AND SEATS

| | Valves (in.)[1] | | | | | | Seats (in.)[1] | | | |
| | Intake | | | Exhaust | | | Intake | | Exhaust | |
P/N	Dia.	Length	Margin	Dia.	Length	Margin	Dia.	Depth	Dia.	Depth
14011076	2.19[3]	5.22	.020	1.88[4]	5.35	.040	2.29	.250	1.945	.250
14044862	2.19[3]	5.42	.020	1.88[4]	5.55	.040	2.29	.250	1.945	.250
10051128[2]	2.40	6.00	.065	1.90	6.15	.100	2.45	.375	2.000	.375

[1]Note: These are recommended valve specifications—all Bow Tie cylinder heads are supplied without valves.
[2]Not supplied with valve seat inserts.
[3]P/N 3969815
[4]P/N 3946077

3946077 for Mark IV heads and PN 14097045 for Gen V versions.

Replacement valve seat inserts are available to repair aluminum cylinder heads as PN 3893268 (2.288-inch diameter for 2.19-inch intake valves) and PN 3946078 (1.942-inch diameter for 1.88-inch exhaust valves). Replacement valve guides (intake PN 3893294 and exhaust PN 3893295) are also available; the valve stem hole must be honed for clearance after installation. If the valve guides are loose in the head, they can be pinned in place with small set screws.

Camshafts

Chevrolet offers several mechanical and hydraulic flat tappet camshafts for big-block V8s that are suitable for street, high-performance and limited competition uses. The accompanying chart summarizes the timing and valve lift specifications for Chevrolet big-block V8 performance profiles, and indicates recommended applications.

The Gen V big-block uses a nonadjustable "net lash" valvetrain. If the camshaft base circle is changed, or if a mechanical lifter camshaft is installed, the nonadjustable valvetrain must be replaced with Mark IV rocker studs, rocker arms, adjusting nuts, and pushrod guideplates. See the "Rocker Arm" section for conversion information.

Chevrolet big-block V8s manufactured in 1965-66 used camshafts with grooved rear bearing journals. This oil groove was eliminated in later years. If you are using a camshaft with a grooved rear journal, it is necessary to remove the rear camshaft bearing, solder the bearing oil hole closed, and redrill it to .060-inch diameter. This groove was required for valve lifter oiling, but it creates a major internal oil leak in Mark IV engines produced after 1966. All currently available Chevrolet high-performance and racing camshafts are manufactured without a groove in the rear cam bearing journal.

All Chevrolet big-block high-performance cams originally used in Mark IV engines are designed to produce split overlap at four crankshaft degrees before Top Dead Center. This means that both valves or lifters should be the same height off of the camshaft base circle when the number one cylinder is four degrees before TDC on the overlap cycle. Installing the camshaft with the timing marks on the camshaft and crankshaft timing chain sprockets aligned will normally produce split overlap at four degrees before TDC.

Many aftermarket specialty companies offer kits to alter the camshaft phasing from these production timing locators. As a general rule, advancing the camshaft improves low-speed torque, while retarding it increases high-speed horsepower.

Loose valve guides in aluminum cylinder heads can be retained with pins or set screws.

Camshaft timing can be adjusted by installing an eccentric bushing in the camshaft sprocket.

TECH SPECS: BIG-BLOCK V8 CAMSHAFTS

Part Number	Description	Crankshaft Duration @ Lash Point, Int./Exh. (degrees)	Crankshaft Duration @ .050" Tappet Lift, Int./Exh. (degrees)	Maximum Lift w/ 1.7:1 Rocker Ratio, Int./Exh. (inches)	Valve Lash (inches)	Lobe Centerlines (degrees)	Notes
10185060	Hydraulic flat tappet	347/347	224/224	.510/.510	———	116	Good street high-performance and marine cam; advanced 5 degrees. Use spring #3970627. Used in 454 HO engine.
14096209	Hydraulic flat tappet	328/324	220/220	.500/.500	———	115	Good street high-performance and marine cam. Use spring #3970627. Used in 502 HO engine.
3904362	Mechanical flat tappet	307/298	242/242	.496/.492	.024/.028	114	LS6 street mechanical lifter cam. Use spring #3970627.
3925535	Mechanical flat tappet	332/333	264/270	.536/.554	.024/.026	112	1967-69 L88 mechanical lifter racing cam; good in 396-427. Use spring #3916164.
3959180	Mechanical flat tappet	327/333	262/273	.556/.594	.024/.026	110	ZL1 and LS7 mechanical lifter competition cam; good in 427-454. Use spring #3916164.

Edge orifice mechanical lifters (PN 5231585) reduce the total oil circulation rate by 10 to 20 percent compared to piddle valve lifters.

The camshaft timing can be changed with offset crankshaft keys or eccentric cam sprocket bushings. It is important that the camshaft phasing be rechecked and verified after installing either an offset crank key or timing gear bushing. This procedure requires an accurate degree wheel and a precision dial indicator. Refer to the engine building section for camshaft installation recommendations.

Flat valve lifters can be made more compatible with the camshaft lobes by polishing the lifter bottoms with #600 grit sandpaper before installation. Good used lifters that retain some crown or convex curvature across the bottom are generally satisfactory for reuse when installed on the same camshaft lobe.

Hydraulic Lifters

Production hydraulic lifters (PN 5232720) are recommended for all high-performance Chevrolet hydraulic flat tappet camshafts. For normal use, the rocker adjusting nuts should be tightened ½ to ¾ turn after all valvetrain lash is taken up. If all new valvetrain parts are being installed, the lifters should be readjusted after 1,000 to 2,000 miles to compensate for run-in wear.

Higher engine operating speeds can often be attained by "zero-lashing" Chevrolet hydraulic lifters. This requires idling a thoroughly warmed up engine and backing off each rocker arm adjusting nut until an audible clicking is heard. Tighten the adjusting nut until the clicking just stops, and then turn the nut ⅛ turn tighter. Repeat this operation until all the lifters have been set to "zero lash."

Mechanical lifters

Two production mechanical (solid) valve lifters are available. PN 5232695 is similar in appearance to a hydraulic tappet. Its overhead oil metering is controlled by an internal inertia flapper valve, also called a "piddle valve."

A second mechanical lifter is offered as PN 5231585. This lifter was original equipment in several high-performance small-block V8s produced from 1959-69. (Lifters are interchangeable between small-block and big-block V8 Chevrolet engines.) This lifter meters oil to the top end of the engine on the basis of the clearance between the lifter body and the block's lifter bore; it is commonly referred to as an "edge orifice" lifter.

An edge orifice lifter has several desirable features which are not available with the piddle valve design. The edge orifice lifter effects a 10 to 20 percent reduction in the total oil circulation rate. Because this lifter limits the flow of oil to the top end of the engine, it can be beneficial in engines equipped with dry sump oiling and engines with limited oil pan capacity. Due to the reduction in oil reaching the rocker arms, edge orifice lifters should be used only with roller bearing rockers.

Pushrods and Guideplates

The demands on pushrods have escalated dramatically as competition engine builders have turned to harsher camshaft profiles and stiffer valve springs in their search for improved performance. The pushrod is a critical link in an overhead valve engine like the big-block V8.

The big-block V8's splayed valve design requires different pushrod lengths for the intake and exhaust valves, as shown in the specifications chart. In addition, the Gen V's non-adjustable valvetrain uses pushrods that are shorter than the pushrods used in Mark IV engines.

TECH SPECS: BIG-BLOCK V8 PUSHRODS

Part Number	Description	Material	Diameter	Length (in.)	Wall Thickness (in.)	Notes
10134307	Intake	1010 steel	⅜"	8.285	.080	One-piece design; recommended for high-performance street engines; use with pushrod guideplate #3860038.
10134308	Exhaust	1010 steel	⅜"	9.256	.080	See above.
10134304	Intake	1010 steel	⁷⁄₁₆"	8.285	.080	One-piece design; recommended for high-performance and limited competition engines; use with pushrod guideplate #3879620.
10134303	Exhaust	1010 steel	⁷⁄₁₆"	9.256	.080	See above.
10134306	Intake	4130 chrome moly steel	⁷⁄₁₆"	8.285	.080	Premium quality one-piece pushrod for maximum effort racing engines; use with pushrod guideplate #3879620.
10134305	Exhaust	4130 chrome moly steel	⁷⁄₁₆"	9.256	.080	See above.
14097068	Intake	1010 steel	⅜"	8.171	.058	For Gen V 454 and 502 HO engines.
14097070	Exhaust	1010 steel	⅜"	9.151	.058	For Gen V 454 and 502 HO engines.

Chevrolet offers heavy-duty pushrods for big-block V8s in ⅜-inch and ⁷⁄₁₆-inch diameters. The larger ⁷⁄₁₆-inch diameter pushrods are recommended for most racing applications, and smaller ⅜-inch pushrods are suitable for many moderate performance engines. However, ⁷⁄₁₆-inch diameter pushrods may not clear some aftermarket roller tappet bodies. In these instances, ⅜-inch Chevrolet pushrods may be substituted.

Chevrolet heavy-duty pushrods are available in two materials. Pushrods made from 1010 mild steel are suitable for high-performance street cars, power boats, street rods, and limited competition applications. Premium quality pushrods made from 4130 chrome moly steel are recommended for maximum-effort racing engines.

Heavy-duty pushrods are case hardened for use with pushrod guideplates. They can be used with all conventional hydraulic and mechanical flat tappets and most aftermarket roller lifters.

One-piece heavy-duty 1010 and 4130 steel pushrods offer significant improvements in reliability and performance over production pushrods.

Tests conducted by GM Motorsports Technology Group engineers have shown that increasing pushrod stiffness improves valvetrain stability. At extreme engine speeds, a pushrod begins to act like a spring, compressing and stretching as the valve opens and closes. Strain gauge tests have shown that the pushrod is actually in tension as the valve approaches its maximum lift and the lifter goes over the nose of cam lobe. A stiff pushrod stabilizes a racing valvetrain by minimizing this undesirable deflection. The extra stiffness provided by increasing a pushrod's wall thickness more than compensates for the few additional grams of weight.

Valvetrain geometry also has a major impact on the reliability and performance of a big-block V8. When the pushrod length is correct, the rocker arm and valve stem will be at a 90-degree angle at one-half of the valve's maximum lift.

The pushrod guideplates must match the pushrod diameter. Use guideplate PN 3860038 with ⅜-inch diameter pushrods and PN 3879620 with ⁷⁄₁₆-inch pushrods. Gen V big-blocks with non-adjustable valvetrains use guideplate PN 14097005 (⅜-inch pushrods only).

Pushrod guideplates should be adjusted during assembly to center the rocker arm

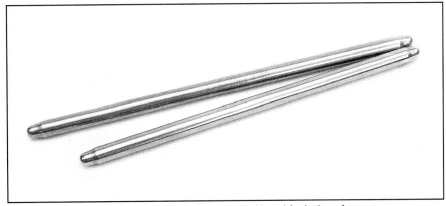

Heavy-duty Chevrolet pushrods are available in 1010 mild steel for high-performance street cars and 4130 chrome moly steel for racing engines. Both versions are hardened for guideplates.

Use guideplate PN 3860038 with ⅜-inch pushrods and guideplate PN 3879620 with ⁷⁄₁₆-inch pushrods.

tip over the valve stem. In applications requiring non-standard valve stem lengths (for example, Bow Tie cylinder head PN 14044861-2 and 10051128), pushrod length may have to be adjusted to restore the correct valvetrain geometry. Custom pushrods can be obtained from aftermarket sources for these heads.

Chevrolet ⁷⁄₁₆-inch diameter screw-in rocker arm studs (PN 3921912) are suitable for high-performance and racing uses. An aftermarket rocker stud girdle may be beneficial in reducing rocker stud flexing and breakage in engines equipped with high-lift or fast action camshafts.

Rocker Arms

The production big-block V8's splayed-valve design uses individual stud-mounted rockers. This system is simple, lightweight, reliable, inexpensive, and effective. The big-block V8's valvetrain is also easy to modify for improved performance. With only minor refinements, the same basic valvetrain design has proven itself in both production motors and high-speed racing engines.

A high-performance "H" rocker arm (PN 3959182) has a longer slot than a standard rocker arm to accommodate more valve lift.

Production Chevrolet big-block rocker arms have a nominal ratio of 1.7:1. A rocker arm assembly consists of a stamped steel rocker arm, a pivot ball, and an adjusting nut. High-performance Chevrolet Mark IV big-block rocker arms (PN 3959182) can be identified by a raised letter "H" or "L" which is forged inside the pallet end. These rockers have longer slots than production rockers to prevent interference between the rocker arm and stud with cams with .600-inch maximum valve lift. Long-slot rocker arms for Gen V engines are available as PN 12508879.

The clearance between the rocker and stud should always be checked before final assembly. This can be done by inserting a gauge made from a wire paper clip between the rocker arm slot and stud when the valve is at its maximum lift. If the clearance is insufficient, elongate the rocker arm slot with a small grinder.

Long-slot Mark IV big-block rocker arms are sold without balls and nuts. Heavy-duty pivot balls (PN 5232762) and adjusting nuts (PN 3896648) are

Gen V Valvetrain Conversion

The production Gen V big-block V8 introduced in 1991 uses a non-adjustable "net lash" valvetrain. This valvetrain uses shouldered bolts instead of threaded studs and adjusting nuts to retain the rocker arms.

The Gen V "net lash" valvetrain presents a challenge to engine builders, however. If the camshaft profile is changed significantly for off-highway applications, the net lash rocker assembly must be replaced with Mark IV rocker studs, rocker arms, adjusting nuts, and pushrod guideplates. This conversion will allow an engine builder to compensate for changes in the camshaft's base circle diameter and to adjust valve lash with mechanical tappets.

The rocker stud bosses on Gen V cylinder heads are machined for ⅜-inch shouldered bolts. To convert to an adjustable valvetrain, the cylinder heads must be disassembled and the bosses drilled and tapped for conventional ⁷⁄₁₆-inch rocker studs.

The Gen V big-block has a "net lash" valvetrain with nonadjustable rocker arms.

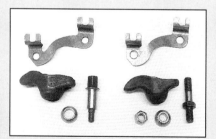

The Gen V valvetrain (left) uses a ⅜-inch shouldered bolt to retain the rocker arm. Conventional big-block ⁷⁄₁₆-inch rocker studs, rocker arms, and pushrod guideplates (right) can be installed for high-performance off-highway applications.

A nonadjustable rocker arm (left) has a wider slot than a high-performance rocker (right). Note the difference in the diameter of the pivot ball holes.

Due to the compound angle of the big-block's rocker studs, this operation should be performed with a multi-axis mill or valve machine. Drill out the ⅜-inch threads with a .375-inch bit, then tap the bosses for ⁷⁄₁₆-14 NC threads. Do not shorten or spot face the rocker stud bosses.

Special rocker arm studs are available from aftermarket suppliers to convert Gen V cylinder heads without machining. These studs have ⅜-inch threads that screw into the production Gen V rocker stud bosses without modification. They are recommended only for valve springs with less than 450 pounds open pressure.

Replace the original rocker arms, nuts, pivot balls, and pushrod guideplates with the parts listed below.

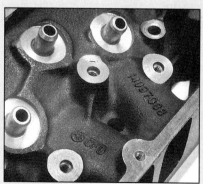

To install adjustable rocker arm studs, drill and tap the rocker stud bosses for ⁷⁄₁₆-14 NC threads. Do not shorten the stud bosses.

To convert to adjustable rocker arms, replace the ⅜-inch diameter shouldered bolt (right) with a conventional ⁷⁄₁₆-inch big-block screw-in rocker arm stud or a special aftermarket stud with ⅜-inch threads.

Heavy-duty one-piece ⅜-inch or ⁷⁄₁₆-inch pushrods should be used in place of production Gen V pushrods in high-performance applications.

The following parts can be used to install an adjustable valvetrain on Gen V big-block Chevrolet V8 engines:

Part Number	Description
10112680	Rocker arm, stamped steel (includes ball and nut)
3959182	Rocker arm, stamped steel, long slot (without ball and nut)
5232762	Rocker arm ball
3896648	Rocker arm adjusting nut
3921912	Rocker arm stud
3860038	Pushrod guideplate (for ⅜" pushrods)
3879620	Pushrod guideplate (for ⁷⁄₁₆" pushrods)

Aftermarket rocker studs with ⅜" threads can convert Gen V cylinder heads to adjustable rocker arms without machining.

available separately to complete the rocker assembly. Production rocker arm adjusting nuts perform well as long as they have enough preload torque to prevent them from loosening while the engine is running. Any nuts with insufficient preload should be discarded.

Significant changes in valve lash may be experienced when new valvetrain components are first run-in. Valve lash should be checked and adjusted frequently until it stabilizes. New rocker arms and balls should be observed closely for overheating and excessive wear during break-in.

If it is necessary to change a rocker and ball, always install a good used rocker arm assembly. If good used rockers and balls are not available, move an intake rocker and ball over to replace a burned exhaust rocker arm. Then install the new components on an intake valve, which runs cooler. Always keep usable rocker arms and balls together during engine disassembly and rebuild.

Roller Rocker Arms

Chevrolet Bow Tie big-block cylinder heads are designed to use aftermarket rocker arms. For example, shaft-mounted rockers are required on symmetrical port cylinder heads, and stud-mounted needle roller rocker arms are recommended for maximum-effort racing engines equipped with Bow Tie heads (PN 14044861-2). Hardened adjusting nuts and $7/16$-inch diameter big-block V8 rocker studs (PN 3921912) should be used whenever possible with stud-mounted roller rockers.

Needle roller rocker arms typically lower the engine oil temperature and require less lubrication than ball-type rockers. Rocker arms should be inspected frequently for signs of failure, and must be checked for adequate spring, retainer, and stud clearance during assembly. Rocker arm studs should be Magnaflux inspected to ensure their quality.

Increasing the rocker arm ratio on high-performance and competition big-block V8s can often improve engine performance. High-ratio rocker arms can be installed on the intake valves, on the exhaust valves, or in both positions. The degree of improvement will vary, however, depending primarily on the camshaft profile and cylinder head airflow. A particular combination should be tested with higher ratio rocker arms in each position separately, and then together.

Big-block valve springs (left to right): PN 3970627 dual spring; PN 3916164 dual with damper; PN 3989354 dual with damper.

Stud-mounted needle roller rocker arms are recommended for racing engines equipped with Bow Tie cylinder heads.

Although high-ratio rockers may offer a performance gain, they also impart higher loads to the rest of the valvetrain. These higher loads can cause valvetrain malfunctions, reduce durability, and contribute to premature valve float.

Valve Lash

Engine failures are frequently caused by problems in the valvetrain. It is essential that the valve lash not change during a race. If the valve lash increases significantly for any reason, valve springs and valves cannot reasonably be expected to survive. Failure of either component can seriously damage an engine.

Valve lash adjustments should be made with the engine hot whenever possible. If this is impractical, a determination of the lash change during warm-up should be made and allowed for when the lash is set cold. Valve lash may increase or decrease during warm-up depending on whether cast iron or aluminum heads are used.

Valve Springs

Valve springs are among the most highly stressed components in a high-performance engine. The valve springs must have sufficient pressure to control valve motion at the intended engine speeds and adequate travel to prevent the coils from stacking solid ("coil binding") at maximum valve lift.

Chevrolet has developed four different valve springs that are suitable for high-performance and competition big-block V8 engines. The chart on page 140 summarizes their specifications.

PN 3970627 is recommended for high-performance street engines. It is a second-design dual spring originally used with LS-6 engines.

PN 3916164 is a production L-88 chrome vanadium steel dual spring with damper. Aluminum valve spring retainers are not recommended for this spring because the damper will erode the retainer material; the preferred steel retainer for this spring is PN 3879613.

PN 3989354 is a large diameter (1.538-inch OD) dual spring manufactured from aircraft quality steel. This spring was designed expressly for competition camshaft PN 3994094. This spring also offers improved durability with L-88 and ZL-1 camshafts (PN 3925535 and 3959180 respectively) if maximum engine speed does not exceed 7000 rpm. This spring must be used with steel valve spring retainer PN 3989353. This retainer does not include a valve stem seal, so a separate seal should be installed on the valve guide for proper oil control.

Hardened steel valve stem locks are recommended for all high-performance big-blocks. These locks are color coded purple, and are available as PN 3947880.

Use hardened valve stem locks (PN 3947880) with the valve spring retainers specified in the chart below on high-performance big-blocks.

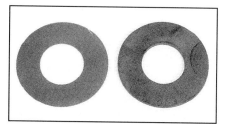

Adjust valve spring installed height by inserting .015-inch and .065-inch shims between the spring and the spring seat.

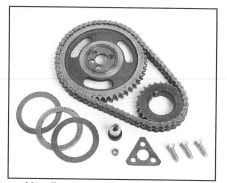

Double roller timing sets with needle thrust bearings to control cam movement are available from aftermarket suppliers.

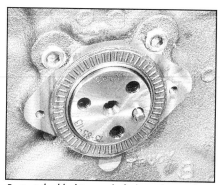

Protect the block's camshaft thrust face with a brass or roller bearing thrust washer when using an iron or steel cam sprocket.

The back of the camshaft sprocket must be machined to accommodate the thickness of a roller thrust bearing.

For maximum performance and reliability, the valve spring installed height should be checked during assembly. Installed height can be measured using a small machinist's rule. Telescoping gauges, valve height micrometers, and specially modified calipers are also suitable for measuring installed height. Valve spring installed heights which are greater than the recommended specification can be adjusted by inserting Chevrolet shims PN 3891521 (.065-inch thick) and PN 3875916 (.015-inch thick) between the spring and spring seat.

In all installations where high-lift camshafts and heavy-duty springs, retainers, and valve stem seals are used, all parts should be checked carefully for adequate clearance. Make a temporary assembly of the complete valvetrain on the engine and check for possible interference between the spring retainer and seal at maximum valve lift, bottoming of the inner, outer, and damper coils at maximum lift, and possible interference between the rocker arm and valve spring retainer. Any of these conditions will re-sult in very short engine life if not corrected before final assembly!

Aftermarket camshafts may require different valve springs and related components. The camshaft manufacturer's recommendations should be followed in these instances.

Timing Sets

Production Chevrolet big-block camshaft sprockets and link-type timing chains are used with good results by many engine builders. However, for durability and extended life at high engine speeds, the GM Motorsports Technology

TECH SPECS: BIG-BLOCK V8 VALVE SPRINGS

Part Number	Description	Outside Diameter (in.)	Pressure @ Installed Height	Solid Height (in.)	Pounds per Inch	Retainer Part Number	Notes
3970627	Dual	1.487	105# @ 1.88"	1.280	450	3964264	Used with high-performance 396/427/454 production engines; LS-6.
3916164	Dual w/ damper	1.487	116# @ 1.88"	1.100	317	3879613	Used with heavy-duty 427/454 engines; L-88, ZL-1, LS-7.
3989354	Dual w/ damper	1.538	128# @ 1.90"	1.260	330	3989353	Used with camshaft #3994094.
14097002	Dual	1.487	110 # @ 1.88"	1.290	400	14096274	Used with 454 and 502 HO engines.

Group recommends a double-roller timing set consisting of a camshaft sprocket (PN 3891517), a steel crankshaft sprocket (PN 3891418), and a double-roller chain (PN 3891519). Aftermarket belt-type timing sets are also suitable for many competition applications.

Many competition engine builders protect the block's camshaft sprocket thrust face with a brass or roller bearing thrust washer when using a cast iron cam sprocket. This precaution is especially important when using a high-volume oil pump, which increases the load on the thrust face. These parts are available from specialty speed equipment suppliers and companies that sell ball and roller bearings. The rear surface of the cam sprocket must be machined in a lathe to accommodate the thickness of the thrust washer.

When using aftermarket roller lifters, the cam should be prevented from moving forward in the block with a needle roller thrust bearing. Suitable bearings to prevent forward cam thrust are available from aftermarket manufacturers. A plate should be brazed to the timing chain cover or other reinforcement provided.

As noted in the camshaft section, changes in camshaft timing can be produced by installing offset cam dowel bushings in the camshaft timing sprocket. The cam bushing should be staked in place to prevent it from turning or falling out after installation.

Rocker Covers

All Chevrolet big-block cylinder heads have the same rocker cover bolt pattern. Chrome plated Chevrolet Bow Tie rocker covers are available as PN 10051176; plain steel Bow Tie covers are PN 10051180. Both Bow Tie covers are taller than production covers to clear af-

termarket rocker stud girdles; they may not clear alternators and air conditioning compressors when installed on production engines.

Chromed spring bar retainers (PN 14044820) should be used under all fasteners when installing stamped steel rocker covers to curtail oil leaks. Steel-reinforced rocker cover gaskets are available as PN 14085759.

Intake Manifolds

Chevrolet offers a high-rise aluminum intake manifold for big-block V8s as PN 3933163. This single four-barrel manifold is a dual-plane design for high-performance cylinder heads with rectangular intake ports. It is installed on H.O. 454 and H.O. 502 engine assemblies. The recommended carburetor for this manifold is a standard flange Holley four-barrel.

BOW TIE TECH — Cast Rocker Covers

Cast aluminum Gen V rocker covers can be modified for use on Mark IV big-block V8s.

The Gen V engine introduced cast aluminum rocker covers for big-block V8s. These rigid covers are the first line of defense against rocker cover oil leaks. They have captured "O"-ring gaskets and screw-in filler caps to prevent oil seepage.

The cast rocker covers' matte black finish adds a high-tech touch to any engine compartment. Four self-adhesive engine displacement emblems are available for cast aluminum rocker covers.

Cast aluminum Gen V rocker covers can be installed on Mark IV cylinder heads with only minor modifications. The cast cover's raised "O"-ring splash shield must be removed to allow the

To install Gen V cast rocker covers on Mark IV cylinder heads, machine off the raised "O"-ring splash shield on the exhaust side of the cover and remove the bosses under the rocker cover hold-down bolts.

cover to seal against the rocker cover rails on early-model cylinder heads. The small bosses beneath the rocker cover hold-down bolts should also be removed; these bosses provide the correct compression for the production "O"-ring gasket. Use conventional Mark IV gaskets in place of the "O"-ring seals with modified Gen V covers.

A vertical mill is recommended for this operation. Protect the top of the cover to prevent damage to the finish when the cover is clamped to the milling table. Support the center of the cover with shims to prevent chattering.

The following parts can be used to install Gen V cast aluminum rocker covers on Mark IV Chevrolet big-block V8 engines:

A modified Gen V rocker cover (top) will seal against the rocker cover rail on a Mark IV cylinder head. Replace the production "O"-ring seal with a flat gasket (PN 14085759).

Part Number	Description
10183745	Cast rocker cover, without oil filler hole
10183746	Cast rocker cover, with oil filler hole
14085759	Rocker cover gasket, steel reinforced
10126726	Screw-in oil filler cap
10126724	Grommet, for PCV valve
14082320	Rocker cover stud, ¼-20 x 1¼", Torx head (14 required)
14051876	Rocker cover stud nut, ¼-20 (14 required)
10126786	"366" rocker cover emblem
10126787	"427" rocker cover emblem
10126790	"454" rocker cover emblem
10185091	"502" rocker cover emblem

Chevrolet Bow Tie rocker covers are taller than production covers to provide clearance for competition valvetrains.

The removable lower housing on a high-capacity mechanical fuel pump (PN 6415748) can be rotated to fit the chassis.

A high-rise dual-plane aluminum intake manifold (PN 3933163) is installed on H.O. 454 and H.O. 502 engine assemblies.

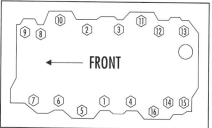
Tighten the intake manifold bolts in the sequence shown. The recommended torque is 25 ft.-lbs.

An increase in high rpm horsepower can be achieved by milling out the manifold's plenum divider, leaving a ¼-inch ridge between the two halves of the plenum. If the plenum divider is removed, an 850cfm Holley with mechanical secondaries and dual accelerator pumps will perform well if it is stagger jetted as follows: Left front #80, right front #76, left rear #76, right rear #78. If a richer or leaner fuel mixture is desired, all four jets should be changed up or down in size.

Most intake manifolds require modification when used with aluminum Bow Tie cylinder heads PN 14044861-2. Match the intake manifold ports to the heads' raised intake runners to take full advantage of the available airflow.

A wide selection of intake manifolds for the big-block Chevrolet is available from aftermarket manufacturers. These include single-plane and ram-type manifolds for competition applications. High-performance manifolds installed on tall-deck blocks require spacers between the manifold and heads to compensate for the wider vee of the tall block.

Chevrolet offers an intake manifold oil splash shield as PN 14096974. This shield mounts in the lifter valley below the manifold and prevents hot oil from heating the incoming air/fuel mixture.

An intake manifold gasket set with blocked heat riser passages is available as PN 12511789. These gaskets will lower the manifold temperature and improve engine performance. They fit big-block heads with rectangular intake ports except Bow Tie heads PN 14044861-2.

Fuel System

A heavy-duty mechanical fuel pump for Mark IV big-block V8 engines is available as PN 6415748. This high-capacity pump has a removable lower housing which can be rotated to position the inlet and outlet fittings as required by the chassis and engine installation. This pump uses a standard big-block fuel pump pushrod (PN 3704817).

Gen V blocks require an electric fuel pump because they do not have provisions to mount a mechanical fuel pump. A late-model in-tank electric pump such as PN 25116279 has sufficient capacity for a high-performance small-block V8. This pump produces 14 psi pressure, and has a built-in check valve to prevent reverse flow. It should be used with a fuel pressure regulator for carbureted engines; adjust the regulator to provide 6 psi fuel pressure at the carburetor needle and seat.

A fuel pressure gauge should be installed between the fuel filter and carburetor. A minimum fuel pressure of at least 4 psi should be maintained at maximum engine speed with a wide open throttle. Fuel lines should be formed from neoprene rubber, steel tubing, or braided steel. *Never* use copper tubing, which will eventually crack from engine vibration.

When installing a Holley four-barrel carburetor, the production sintered bronze fuel filters located inside the fuel inlet nuts should be removed and discarded. Install a single large paper element replaceable filter (PN 854619) between the fuel pump and carburetor. The fuel pressure drop through the sintered bronze filters cannot be detected because they are located after any fuel pressure gauge connection. Clogged fuel filters are frequently responsible for engine failures and poor performance.

Carburetor heat shields are available from Chevrolet for Holley four-barrel carburetors (PN 3969835) and Quadrajet carburetors (PN 3969837). These shields should be installed between the carburetor and the manifold flange to isolate the fuel in the carburetor float bowls from engine heat. A carburetor heat shield can be especially effective in curing fuel percolation problems.

A foam or paper element low-restriction air cleaner element should always be used to diffuse the air entering the carburetor. The fuel mixture distribution can be upset if no diffuser is used, causing poor power and misfiring at high engine speeds. A 14-inch diameter open element chromed air cleaner assembly for single four-barrel carburetors is available from Chevrolet as PN 12341859. This air cleaner assembly is supplied with a three-inch tall filter element (PN 6421746, AC #A212CW). A taller four-inch element is available as PN 8997189 (AC #A697C).

Lubrication System

The information in this section applies specifically to the Chevrolet big-block V8. Refer to the chapter on lubrication systems for general information on oil system requirements, wet sump and dry sump design, and oil recommendations.

When properly assembled and installed in a vehicle with the correct oil pan, pump, coolers, and filters, the Chevrolet big-block V8 is remarkably free of failures caused by inadequate lubrication.

Two different oil systems are used in Chevrolet big-blocks. The main oil gallery in Mark IV blocks is located above

Oil pump pickups are tack-welded in place on high-volume Mark IV (left) and Gen V oil pumps to prevent vibration damage.

Oil pump drives are interchangeable between Mark IV and Gen V big-blocks. An all-steel shaft is available as PN 3865886.

the driver's side oil pan rail. Connecting passages drilled from the side of the block deliver oil to the main bearings. In Gen V blocks, the main oil gallery is located next

to the camshaft tunnel, with vertical oil passages to the main bearings. While both systems are generally trouble-free, the Gen V oiling system is less susceptible to

---

BOW TIE TIPS: Oil Pump Pointers

The Chevrolet big-block V8 engine family is justifiably famous for its dependable oiling system. There are significant differences in the lubrication systems of the Mark IV and the Gen V designs, however. Engine builders should be aware of differences in Mark IV and Gen V main bearing caps that may affect the oil pump mounting.

One of the features of the Gen V big-block is a one-piece rear crankshaft seal. The rear main bearing cap and the rear bulkhead were revised to accommodate this one-piece seal design, which has a larger outside diameter than the previous two-piece seal. The nominal height of the main cap bolt bosses was increased .183-inch as shown in the following comparison:

	Outboard Bolt Boss Height	Inboard Bolt Boss Height
Gen V Main Cap	2.043"	2.583"
Mark IV Main Cap	1.860"	2.400"
Difference	.183"	.183"

Production GM oil pumps are interchangeable between Mark IV and Gen V blocks. The high-volume Mark IV oil pump (PN 3969870) used on ZL-1 and LS-7 big-blocks and the Gen V oil

The bolt bosses on a Gen V main cap (right) are .183-inch taller than a Mark IV cap. A Gen V rear cap can be machined .183-inch to duplicate the Mark IV's bolt boss height when using an aftermarket oil pump.

pump (PN 14097007) used on H.O. 454 and H.O. 502 engines have similar pump body castings. The two pumps also use 1.30-inch gears, but have different pickups and screens. Both pumps will fit a Gen V rear main cap.

Oil pump drives are also interchangeable. The production Gen V drive uses a steel shaft (PN 3860365) and plastic sleeve (PN 3764554). A heavy-duty Mark IV pump shaft with a steel collar is available as PN 3865886.

High-volume aftermarket oil pumps may require modification to clear the pump mounting bolt (or stud) when installed on a Gen V block. If main cap bolts are used, the boss can be machined down .183-inch to duplicate the height of a Mark IV rear cap and eliminate the interference problem. Be sure to use a radiused cutter when performing this modification. If you are using main cap studs, the pump body must be ground to clear the stud and nut.

Mark IV ZL-1/LS-7 and Gen V H.O. oil pumps can be installed on a Gen V block without modification. A high-volume Mark IV oil pump (PN 3939870–left) and a Gen V H.O. oil pump (PN 14097007–right) use similar castings and 1.300-inch long gears; the pickups and screens are different.

An aftermarket oil pump may require grinding to clear a rear main cap stud on a Gen V block.

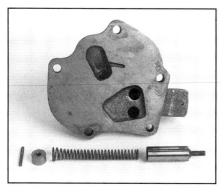

Shim the oil pump bypass spring in the oil pump cover to increase pressure; 65 psi oil pressure is usually sufficient.

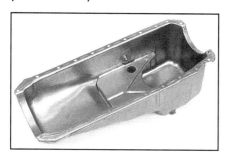

A four-quart oil pan (PN14081027) was used on Mark IV LS-6 engines. This pan fits early-model Camaros and Chevelles.

oil leaks, and permits the pan rails and main bearing bulkheads to be machined extensively for crankshaft and connecting rod clearance.

Production big-block oiling systems are suitable for high-performance and most moderate competition uses. Gen V Bow Tie blocks are available with rear-inlet main oil galleries for dry sump applica-

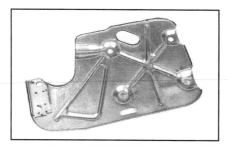

Use windage tray PN 3967854 with oil pan PN 14091356 to control slosh and prevent aeration of the oil in the sump.

tions. See the cylinder block section on page 116 for information on these blocks.

Oil Pump

Several heavy-duty oil pumps are available for the big-block Chevrolet. The high-performance LS-6 oil pump has 1.1-inch long pump gears, while the high-volume LS-7 and Gen V oil pumps have 1.3-inch gears. The longer gears of the LS-7/Gen V pumps increase their capacity by 25 percent at standard pressure. This additional oil volume can extend engine life by enhancing internal cooling and ensuring adequate lubrication under severe operating conditions.

The production Gen V oil pump intermediate driveshaft (PN 3860365) is attached to the oil pump with a plastic retaining sleeve (PN 3764554). The sleeve should be replaced whenever the pump and driveshaft are disassembled for service. Chevrolet offers a heavy-duty oil pump driveshaft with a steel coupler for big-block oil pumps as PN 386588.

Gen V H.O. big-block engine assemblies use oil pan PN 10198992. This six-quart pan must be modified to fit some chassis.

Shafts with steel couplers are also available from aftermarket suppliers. If you are using an all-steel shaft, make sure that the coupler is securely pinned to the shaft.

Oil pressure is regulated by a bypass spring located in the oil pump cover. Any oil pressure above 65 psi at operating speeds is usually sufficient for high-performance use. (A general rule of thumb is that a racing engine requires 10 psi oil pressure for every 1,000 rpm. Using this formula, an engine that runs 7,000 rpm needs approximately 70 psi oil pressure.) Inadequate oil pressure can result in bearing failures and engine damage.

If the oil pressure is insufficient, the pump bypass spring can be shimmed to increase oil pressure by inserting small washers or a Holley carburetor jet inside the bypass piston. Be careful not to use so many spacers that the bypass piston will not uncover the bypass port in the oil pump cover. If the bypass port is blocked by the piston, very high cold oil pressure may blow out the oil filter seal or cause excessive distributor gear wear due to high loading.

Oil pump pickups should always be tack-welded or brazed to the pump body. This will prevent the pickup from vibrating loose. (Remove the oil pressure regulating spring before brazing to prevent heat damage.)

Oil Pan

When selecting an oil pan for a big-block Chevrolet V8, the pan must be matched to the block's rear crankshaft seal. Oil pans are not interchangeable between Mark IV and Gen V blocks due to differences in the design of the rear main bearing caps.

A five-quart capacity oil pan for Mark IV V8s is available as PN 14091356. This pan was originally used on 1965-74 Corvettes and LS-7 engine assemblies. It has a trap door baffle to control oil slosh during cornering and heavy braking.

BOW TIE TIPS Oil Pump Pickups

Production Chevrolet oil pump pickups are designed to strain out large dirt particles and metal fragments before they reach the pump gears. A properly designed pickup also inhibits the formation of a vortex in the sump that would allow the pump to pull in air.

Several big-block oil pumps are supplied with pickups. The distance from the pump mounting surface to the bottom of the screen on the high-volume LS-7 oil pump (PN 3969870) is 4.94-inch. The pickup is tack-welded to the pump body. This pump is used with Corvette oil pan PN 3965774.

LS-6 oil pump PN 475908 includes a pickup that measures 4.88-inch from the mounting surface to the lowest point of the screen. This pump is used with oil pan PN 14081027.

The pickup should be positioned ¼ to ⅜-inch from the bottom of the pan. This can be verified by measuring from the block's oil pan flange to the pickup. You can also check the pickup location during a trial assembly by placing clay on the pickup, installing the pan, and then measuring the thickness of the clay after the pan is removed.

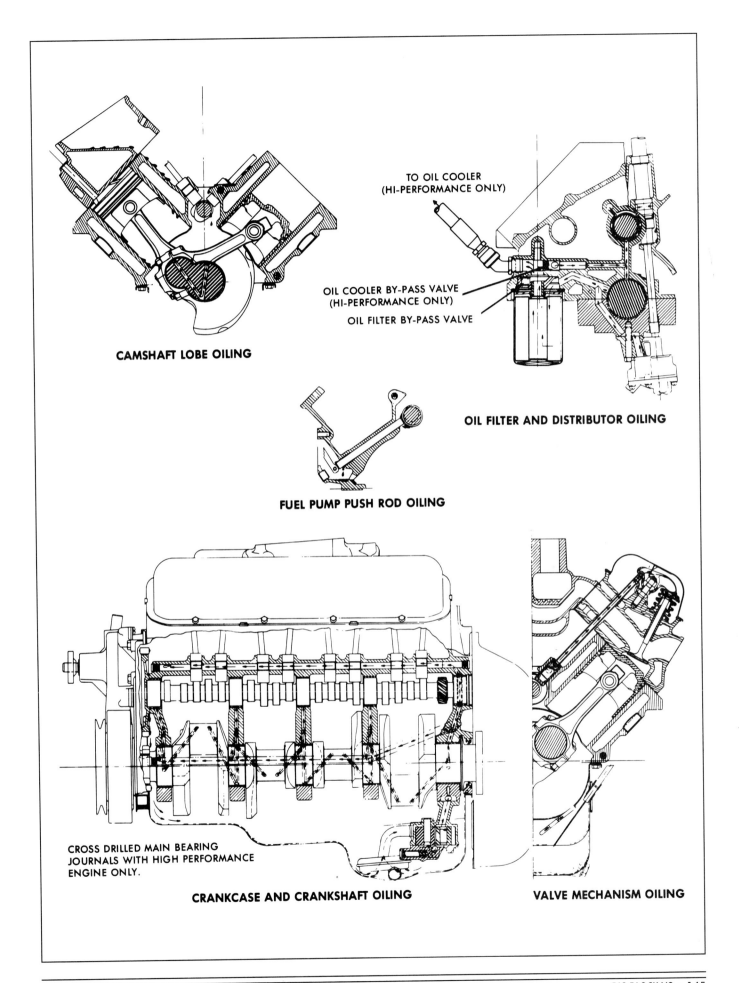

CAMSHAFT LOBE OILING

TO OIL COOLER
(HI-PERFORMANCE ONLY)

OIL COOLER BY-PASS VALVE
(HI-PERFORMANCE ONLY)

OIL FILTER BY-PASS VALVE

OIL FILTER AND DISTRIBUTOR OILING

FUEL PUMP PUSH ROD OILING

CROSS DRILLED MAIN BEARING
JOURNALS WITH HIGH PERFORMANCE
ENGINE ONLY.

CRANKCASE AND CRANKSHAFT OILING

VALVE MECHANISM OILING

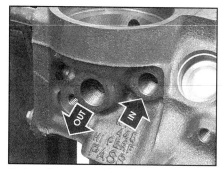

High-performance Mark IV blocks have provisions for oil cooler lines. Install a bypass valve in the rear hole.

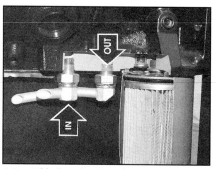

A Gen V block's oil cooler inlet and outlet connections are located on the oil pan rail. Oil returns through the front hole.

A lightweight aluminum Chevrolet water pump (PN 14058915) is a direct replacement for a cast iron Corvette pump.

H.O. engine assemblies use a standard rotation cast iron water pump (PN 12521038).

A flat sheetmetal windage tray (PN 3967854) is included with this pan to separate the oil in the sump from the rapidly spinning crankshaft assembly. This tray requires four special mounting studs (PN 3902885) that replace the main cap bolts on the No. 3 and 4 main bearings.

Mark IV oil pan PN 14081027 is recommended for early-model Chevelle and Camaro chassis. This four-quart pan has a smaller sump than the Corvette pan, and will clear the front crossmember in these vehicles. This pan was also used with the LS-6 engine assembly. This pan does not have clearance for a windage tray.

A six-quart oil pan is available for Gen V big-blocks as PN 10198992. This pan is original equipment on H.O. 454 and H.O. 502 engine assemblies; it uses windage tray PN 14097040. Note that this pan will not clear the front crossmembers in early-model Chevelle/Camaro chassis; Chevrolet does not offer a four-quart Gen V oil pan to fit these models. However, a six-quart Gen V pan can be modified by shortening its sump and relocating the oil pump pickup.

Overfilling a wet sump oil pan to increase its oil capacity is not recommended. Adding oil beyond the pan's designed capacity may cause the lubricant

to overheat and the oil pressure to fluctuate if the oil is aerated by the spinning crankshaft assembly.

A magnetic oil drain plug (PN 23011420) is inexpensive insurance for any engine. It will collect and hold small particles of engine debris until they can be removed during oil changes. Close inspection of the metal chips can also reveal internal engine problems before they reach a critical stage.

Oil Cooler

An oil cooler may be necessary in some applications to maintain the desired oil temperature. If a remote-mounted oil filter is used, it should be plumbed so the oil is filtered before it is returned to the engine to prevent contamination of the engine bearings. The remote filter adapter should be designed to use a non-bypassing filter. Check the adapter to make sure that the upper cavity of the block's oil filter pad is completely sealed to eliminate partial bypassing.

An oil cooler with its inlet and outlet fittings on opposite ends is preferred. This design minimizes restrictions and pressure loss as the oil flows through the cooler core. Oil cooler lines should have a minimum inside diameter of ½-inch in all installations.

All high-performance Mark IV blocks have provisions for oil cooler fittings located above the oil filter pad. To connect an oil cooler, first remove the two factory-installed pipe plugs. Then install an oil filter bypass valve (PN 5575416) in the rear hole behind the oil filter adapter bolt to route oil through the cooler.

The oil cooler holes are located next to the oil pan rail on Gen V blocks. Oil is routed out of the block through the rear hole, and returns from the cooler through the front hole.

Ignition System

Distributors are interchangeable between small-block and big-block Chevrolet V8s, except on engines using tall-deck blocks. A distributor with a longer shaft is required for these engines due to the higher deck height of these tall blocks. Chevrolet does not offer high-performance distributors for tall-deck big-blocks, but they are available from several aftermarket sources.

See the ignition section of the small-block V8 chapter for information and recommendations on distributors, spark plug wires, and related components for big-block V8 engines.

Starters

Starters are interchangeable between small-block and big-block V8 engines. Refer to the small-block V8 chapter for information on starter motors and related components.

Cooling System

A lightweight aluminum water pump for the big-block Chevrolet is available as PN 14058915. This pump has a reinforced snout and a large diameter hub with dual pulley bolt patterns. The pump casting has short mounting legs; water pump spacers are available from aftermarket manufacturers for applications that require long mounting legs.

A cast iron water pump (PN 12521038) is used with H.O. 454 and H.O. 502 engine assemblies. This pump is a good choice for applications that require a standard-rotation pump.

Deep-groove pulleys are recommended to prevent belt loss at high rpm. A 6-inch two-groove cast iron crankshaft pulley for short water pumps is available as PN 3899660. This small-diameter pulley also reduces parasitic power losses. The corresponding two-groove water pump pulley is PN 3995641.

Exhaust System

A big-block racing engine should be equipped with headers whenever a non-production exhaust system is legal. The exact pipe diameter and length that will produce the best engine performance depends on several factors, including engine displacement, operating rpm range, camshaft profile, induction system, and cylinder head selection. The chassis configuration must also be considered when designing a header system.

For street performance and limited competition applications, primary pipe dimensions of 2-inch OD x 34-inch length feeding 3½ to 4-inch collectors have proven successful. Large displacement and high-rpm engines generally respond well to 2⅛ or 2¼-inch primary tubes, measuring 30 to 32 inches in length. Big-block racing engines with displacements over 500 cubic inches and operating at extremely high engine speeds may require 2⅜ to 2½-inch diameter primary tubes and 5-inch collectors for peak performance.

Header systems designed to these dimensions are made by specialty manufacturers

Headers for Pro Stock big-block engines have 2⅜-inch diameter primary pipes and huge 5-inch collectors.

and independent shops. These sources can supply specific information on tubing sizes for your intended usage. ⌐

TECH SPECS: CAST IRON BIG-BLOCK V8 RECOMMENDED BOLT TORQUE AND LUBRICANT SPECIFICATIONS

	Torque	Lubricant
Main Bearing:		
Inner	110 ft.-lbs.	Oil
Outer	110 ft.-lbs.	Oil
Connecting Rod Bolt (⁷⁄₁₆"), Rod #3969804	67-73 ft.-lbs. (.009" stretch preferred)	Oil
Cylinder Head Bolt	70	Sealant (Use oil in blind-tapped bolt holes in Bow Tie blocks.)
Head Studs (⁷⁄₁₆" NF Thread)	65	Oil
Rocker Arm Stud	50	Oil
Camshaft Sprocket	20	Oil
Intake Manifold	25	Oil
Flywheel	60	Oil
Spark Plugs:		
Conventional Gasket, Alum. Head	25	Anti-Seize
Tapered Seat, Alum. Head	15	Anti-Seize
Tapered Seat, Iron Head	15	Dry
Exhaust Manifold	20	Anti-Seize
Oil Pan Bolt	165 in.-lbs.	Oil
Front Cover Bolt	75 in.-lbs.	Oil
Rocker Cover	25 in.-lbs.	Anti-Seize

TECH SPECS: BIG-BLOCK V8 SPECIFICATIONS FOR HIGH-PERFORMANCE USE

Firing Order	1-8-4-3-6-5-7-2
Spark Advance	Maximum of 36-40 degrees BTDC
Maximum Oil Temp	270 degrees in oil pan
Minimum Fuel Pressure	4-5 psi at maximum engine speed
Piston to Bore	.0065-.0075" measured at centerline of wrist pin hole, perpendicular to pin, for Chevrolet forged pistons. Follow manufacturer's recommendations for other pistons. Finish bores with 400 grit stones or equivalent.
Minimum Piston Ring End Gap	Top .018"; 2nd .016"; oil rails .016"
Wrist Pin	.0006-.0008" in piston. (.0005-.0008" in bushed rod for floating pin; 0-.005" end play preferred.)
Rod Bearing	.002-.003"; side clearance .015-.025"
Main Bearing	.002-.003"
Crank End Play	.005-.007"
Piston to Cylinder Head	.035/.040" minimum (steel rod)
Valve Lash	As specified by camshaft manufacturer. See text for recommended lash for Chevrolet camshafts.
Valve to Piston Clearance	.045" exhaust and intake at running valve lash. NOTE: These are absolute minimum clearances for an engine running below the valvetrain limiting speed. More clearance must be allowed for engines operating at valvetrain limiting speed; allow .080" intake and .100" exhaust valve clearance for high rpm engines.

NOTE: These specifications are intended as general guidelines for high-performance and competition applications. Different clearances and specifications may be required depending on operating conditions and components used. Always follow manufacturer's recommendations when installing aftermarket components.

Chevrolet 90-Degree V6

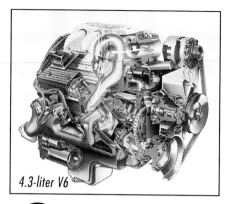
4.3-liter V6

Chevy's Championship V6

The "Three-Quarter" Small-Block

V6 Firing Sequences

High-Tech Cylinder Heads

Chevrolet launched a revolution in auto racing with the 90-degree V6. Originally developed to meet the need for a compact and economical production engine, the Chevy V6/90 has become a formidable force in motorsports. The V6/90's potential as a racing engine has been widely recognized by enthusiasts because of its similarity to the Chevrolet small-block V8. The V6/90 has found favor with street rodders, powerboat owners, oval track racers, drag racers, and road racers. It has won races and championships in a wide variety of venues, including the SCCA (Trans-Am), IMSA (GTP, GTO, and GTU), NHRA (Competition and Super Stock eliminators), NASCAR (Grand National), ASA, USAC (sprint cars) and other major sanctioning bodies.

The V6/90 has been aptly described as a "three-quarter" small-block. GM engineers created the V6 by deleting the No. 3 and No. 6 cylinders from a small-block V8. The two engines share the same basic architecture (block height, bore centers, camshaft location, crankshaft main journal diameter, etc.). Consequently many of the modifications and preparation techniques developed for the Chevrolet V8 also apply to the V6/90.

The specifications and procedures in this chapter are intended primarily to aid enthusiasts in preparing the Chevrolet V6/90 engine for "off-highway" and emission-exempt operation. Due to the diversity of sanctioning bodies' rules and the special demands of various types of

Chevrolet's compact and powerful 90-degree V6 is a proven winner in NASCAR, ASA, SCCA, and IMSA competition.

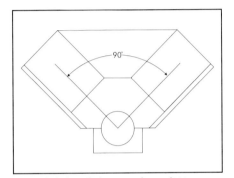

The included angle between the V6/90's cylinder banks is 90 degrees—thus the engine is designated a "90-degree V6."

Chevrolet Berettas swept the 1990 SCCA Trans-Am driver's and manufacturer's championships with 4.5-liter V6/90 engines equipped with splayed-valve Bow Tie cylinder heads.

Johnny Benson, Jr. drove his Chevy V6-powered Lumina to the 1993 ASA AC-Delco Challenge Series championship.

TECH SPECS: V6/90 DESIGN FEATURES

Engine Displacement	Model Year	Bore	Stroke
200ci	1978-79	3.50"	3.48"
229ci	1980-84	3.74"	3.48"
262ci (4.3L)	1985-94	4.00"	3.48"

motorsports, an engine may require specific preparation procedures and accessories not covered in this manual. These specifications and recommendations are intended as guidelines that have been tested and proven by leading competitors.

V6 and V8 Interchangeability

Many components are readily interchangeable between Chevrolet V6/90 and small-block V8 engines. These items include valvetrain parts (valves, springs, rocker arms, pushrods, timing sets, and lifters); camshaft and crankshaft main bearings; piston assemblies (pistons, wrist pins, and rings); lubrication systems (oil pumps, pickups, and drives); and external accessories (front covers, torsional dampers, flywheels, and water pumps). This commonality of design means that many heavy-duty V8 parts can be used without modification, or easily adapted to the V6/90 Chevrolet.

This chapter describes parts and procedures that are unique to V6/90 engines.

Refer to the small-block V8 chapter for recommendations on other components. For information on general engine building and blueprinting procedures, ignition systems, and lubrication requirements for racing applications, see the respective chapters on these topics.

V6/90 Engine Design

The Chevrolet 90-degree V6 ("V6/90") owes its basic design to the small-block V8. The term "90-degree V6" refers to the included angle between the engine's two cylinder banks. In the V6/90 Chevrolet, the vee angle is 90 degrees—the same vee angle used in small-block and big-block Chevrolet V8s. The "90-degree" designation does *not* refer to the number of degrees of crankshaft rotation between cylinder firings. In fact, there are three different firing sequences for the V6/90 Chevrolet, as will be discussed later.

Production Chevrolet 90-degree V6s have been manufactured with three displacements. The V6/90 was introduced in 1978 with 200 cubic inches (3.50-inch bore x 3.48-inch stroke). In 1980, the bore

diameter was increased to 3.74-inch to yield 229 cubic inches. In 1985, a 4.3-liter (262ci) V6/90 replaced the 229ci version in Chevy's engine lineup. The 4.3-liter V6/90 has the same internal dimensions as a 350ci small-block V8 (4.00-inch bore x 3.48-inch stroke).

Firing Order

Production V6/90 Chevrolets are also distinguished by their firing sequences. All 1978-84 200ci and 229ci V6/90 engines had a "semi-even" firing sequence. Each pair of adjacent connecting rods shared a crankshaft throw; however, the individual rod journals were offset 18 degrees. This offset produced a firing sequence of 132 degrees/108 degrees throughout the engine's firing order.

The big ends of the connecting rods in 200ci and 229ci V6/90 engines are .050-inch narrower than small-block V8 rods to accommodate a thrust flange between adjacent rod journals. The rod bearing inserts are also correspondingly narrower than V8 bearings.

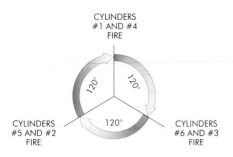

CYLINDERS #1 AND #4 FIRE

120° 120°

CYLINDERS #5 AND #2 FIRE

120°

CYLINDERS #6 AND #3 FIRE

EVEN-FIRE V6

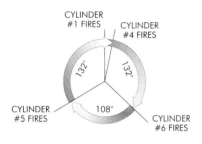

CYLINDER #1 FIRES

CYLINDER #4 FIRES

132° 132°

CYLINDER #5 FIRES

108°

CYLINDER #6 FIRES

SEMI-EVEN FIRE V6

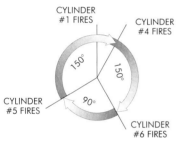

CYLINDER #1 FIRES

CYLINDER #4 FIRES

150° 150°

CYLINDER #5 FIRES

90°

CYLINDER #6 FIRES

ODD-FIRE V6

These diagrams illustrate the three firing sequences used in Chevrolet 90-degree V6s. The arrows represent the number of crankshaft degrees between cylinder firings for even-fire, semi-even fire, and odd-fire crankshafts. For clarity, only one crankshaft revolution (360 degrees) is shown for the semi-even fire and odd-fire sequences.

The 4.3-liter V6/90 introduced in 1985 is a true "even-fire" engine. Its rod throws are offset 30 degrees to produce 120-degrees of crankshaft rotation between cylinder firings. This uniform firing sequence provides exceptional smoothness in passenger cars and light-duty trucks. The rod bearing journal diameter was enlarged to 2.250-inch on even-fire 4.3-liter crankshafts to maintain strength with the increased offset of the rod journals.

Finally, a heavy-duty "common-pin" crankshaft was developed for V6/90 racing engines. There is *no* offset in the rod

Semi-even and even-fire cranks have offset rod journals (left); an odd-fire crank (right) has common-pin journals like a small-block V8.

journals of a common pin crankshaft. This design produces an "odd-fire" sequence with alternating 150-degree and 90-degree intervals between cylinder firings. No production V6/90 Chevrolets have been manufactured with odd-fire common pin crankshafts; however, the vast majority of Chevy V6/90s used in competition are equipped with common-pin odd-fire crankshafts.

Thus there are *three* possible firing sequences for Chevrolet V6/90 engines. The firing sequence is determined by the crankshaft. *Each firing sequence requires a specific distributor and camshaft to produce the proper spark and valve timing.*

Although the *interval* in degrees of crankshaft rotation between the cylinder firings is different with the three types of crankshafts, the firing *order* does not change. All Chevrolet V6/90 engines use the same 1-6-5-4-3-2 firing order regardless of the crankshaft used.

Design Features

Production Chevrolet V6/90 engines use lightweight cast iron blocks with two-bolt main bearing caps, cast nodular iron crankshafts, and forged connecting rods. The 229ci V6/90 featured 1.84-inch diameter inlet valves and 1.50-inch exhausts; intake valve size was increased to 1.94-inch diameter in 4.3-liter engines.

Both the 200ci and 229ci V6/90 engines were equipped with aluminum intake manifolds and two-barrel Rochester "dual jet" carburetors; manifolds on 229ci V6s had open plenums. Induction systems for late-model 4.3-liter engines include Quadrajet carburetors, throttle body fuel injection (TBI), and central port fuel injection (CPI).

Production 4.3-liter V6/90 Chevrolets are equipped with swirl port cast iron

An enhanced 200hp version of the 4.3-liter V6/90 debuted in mid-1992 with a gear-driven balance shaft and central port fuel injection.

cylinder heads that yield a 9:1 compression ratio. These heads have raised rocker cover rails that are designed to reduce oil leakage through the valve cover gaskets. The rocker cover attaching bolts are located in the center of the covers to distribute clamping loads evenly.

1986 and later 4.3-liter V6/90 engines have one-piece rear crankshaft seals and use one-piece molded rubber oil pan gaskets. Heavy-duty cast iron Bow Tie cylinder blocks manufactured since 1987 are also machined for one-piece rear seals.

Hydraulic roller tappets were introduced on production Chevrolet V6/90 engines in 1987. This change from conventional flat tappets reduced internal engine friction, increased fuel economy, and improved engine reliability. Revisions in the V6/90 block to accommodate roller tappets included longer lifter bosses with machined tops, mounting bosses in the lifter valley for a lifter guide retainer, and a front-mounted cam thrust plate.

Engine Blocks

Production Chevrolet V6/90 cylinder blocks are suitable for high-performance street use, powerboats, and limited competition applications. The chief differences between production V6/90 blocks are the rear main seal design and the machining in the lifter valley for either flat or roller tappets.

There are significant differences in the oiling systems of production V6/90 and small-block V8 engines. Chevrolet small-block V8s have three oil galleries above the camshaft; the central gallery feeds the camshaft and crankshaft bearings, while the two side galleries lubricate the lifters and valvetrain. In contrast, production V6/90 engines have only *two* oil galleries. The passenger's side gallery

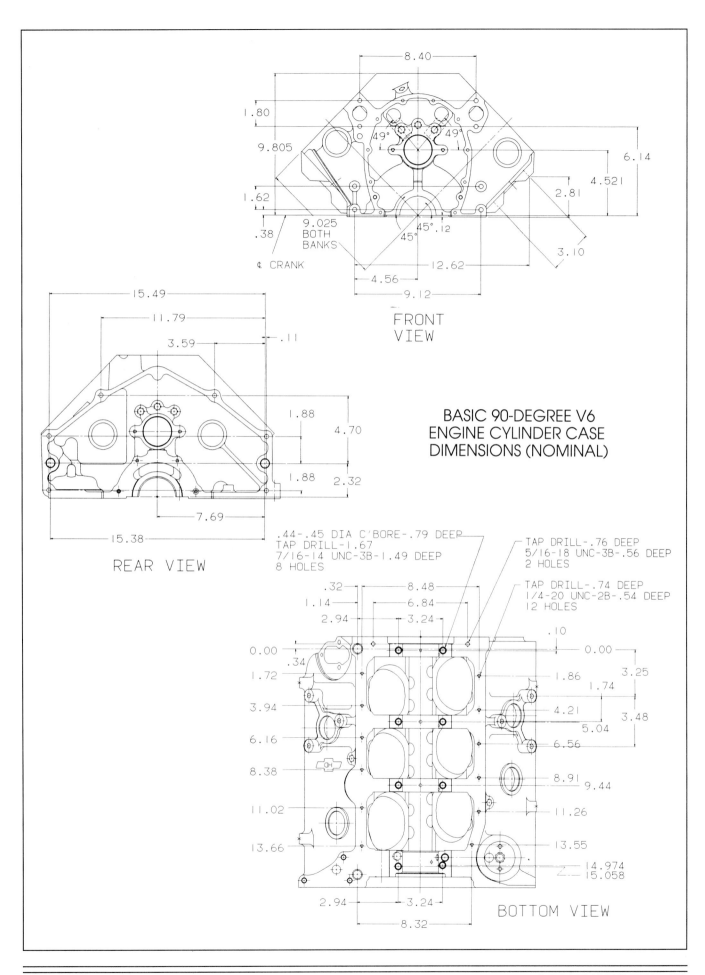

FRONT
VIEW

REAR VIEW

BASIC 90-DEGREE V6
ENGINE CYLINDER CASE
DIMENSIONS (NOMINAL)

.44-.45 DIA C'BORE-.79 DEEP
TAP DRILL-1.67
7/16-14 UNC-3B-1.49 DEEP
8 HOLES

TAP DRILL-.76 DEEP
5/16-18 UNC-3B-.56 DEEP
2 HOLES

TAP DRILL-.74 DEEP
1/4-20 UNC-2B-.54 DEEP
12 HOLES

BOTTOM VIEW

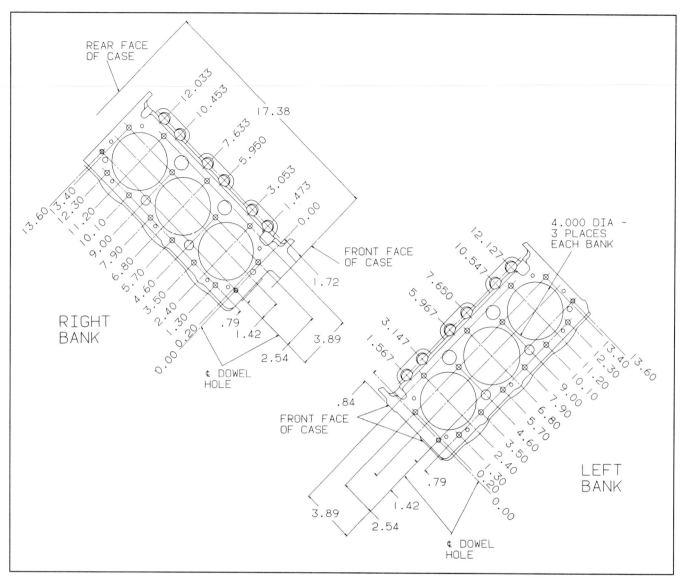

The production V6/90 oiling system has proven trouble-free in many engines used in competition. Although heavy-duty V6/90 blocks have provisions for V8-style oiling, the production V6 oiling system is generally satisfactory if the engine will be operated below 7000 rpm.

Cast Iron Bow Tie Blocks

10134387	Cast Iron Bow Tie Engine Block, 2-bolt Iron Main Bearing Caps
10185051	Cast Iron Bow Tie Engine Block, 4-bolt Steel Main Bearing Caps

The GM Motorsports Technology Group has developed two cast iron Bow Tie V6/90 cylinder blocks for competition applications. Bow Tie blocks have thicker main bearing bulkheads than production versions, and their solid lifter valleys are similar to a small-block V8.

Two versions of the cast iron Bow Tie V6/90 block are available. PN 10134387 has production-type two-bolt main bear-

ing caps and a semi-machined oiling system. PN 10185051 has billet steel main bearing caps and a fully machined oiling system. Except for these differences in bearing caps and lubrication systems, the cast iron Bow Tie blocks are identical.

Semi-machined versions of the Bow Tie V6/90 blocks are manufactured with production two-bolt iron caps. These caps are suitable for moderate performance applications, such as street rods and power boats. Production caps can be replaced easily if an engine builder prefers aftermarket bearing caps.

Steel bearing caps are used on all four main bearings on a fully machined Bow Tie block. The two middle four-bolt bearing caps have angled outer bolt holes. The two-bolt steel rear bearing cap uses a one-piece crankshaft seal. A seal adapter (PN 10051118) is required when installing a crank designed for a two-piece seal.

1987 and later production blocks have lifter bosses with machined tops and mounts for hydraulic roller lifter guide retainers.

feeds the right bank of lifters, just as in a small-block V8. A large diameter gallery on the driver's side feeds the left lifter bank *and* the camshaft and crankshaft bearings. This driver's side oil passage is offset from the lifter bore centerline to allow oil to flow around the lifter bodies. The lifter valley in production V6/90 blocks has open webs above the camshaft because there is no center oil gallery.

TECH SPECS: V6/90 BLOCKS

Part Number	10134387	10185051	10134371	10134351
Block Material	Cast Iron	Cast Iron	A356-T6 Aluminum	A356-T6 Aluminum
Cylinder Wall Type	Siamesed	Siamesed	Siamesed	Siamesed
Cylinder Deck Height	9.025"	9.025"	9.025"	9.025"
Cylinder Bore Range	4.000-4.180"	4.000-4.180"	4.125"	4.125"
Bearing Cap Bolts	2	4	4	4
Cap Bolt Orientation	Straight	Splayed	Splayed 20°	Splayed 20°
Bearing Cap Type	Gray Cast Iron	Steel	8620 Steel	8620 Steel
Crankshaft Journal Diameter (in.)	2.45	2.45	2.45	2.65
Oil Sump Type	Wet	Dry	Dry	Dry
Crankshaft Seal Type	1 or 2 piece*	1 or 2 piece*	2 piece	2 piece
Design Max. Stroke	4.00"	4.00"	3.75"	4.00"
Weight (lbs.—bare)	160	163	78	78
Intended Usage	Street	Professional Competition	Professional Competition	Professional Competition
Notes	Semi-machined oil system	Fully-machined V8-type oil system.	No mechanical fuel pump boss.	No mechanical fuel pump boss.
	*Block is machined for 1-piece seal; 2-piece seal requires adapter PN 10051118.			

Cast iron V6/90 Bow Tie blocks have siamesed cylinder walls and reinforced decks with blind-tapped head bolt holes. Bow Tie blocks are available with two-bolt and four-bolt main bearing caps.

Fully-machined V6/90 Bow Tie blocks have steel main bearing caps; the outer bolts in the two middle caps are angled outward.

This Bow Tie block has been outfitted with a rear camshaft block-off plate, a crankshaft seal adapter, and a valley oil scavenge line.

Both Bow Tie V6/90 blocks have sufficient material in the oil pan rails to permit the installation of four-bolt front and rear caps.

The semi-machined two-bolt Bow Tie V6/90 block has provisions for a central oil gallery, and will accommodate a V8-type oiling system. Only the passenger side oil gallery is drilled, however. To convert to V8-type oiling, the engine builder must drill holes for the central oil gallery and left-side lifter gallery. Oil holes must also be drilled from the central gallery to the cam and main bearings.

The oiling system is fully machined in a four-bolt Bow Tie block. Oil is routed from the center oil gallery to the intermediate main bearings through two intersecting passages, eliminating the annular grooves behind the camshaft bearings that are used in production blocks. The cam bearing oil holes are drilled at the 2 o'clock position. Make sure they align with the holes in the cam bearing inserts.

A boss at the front of the block allows oil from an external pump to be pumped directly into the main oil gallery. This boss is drilled and tapped in fully machined Bow Tie V6/90 blocks. A front oil inlet simplifies the plumbing for a dry sump oil system with a remote-mounted filter. This system also eliminates several 90-degree turns in the engine's internal oil system, and provides a more direct path for the oil to reach the bearings.

Cast iron Bow Tie V6/90 blocks share many technical features (siamesed cylinders, reinforced decks, enlarged lifter bosses, etc.) with their small-block V8

Lightweight aluminum Bow Tie V6/90 blocks have 4.125-inch diameter cylinder liners and V8-style oiling.

Aluminum Bow Tie blocks are equipped with billet steel four-bolt main bearing caps. Screw-in plugs seal the water jackets.

Grooved main bearing saddles improve connecting rod oiling. Drill additional oil feed holes in the upper main bearing inserts.

counterparts. See the small-block V8 chapter for more information on cast iron Bow Tie blocks.

Aluminum Bow Tie Blocks

10134371	V6/90 Aluminum Bow Tie Engine Block (350-type Main Bearings)
10134351	V6/90 Aluminum Bow Tie Engine Block (400-type Main Bearings)

Aluminum Bow Tie V6/90 engine blocks combine light weight with the strength to withstand the power levels of today's racing engines. The front and rear bulkheads are reinforced, and the main bearing bulkheads are tapered to buttress the cylinder barrels. Solid aluminum above the oil pan rails strengthens the bottom end and eliminates the need for supplemental girdles and main bearing supports. The cam bearing tunnel is also augmented with additional material.

The two aluminum Bow Tie blocks are identical except for their main bearing diameters. V6/90 aluminum blocks are available with standard 2.450-inch di-

ameter main bearings (350-type) and extra-large 2.650-inch (400-type) main bearings. The larger 400-type bearings enhance reliability when using a long-stroke crankshaft.

V6/90 aluminum Bow Tie blocks are similar to aluminum small-block V8s. See the small-block V8 chapter for technical details on aluminum blocks.

Main Bearing Caps

All cast iron production and Bow Tie V6/90 blocks use 2.45-inch main bearings. Aluminum blocks are available with 2.45 and 2.65-inch mains. Main caps are interchangeable between V6/90 and small-block V8 engines; however, the main bearing housings *must* be align bored whenever replacement caps are installed. Refer to the small-block V8 chapter for additional information on main bearing caps.

The GM Motorsports Technology Group has developed a lubrication system modification that improves rod oiling at high speeds. This modification is

highly recommended for V6/90 engines that are operated for sustained periods above 7500 rpm.

The main bearing saddles (in the block only) should be grooved through the oil hole with a slot .150-inch wide and .150-inch deep. Modify the upper main bearing inserts by drilling two equally spaced ⅛-inch diameter oil feed holes on both sides of the original oil hole; this produces a total of five oil holes in each upper bearing half.

This modification pressurizes the oil groove in the bearing insert from end to end. This ensures that the connecting rod oil feed hole receives pressurized oil whenever it is exposed to the main bearing groove as the crankshaft rotates.

Rear Crankshaft Seals

V6/90 Chevrolets produced from 1978 through 1985 used two-piece rear crankshaft seals. At the start of the 1986 model year, a new one-piece rear main seal was developed for the Chevrolet V6/90 and small-block V8. The one-piece rear main seal required revisions to the V6 engine case, crankshaft, and oil pan. As a result of these design changes, these components are not interchangeable with V6/90 engines produced before 1986.

See the sections on crankshafts, rear seal adapters, and flywheels in the small-block V8 chapter for more information on design revisions for one-piece rear seals.

Crankshafts

As noted previously in the "Firing Order" section, three different crankshaft designs are used in Chevrolet 90-degree V6s. 1978-84 200ci and 229ci V6s use "semi-even fire" cranks with alternating 132 and 108 degree intervals between cylinder firings. 1985 and newer 4.3-liter engines have true "even-fire" cranks with 120-degrees of crankshaft rotation between cylinder firings. Finally, heavy-duty Chevrolet unfinished forged steel cranks have an "odd-fire" design that produces an alternating 150-degree/90-degree firing sequence.

Production Crankshafts

All production V6/90 crankshafts are cast nodular iron. These crankshafts are suitable for mildly modified high-performance engines and limited competition applications.

Although both "even-fire" and "semi-even fire" production V6/90 crankshafts have 3.48-inch strokes, there are several important differences between these crankshafts. The rod journal offset in a 200/229ci crank is 18 degrees; the journal offset is 30 degrees in an even-fire 4.3-liter crank. Early-model 200/229ci cranks have 2.100-inch diameter rod bearing journals, while 4.3-liter crankshafts have larger 2.250-inch diameter rod journals. This difference in journal diameter also requires different connecting rods.

Production 4.3-liter crankshafts were redesigned at the start of the 1986 model year to accommodate one-piece rear oil seals. This change required a smaller diameter flywheel flange bolt pattern; flywheels and flexplates with this revised bolt pattern must be used with 1986 and later V6/90 production crankshafts.

Heavy-Duty Forged Steel Crankshaft

A forged steel common-pin crankshaft is recommended for all maximum-effort Chevrolet V6/90 racing engines. A suitable competition crankshaft can be machined from a steel billet or a Chevrolet unfinished crankshaft forging (PN 14044838). Unmachined Chevy V6/90 cranks are forged from vacuum degassed 5140 steel, and can be ground to produce strokes from 3.25-inch to 3.75-inch.

The rod journals on a common-pin V6 crankshaft are not offset; the connecting rods on each throw are side-by-side, similar to a small-block V8. This design provides more bearing area and requires less rod offset than a splayed-pin crank. V6/90 racing engines equipped with "odd-fire" common-pin crankshafts actually exhibit less vibration and better durability at high speeds than even-fire and semi-even fire engines.

The ignition system and camshaft must be compatible with the odd-fire crankshaft design. Chevrolet offers heavy-duty distributors for common-pin cranks, and aftermarket manufacturers can supply camshafts ground for the 150-degree/90-degree firing sequence.

When balancing an odd-fire V6/90 crankshaft, the bobweight should be calculated using 50 percent of the engine reciprocating weight plus 100 percent of the rotating weight.

Torsional Dampers

V6/90 Chevrolet engines used in competition do not have the same torsional

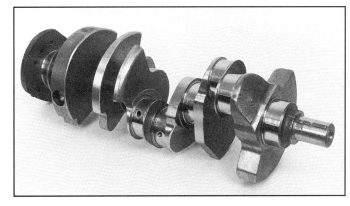

Production 4.3-liter crankshafts are available for one-piece and two-piece rear seals. The rod journals are offset 30 degrees.

Unmachined Chevrolet heavy-duty odd-fire crankshafts for V6/90 competition engines are forged from 5140 alloy steel.

damper requirements as a small-block V8. The GM Motorsports Technology Group recommends 8-inch diameter dampers only for V6/90 engines equipped with production cast iron crankshafts. A production 6.75-inch diameter damper (PN 6272221) works well with a forged steel odd-fire crankshaft. Note that some sanctioning bodies prohibit the use of stock-type dampers on racing engines because of the possibility of inertia ring failure at high rpm; check the rulebook before installing a production damper on a competition V6/90. A torsional damper is usually not required for Chevrolet V6/90 engines used in drag racing and applications that do not require a flywheel (sprint cars, for example).

Flywheels

Two different flywheel flange bolt patterns have been used on Chevrolet V6/90 V8 engines. All 1978-85 production crankshafts have a 3.58-inch diameter bolt pattern. 1986 and later production cranks designed for one-piece rear crankshaft seals have a smaller 3.00-inch diameter flywheel flange bolt pattern. The larger 3.58-inch bolt pattern is preferred for high-performance use, and is recommended for V6/90 crankshafts machined from Chevrolet raw forgings.

The flywheel (or flexplate) must be matched to the crankshaft. 1978-85 V6/90 production and heavy-duty crankshafts with two-piece rear seals are inter-

A 4.3-liter V6 damper (right) is suitable for street engines; a 6.75-inch diameter V8 damper (left) is recommended for racing.

nally balanced; neutral balanced flywheels and torsional dampers should be used with these cranks. 1986 and later crankshafts designed for one-piece seals are externally balanced, and require a counterweighted flywheel for proper engine balance.

Flywheels and automatic transmission flexplates are interchangeable between V6/90 and small-block V8 engines. See the "Flywheels" section of the small-block V8 chapter for part numbers and specifications.

Connecting Rods

Connecting rods used in 200/229ci V6/90 engines are similar to small-block V8 connecting rods. They have the same center-to-center length (5.70-inch), the same wrist pin diameter (.927-inch), and the same rod journal diameter (2.10-inch). However, because of the V6/90 crankshaft's offset rod journals, the big

Production cast iron 4.3-liter V6/90 cylinder heads have raised rocker cover rails and "swirl port" intake runners.

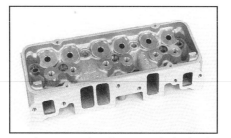

Raised runner V6/90 aluminum cylinder heads are available without seats, guides, and pushrod holes as PN 14044883.

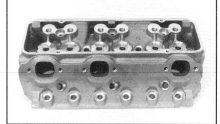

18-degree Bow Tie heads have raised and widened exhaust ports. Special header flanges are required to fit the revised bolt pattern.

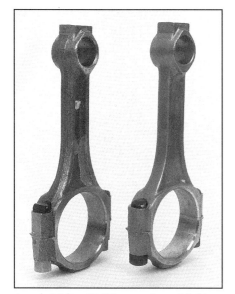

A stock 4.3-liter V6/90 connecting rod (left) fits a 2.25-inch diameter crank journal. Grind and shotpeen the beams on production rods.

ends of the rods are .050-inch narrower and the rod bearing inserts are .130-inch narrower than standard small-block V8 components. The beam of a V6/90 connecting rod is also slightly more offset relative to its big end bore than a small-block V8 rod.

Any small-block V8 connecting rod with a 2.10-inch bearing ID can be reworked for a high-performance 1978-84 200/229ci V6 engine by narrowing the big end approximately .050-inch to .890-inch (plus-or-minus .002-inch). A .0625-inch chamfer must be machined on both sides of the big end bore for crank fillet clearance. Make sure that the V6 rod bearing is centered in the rod bore during assembly; if it rides up on either fillet, the bearing will fail quickly.

Production connecting rods for 1985 and newer 4.3-liter V6/90 engines have the same center-to-center length and pin bushing diameter as other V6 and small-block V8 components. The rod bearing diameter is different, however. 4.3-liter

V6 connecting rods use 2.250-inch bearings (.150-inch larger than other V6 and small-block V8 rods). Connecting rods used in 4.3-liter V6s are not interchangeable with other Chevrolet engines because of this difference in rod bearing bore diameter.

Production 4.3-liter V6 connecting rods are satisfactory for high-performance and limited competition applications. See the engine building chapter for recommendations on preparing production connecting rods.

Chevrolet V6/90 engines equipped with common-pin odd-fire crankshafts can use production or Bow Tie small-block V8 connecting rods and bearings if the crankshaft's rod journals are ground to 2.10-inch diameter.

Pistons

Chevrolet does not offer heavy-duty forged pistons for standard bore 200ci (3.50-inch cylinder diameter) and 229ci (3.74-inch) V6/90 engines.

A variety of Chevrolet pistons are available for 1985 and newer 4.3-liter V6s. Production 4.3-liter pistons are cast aluminum with a dished top and four valve notches. Forged aluminum small-block V8 pistons can be installed in high-performance V6/90 engines with 4.00-inch diameter and larger cylinders.

If you are ordering pistons with asymmetrical domes for use in a V6/90 racing engine, make sure that the domes and valve pockets correspond to the cylinder head layout. Cylinder Nos. 1, 3, 4, and 6 require pistons with the intake valve relief on the right; cylinder Nos. 2 and 5 use pistons with the intake valve on the left. Of course, flat-top pistons and pistons with "universal" domes can be installed in any cylinder in a V6/90.

See the small-block V8 chapter for additional information on selecting and preparing pistons.

Cylinder Heads

Chevrolet V6/90 cylinder heads are based on the successful small-block V8 design. Most valvetrain components are interchangeable between the two engines, and many of the porting techniques developed for the V8 are directly applicable to the V6. It should be noted, however, that a V6 head is not simply a shortened V8 casting. The combustion chambers in a V6/90 cylinder head correspond to the Nos. 1, 5, and 7 chambers in a small-block V8; it is the No. 3 chamber that is "missing" in a V6.

Production Cylinder Heads

Production cast iron cylinder heads installed on 200/229ci Chevrolet V6/90 engines have intake and exhaust ports that are similar in both size and shape to the runners found in conventional small-block V8 production heads. Production heads for these engines have 1.84-inch diameter intake valves and 1.50-inch diameter exhausts. The intake valve diameter can be increased to 1.88-inch diameter before encountering interference with these engines' 3.74-inch diameter cylinder bores.

Early-model production cast iron heads have limited potential for high-performance applications. Standard V8 porting techniques can be applied, but significantly enlarging either the intake or exhaust ports runs the risk of breaking through to the water jacket.

Production cast iron cylinder heads used on 4.3-liter even-fire V6/90 engines employ a "swirl port" design that promotes turbulence in the combustion chamber to enhance combustion. The spark plugs are also centrally located in the chambers to establish a uniform flame pattern. The combination of this swirl port technology and fast-burn combustion chamber permits a relatively high compression ratio with regular unleaded

Part Number	Description	Casting Number	Material/ Weight (lbs.)	Port Volume Int./Exh. (cc)	Combustion Chamber Volume (cc)	Valve Diameter Int./Exh. (in.)	Notes
14044883	Raised Runner Bow Tie (bare)	14044883	356 Aluminum/ 15	195/64	53	N/A	No seats, guides, or intake pushrod holes.
14044884	Raised Runner Bow Tie	14044883	356 Aluminum/ 15	195/64	53	2.10/1.60	Intake ports .200" higher than standard location.
10134359	18° Bow Tie	10134359	355 Aluminum/ 17	210/80	43	N/A	18° valve angle; no seats, guides.
24502523	CNC-ported 18° Bow Tie	10134359	355 Aluminum/ 16	245/95	48	2.15/1.625	Fully ported with seats and guides.
10134394	Splayed-valve Bow Tie	10134394	355 Aluminum/ 19	253/80	45	N/A	Splayed valve design; no seats or guides.

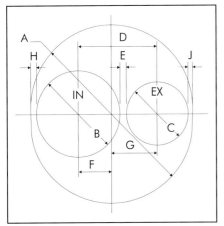

This chart shows the valve spacing for V6/90 Bow Tie heads. "H" and "J" are the clearances between the valves and cylinder wall.

P/N	A	B	C	D	E	F	G	H	J
10134359	4.125	2.15	1.625	1.935	.048	.825	1.13	.163	.120
14044883	4.00	2.10	1.60	1.91	.050	.850	1.06	.100	.140

The raised intake runners in 18-degree V6/90 Bow Tie cylinder heads are located .650-inch above the deck surface.

gasoline. V6/90 engines equipped with swirl port heads typically require only 23 to 25 degrees of spark advance to produce maximum power.

Swirl-port heads for 4.3-liter V6/90 engines have 1.94-inch diameter intake valves and 1.50-inch diameter exhausts. Production 4.3-liter cylinder heads also feature raised rocker cover rails with machined gasket surfaces to minimize oil leaks. The performance potential of these production heads is limited, however, by their port size. The thickness of the material around the runners does not permit large increases in port volume.

Aluminum Bow Tie Cylinder Heads

The GM Motorsports Technology Group responded to the need for heavy-duty V6/90 cylinder heads by developing several high-performance aluminum Bow Tie castings. Heavy-duty V6/90

heads are manufactured from 356 T-6 or 355 T-71 aluminum (see chart above for alloy). The "first design" aluminum Bow Tie V6 head had conventional intake runners, and the "second design" head featured raised inlet ports. As cylinder head technology advanced, 18-degree and splayed-valve Bow Tie heads were introduced for V6/90 racing engines.

18-Degree Bow Tie Cylinder Head PN 10134359

A new generation of competition cylinder heads for 90-degree Chevrolet V6 engines was introduced in 1989. These heads have an 18-degree valve angle instead of the 23-degree angle used in conventional Chevrolet V6/90 and small-block V8 heads.

The valves in 18-degree heads are located on the cylinder bore centerline to minimize cylinder wall shrouding at high

valve lift. The valve centerlines are also moved laterally to enhance intake flow and to allow the use of intake valves up to 2.20-inch in diameter (depending on cylinder bore diameter).

The intake runners in the 18-degree head are .650-inch above the deck surface (.200-inch higher than the ports in "raised runner" V6/90 cylinder heads). The intake manifold flange was lengthened to realign the higher ports with the runners in existing intake manifolds. A two-piece Bow Tie cross-ram intake manifold (PN 10051125-6) is recommended for engines that require a single four-barrel induction system.

Except as noted above, 18-degree V6/90 and small-block V8 cylinder heads are identical. See the small-block V8 chapter for more information on 18-degree Bow Tie heads.

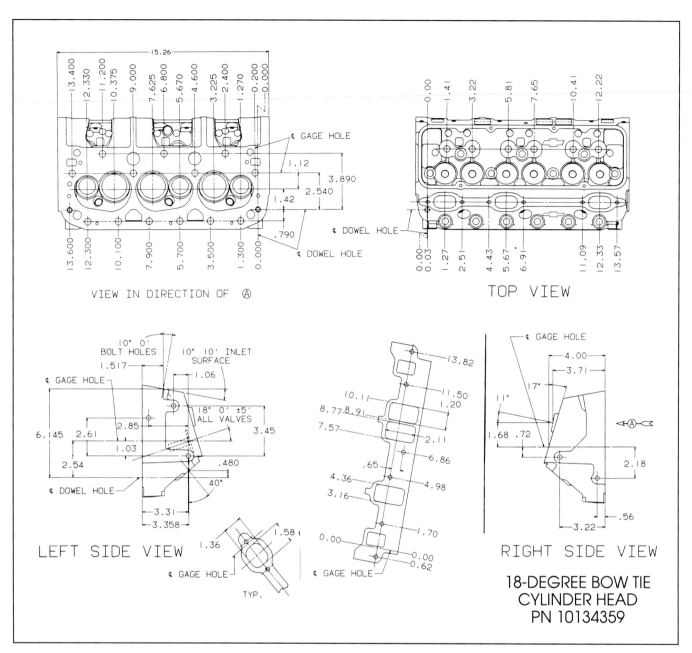

VIEW IN DIRECTION OF Ⓐ

TOP VIEW

LEFT SIDE VIEW

TYP.

RIGHT SIDE VIEW

18-DEGREE BOW TIE
CYLINDER HEAD
PN 10134359

Race-Prepared 18-Degree Bow Tie Cylinder Head
PN 24502523

The intake runners, combustion chambers, and exhaust ports in race-prepared 18-degree V6/90 cylinder heads are modified for maximum performance using sophisticated CNC (Computer Numerical Control) machinery. The CNC-ported cylinder head's port volumes and cross-sectional areas are optimized for 4.5-liter (274 cubic inch) V6s with 4.100-inch and larger cylinder bores.

CNC porting programs were written specifically for the V6/90 cylinder head. The V6 head's intake runners differ significantly from small-block V8 versions in both size and position. In accordance

with NASCAR Grand National rules, the roofs of the V6 head's intake ports are three inches above the deck surface. This lower runner entrance (compared to a high-port V8 head) required a different treatment to maximize airflow. However, the V6's exhaust ports closely resemble the runners in CNC-ported V8 heads.

The recommended intake and exhaust valve diameters for CNC V6 cylinder heads are 2.150-inch and 1.625-inch respectively. Overall valve length should be 5.35-inch (.100-inch shorter than valves for high-port V8 heads). Modified small-block V8 cast aluminum rocker covers (PN 24502527) must be used with CNC-ported V6/90 heads.

The head bolt holes adjacent to the intake ports' "long walls" are drilled for

⅜-inch studs; stepped head studs are available from aftermarket sources to fit the block's ⁷⁄₁₆-inch head bolt threads.

Race-prepared V6/90 heads are designed to use aftermarket shaft-mounted rocker arms. The intake rockers for the end cylinders (Nos. 1, 2, 5, and 6) should be offset .550-inch; rockers for the center cylinders (Nos. 3 and 4) should be offset .650-inch. Roller lifters with .150-inch offset are recommended to provide adequate pushrod clearance.

Three-angle valve seats are installed in the modified combustion chambers. The 48cc chamber volume accommodates the 9.5:1 compression ratio required in several racing series that use V6 engines, as well as the unrestricted ratios used in

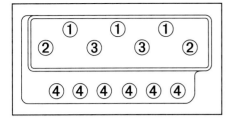

TECH SPECS: V6/90 CYLINDER HEAD BOLT BOSS HEIGHTS

Part Number	1	2	3	4
14044883/4	3.06"	2.32"	3.06"	1.12"
10134359	3.60"	2.32"	3.10"	1.12"
10134394	1.03"	2.96"	2.96"	1.01"

The height of the head bolt columns is different in various cylinder head castings. Use the chart above to find the column height for specific V6/90 heads.

TECH SPECS: V6/90 VALVES AND SEATS

| | Valves (in.)[1] | | | | | | Seats (in.)[1] | | | |
| | Intake | | | Exhaust | | | Intake | | Exhaust | |
P/N	Dia.	Length	Margin	Dia.	Length	Margin	Dia.	Depth	Dia.	Depth
14044883[2]	2.10	5.15	.065	1.600	5.50	.100	2.20	.312	1.65	.312
14044884	2.10	5.15	.065	1.600	5.15	.100	2.20	.312	1.65	.312
10134359[2]	2.15	5.35	.065	1.625	5.35	.100	2.20	.312	1.65	.312
24502523	2.15	5.35	.065	1.625	5.35	.100	2.25	.312	1.68	.312
10134394[2]	2.20	5.70	.065	1.625	5.70	.100	2.25	.375	1.68	.375

[1]Note: These are recommended valve specifications—all Bow Tie cylinder heads are supplied without valves.
[2]Not supplied with valve seat inserts.

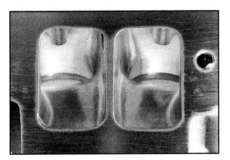

The port shapes and valve sizes in CNC-ported V6/90 cylinder heads are optimized for 274ci (4.5-liter) racing engines.

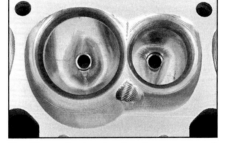

The 48cc combustion chambers in race-prepared V6/90 cylinder heads are CNC-machined to fit 4.100-inch and larger bores.

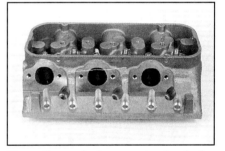

The equally spaced exhaust ports in splayed-valve V6/90 Bow Tie heads require special flanges and fabricated headers.

NASCAR Grand National competition. See the CNC cylinder head section in the small-block V8 chapter for valve preparation recommendations for CNC-ported Bow Tie heads.

Splayed-Valve Bow Tie Cylinder Head PN 10134394

Splayed-valve Bow Tie V6/90 cylinder heads were developed for unlimited classes in road racing, oval track, and drag racing classes. The influence of big-block V8 airflow technology is readily apparent in the splayed-valve V6's ports and combustion chambers.

The intake and exhaust valves are inclined in *two* axes relative to the cylinder bore centerline. The intake valves are angled 16 degrees to the deck surface, and tilted ("splayed") four degrees. The ex-

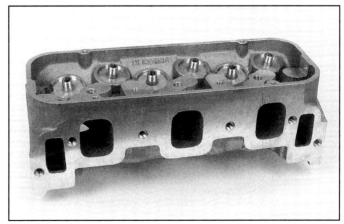

Splayed-valve cylinder heads brought Pro Stock airflow technology to 90-degree V6 engines. The intake runner entrances are 1.88-inch above the deck surface, 2.00-inch high, and 1.60-inch wide.

haust valve angle is 11 degrees, with a four-degree tilt. These compound valve angles offer several significant advantages over the in-line valves used in conventional Chevrolet V6/90 cylinder heads. In-line valves in a wedge-type cyl-

inder head open parallel to the cylinder bores; in a splayed-valve head, the valves move away from the cylinder walls as they open. This unshrouds the valves heads at maximum lift, offering a potential increase in flow.

Part Number	Description	Crankshaft Duration @ Lash Point, Int./Exh. (degrees)	Crankshaft Duration @ Tappet Lift, Int./Exh. (degrees)	Maximum Lift w/ 1.5:1 Rocker Ratio, Int./Exh. (in.)	Valve Lash	Lobe Centerline (degrees)	Notes
6269733	Hydraulic flat tappet	294/306	202/210	.410/.410	——	113	Marine cam for 229ci V6 with 108-132° semi-even fire crankshaft. Good street performance cam.
14011097	Hydraulic flat tappet	326/326	224/224	.456/.465	——	112	High-performance hydraulic cam for 229ci V6 with 108-132° semi-even fire engine. Good torque, excellent power.
10051165	Hydraulic flat tappet	320/320	222/222	.447/.447	——	114	V6/90 version of L79 small-block V8 cam for 4.3L even-fire engine. Excellent power and torque.
10051147	Hydraulic roller tappet	318/318	222/222	.447/.447	——	114	V6/90 version of L79 small-block V8 cam for 4.3L even-fire engine. Use only with roller tappet block.
10134321	Hydraulic roller tappet	321/316	224/224	.450/.460	——	112	High-performance street and marine cam for 4.3L even-fire engine. Use only with roller tappet block.

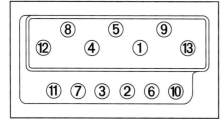

Tighten V6/90 cylinder head bolts in the sequence shown. The recommended bolt torque is 65 ft.-lbs.

Heavy-duty Chevrolet cylinder head gasket PN 14011079 fits bores sizes up to 4.125-inch. This gasket has integral wire "O"-rings.

The symmetrical intake ports are located above the top row of head bolts. Holes in the roofs of the intake runners provide access to short socket-head capscrews that replace the top three head bolts on each cylinder bank. A rocker arm mounting bar is bolted to the threaded access holes to seal the intake runners after the capscrews are torqued.

Splayed-valve V6/90 cylinder heads are designed to meet the airflow requirements of a 4.5-liter (274ci) racing engine. The combustion chambers will accommodate 2.20-inch diameter intake valves and 1.625-inch exhausts. The nominal combustion chamber volume is 50cc, depending on the valves and seat inserts installed by the engine builder. The increased overall height of the new head requires 5.70-inch long valves (.750-inch longer than production V6/90 valves). The spark plug holes are machined for .708-inch reach plugs with tapered seats (Champion S series or equivalent).

Splayed-valve V6 heads use unique valvetrain hardware. A mounting bar (PN 10134395) is available for aftermarket shaft-type rocker arms. The conversion to splayed-valve heads also requires special pistons, pushrods, an intake manifold, headers, rocker covers, and a camshaft with lobes ground to match the revised valve layout. Cast aluminum rocker covers (PN 10185010) and gaskets (PN 10185008) are available from Chevrolet for splayed-valve heads.

Head Gaskets

Chevrolet offers a heavy-duty Teflon-coated composition gasket for V6/90 engines as PN 14011079. This gasket has solid wire "O"-rings around each cylinder bore. It fits bore sizes from 4.00 to 4.125-inch, and its compressed thickness is .040-inch.

Camshafts

Several Chevrolet flat and hydraulic roller lifter camshafts are suitable for street, marine, and high-performance V6/90 engines. The camshaft specification chart summarizes the timing and valve lift specifications for Chevrolet V6/90 performance profiles, and indicates recommended applications.

Some types of mechanical valve lifters cannot be used in production V6/90 blocks due to the design of the oiling system. Unlike a small-block V8, the driver's side lifter oil gallery cannot be restricted to control overhead oil flow because this gallery also feeds the crankshaft bearings.

Production V6/90 engines with mechanical lifter cams require piddle valve lifters. Chevrolet mechanical lifter PN 5232695 is not suitable for V6/90 engines due to oil leakage around its pushrod seat. Sealed Power PN AT-992 is a satisfactory lifter for the Chevrolet V6/90.

A semi-circular notch identifies pushrod guideplate PN 14011057 used on cylinders No. 3 and 4 with aluminum Bow Tie cylinder heads.

Beginning in the 1987 model year, production V6/90 engines were equipped with hydraulic roller valve lifters in place of conventional flat hydraulic lifters. See the small-block V8 chapter for information on hydraulic roller lifters.

Valvetrain

Most valvetrain components (valves, rocker arms, pushrods, valve springs, retainers, etc.) are interchangeable between Chevrolet V6/90 and small-block V8 engines. See the small-block V8 chapter for recommendations and specifications.

Special pushrod guideplates are required on aluminum Bow Tie cylinder heads PN 14044802, 14044883, and 14044884. The cylinders at the "corners" of the block (Nos. 1, 2, 5, and 6) use guideplate PN 14011051, which can be identified by the stamped numerals "05". This guideplate must be relieved to clear the valve cover hold-down bolts by grinding a notch between the pushrod slots. The two center cylinders (Nos. 3 and 4) require guideplate PN 14011057. This guideplate can be identified by a semi-circular notch between its pushrod slots.

Aftermarket shaft-mounted rocker arms are required for 18-degree Bow Tie cylinder heads (PN 10134359 and 24502523) and splayed-valve Bow Tie heads (PN 10134394).

Timing Sets

Timing sets are interchangeable between Chevrolet V6/90 and small-block V8 engines. 1987 and newer production engines with hydraulic roller camshafts require a special camshaft sprocket to clear the camshaft thrust plate on the front of the block. See the small-block V8 chapter for details.

A camshaft gear drive is recommended for V6/90 competition engines. This three-gear drive uses a standard rotation cam.

A camshaft gear drive is recommended for competition V6/90 engines equipped with odd-fire crankshafts. Gear drives have proven more reliable than chains at high engine speeds.

Rocker Covers

Two different rocker cover bolt patterns have been used on in-line valve Chevrolet V6/90 cylinder heads. 1978-84 production cylinder heads and all heavy-duty Bow Tie heads have four hold-down bolts on the rocker cover flange. A new rocker cover design with three central hold-down bolts was introduced on production cylinder heads in 1985.

Stamped steel Bow Tie rocker covers are available for V6/90 cylinder heads with hold-down bolts on the rocker cover rails. A plain steel tall Bow Tie rocker cover is available as PN 10134319; a chrome plated version is PN 12341005. These tall valve covers will not clear alternators and air conditioning compressors. A stock height Bow Tie rocker cover is available as PN 12341006 for high-performance street V6s.

CNC-ported V6/90 cylinder heads have a unique rocker cover bolt pattern. Modified small-block V8 cast aluminum rocker covers are available as PN 24502527 for these heads.

Intake Manifolds

All 1978-84 200/229ci V6/90 engines were equipped with aluminum two-barrel intake manifolds. These manifolds were designed for a Rochester "Dual Jet" carburetor, which is similar to the primary side of a Quadrajet four-barrel. Manifolds installed on 229ci V6s had open plenums under the carburetor.

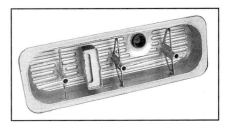

Rocker covers with three central hold-down bolts were introduced on production 4.3-liter V6 cylinder heads in 1985.

Tall V6/90 Bow Tie stamped steel rocker covers are designed to clear aftermarket stud girdles and racing valvetrains.

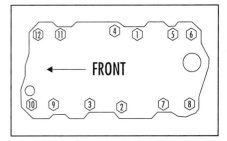

Tighten the intake manifold bolts in the sequence shown. The recommended torque is 30 ft.-lbs for iron heads.

At the start of the 1985 model year cast iron Quadrajet four-barrel intake manifolds were used on 4.3-liter V6/90 engines in Chevrolet Astro vans and light trucks. A low-profile cast iron Quadrajet intake manifold for marine applications is available as PN 14097284. An aluminum two-barrel throttle body fuel injection manifold was introduced in 1988. Both the TBI and four-barrel intake manifolds have been used successfully in restricted V6 racing classes.

A "cross-ram" single four-barrel aluminum intake manifold was developed for raised runner and 18-degree Bow Tie cylinder heads. The inlet runners cross over the engine valley to feed the cylinders on the opposite cylinder bank, producing a wide, flat torque curve. This box-style intake manifold assembly consists of a base (PN 10051125), a removable lid (PN 10051126), and a gasket (PN 10134325).

The manifold lid mounts a standard flange Holley four-barrel with its float

A Quadrajet four-barrel cast iron intake manifold was used on 4.3-liter V6s installed in Astro vans and light trucks.

Install a flat aluminum plate in the cross-ram manifold's plenum between the runner entries. Radius the edges of the plate.

An even-fire HEI distributor can be converted to direct 12-volt operation by installing a two-prong module (PN 990F26).

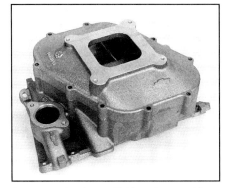

A cross-ram intake manifold produces a wide torque curve. This two-piece manifold fits raised runner and 18-degree heads.

The mechanical fuel pump on a V6/90 Chevrolet is mounted upside down. Do not use an externally vented pump.

bowls at the front and rear of the engine. The carburetor mounting pad is large enough to accommodate a Holley model 4500 (Dominator-type) four-barrel; however, new hold-down holes must be drilled and tapped for the 4500 carburetor's larger bolt pattern. This manifold will clear HEI distributor caps.

A cross-ram manifold requires very little preparation for competition use. The runner cross-sections and volume were optimized during the manifold's development phase. The runner exits should be matched to the cylinder head ports, and the side of the plenum relieved as required for rocker cover clearance. A flat aluminum plate (½-inch thick x 1¾-inch wide) should be fabricated and installed in the manifold plenum between the runner entries. Attach this plate with two 10-32 socket head screws. Apply permanent thread adhesive to the bolt threads during final assembly.

Fuel Pump

Small-block V8 mechanical fuel pumps can be installed on a V6/90 engine if the pump is not externally vented. However, Chevrolet heavy-duty fuel pump PN 6415325 is not suitable for V6/90 engines because it will leak oil when mounted upside down on the V6 block. Chevrolet offers a fuel pump block-off plate (PN 14094068) to seal the pump cavity when a mechanical pump is not used.

Lubrication System

The production V6/90 oiling system is similar to a small-block V8, with one important exception: The left-hand (driver's side) oil passage serves as both a lifter gallery and the main oil gallery. This left-hand oil gallery is deleted in a semi-machined cast iron Bow Tie V6/90

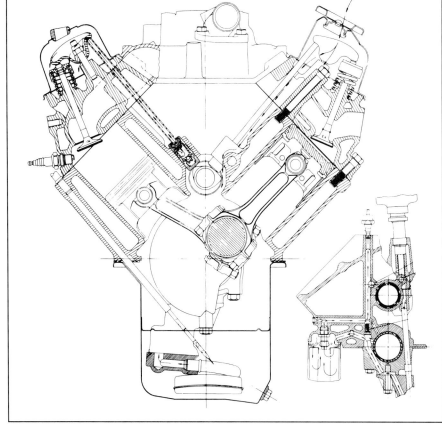

Production V6/90 engines have two oil galleries. The large gallery on the driver's side feeds the left lifter bank and the cam and crankshaft bearings.

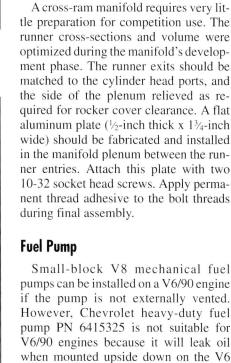

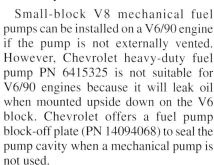

Heavy-duty Chevrolet distributors for odd-fire and semi-even fire V6/90 engines are identical except for their reluctor wheels.

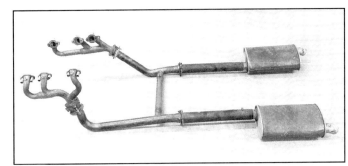

A high-performance street dual exhaust system can be fabricated with production tubular manifolds, a cross-over pipe, and low-restriction Corvette mufflers.

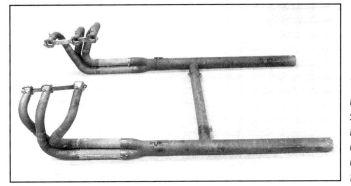

This well-designed racing V6 exhaust system has equal length primary tubes, a cross-over pipe, and extended tailpipes.

block (PN 10134387) to simplify the conversion to V8-type oiling.

Fully machined cast iron Bow Tie blocks (PN 10185051) and aluminum Bow Tie blocks are supplied with three V8-style oil galleries. If a V8-type oiling system is used, the two lifter galleries can be restricted to reduce overhead oil if needle bearing rocker arms are used.

Oil pumps are interchangeable between the V6/90 and small-block V8. Production and cast iron Bow Tie V6/90 blocks produced since 1986 require an oil pan designed for a one-piece rear main bearing seal. Aluminum Bow Tie blocks have special rear main bearing caps that use a pre-1986 oil pan design.

V6/90 Chevrolet engines use a small diameter spin-on oil filter. Production-type oil filters have adequate capacity for high-performance street and limited competition engines; a remote-mounted filter is preferred for all-out racing applications, however.

An adapter is required to connect a remote oil filter or cooler to a V6/90 block. Most adapters for small-block Chevrolet V8s will not fit because of the smaller diameter of the production V6 filter canister. Adapters designed specifically for V6/90 blocks are available from aftermarket sources.

Ignition System

Three firing sequences are used in V6/90 engines: even-fire (1985 and newer 4.3-liter production V6s); semi-even fire (1978-84 production V6s); and odd-fire (competition V6s with heavy-duty common-pin crankshafts). The distributor and ignition system must match the crankshaft's firing sequence for proper engine operation.

Even-fire 4.3-liter Chevrolet V6s have a firing sequence with a uniform 120 degrees of crank rotation between sparks. These engines can use production HEI distributors for most performance and limited competition applications.

The semi-even fire Chevrolet V6 firing sequence alternates between 132 and 108 degrees of crankshaft rotation between sparks. Chevrolet offers a high-performance distributor for semi-even fire engines as PN 10051134. This high-quality racing distributor has an aluminum housing, a hardened shaft, and a ground and hardened centrifugal advance cam. It employs a high-output magnetic pickup to trigger a heavy-duty ignition amplifier (PN 10037378), and uses a standard small diameter distributor cap.

V6/90 engines equipped with Chevrolet odd-fire heavy-duty crankshafts have an alternating 150/90/150 degree firing sequence. A semi-even fire HEI distributor can be converted to the odd-fire sequence by installing a magnetic pickup coil from a 1976-77 odd-fire Buick V6 (PN 1891209 or D1912).

Chevrolet also offers a heavy-duty distributor for odd-fire engines as PN 10051133. This distributor is identical to the semi-even fire heavy-duty distributor described earlier, except for its reluctor (trigger) wheel.

When installing the spark plug wires in a V6/90 distributor cap, start with the wire for the No. 1 spark plug nearest the cap's locating notch. Then proceed clock-wise around the cap as you follow the firing order (1-6-5-4-3-2). Note that the same firing order is used for *all* Chevrolet V6/90 engines, regardless of which crankshaft is used. Remember that the first step of the firing sequence on odd-fire V6 Chevrolets is always 150 degrees (132 degrees on semi-even fire V6s) between the No. 1 and No. 6 cylinders.

Examine the spark plug wire contacts inside the distributor cap on odd-fire V6s to make sure that the rotor tip is positioned properly to prevent cross-firing between successive cylinders in the firing order. If there is evidence of spark marks on the edges of three terminal contacts, and if the engine misfires, you may need to rotate and reposition the magnet or pickup slightly.

Exhaust System

Production 4.3-liter Chevrolet V6s are equipped with tubular exhaust manifolds that are suitable for engine swaps, street rods, and other non-stock installations. A dual exhaust system with low-restriction Corvette mufflers and a cross-over pipe ahead of the mufflers will perform well on V6/90 engines that are not subject to emission control regulations.

Chevrolet V6/90 engines used in competition should be equipped with a fabricated exhaust system. The exact pipe diameter and length that will produce the best engine performance depends on several factors, including engine displacement, operating rpm range, cam profile, induction system, and cylinder head selection. Chassis design must also be considered when designing a tubular header system.

Primary pipe dimensions of 1¾-inch OD x 30 inches long feeding 2¾ to 3-inch collectors have proven successful. Large displacement and high-rpm engines will often respond to an increase in the size of the primary and collector tube diameters.

Header systems designed to these dimensions are available from aftermarket manufacturers and independent shops. These sources can supply information on tubing sizes and chassis considerations based on your intended usage. ⌐◊

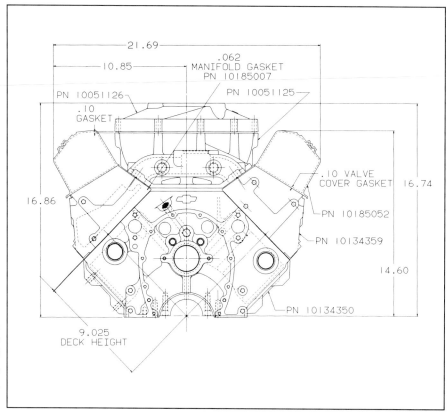

This diagram shows the overall dimensions of a Chevrolet V6/90 equipped with 18-degree heads and a Bow Tie cross-ram intake manifold.

TECH SPECS: CHEVROLET V6/90 SPECIFICATIONS FOR HIGH-PERFORMANCE USE

Firing Order	1-6-5-4-3-2
Spark Advance	Maximum of 40-44 (32-34 degrees w/18° heads)
Maximum Oil Temp	270 degrees in oil pan
Minimum Fuel Pressure	4-5 psi at maximum engine speed
Piston to Bore	.006-.007" measured at centerline of wrist pin hole perpendicular to pin for Chevrolet heavy-duty forged piston; .002-.003" for cast pistons. Follow manufacturer's recommendations for other pistons. Finish bores with 400 grit stones or equivalent.
Minimum Piston Ring End Gap	Top .018"; Second .016"; Oil Rails .016"
Wrist Pin	.0006-.0008" in piston. (.0005-.0008" in bushed rod for floating pin. 0-.005" end play preferred.)
Rod Bearing	.002-.0025"; side clearance .010-.020" (common pin); .005-.010" (offset pin)
Main Bearing	.002-.003"
Crank End Play	.005-.007"
Piston to Cylinder Head	.035" minimum (steel rods)
Valve Lash	As specified by camshaft manufacturer. See text for recommended lash for Chevrolet camshafts.
Valve to Piston Clearance	.045" exhaust and intake at running valve lash. NOTE: These are absolute minimum clearances for an engine running below the valvetrain limiting speed. More clearance must be allowed for engines operating at valvetrain limiting speed; allow .080" intake and .100" exhaust valve clearance for high rpm engines.
Valve to Guide	Inlet .0018" and Exhaust .0025" minimum for racing.

NOTE: These specifications are intended as general guidelines for high-performance and competition applications. Different clearances and specifications may be required depending on operating conditions and components used. Always follow manufacturer's recommendations when installing aftermarket components.

TECH SPECS: CAST IRON V6/90 BOLT TORQUE AND LUBRICANT RECOMMENDATIONS

	Torque	Lubricant
Main Bearing Cap:		
Inner Bolt ($^7/_{16}$")	70 ft.-lbs.	Molykote
Outer Bolt ($^7/_{16}$")	65	Molykote
Inner Stud ($^7/_{16}$")	65	Oil
Outer Stud ($^3/_8$")	60	Oil
Outer Bolt ($^3/_8$")	40	Oil
Connecting Rod Bolt ($^3/_8$")	45-50 ft.-lbs. (.006" stretch preferred)	Oil
Bow Tie Connecting Rod Bolt ($^7/_{16}$")	70 ft.-lbs. (.005-.006" stretch preferred)	Oil
Cylinder Head Bolt	65 ft.-lbs.	Sealant (Use oil in blind-tapped bolt holes in Bow Tie blocks)
Rocker Arm Stud:		
Cast Iron Head	50	Sealant
Aluminum Head	50	Oil
Camshaft Sprocket	20	Oil
Intake Manifold, Iron Head	30	Oil
Flywheel	60	Oil
Bellhousing	25	Oil
Spark Plugs:		
Conventional Gasket, Iron Head	25	Dry
Conventional Gasket, Alum. Head	25	Anti-seize
Tapered Seat, Iron Head	15	Dry
Tapered Seat, Alum. Head	15	Anti-seize
Exhaust Manifold	25	Anti-seize
Oil Pan Bolt	165 in.-lbs.	Oil
Front Cover Bolt	75 in.-lbs.	Oil
Rocker Cover	25 in.-lbs.	Oil

TECH SPECS: ALUMINUM V6/90 BOLT TORQUE AND LUBRICANT RECOMMENDATIONS

	Torque	Lubricant
Main Bearing:		
Inner Stud ($^7/_{16}$")	65 ft.-lbs.	Oil
Outer Stud ($^3/_8$")	45	Oil
Outer Bolt ($^3/_8$")	40	Oil
Bow Tie Connecting Rod Bolt ($^7/_{16}$")	70 ft.-lbs. (.005-.006" stretch preferred)	Oil
Head Studs—$^7/_{16}$" NF Thread:		
Long	65	Oil
Short	60	Oil
Rocker Arm Stud	50	Oil
Camshaft Sprocket	20	Oil
Intake Manifold, Alum. Head	25	Anti-Seize
Flywheel	60	Oil
Bell Housing	25	Anti-Seize
Spark Plugs:		
Conventional Gasket, Alum. Head	25	Anti-seize
Tapered Seat, Alum. Head	15	Anti-seize
Exhaust Manifold	20	Anti-seize
Oil Pan Bolt	165 in.-lbs.	Anti-seize
Front Cover Bolt	75 in.-lbs.	Anti-seize
Rocker Cover	25 in.-lbs.	Anti-seize

Chevrolet 60-Degree V6

Gen II V6/60

The Chevrolet 60-degree V6 has earned a solid reputation for performance and reliability in competition. The V6/60 Chevrolet has won championships in off-road racing, set records in drag racing, and won honors in midget oval track competition. The light weight and ample traction of a front-wheel-drive V6/60 powertrain has made this compact Chevy engine a favorite in autocrossing and other forms of motorsports that emphasize precise handling and quick response. The 60-degree V6 has also found favor with innovative street rodders seeking a lightweight, fuel-efficient powerplant.

The 60-degree V6 is a unique member of the family of Chevrolet engines. It is the only Chevrolet engine used in both transverse and longitudinal installations, and it is the only motor in the Chevy lineup with a 60-degree included angle between its cylinder banks. (Small-block V8s, big-block V8s, and 4.3-liter V6 engines all have 90-degree vee angles).

The specifications and procedures in this chapter are intended primarily to aid enthusiasts in preparing the Chevrolet V6/60 engine for "off-highway" and emission-exempt operation. Due to the diversity of sanctioning bodies' rules and the special demands of various types of motorsports, an engine may require specific preparation procedures and accessories not covered in this manual. These specifications and recommendations are intended as guidelines that have been tested and proven by leading competitors.

This chapter describes parts and procedures that are unique to V6/60 engines. For information on engine building and

- Chevy's Versatile V6

- Compact and Powerful

- A Lightweight Contender

- DOHC and Splayed-Valve Variations

Savvy street rodders have discovered that the Chevrolet V6/60 is a contemporary alternative to traditional V8 powerplants.

The sophisticated 3.4-liter/210hp Twin Dual Cam V6/60 debuted in 1991 with dual overhead cams and four valves per cylinder.

blueprinting procedures, ignition systems, and lubrication requirements, see the respective chapters on these topics.

V6/60 Engine Design

The Chevrolet 60-degree V6 ("V6/60") was introduced in 1980 as a 2.8-liter (173ci) transverse-mounted engine in the front-wheel-drive Citation chassis. A rear-wheel-drive version of the V6/60 debuted in 1982 in the S-10 pickup, S-10 Blazer, and Camaro. This dual application accounts for several minor differences between V6/60 engines, including starter location, motor mounts, and manifold water inlet locations. All specifications in this chapter apply to both configurations, however.

The term "60-degree V6" refers specifically to the included angle between the engine's cylinder banks. In the V6/60 Chevrolet, this angle is 60 degrees. (Chevrolet's "other" V6 has a 90-degree Vee angle.) The "60-degree" designation does *not* refer to the number of degrees between cylinder firings. The Chevrolet V6/60 is a true "even-fire" engine, with a

Nelson & Nelson Racing's Chevy pickup flies high in the MTEG stadium racing series with a 3.0-liter 60-degree Chevy V6.

Chevrolet General Manager Jim Perkins paced the 1990 Indianapolis 500 with a V6/60-powered Beretta.

The 1990 Indy 500 Beretta pace car's 3.4-liter V6 produced 225 horsepower with Generation II aluminum heads and electronic fuel injection.

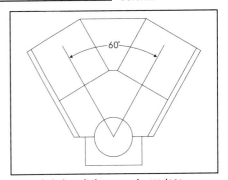

The included angle between the V6/60's two cylinder banks is 60 degrees—hence the engine is referred to as a "60-degree V6."

uniform 120 degrees of crankshaft rotation between each cylinder firing.

The V6/60 was Chevrolet's first all-metric engine. The bolts and fasteners used in V6/60 engines have metric threads exclusively. The dimensions shown on the V6/60 blueprint are expressed in metric units. To convert millimeter dimensions to inches, divide by 25.4 or multiply by .03937.

2.8-liter V6/60 Chevrolets have 89mm (3.50-inch) cylinder bores and 76mm

(2.99-inch) strokes. A 3.1-liter V6/60 was introduced in 1990 with an 84mm (3.31-inch) stroke, and a 3.4-liter version debuted in 1991 with 92mm (3.62-inch) cylinder bores. All V6/60 engines have the same cylinder bore spacing (111.8mm/4.40-inch) and the same block height (224mm/8.819-inch).

The V6/60 has been continuously updated and improved since its introduction. In 1985, the crankshaft journal diameter was increased 4mm to improve

TECH SPECS: V6/60 DESIGN FEATURES			
Engine Displacement	Model Year	Bore	Stroke
2.8-liter (173ci)	1980-89	3.50" (89 mm)	2.99" (76 mm)
3.1-liter (191ci)	1990-94	3.50" (89 mm)	3.31" (84 mm)
3.4-liter (207ci)	1991-94*	3.62" (92 mm)	3.31" (84 mm)
	*DOHC introduced 1991; OHV introduced 1993		

A production cast iron engine block is a good choice for off-road competition. A rear-wheel-drive V6/60 bare block weighs 106 pounds.

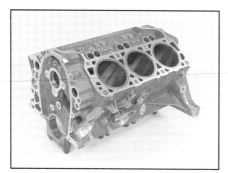

Chevy's lightweight V6/60 aluminum Bow Tie block has 89mm cast nodular iron cylinder liners and four-bolt intermediate bearing caps.

An aluminum Bow Tie block has V8-style oiling with three oil galleries. The center gallery feeds the cam and main bearings.

durability, and multi-port fuel injection was developed to enhance performance. New aluminum cylinder heads with high-flow ports and splayed valves signaled the arrival of the "Generation II" V6/60 in front-wheel-drive applications at the start of the 1987 model year. A dual overhead cam version with four valves per cylinder followed in 1991.

Engine Blocks

All production V6/60 engine blocks are cast iron. Unlike other Chevrolet engines, the V6/60's *right-hand* cylinders (when viewed from the rear of the block) are forward of the left-hand cylinders. The right-hand cylinders (passenger's side in fore-and-aft installations) are numbered 1, 3, 5 from front to rear. The left-hand cylinders are numbered 2, 4, 6 from front to rear. The firing order is 1-2-3-4-5-6.

A production cast iron block (with main caps and bolts) for a front wheel drive chassis weighs approximately 101 pounds. A rear-wheel-drive block is five pounds heavier. The nominal cylinder wall thickness for production V6/60 blocks is 4.5mm (.175-inch).

An important difference between early-model (1980-84) and late-model (1985 and newer) V6/60 blocks is the diameter of the main bearings. 1980-84 engines have 63.35mm (2.494-inch) mains, while 1985 and later engines use 67.25mm (2.648-inch) main bearings. (Note: The diameter of the No. 3 main bearing was changed to 63.13mm in 1982; in 1985, it was enlarged to 67.25mm.) All 1985 and later 2.8-liter V6/60 engines with multi-port fuel injection have large diameter main bearings; S-10 pickups, Blazers, and carbureted engines manufactured in 1985 can have either large or small main bearings. A block with large diameter crankshaft

journals can be easily identified by its one-piece rear crankshaft seal.

Production V6/60 blocks are suitable for high-performance street use, off-roading, and limited competition applications. Production V6/60 blocks used in SCORE/HDRA off-road racing routinely produce over 270 horsepower and provide hundreds of miles of trouble-free operation at high engine speeds. A late-model block with large main bearings is recommended for all high-performance applications.

Aluminum Bow Tie Block
PN 10051141

An aluminum Bow Tie V6/60 cylinder block (PN 10051141) is recommended for all maximum-effort competition engines. This block offers improved durability, lighter weight, and more displacement options than production cylinder cases. Aluminum V6/60 blocks are suitable for competition engines with displacements ranging from 2.5 to 3.0-liters, depending on the bore and stroke dimensions selected by the engine builder.

A bare aluminum Bow Tie block (with main caps) weighs 59 pounds—a weight savings of 47 pounds over a rear-wheel-drive production block. The aluminum Bow Tie engine block has extra-thick cylinder walls with dry cylinder liners. These cast nodular iron cylinder sleeves are rough-bored at the factory to 89mm (3.504-inch) diameter; they can be safely enlarged to 91mm (3.582-inch). A 3.0-liter V6/60 racing engine can be assembled by installing a production 76mm (2.99-inch) stroke crankshaft in a Bow Tie block that has been bored to 91mm.

The Bow Tie block has reinforced head bolt bosses that improve head gasket sealing. The main bearing bulkheads are thicker than production blocks to increase bottom end strength. Cast iron front and

rear caps and billet steel intermediate caps are installed at the factory. The four-bolt intermediate main bearing caps (Nos. 2 and 3) have angled outer studs. High-strength 11mm studs are supplied with the Bow Tie block.

The heavy-duty aluminum Bow Tie V6/60 block has an oiling system that is similar to a production small-block V8's lubrication system. Three oil galleries are drilled above the camshaft; annular grooves in the camshaft bearing bores carry oil from the center oil gallery to the main bearing saddles. (Production V6/60 blocks have only two oil galleries above the camshaft. The large left-hand lifter oil gallery feeds the lifters, the camshaft bearings, and the main bearings.)

The Bow Tie block's revised lubrication system routes most of the oil directly to the crankshaft bearings to improve reliability at high engine speeds. This design also allows an engine builder to restrict the flow of oil to the lifter galleries.

The aluminum Bow Tie block has motor mount bosses for both front-wheel-drive and rear-wheel-drive applications. The starter motor can be mounted on either side of the block to accommodate a variety of chassis configurations. Aluminum blocks also have provisions for production ignition timing sensors, coil packs, and mechanical fuel pumps. The oil filter bypass spring is deleted.

Block Preparation

If new cam bearings are being installed, bearings from a small-block V8 may be substituted. These bearings are wider than production V6/60 cam bearings, so make sure that the longitudinal position is correct. The oil feed hole in the cam bearings should be positioned between 4 o'clock and 5 o'clock when viewed from the front of the block.

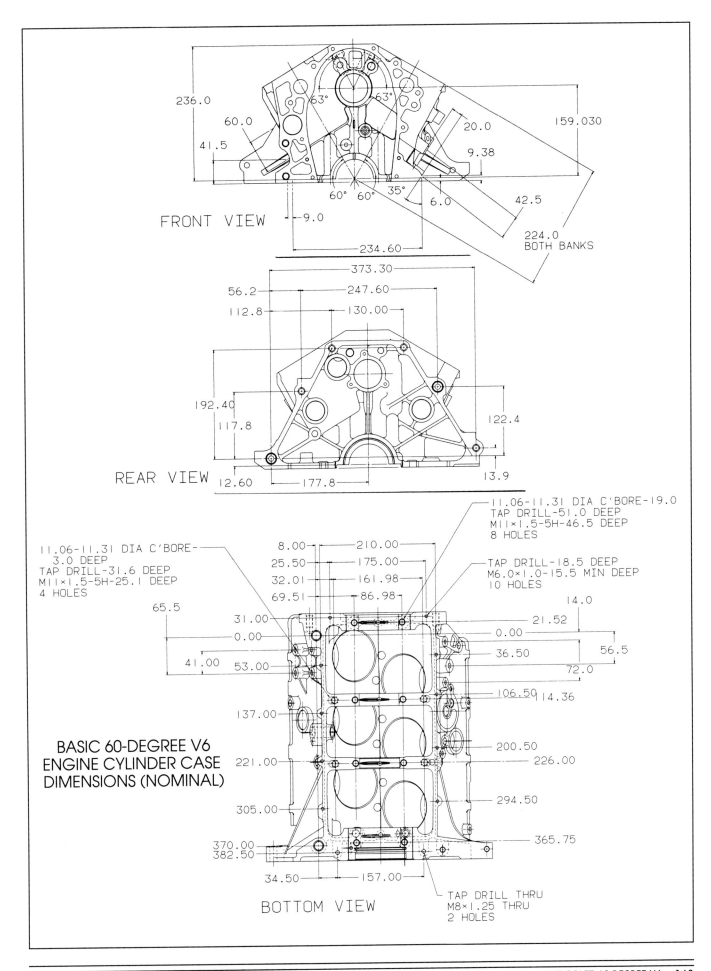

FRONT VIEW

236.0
60.0
41.5
63° 63°
20.0
9.38
159.030
60° 60° 35°
6.0
9.0
42.5
234.60
224.0
BOTH BANKS

REAR VIEW

373.30
56.2
247.60
112.8
130.00
192.40
117.8
122.4
12.60
177.8
13.9

11.06-11.31 DIA C'BORE-3.0 DEEP
TAP DRILL-31.6 DEEP
M11×1.5-5H-25.1 DEEP
4 HOLES

11.06-11.31 DIA C'BORE-19.0
TAP DRILL-51.0 DEEP
M11×1.5-5H-46.5 DEEP
8 HOLES

TAP DRILL-18.5 DEEP
M6.0×1.0-15.5 MIN DEEP
10 HOLES

65.5
8.00
210.00
25.50
175.00
32.01
161.98
69.51
86.98
14.0
31.00
21.52
0.00
0.00
41.00
36.50
56.5
53.00
72.0
106.50
114.36
137.00
BASIC 60-DEGREE V6
ENGINE CYLINDER CASE
DIMENSIONS (NOMINAL)
200.50
221.00
226.00
294.50
305.00
365.75
370.00
382.50
34.50
157.00
TAP DRILL THRU
M8×1.25 THRU
2 HOLES

BOTTOM VIEW

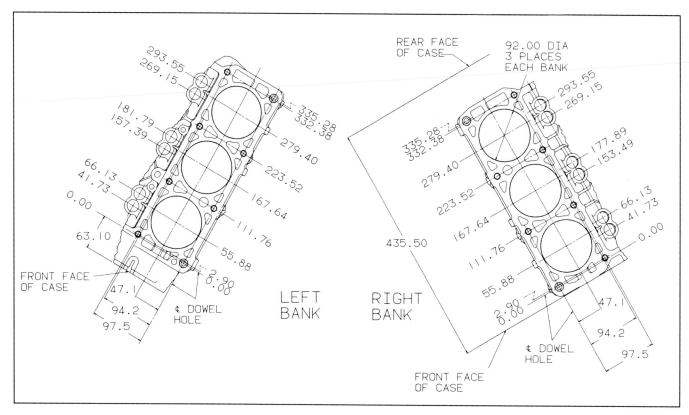

Early-model V6/60 iron blocks should be modified to improve rod bearing oiling by machining grooves in the main bearing saddles.

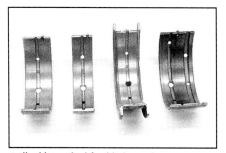

Drill additional oil feed holes in the upper main bearing inserts to ensure that full oil pressure reaches the rod bearings.

The GM Motorsports Technology Group recommends an oiling system modification for pre-1985 V6/60 engines that are operated for sustained periods above 7000 rpm. This modification, which improves connecting rod oiling at high speeds, is already incorporated in production V6/60 blocks with large journal main bearings and all heavy-duty Bow Tie blocks.

The main bearing bores (in the block only) should be grooved through the oil hole with a slot .125-inch wide and .125-inch deep. This groove should extend 180 degrees on the front three main bearing saddles; on the rear main bearing bore, this groove should extend approximately 135 degrees. It should intersect the oil feed hole from the cam bearing, but it must not connect to the main oil feed passage that also enters the rear main bearing bore.

Modify the upper main bearing inserts by drilling two equally spaced .125-inch diameter oil feed holes on both sides of the original oil hole. (On the rear main bearing, drill only one hole where the groove in the block does not extend up to the bearing cap mating surface). This will produce a total of five oil holes in each upper bearing half (four holes in the rear bearing). This bearing modification ensures that full oil pressure reaches the connecting rod journal oil hole whenever it is exposed to the main bearing oil groove as the crankshaft rotates.

Crankshafts

Production V6/60 crankshafts are cast nodular iron. The six crankpins and the center main bearing journals have deep rolled fillets that increase the crankshaft's fatigue life.

Crankshafts with two different main journal diameters have been installed in Chevrolet V6/60 engines. Engines produced in 1980-84 have 63mm main bearings, while most 1985 and later engines have 67mm mains. Production V6/60 nodular iron crankshafts with 67mm main bearings are extremely durable and have performed without failure in many racing applications.

V6/60 crankshafts manufactured through the 1986 model year are externally balanced and require a counterweighted flywheel or flexplate for proper engine balance. In 1987, a new crankshaft with an integral timing disc was introduced in 2.8-liter engines with aluminum cylinder heads. Crankshafts with timing discs are internally balanced, and do not require a counterweighted flywheel.

This slotted timing disc provides reference signals for an electronic control module in the ignition coil assembly in production front-wheel-drive applications. The timing disc can be recontoured to serve as a crankshaft counterweight in V6/60 racing engines. The disc should not be modified, however, if you intend to use a block-mounted ignition sensor.

The GM Motorsports Technology Group recommends cross-drilling the

Externally balanced V6/60 crankshafts use counterweighted flywheels and neutral balanced torsional dampers.

A late-model production V6/60 crankshaft has an integral slotted timing disc that triggers the ignition system.

Lead-in grooves in the main bearing journals channel oil to the rod bearing oil feed holes in late-model V6/60 crankshafts.

1985 and newer cranks with large 67mm main bearing journals and one-piece oil seals are recommended for competition V6/60 engines.

center two main bearing journals on V6/60 crankshafts used in competition engines. This modification provides additional oil flow to the connecting rod bearings at high engine rpm. After drilling the journals, chamfer and deburr the holes at the bearing surfaces and inspect the oil holes for metal chips.

Production V6/60 crankshafts used in 1987 and later front-wheel-drive engines have lead-in grooves in the main bearing journals that channel oil to the feed holes for the rod bearings. All other V6/60 crankshafts should be modified for competition by machining similar lead-in grooves in the main journals. These lead-in grooves should start approximately ½-inch before the rod feed holes, tapering to a depth of .125-inch and a width of .200-inch. When polishing the journals after this machining operation, turn the crankshaft in the direction of normal rotation.

All 1980-84 and some 1985 Chevrolet 2.8-liter V6/60 engines used a rope rear main bearing seal. A one-piece neoprene lip seal that fits into the rope seal groove without modification is available as PN 14081761. This lip seal is more dependable than the rope seal, and is recommended for all high-performance V6s. 1985 and later V6/60 engines with large diameter main bearings use a one-piece rear main seal (PN 14085829).

Flywheels

The mass required to internally balance some 2.8-liter engines could not be included in the rear crankshaft counterweight due to limited clearance in the engine block. All 1982-87 rear-wheel-drive V6/60 engines and all 1980-86 front-wheel-drive V6/60s are externally balanced. These engines require a counterweighted flywheel or flexplate for proper crankshaft balance. 1987 and later V6/60 engines installed in front-wheel-

drive vehicles are internally balanced, and use neutral balanced flywheels.

The flywheel or flexplate and its counterweight is an integral part of the balance system in externally balanced V6/60 engines. If an externally balanced crankshaft is rebalanced, or if your particular application requires a special flywheel or flexplate, these components must be balanced with the crankshaft. Alternatively, an externally balanced crankshaft can be internally balanced by adding slugs of heavy metal to its rear counterweight. These slugs of metal should be located horizontally (parallel to the crankshaft centerline) so that centrifugal force will not dislodge them. A crank which has been internally balanced with heavy metal requires a neutral balanced flywheel or automatic transmission flexplate.

V6/60 engines used in midget race cars and other applications that do not normally use a flywheel should use an internally balanced crankshaft. If an internally balanced crank is not available, a bobweight can be sandwiched between the crankshaft and driveshaft connector to achieve the proper engine balance. (In applications where no flywheel is used, the harmonic damper's outer inertia ring should be removed. The damper hub can

then be marked for timing the engine's spark advance.)

When balancing a V6/60 crankshaft, calculate the bobweight using 50 percent of the engine reciprocating weight and 100 percent of the rotating weight.

Connecting Rods

Production forged steel V6/60 connecting rods are heat-treated at the factory. These connecting rods are suitable for high-performance and limited competition applications when engine speeds do not exceed 7000 rpm.

If you are building a competition V6/60 Chevrolet on a limited budget, engine durability can be improved by installing production connecting rods used in 1967 and earlier small-block Chevrolet V8s. Although some machining is required for this conversion, the total expense is typically less than the cost of aftermarket connecting rods. These "small journal" V8 rods have the same center-to-center length (5.70-inch) and the same rod bearing ID as production V6/60 rods. The small-block V8 rods have wider, thicker beams than stock V6/60 rods, and use $^{11}/_{32}$-inch bolts instead of the V6's standard 9mm (.354-inch) fasteners.

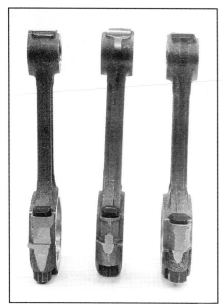

A production V6/60 rod (left) is reliable to 7000 rpm; a small-block V8 rod (center) can be narrowed to fit a V6/60 crankshaft. A small-block V8 rod (right) has the same bearing bore and center-to-center length as a V6/60 rod.

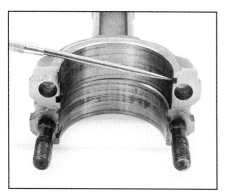

Machine new bearing tang grooves in modified small-block V8 rods to center the bearing inserts on the V6/60's rod journal.

Production connecting rods and cast aluminum pistons (left) are suitable for moderate performance applications. Aftermarket steel connecting rods and Chevrolet heavy-duty pistons (right) are recommended for racing.

TECH SPECS: V6/60 HIGH-PERFORMANCE PISTONS

Part Number	Engine	Compression Ratio	Size	Pin Type	ID#	Notes
14033129	2.8L	9:1	Standard	Pressed	14033123 or 14031340	High Output piston. Piston OD 88.961–88.999mm.
14033131	2.8L	9:1	+0.5mm	Pressed	14033125	High Output piston. Piston OD 89.474–89.525mm.
14033132	2.8L	9:1	+1.0mm	Pressed	14033127	High Output piston. Piston OD 89.974–90.150mm.
14044833	2.8L	12.5:1	Standard	Floating	14044829	Heavy-duty off-highway piston. Use with cast iron heads.
14044834	2.8L	12.5:1	+0.5mm	Floating	14044830	Heavy-duty off-highway piston. Use with cast iron heads.
14044835	2.8L	12.5:1	+1.0mm	Floating	14044831	Heavy-duty off-highway piston. Use with cast iron heads.

One important difference between V6/60 and small-block V8 connecting rods is the diameter of their wrist pin holes. V6 rods have .912-inch diameter pin bores; V8 rods have .927-inch wrist pin holes. In order to use V8 rods with stock or heavy-duty Chevrolet V6/60 pistons, the small ends of the V8 rods must be bushed to fit the V6 wrist pins. (If aftermarket pistons are ordered with .927-inch diameter wrist pins, the small-block rods will not require bushings.)

The big ends of the V8 rods must also be narrowed from .940-inch wide to .854-inch wide to fit the V6/60 crankshaft journals. Machine .086-inch off the side of the big end bore which is next to the crankshaft cheek in a V8 installation. Then machine new bearing tang notches in the rod, taking care to center the bearing insert on the rod journal. See the engine building chapter for additional information on connecting rod preparation.

V6/60 Chevrolet engines used in endurance racing and long-distance off-road events should be equipped with aftermarket connecting rods designed specifically for competition. V6/60 connecting rods are dimensionally similar to small-block V8 rods, so racing connecting rods are readily available from sev-eral aftermarket sources. The manufacturer's recommendations on bolt torque and rod installation procedures should be followed to ensure satisfactory service.

Pistons

Both standard and High Output versions of the V6/60 Chevrolet equipped with cast iron cylinder heads use flat-top pistons. These cast aluminum pistons are an "autothermic" design which provides uniform clearances through a wide range of engine operating temperatures. Pistons installed in High Output engines have a .020-inch taller compression height than standard V6/60 pistons. This change raises the compression ratio from 8.5:1 in standard 2.8-liter engines to 8.9:1 in H.O. and fuel-injected motors.

1987 and later "Generation II" V6/60 Chevrolets with aluminum cylinder heads use dished pistons. This sump head design maintains an 8.9:1 compression ratio with the aluminum head's smaller combustion chamber volume (28cc). Flat-top pistons used in 3.4-liter DOHC V6/60 engines have machined valve reliefs.

Chevrolet offers heavy-duty forged pistons with 12.5:1 compression for 2.8-liter V6/60 engines used in off-highway applications. Heavy-duty V6/60 pistons are machined for 1.5mm (.059-inch) wide compression rings; these rings provide an effective seal at high speeds and reduce internal friction.

Heavy-duty Chevrolet forged aluminum V6/60 pistons should be used only with cast iron cylinder heads. Their dome design is not compatible with an aluminum head's splayed valves and heart-shaped combustion chambers.

Chevrolet heavy-duty pistons use round wire pin locks that are more resistant to pound-out than other pin retaining systems. The full-floating wrist pins supplied with these pistons are chamfered on both ends to accommodate these round wire pin locks. Replacement 1.07-inch OD x .064-inch round wire retainers (PN 14011033) are available for rebuilds. Wrist pin retainers should never be reused when an engine is rebuilt.

Heavy-duty Chevrolet pistons may require machining to provide valve clearance for long duration camshafts. The piston valve reliefs should correspond to the valve layout in the cylinder heads. A complete V6/60 piston set consists of *four* pistons with valve reliefs matching the No. 1 combustion chamber (used in cylinder Nos. 1, 3, 4, and 6), and *two* pistons corresponding to the No. 2 combustion chamber's layout (cylinder Nos. 2 and 5).

Piston Rings

Chevrolet markets high-performance piston ring sets for heavy-duty V6/60 pistons. These sets include 1.5mm (.059-inch) wide moly-filled compression rings with radiused faces. They are offered in standard, .5mm oversize, and 1mm oversize diameters for 89mm (3.50-inch) cylinder bores.

Measure the piston ring end gaps before installation with each ring square in its assigned cylinder bore. If the end gaps are under the minimum recommended dimension (.016-inch top, .014-inch second, .014-inch oil), the end gaps must be filed to prevent ring scuffing.

Cylinder Heads

Cast iron and aluminum cylinder heads are used on production V6/60 Chevrolet engines. All 1980-86 front-wheel-drive and 1982 and newer rear-wheel-drive V6/60 engines are equipped with cast iron cylinder heads; 1987 and later "Generation II" and DOHC front-wheel-drive V6/60s have aluminum cylinder heads. Cast iron and aluminum heads are not

Chevrolet forged aluminum pistons with 12.5:1 compression are supplied with chamfered wrist pins and round wire pin locks.

Production V6/60 cast iron cylinder heads have vanes in the intake runners that increase airflow. These vanes should not be removed.

interchangeable due to differences in the combustion chamber design and valve geometry of the two castings.

Cast Iron Cylinder Heads

Several cast iron cylinder head assemblies have been used on production V6/60 engines. Heads installed on standard performance V6s have 1.60-inch diameter intake valves and 1.30-inch exhaust valves. High Output and fuel-injected versions are equipped with 1.72-inch diameter intakes and 1.42-inch exhausts. The larger valves of the H.O. cast iron cylinder head (PN 14054884) provide an increase in airflow over the standard head, and are preferred for competition V6/60 engines. The only difference between the standard and H.O. cast iron heads is the size of the valves; the ports and combustion chambers are the same in both cylinder heads.

Cast iron V6/60 cylinder heads were designed for production applications, and extra material was not included in the port walls to allow extensive enlargement of

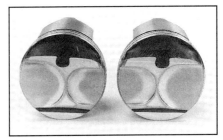

Make sure the pistons' valve notches match the cylinder head layout when machining reliefs for valve clearance.

A cast iron V6/60 head (left) has two siamesed intake ports; the ports in a Generation II aluminum head (right) are equally spaced.

the runners. Nevertheless, V6/60 racing engines with production cylinder heads are capable of producing over 1.5 horse-power-per-cubic inch.

Production V6/60 intake runners have a "vane" in the port floor. This vane produced a 17 percent increase in airflow over a conventional port design, and should be retained in competition-prepared cast iron cylinder heads. The intake port entrances should be matched to the intake manifold gasket and casting irregularities removed from the port walls. Blend the sharp edges and machined steps in the valve bowl to form a smooth approach to the valve seat. Contour the exhaust valve bowl to form a smooth venturi under the valve seat.

Cast iron V6/60 cylinder heads have four-angle valve seats. This seat design provides optimum airflow, and should be retained in heads which have been modified for competition use.

V6/60 cylinder heads should be milled as little as possible to prevent a mismatch between the intake manifold ports and the

A cast iron head (left) has in-line valves and open-style combustion chambers; an aluminum head (right) has splayed valves and shallow heart-shaped chambers.

Small-block V8 dual valve springs (PN 330585) and aluminum retainers can be installed on modified cast iron V6/60 cylinder heads.

TECH SPECS: V6/60 CAMSHAFTS

Part Number	Description	Crankshaft Duration @ Lash Point, Int./Exh. (degrees)	Crankshaft Duration @ Tappet Lift, Int./Exh. (degrees)	Maximum Lift w/ 1.5:1 Rocker Ratio, Int./Exh. (inches)	Valve Lash	Lobe Centerline (degrees)	Notes
14024278	Hydraulic flat tappet	258/276	178/196	.347/.394	N/A	107	Base 2.8L V6, S-10 and Camaro.
14034378	Hydraulic flat tappet	276/293	196/203	.394/.410	N/A	109	High-performance 2.8L

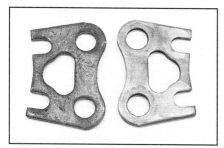

A stock V6/60 pushrod guideplate (left) fits 11mm rocker arm studs. Holes must be enlarged to fit 7/16-inch big-block studs.

A production silent link timing set is suitable for competition V6/60 engines. Use a thrust bearing to limit cam movement.

rocker cover gasket surface. Milling the head more than the minimum required to straighten the deck surface may reduce head gasket clamping and lead to premature gasket failure because the V6/60 has only four head bolts around each bore.

Aluminum Cylinder Heads

Lightweight aluminum cylinder heads were introduced in 1987 on "Generation II" 2.8-liter V6/60 engines installed in Celebrity, Corsica, Beretta, and Cavalier front-wheel-drive chassis. Production aluminum V6/60 cylinder heads incorporate a heart-shaped "fast burn" combustion chamber with splayed valves. The size and shape of the inlet port and the shrouding around the intake valve seat direct the incoming air/fuel mixture in a concentrated stream. This stream promotes swirl in the combustion chamber and spreads the flame front quickly to all parts of the chamber. The resulting fast combustion produces a smooth but rapid rise in cylinder pressure. The spark plug is also centrally located in the combustion chamber to promote propagation of the flame front throughout the chamber.

The intake and exhaust valves are canted relative to each other and to the head's deck surface. This splayed-valve design is similar to a big-block Chevrolet V8; it promotes efficient breathing by

unshrouding the valve heads as lift increases. Production aluminum V6/60 heads have 1.72-inch diameter intake valves and 1.42-inch exhaust valves. Valve stem diameter is 8mm (.315-inch).

Valvetrain

Valve timing for standard production and H.O. V6/60 hydraulic lifter camshafts are listed in the specifications chart.

Several aftermarket manufacturers offer camshafts that are suitable for high-performance and competition V6/60 engines. As a general guideline, a good street hydraulic cam for the 2.8-liter V6 should have approximately 205 to 210 degrees of intake duration at .050-inch tappet lift and 215 to 220 degrees exhaust duration at .050-inch tappet lift. A mechanical lifter cam with 270/280 degrees intake duration and 275/280 degrees exhaust duration is recommended for most competition applications. Maximum valve lift should be approximately .560-inch. Street and competition cams should be ground with lobe centers between 106 and 110 degrees.

Valve Lifters

Some types of mechanical lifters cannot be used in V6/60 Chevrolets due to the design of the production lubrication system. The left-hand lifter oil gallery in production engine blocks also feeds the crankshaft bearings. It is larger in diameter than the right lifter gallery and offset from the lifter bore centerline. Since this gallery also supplies lubrication to the main and connecting rod bearings, it cannot be restricted like a V8 gallery to control overhead oil flow. (Aluminum Bow Tie V6/60 blocks have V8-style oil systems with three oil galleries. The oil flow to the lifter galleries can be restricted when roller bearing rocker arms are used without reducing the oil supply to the crankshaft bearings.)

Production V6/60 engines equipped with mechanical lifter cams require a piddle valve lifter. Chevrolet mechanical lifter PN 5232695 is not suitable for V6/60 engines due to oil leakage around its pushrod seat. Sealed Power lifter PN AT-992 is satisfactory for V6/60 engines equipped with mechanical tappet cams.

Before installing new lifters in an aluminum block, deburr or sand off any sharp edges in the grooves around the lifter bodies. These edges tend to gall and wear the aluminum lifter bores rapidly.

Valve Springs

Production V6/60 valve springs and retainers are satisfactory for hydraulic camshaft profiles with .420-inch or less maximum valve lift. Chevrolet dual valve spring PN 330585 and aluminum retainer PN 330586 can be used with mechanical cams with .560-inch or less net valve lift. This spring is 1.379-inch in diameter, and produces 135 pounds of seat pressure at an installed height of 1.72-inch. V6/60 cylinder heads must be modified to accommodate this spring by enlarging and deepening the valve spring pockets. Install aftermarket valve stem seals for oil control when using these springs.

Rocker Arms

Production V6/60 stamped steel rocker arms are mounted on individual rocker studs with pivot balls and adjusting nuts. This lightweight, rugged valvetrain is similar to the small-block Chevrolet V8. Production V6/60 valvetrain components are suitable for many applications.

The reliability of a V6/60 engine equipped with racing valve springs can be improved by installing 7/16-inch diameter big-block V8 rocker arm studs (PN 3921912). To perform this conversion on cast iron V6/60 cylinder heads, the stock studs must be removed and the 11mm

Check for interference between adjacent rocker arms when using aftermarket needle bearing rockers on V6/60 cylinder heads.

rocker arm stud holes drilled and tapped with 7/16-14 threads. The rocker stud bosses will have sufficient strength to support the big-block rocker studs after they are re-tapped.

The pushrod guideplate holes must also be enlarged slightly to fit the 7/16-inch studs. The guideplates are hardened, so the holes should be enlarged by grinding or drilling with a carbide drill bit.

Aftermarket needle bearing rocker arms for a small-block V8 with 7/16-inch trunions should be installed on cast iron V6/60 cylinder heads that have been converted to 7/16-inch rocker studs. Due to limited clearance between adjacent rockers, narrow aluminum rockers are required. Aftermarket rocker arms with 1.260-inch wide trunions (Crane PN 11756 or equivalent) are suitable.

Head Gaskets

Head gasket sealing is critical on V6/60 engines because the block has only four head bolts around each cylinder bore. The span between bolts is relatively short, however, and V6/60 Chevrolet racing engines seldom experience problems with leaking head gaskets.

The block and cylinder head surfaces should be as straight as possible to promote an effective seal. Only the minimum amount of material necessary to straighten the sealing surfaces should be removed when machining the decks.

Cast iron blocks used for endurance racing should be machined for .041-inch stainless steel "O"-rings and assembled with .035-inch thick production head gaskets. The outer diameter of the "O"-ring groove should be 3.750-inch, and the wire should protrude .005 to .007-inch above the deck surface. Modify the production head gasket by enlarging the small water passage holes for the end cylinders to 9/32-inch diameter. Enlarge the two center water holes to 1/4-inch.

The intake ports in Generation II aluminum cylinder heads are tapered to provide pushrod clearance. Splayed valves improve breathing.

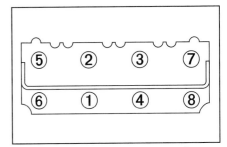

Tighten the head bolts in the sequence shown when installing or retorquing V6/60 cylinder head gaskets.

Aftermarket fuel injection manifolds are available for cast iron and Generation II aluminum V6/60 cylinder heads.

Install the head gasket without sealer. Tighten the head stud nuts to 65 ft.-lbs., and retorque the head studs after the engine has been run.

Intake Manifolds

The location of the intake manifold water outlet is different on V6/60 engines used in front-wheel-drive and rear-wheel-drive chassis. Make sure that the manifold's water outlet is in the correct location for your vehicle.

Induction systems for production Chevrolet V6/60 engines range from two-barrel carburetion to multi-point

A production two-barrel intake manifold can be modified with an adapter plate to mount a 500cfm Holley carburetor.

Aftermarket adapters are available to install three downdraft Weber two-barrel carburetors on a fuel injection manifold.

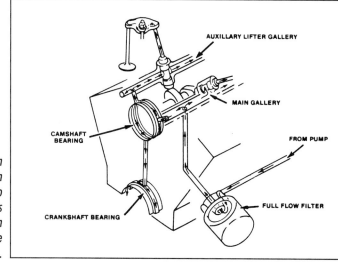

The production V6/60 lubrication system uses two galleries. Oil is routed to the main bearings through the left-hand gallery.

Eliminate the vacuum advance and connect the magnetic pickup in an S-10 distributor directly to a heavy-duty ignition box for racing.

An aluminum V6/60 water pump housing can be modified to increase coolant flow by enlarging its inlet passage.

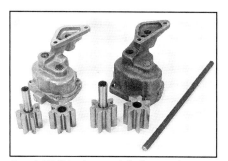

A stock V6/60 oil pump (left) has an aluminum housing; a high-volume pump (PN 10051104— right) has a cast iron housing and longer gears.

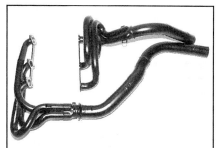

A three-into-one header system with 1⅝-inch primary pipes is recommended for competition Chevrolet V6/60 engines.

electronic fuel injection. Several aftermarket manufacturers also offer competition intake manifolds for V6/60 engines.

A production two-barrel manifold will perform well in restricted racing classes. Install an adapter for a Holley two-barrel, plug the EGR passages, and enlarge (or remove) the stock throttle bores.

Lubrication System

Production Chevrolet V6/60 oil pumps have lightweight aluminum housings. Oil pressure is regulated by a bypass spring located in the oil pump cover. A high-pressure spring (PN 10044435, color coded with a blue stripe) will produce approximately 70 psi oil pressure.

Remove and discard the gasket between the cover and pump body. Machine the ends of the pump gears to produce .001 to .002-inch clearance between the gears and the pump cover.

A heavy-duty cast iron oil pump for the V6/60 is available as PN 10051104. This pump has longer gears than a production pump, and offers a significant increase in oil volume for competition V6/60 Chevrolets. Modify this pump by enlarging the hole between the pickup and the pressure bypass to .410-inch diameter; a larger plug is required after drilling out this hole. The hole in the pump cover that feeds the oil pressure relief should also be enlarged to .410-inch. Relocate the pin that retains the oil pressure relief spring to the edge of the pump cover, and install a low-pressure Weaver pump spring (color coded green) with a .050-inch spacer. A cast iron oil pump modified in this manner will provide a steady supply of oil at approximately 80 psi.

Chevrolet does not offer windage trays for V6/60 oil pans. However, a semi-circular small-block V8 tray (PN 3927136) can be modified for use in a V6/60 by cutting off the front section. Three main cap bolts must also be modified by welding mounting studs to the bolt heads. The length of these mounting studs should be adjusted to provide sufficient clearance for the oil pan, crankshaft, and connecting rods you are using.

Ignition System

Production V6/60 engines are equipped with HEI (High Energy Ignition) systems. The spark timing in 1981 and later passenger cars equipped with V6/60 engines is controlled entirely by the vehicle's electronic control module.

1982-84 S-10 pickups and Blazers used conventional mechanical and vacuum controls for spark timing. This conventional ignition system can be easily modified for racing and high-performance applications. S-10 truck distributors also have remote-mounted coils, and are recommended for installations that require a small diameter distributor cap.

Cooling System

The production V6/60 water pump is a lightweight aluminum casting with a rib-reinforced snout. This pump should be modified for endurance racing to increase coolant flow. Disassemble the pump and enlarge the water pump inlet by machining off the outside wall of the cast aluminum housing. Fabricate a new water inlet passage from sheet aluminum and weld it to the pump casting. This new inlet should be approximately twice as deep as the original passage. Radius the inlet where it joins the impeller chamber and remove the impeller dust collar.

Exhaust System

Cast iron exhaust manifolds from an S-10 truck can be used for engine swaps, street rods, and similar installations. A dual exhaust system with low-restriction Corvette mufflers and a cross-over pipe will perform well on high-performance V6/60 engines that are not subject to emission regulations.

The preferred exhaust system for a competition V6/60 Chevrolet is a three-into-one header system for each cylinder bank. Primary pipe dimensions of 1⅝-inch OD x 26 inches long feeding 2½-inch diameter collectors have proven successful. Tailpipe length should be at least 33 inches. If the engine operating range is above 4000 rpm, a 2¼-inch diameter crossover pipe between the two collectors may be beneficial. Position this crossover at the front of the collectors.

Header systems designed to these dimensions are available from specialty manufacturers and independent shops. These sources can supply specific information on tubing sizes and chassis considerations for your usage. ⌐

NOTES:

TECH SPECS: V6/60 SPECIFICATIONS FOR HIGH-PERFORMANCE USE	
Firing Order	1-2-3-4-5-6
Spark Advance	Maximum 36-40° BTDC
Maximum Oil Temp	270° in oil pan
Minimum Fuel Pressure	4-5 psi at maximum engine speed
Piston to Bore Clearance	.006-.007" measured at centerline of wrist pin hole perpendicular to pin for Chevrolet heavy-duty forged pistons; .002-.003" for cast pistons. Follow manufacturer's recommendations for other pistons. Finish bores with 400 grit stones or equivalent.
Minimum Piston Ring End Gap	Top .016"; Second .014"; Oil Rails .016"
Wrist Pin Clearance	.0006-.0008" in piston; .0010-.0012" in rod (.0005-.0008" in bushed rod for floating pin, 0-.005" end play preferred)
Rod Bearing Clearance	.002-.0025"
Rod Side Clearance	.008-.012"
Main Bearing Clearance	.002-.0025"
Crank End Play	.004-.007"
Piston to Cylinder Head	.035" minimum (steel rods)
Valve to Piston Clearance	.045" for intake and exhaust at running valve lash. NOTE: These are absolute minimum clearances for an engine running below the valvetrain limiting speed. More clearance must be allowed for engines operating at valvetrain limiting speed; allow .080" intake and .100" exhaust valve clearance for high rpm engines.

NOTE: These specifications are intended as general guidelines for high-performance and competition applications. Different clearances and specifications may be required depending on operating conditions and components used. Always follow manufacturer's recommendations when installing aftermarket components.

Lubrication System

Mark IV oil pump

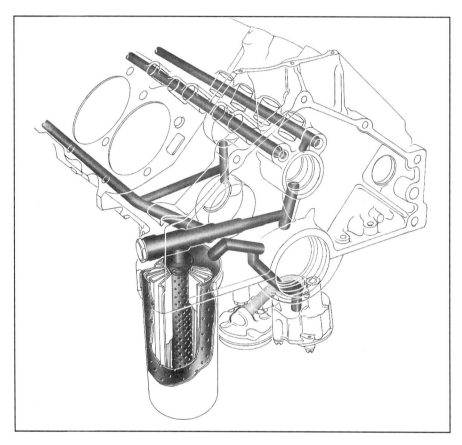

Oil is the lifeblood of every engine. Without a constant supply of clean oil, delivered at the proper pressure and the recommended temperature, an engine cannot survive the heat and stress of competition.

Oil both lubricates and cools internal components. It prevents metal-to-metal contact between moving parts, and transfers heat away from high-temperature areas. A properly designed and correctly installed lubrication system is essential to the health of any high-performance Chevrolet engine.

This chapter will describe the general requirements for an effective lubrication system. For specific information on recommended modifications for Chevrolet motors, refer to the sections on block preparation, crankshafts, and lubrication systems in the appropriate chapter.

There are two basic types of lubrication systems: wet sump and dry sump. In a wet sump system, the oil supply is stored in the pan; in a dry sump, it is held in an external reservoir or tank. The choice between a wet sump and dry sump lubrication system depends on both the engine builder's budget and the motor's intended usage. Dry sump systems are required in some racing classes and prohibited in others, so the rulebook may determine the final decision in many instances.

Wet Sump Oil Systems

All Chevrolet production engines use wet sump oil systems. A wet sump is simple, relatively inexpensive, and completely reliable in many high-performance applications. Wet sump oil systems are suitable for modified street engines,

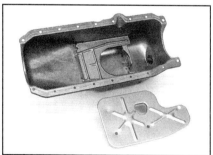
Baffles and windage trays can be installed in wet sump pans to control oil slosh under hard acceleration, braking, and cornering.

Aftermarket oil pans are available for racing classes that require wet sump systems. A deep, wide pan minimizes windage losses.

Many high-performance Chevrolet engines are equipped with a windage tray to separate the oil in the sump from the crankshaft assembly.

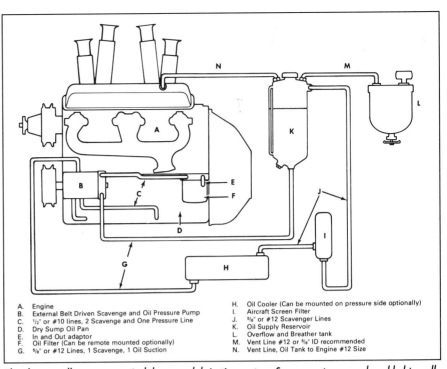

A. Engine
B. External Belt Driven Scavenge and Oil Pressure Pump
C. ½" or #10 lines, 2 Scavenge and One Pressure Line
D. Dry Sump Oil Pan
E. In and Out adaptor
F. Oil Filter (Can be remote mounted optionally)
G. ⅝" or #12 Lines, 1 Scavenge, 1 Oil Suction
H. Oil Cooler (Can be mounted on pressure side optionally)
I. Aircraft Screen Filter
J. ⅝" or #12 Scavenger Lines
K. Oil Supply Reservoir
L. Overflow and Breather tank
M. Vent Line #12 or ⅝" ID recommended
N. Vent Line, Oil Tank to Engine #12 Size

This diagram illustrates a typical dry sump lubrication system. Scavenge stages can be added to pull oil from the lifter valley and heads.

pleasure boats, and many classes in both oval track and drag racing competition.

The chief shortcoming of a wet sump is oil control. During hard braking, acceleration, and cornering, the oil pump pickup may be uncovered, interrupting the flow of lubricant to the bearings. The oil in a poorly designed wet sump system can also be aerated by the rapidly spinning crankshaft assembly; the resulting air bubbles in the oil supply reduce its lubricating qualities.

Racing engines equipped with wet sump systems may have high internal friction caused by windage losses if the oil in the pan is not effectively separated from the crankcase. The restricted capacity of most production pan designs also limits the total engine oil supply to four or five quarts. In a long-distance event, the oil may become overheated unless an auxiliary cooler is used to maintain the recommended oil temperature.

A properly designed wet sump oil system can remedy many of these shortcomings. Baffles can be installed in the pan to reduce oil slosh and to keep the oil pump pickup covered. Oil pump pickups can be modified to ensure a constant flow of oil. Windage trays can be fabricated to separate the oil in the sump from the crankshaft assembly. Wet sump pans can be deepened and widened to increase their capacity, and auxiliary coolers can be added to keep the oil temperature within the recommended range.

Dry Sump Oil Systems

Dry sump oil systems avoid many of the pitfalls of the wet sump design. In a typical dry sump system, the oil is scavenged from the engine by an externally mounted pump and stored in a remote-mounted tank. The oil is drawn from this reservoir, filtered, and then pumped back into the engine.

A dry sump system has several advantages over a wet sump. The storage tank provides an ample supply of oil for the pressure pump regardless of the vehicle's attitude or cornering speed. The oil capacity can be several times greater than a wet sump. An efficient scavenging system reduces windage losses by minimizing the volume of oil inside the engine. A shallow dry sump oil pan also allows the engine to be mounted low in the chassis to improve handling. Many racing organizations require dry sump systems to limit the loss of oil onto the track surface in the event of a blown engine.

Dry sump oil systems do have drawbacks, of course. They are more expensive, more complex, and heavier than wet sumps. They require a pump drive, mounting brackets, hoses, and a storage tank. Nevertheless, the advantages of a dry sump oil system usually outweigh the disadvantages for a maximum-effort racing engine. Dry sump lubrication systems have become standard in stock car racing, road racing, offshore boat racing, and professional drag racing.

Dry Sump Design

The GM Motorsports Technology Group recommends the following procedures when selecting and installing dry sump oil system components:

1. Eliminate the internal engine pump and plug the oil pump passage in the cylinder block. Install a non-bypassing in-and-out adapter on the oil filter pad.

2. Most dry sump oil pumps consist of a series of scavenge and pressure stages contained in a single belt-driven unit. The GM Motorsports Technology Group recommends a pump with at least two (and preferably three) scavenge stages, plus one pressure section.

3. A minimum of two scavenge stages should be plumbed to the oil pan. If a third scavenge stage is used, it should be connected to the lifter valley or the rear of the valve cover on the outboard side of the car. (On oval tracks that are run in a counter-clockwise direction, the passenger side is outboard; on road courses, the predominantly outboard side depends on the course layout and the direction which the course is run.)

4. If the capacity of the oil pump scavenge stages is adequate, the scavenged oil can be pumped through an oil cooler before it is returned to the supply tank. This routing requires low-restriction coolers.

Oil coolers should not be connected in series; if more than one cooler is used, they should be plumbed in parallel. To connect coolers in parallel, install a tee fitting in the scavenge return line and route the oil through both filters simultaneously. The minimum recommended inside diameter for oil scavenge lines is ¾-inch (#12 hose).

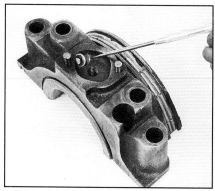

Remove the internal oil pump and plug the pump passage in the rear main bearing cap when converting a block to dry sump oiling.

A belt-driven dry sump oil pump contains a series of scavenge and pressure stages. The oil pressure can be adjusted externally.

Low-restriction oil coolers can be installed in scavenge and pressure lines. Engine oil temperature should not exceed 270 degrees.

Install screen-type filters in the scavenge lines to prevent metal particles from damaging the oil pump and contaminating the dry sump storage tank.

Install fine screen-type filters in the scavenge lines. These filters will prevent metal particles from reaching the supply tank, pressure pump, and pressure bypass valve. A screen-type filter should be examined frequently to check for bearing material and other debris that may indicate internal engine problems.

5. Use ¾-inch ID line (#12 hose) from the supply tank to the pressure stage of the oil pump.

6. Route the pressurized oil from the oil pump through a remote-mounted oil filter and then into the engine block. An oil cooler may be installed between the pressure pump and the remote oil filter. (See item No. 4 above for alternate oil cooler plumbing.) Use ½-inch ID line (#10 hose) for high pressure oil plumbing.

7. Excessive oil pressure will increase total oil flow through the engine and reduce the efficiency of the oil scavenging system. The minimum recommended oil pressure for Chevrolet racing engines is 65 psi. Many successful engine builders specify 10 psi oil pressure for every 1000 rpm. Using this formula, an engine running at 8000 rpm should have at least 80 psi oil pressure.

8. Install a full-length semi-circular windage tray baffle under the crankshaft. This tray should be louvered to draw oil away from the crankshaft assembly. The baffle can be mounted on the main cap studs or installed in the oil pan.

9. A round oil sump tank is recommended. This tank should be as small in diameter and as tall as the available space allows. It should have a minimum capacity of eight quarts when two-thirds full. The tank should have a cone-shaped bottom with the oil outlet to the pressure pump located at the bottom of the cone. This tank design assures that the oil outlet will be covered regardless of the g-loads the vehicle may encounter.

The scavenged oil should be returned at the top of the supply tank through a fitting which is tangent to the side of the tank. This will circulate the oil around the side of the tank, separating air from the scavenged oil. The tank should also incorporate a horizontal baffle perforated with ³⁄₁₆-inch to ¼-inch diameter holes. This baffle design also de-aerates the oil, and stops the swirling of the lubricant.

The preferred location for the dry sump tank is in the engine compartment. This location minimizes oil line lengths.

10. The engine should be assembled with the proper valve lifters, rocker arms, and bearing clearances to minimize oil flow. Reducing the engine's oil requirements is a tremendous advantage for a properly functioning dry sump system. Oil flow in a properly assembled competition Chevrolet V8 should be approximately eight gallons per minute. A V6's oil flow should be approximately six gallons per minute.

11. Both the engine and the supply tank should be vented to the atmosphere. The engine can be vented to the supply tank if the tank is properly vented. The vent lines must be large enough to prevent pressure build-up in the crankcase; a single #12 line or two #10 vent lines are recommended. The engine may be vented through existing breather holes in the rocker covers; install oil separators (baffles) to prevent oil from being pulled into the vent lines.

12. The oil pan should be as deep as the chassis design allows. (Some sanctioning bodies also enforce minimum ground clearance rules which should be observed when designing a dry sump oil pan.) It is easier to scavenge oil effectively from a six-inch deep pan than from a four-inch deep pan.

If the pan is equipped with two oil scavenge pickups, it should be divided in half. The pickups should be located at the rear of each compartment. Don't be concerned about how well the pan is scavenged under braking; it is unimportant how much power the engine produces when the driver is off the throttle.

13. The GM Motorsports Technology Group recommends that screens *not* be used on the scavenge pickups. Many engines have been damaged and races lost

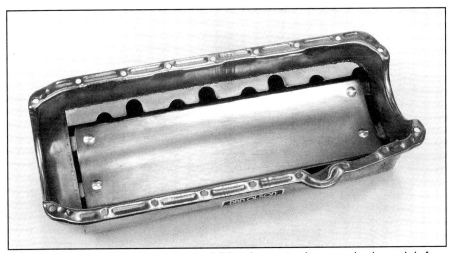

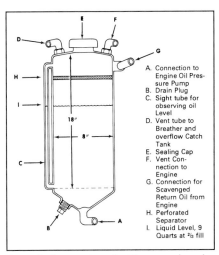

A dry sump oil pan should be equipped with a full-length, semi-circular tray under the crankshaft. Notch the oil scraper for connecting rod clearance.

A round oil reservoir tank with a cone-shaped bottom is recommended.

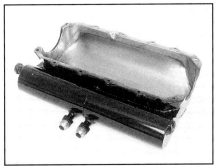

The oil return line fitting should be tangent to the side of the dry sump reservoir tank to swirl and de-aerate the scavenged oil.

To maximize scavenging efficiency, divide a dry sump oil pan into two parts with baffles and use one pickup for each half of the pan.

Check the effectiveness of a dry sump system by observing fluctuations in the oil level in a sight gauge on the dry sump reservoir tank.

because scavenge pickups have been plugged by RTV, cork, and aluminum particles. To keep contaminants out of the scavenge sections, install screens over the oil drainback holes in the engine block. Magnets can also be installed near the oil drainback holes and in the rear of the oil pan to catch stray steel particles.

14. If possible, run the complete dry sump system on a dynamometer and observe fluctuations in the oil level with a simple sight gauge installed on the side of the sump tank. This will reveal the effectiveness of the oil pan, baffle, and scavenging system. There should be no more than a one or two quart drop in the oil level in the tank between idle and maximum engine speed.

A similar test of the dry sump system can be performed in the vehicle by shutting off and declutching the engine at high speed. Drain the oil pan to determine how much oil is circulating in the engine and crankcase at high rpm.

A dry sump oil system does *not* guarantee trouble-free engine lubrication. A dry sump system should be checked for proper operation, and maintained in peak condition. An oil pressure gauge should be installed to reveal any fluctuations in oil pressure, and the scavenging system tested to determine its efficiency.

Racing Oil

The GM Motorsports Technology Group recommends 30 to 50 weight ashless racing oil or a 20W-50 multi-viscosity oil with ashless detergent additives. If you are uncertain whether a particular brand of oil is ashless, check with the oil manufacturer. Avoid all oils that contain even a small percentage of barium or calcium. These materials promote destructive pre-ignition and can cause

burned pistons when they are present in carbon deposits in the cylinder.

Synthetic oils have shown excellent performance at high engine temperatures. Although synthetic oils are generally more expensive than petroleum-based lubricants, they are worth your consideration if you are running a maximum-effort competition engine.

Ignition System

HEI Ignition

An electronic distributor's "star wheel" reluctor induces voltage in a magnetic pickup as the distributor shaft rotates.

The self-contained HEI distributor includes a magnetic pickup, module, and coil. PN 1103436 has mechanical and vacuum advance.

H igh-performance and competition engines typically operate at higher speeds and with greater cylinder pressures than production engines. These severe operating conditions place heavy demands on the ignition system.

The ignition system must be capable of producing hundreds of accurately timed sparks every second; an eight-cylinder engine running at 8000 rpm requires 32,000 ignition discharges per minute! Moreover, these sparks must have sufficient energy to ignite the fuel/air mixture in the combustion chambers. Misfires, erratic spark timing, and incomplete combustion caused by an inadequate or poorly maintained ignition system can impair engine performance.

Many factors affect the efficiency of an engine's ignition system. The battery and charging system must have adequate capacity to satisfy the ignition's voltage and amperage requirements. The switches, fuses, and wires in the primary ignition system must be installed correctly and serviced periodically. The secondary spark plug wires, terminals, and boots must have adequate insulation to prevent voltage leaks and cross-firing.

The engine's mechanical characteristics also play a role in the combustion process. The location of the spark plugs in the cylinders, the width of the plug gaps, the design of the electrodes, the height of the piston domes, and even the shape of the combustion chambers can have an impact on the ignition's ability to establish a flame front.

Advances in electronics have improved the accuracy, reliability, and performance of Chevrolet heavy-duty ignitions. Magnetically triggered ignition systems have made conventional breaker points obsolete. A mag-triggered ignition eliminates the mechanical limitations imposed by points, springs, and distributor cams. Magnetically triggered ignitions are immune to changes in dwell and spark timing caused by worn rubbing blocks, pitted breaker points, and point bounce at high rpm. Point-type distributors are suitable only for restorations that require original equipment. The GM Motorsports Technology Group strongly recommends the use of modern magnetically triggered ignitions in all other applications.

Production and heavy-duty Chevrolet magnetically triggered ignitions are similar in their operating principles. The teeth on the distributor's timing core (often referred to as the "star wheel" or "reluctor") induce voltage in a magnetic pickup as the distributor shaft rotates. The ignition module or amplifier senses this voltage and then discharges a high-voltage secondary spark from the coil. This design has proven trouble-free in millions of production engines, and it is capable of producing sparks with excellent timing accuracy at high engine speeds.

High Energy Ignition

Chevrolet introduced the High Energy Ignition (HEI) in 1975 as a replacement for conventional point-type distributors. The HEI distributor assembly is a self-contained ignition system that includes a magnetic pickup, a module, a coil, a rotor, and a cap. The HEI's large diameter cap minimizes arcing and cross-firing between adjacent spark plug terminals. (Some Chevrolet production engines use HEI ignitions with small diameter distributor caps and remote-mounted coils to provide additional induction system clearance.) The cap's male wire terminals provide a reliable, positive connection for the spark plug leads.

Early-model HEI ignitions with conventional centrifugal and vacuum advance mechanisms are recommended for moderate performance applications such as street rods, pleasure boats, limited oval track classes, and bracket racing. The spark advance curve in these ignitions can be tailored to suit a particular car and engine combination by installing various centrifugal weights, springs, and vacuum canisters. The spark curve in late-model HEI ignitions without mechanical advance mechanisms is controlled by the vehicle's PCM (Powertrain Control Module).

The HEI distributor assembly (PN 1103436) included with the H.O. 350 engine assembly is a good choice for most high-performance applications. This distributor has conventional centrifugal and vacuum advance mechanisms, and its spark curve is suitable for most emissions-exempt engines.

The HEI distributor's magnetic pickup assembly includes a permanent magnet, a pole piece with internal teeth, and a pickup coil. When the teeth of the rotating timer core pass by the teeth of the pole piece, an induced voltage in the pickup coil signals the electronic module to open the ignition coil primary circuit. The primary current drops, and a high voltage is induced in the ignition coil secondary wiring. This voltage is routed through the rotor and plug wires to fire the spark plugs. A capacitor in the distributor suppresses radio interference.

The magnetic pickup assembly is mounted over the upper distributor housing bearing. The pickup on early-style HEI distributors with mechanical advance mechanisms is connected to the diaphragm in the vacuum canister to provide vacuum advance. The timer core is also rotated by conventional advance weights to provide centrifugal advance.

A 10 or 12 gauge ignition lead wire should be used with HEI ignitions in high-performance applications. No other electrical devices should be connected to the ignition switch. Use a separate switch and circuit for electric fuel pumps, blower motors, and other equipment. Although the HEI does not have a high average current draw, it does have a high *instantaneous* amperage draw which requires a large ignition wire lead.

If you are replacing a point-type distributor with an HEI ignition, the ballast resistor or resistance wire from the old system should be eliminated. Unlike point-type ignitions that operate at lower voltage levels, the HEI requires full battery voltage for proper operation.

Misfiring at high engine speeds can often be cured by replacing the production carbon core resistance wires with solid core spark plug wires. High-performance spark plug wires with spiral-wound monel cores are also available; this design minimizes electrical interference with radios, rev limiters, data recorders, and other electronic components.

HEI Service Procedures

The HEI magnetic pickup and module do not require maintenance in normal service. The cap, rotor, advance weights,

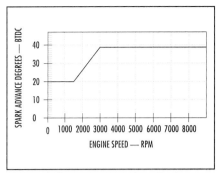

This graph illustrates a typical spark advance curve for a competition engine. Engines with efficient combustion require less total advance.

The ignition advance curve in conventional Chevrolet distributors is controlled by centrifugal weights and springs.

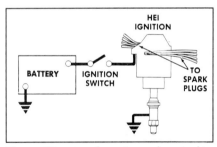

Wire an HEI ignition for racing as shown in this diagram. Use 10 or 12 gauge wire, and do not connect other devices to the circuit.

and weight pins should be inspected periodically for signs of wear to keep the ignition in peak operating condition.

Observe the following precautions when servicing an HEI ignition system:

1. Disconnect the ignition switch feed wire at the distributor before engaging the starter when testing compression on an engine equipped with HEI ignition. When disconnecting this connector, *do not* use a screwdriver or tool to release the locking tab, as it may break.

2. An HEI distributor does not require periodic lubrication. Engine oil lubricates the lower bushing, and an oil-filled reservoir provides lubrication for the upper shaft bushing.

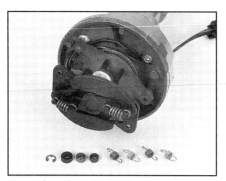

Heavy-duty Chevrolet distributors include an assortment of advance springs and limiting bushings to adjust the spark curve.

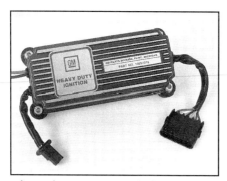

A heavy-duty GM capacitive-discharge ignition amplifier will provide reliable ignition at 10,000 rpm.

An electronic rev limiter is calibrated to the number of cylinders with a chip. Plug-in rpm modules determine the maximum engine speed.

A changeover switch allows the driver to select a back-up amplifier and rev limiter during a race in the event of an ignition malfunction.

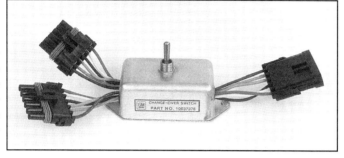

3. The tachometer (TACH) terminal is next to the ignition switch (BAT) connector on the distributor cap or on the remote coil. The tachometer terminal must *never* be connected to ground, as damage to the module and/or ignition coil can result.

Some aftermarket tachometers may not be compatible with the High Energy Ignition system. Consult the tachometer manufacturer if questions arise.

4. Dwell is controlled by the module, and cannot be adjusted.

Electronic Ignition

Chevrolet markets a complete heavy-duty ignition system that is suitable for many high-performance and racing engines. This system includes an ignition amplifier, a heavy-duty coil, an electronic rev limiter, an electronic tachometer, wiring harnesses, and related components. Heavy-duty distributors for Chevrolet V8 and 90-degree V6 engines are also available. This coordinated heavy-duty ignition system is designed to provide dependable off-highway performance under severe operating conditions.

The heart of the Chevrolet heavy-duty ignition is a capacitive-discharge ignition amplifier (PN 10037378). This control box is suitable for all high-compression racing engines with a maximum engine speed of 10,000 rpm. It has multi-spark capabilities, producing a series of sparks

for 20 degrees of crankshaft rotation. The control box has special internal bracing and rubber shock mounts to dampen vibrations. The heavy-duty ignition amplifier has a maximum current draw of 10 amperes. It plugs directly into Chevrolet heavy-duty distributors.

The ignition control has a connector for an electronic rev limiter (PN 10037379). This rev limiter will prevent an engine from overspeeding in the event of a missed shift, a driveline failure, or a loss of traction. It does not shut down the engine, but instead cuts the current to individual cylinders until the engine speed falls below the chosen rpm limit. This "soft touch" rev limiter includes a set of chips, or modules, which adapt the unit to four-, six-, and eight-cylinder engines.

The engine's maximum rpm point is determined by plugging a second chip into the rev control. Three chips are supplied with the rev control to limit engine speed to 6000, 7000, or 8000 rpm. Additional chips are available to set the maximum engine speed in 200 rpm increments. Each kit includes five chips.

Two wiring harnesses are available for the heavy-duty ignition control. PN 10039932 should be used when the control box is mounted in the engine compartment. PN 10037377 has longer wires to allow the box to be mounted in the passenger compartment, where it is protected from high temperatures.

A changeover switch is available as PN 10037376. This switch enables the driver to select a back-up control box in the event of an ignition malfunction during a race. A second ignition box and rev limiter are required when a changeover switch is installed.

The recommended ignition coil for the heavy-duty Chevrolet ignition is PN 10037380. This coil has an alkyd top that prevents arcing to the terminals. It is oil-filled to dissipate heat under severe operating conditions.

Chevrolet heavy-duty distributors do not have provisions for a mechanical tachometer drive. A five-inch diameter electronic tachometer (PN 10038474) is recommended for use with these distributors. This tachometer reads to 10,000 rpm, and has an electronic memory feature that recalls the highest engine speed by flipping a switch on the tachometer face. A pushbutton on the tach resets the memory. Two 8000 rpm electronic tachometers are also available: PN 10185001 has a 3¾-inch diameter dial, and PN 10185002 has a 5-inch dial.

Heavy-duty ignition systems should be wired directly to the battery using a high-quality toggle switch, a fuse or circuit breaker, and heavy-gauge wire. Do not connect the ignition control to the vehicle's common fuse panel or terminal strip, and do not share the wiring for the ignition box with other components.

Do not use solid core spark plug wires with a heavy-duty electronic ignition if your car is equipped with rev limiters, pit radios, data recorders, or other devices that are susceptible to electrical "noise." High-performance radio suppression wires with spiral-wound cores are recommended to eliminate electrical interference caused by high-output ignitions.

This well-prepared race car has a complete spare ignition system. Flipping the changeover switch activates the second ignition control box.

An oil-filled coil (PN 10037380) is recommended for heavy-duty ignitions. This coil has an alkyd top to prevent arcing.

A GM 10,000 rpm electronic tachometer (PN 10038474) has a memory feature that recalls the highest engine speed.

An "E" gap rotor (right) has a shorter blade than a high-performance rotor. The "E" gap can cause misfire by increasing resistance.

Ignition System Troubleshooting

Distributors and ignition systems are frequently neglected until some engine problem appears. New components may have hidden defects, and used parts can deteriorate with use. The following troubleshooting tips and installation recommendations apply to most Chevrolet point-type, HEI, and heavy-duty electronic ignitions.

If the ignition system is malfunctioning, first make sure that the battery is properly charged and that all connections are tight and free of corrosion. Check the voltage at various points to verify that fuses, switches, and wires are in good condition. If the problem persists, check for the following defects:

1. Examine the distributor for loose or worn centrifugal advance weights, pins, and broken welds in the centrifugal advance mechanism and distributor driveshaft. Inspect the rotor blade tip.

2. Check for a worn, damaged, or missing centrifugal advance limiting bushing (not used in HEI distributors). Loss of this bushing on the advance stop pin during a race advances ignition timing several degrees. This in turn cause detonation and serious engine damage. Production plastic advance limiting bushings can be replaced with a metal bushing which can be brazed or soldered to the pin.

3. Damage to the pickup coil or breaker point lead wires. A clean, positive connection should be maintained between the distributor and the wiring harness. An intermittent connection can produce random misfiring and spark scatter. Pickup coil lead wires are occasionally pinched inside the distributor; a grounded wire can cause distributor failure.

All ignition wiring should be examined for brittle or cracked insulation, broken strands, and loose or corroded connections. The secondary leads in the coil and distributor cap should be checked to make sure they are pressed all the way down in their inserts. Rubber boots should be tight in place over the connections. Inspect the distributor cap and coil for cracks which would allow high voltage to jump to ground. The rotor and the inside of the cap should be checked for cracks and carbon paths.

Engine Build Specifications

Photocopy these forms and use them to record information about your engine.

ENGINE BUILD-UP AND CHECK RECORD

Engine Number	
Build Date	
Engine Type	
Displacement	
Fuel Requirement	
Build or Rebuild Number	

Special Assembly/Disassembly Notes:

PISTON SIZE AND BORE CLEARANCE

Cylinder #	1	3	5	7
Bore Size				
Piston Size				
Clearance				

Cylinder #	2	4	6	8
Bore Size				
Piston Size				
Clearance				

NOTES:

PISTON DATA

Piston Make/Type	/
Compression Height	
Wrist Pin Type/Length	/
Wrist Pin Diameter	
Wrist Pin Clearance in Piston	
Wrist Pin Retainer Type/Size	/

PISTON RING DATA

Make of Ring Set	
Part Number	
Top Ring Type	
Width	
Gap	
Material	
2nd Ring Type	
Width	
Gap	
Material	
Oil Ring Type	
Width	
Gap	
Material	

PISTON DECK CLEARANCE

Cylinder Number	1	3	5	7
Deck Clearance				

Cylinder Number	2	4	6	8
Deck Clearance				

ENGINE BEARING DATA

Main Bearing, Make/Type	/
Rod Bearing, Make/Type	/
Camshaft Bearing, Make/Type	/

CRANKSHAFT DATA

Crankshaft Make/Type	/				
Stroke					
End Play					
Main Bearing Number	1	2	3	4	5
Housing Diameter					
Housing Diameter w/Bearing					
Crankshaft Main Journal Diameter					
Main Bearing Clearance					

COMPRESSION RATIO DATA

Swept Volume*	
Dome (-) or Dish (+) Volume	
Ring Land Volume	
Deck Volume	
Head Gasket Volume	
Head Chamber Volume	
Total Volume	

$$CR = \frac{TOTAL\ VOLUME}{TOTAL - SWEPT\ VOLUME}$$

$$CR = \underline{\hspace{2cm}} : 1$$

* SWEPT VOLUME (CC) = BORE² x STROKE x 12.87

CONNECTING ROD DATA

Rod Make/Type	/
Length (Center to Center)	
Side Clearance	
Wrist Pin Bore Diameter	
Wrist Pin Clearance in Rod	
Rod Bolt Make/Size	/
Rod Bolt Torque	

Connecting Rod Number	1	3	5	7
Housing Diameter				
Housing Diameter w/ Bearing				
Crankshaft Rod Journal Diameter				
Rod Bearing Clearance				

Connecting Rod Number	2	4	6	8
Housing Diameter				
Housing Diameter w/Bearing				
Crankshaft Rod Journal Diameter				
Rod Bearing Clearance				

NOTES:

_____

_____

_____

_____

_____

CYLINDER HEAD DATA

Source/Part Number	/
Prepared By/Date	/
Intake Port Volume (cc)	
Intake Valve Type/Size	/
Exhaust Valve, Type/Size	/
Valve Spring Make	
Diameter/Type	/
Valve Spring Installed Height (Int./Exh.)	/
Valve Spring Seat Pressure (Int./Exh.)	/
Valve Spring Open Pressure (Int./Exh.)	/
Coil Bind Height (Int./Exh.)	/
Retainer, Make/Material	/
Keeper Type	
Chamber Volume	
Head Gasket, Type/Thickness	/
Valve Seal Make/Type	/

NOTES:

_____

_____

_____

_____

_____

_____

_____

_____

_____

_____

_____

_____

CYLINDER HEAD AIRFLOW DATA

Serial Number		Casting Number	
Air Bench Model		Test Pressure	
Barometer		Temperature	
Intake Valve Diameter		Intake Port Volume	
Exhaust Valve Diameter		Combustion Chamber Volume	
Bore Diameter		Date	

INTAKE AIRFLOW (AVERAGE)

Lift (in.)	% Flow	Orifice #	Correction
.100			
.200			
.300			
.400			
.500			
.600			
.700			

EXHAUST AIRFLOW (AVERAGE)

Lift (in.)	% Flow	Orifice #	Correction
.100			
.200			
.300			
.400			
.500			
.600			
.700			

_____

_____

_____

_____

_____

_____

_____